Northern Edge

NORTHERN EDGE

HOW CANADIANS CAN TRIUMPH IN THE GLOBAL ECONOMY

◀ ◀ ◀

Thomas Paul d'Aquino
David Stewart-Patterson

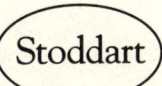

Copyright © 2001 by Thomas d'Aquino and David Stewart-Patterson

All rights reserved. No part of this publication may be reproduced or transmitted in any form or by any means, electronic or mechanical, including photocopying, recording, or any information storage and retrieval system, without permission in writing from the publisher.

Published in 2001 by
Stoddart Publishing Co. Limited
895 Don Mills Road, 400-2 Park Centre
Toronto, Canada M3C 1W3

Distributed by:
General Distribution Services Ltd.
325 Humber College Blvd.,
Toronto, Ontario M9W 7C3
Tel. (416) 213-1919   Fax (416) 213-1917
Email cservice@genpub.com

05 04 03 02 01 1 2 3 4 5

Canadian Cataloguing in Publication Data

d'Aquino, Thomas, 1941– .
Northern edge: how Canadians can triumph in the global economy

Includes bibliographical references and index.

ISBN 0-7737-3267-5

1. Canada — Economic conditions — 1991– .
2. Canada — Economic policy — 1991– .*
3. Canada — Foreign economic relations.
4. Competition — Canada.
I. Stewart-Patterson, David, 1958– . II. Title.

HC115.D238 2001   338.971   C00-931362-1

Every reasonable effort has been made to contact the holders of copyright for materials quoted in this book. The authors and publisher will gladly receive information that will enable them to rectify any inadvertent errors or omissions in subsequent editions.

Jacket design: Angel Guerra
Text design: Kinetics Design & Illustration

We acknowledge for their financial support of our publishing program the Canada Council, the Ontario Arts Council, and the Government of Canada through the Book Publishing Industry Development Program (BPIDP).

Printed and bound in Canada

To Susan, a fellow traveller in search of sound public policies for our country, and to the enterprising men and women who have built Canada for future generations.

— THOMAS PAUL D'AQUINO

To Ivanka, whose love and support make all else possible, and to Ruth and others of the next generation who are counting on us to do what's right.

—DAVID STEWART-PATTERSON

◀ ◀ ◀

Contents

	PREFACE	ix
	INTRODUCTION: ON THE EDGE	1
1	RIDING THE GLOBALIZATION WAVE	25
2	MAKING SMART CHOICES	49
3	DEVELOPING HUMAN ADVANTAGE	93
4	COMPETING FOR TALENT	137
5	CREATING AN INNOVATION SOCIETY	171
6	BUILDING GLOBAL CHAMPIONS	217
7	WALKING TALL AMONG NATIONS	263
8	HOW CANADIANS CAN TRIUMPH	297
	Notes	333
	Index	353

PREFACE

In the last decade of the twentieth century, Canadians conquered inflation, implemented a winning free-trade agreement with the United States, turned huge public deficits into surpluses, created immense numbers of new jobs, and, according to the United Nations Human Development Index, ranked first in the world for seven years in a row.

Despite this remarkable progress, the after-tax income of most Canadians remained flat throughout the decade, Canada's currency in relation to that in the United States continued its twenty-two-year decline, an increasing number of the country's brightest graduates migrated south to beckoning opportunities, and Canadian corporate head offices came under growing pressure to move elsewhere.

Two years ago we asked ourselves: "What are the reasons for these failings and what can be done to correct them?" This book endeavours to provide some answers while at the same time presenting a bold challenge. It dares Canadians to lead the world in the quality of their values, institutions, and enterprises.

The views expressed throughout are our own, but our work would not have been possible without the support and cooperation of the Business Council on National Issues. The inspiration for the book came from the BCNI's Canada Global Leadership Initiative, launched in April 1999, which had the ambitious goal of making Canada "the best place in the world to live, to work, to invest and to grow." Assisted by a generous gift from long-standing BCNI member Ronald Mannix, the initiative involved the member chief executives of the BCNI in an intensive twelve-month study of a wide range of issues relevant to Canada's domestic and global performance. The areas studied included monetary and fiscal policy, productivity, innovation, human capital, connectedness, e-commerce, digital capital, venture capital, internal and external trade and investment, social policy, competition policy, governance, environmental sustainability, and defence and security. CEO roundtables across Canada in the autumn of 1999 engaged BCNI members in an assessment of the studies and the various options for moving forward.

We are grateful to the BCNI for permitting and encouraging this expression of our independent views while we continued in the employ of the organization. Much of what we say accords with the strong consensus among BCNI members emerging from the Canada Global Leadership Initiative. Some of what we say goes beyond that consensus, tests new ideas, and offers fresh prescriptions.

Northern Edge was written during the last six months of 2000. The challenge was a mighty one, given that we had to meet exacting research and writing requirements while still executing our full-time responsibilities at the BCNI. The task would have been impossible without the assistance and encouragement of many people.

First, we salute the members of the BCNI for their support and help. More than sixty individual chief executives agreed to be interviewed, providing the rich collection of insight and experience that is reflected throughout the book. We also extend our appreciation to the more than one hundred chief executives who participated in roundtables and meetings across Canada linked to the Canada Global Leadership Initiative. Their questions and advice helped us to hone our analysis and to give better shape to our arguments.

We are particularly indebted to the members of the Executive Committee of the BCNI: Chairman David O'Brien, Vice-Chairmen Jacques Bougie, John Cleghorn, and Jean Monty. As chief executives of Canadian Pacific, Alcan, the Royal Bank, and BCE, respectively, they took time from their busy schedules to discuss many of the ideas contained in this book. We add a special note of gratitude to Nortel Networks chief executive, John Roth, for his role in inspiring both the initiative and the book, and for courageously speaking out publicly on the need for new thinking.

Our thanks go to each member of the Canada Global Leadership Initiative Board of Advisors who assisted with the analysis, and in some cases with the research, over the eight-month period leading up to the CEO Summit 2000 hosted by the BCNI in Toronto in April of that year:

Preface

Fred Bergsten, Jocelyne Bourgon, Sherry S. Cooper, Thomas J. Courchene, Marcel Côté, Kenneth S. Courtis, Donald G.M. Coxe, John W. Crow, Richard Harris, Michael Hart, John F. Helliwell, Dezsö J. Horváth, Tsun-Yan Hsieh, Harvey Lazar, John McCallum, Jack Mintz, J. Fraser Mustard, Angus E. Reid, David W. Strangway, Donald Tapscott, and David Zussman. Many other people contributed important insights and comments that strengthened our work. We mention in particular Lawson Hunter, Penny Milton, Neville Nankivell, Edward Neufeld, and Helen Raham.

We express our deepest gratitude to the hard-working team at the BCNI who did so much to make this book possible: to Patricia Longino, BCNI vice-president, finance and administration, for proofreading draft after draft of the text; to Nancy Wallace, director of the president's office, for organizing the CEO interviews and roundtables as well as the meetings of the Board of Advisors, and for assisting in the preparation of the manuscript; to Sam Boutziouvis, vice-president, international trade and global economics, for offering analytical support, valuable insights, and graphic material; to John Dillon, vice-president, environment and legal counsel, for helpful comments; to Alexandra Laverdure, policy and research associate, for assistance with fact-finding and for useful comments on the manuscript; to Karen Burton, administrative associate, for assisting in the preparation of the manuscript and graphics and for checking quotations; to Silvana Di Tullio, administrative associate, for assisting with organizational aspects of the project; and to Janice Gardner, librarian, for providing texts and reading materials from around the world.

To Jack Stoddart, we offer a bow for expressing faith in our abilities to produce a book when not one word had been committed to paper. And to the Stoddart editorial team of Don Bastian, Jim Gifford, Rosemary Shipton, and Jane McWhinney we express our special thanks for guiding us through the planning and writing stages in producing this book.

Last but not least we salute our spouses, Susan and Ivanka, for tolerating with grace and good humour our frequent absences and late-night toil. Their encouragement helped us across the finish line.

Thomas Paul d'Aquino and David Stewart-Patterson

INTRODUCTION: ON THE EDGE

> Let him appoint officers over the land, and take up the fifth part of the land of Egypt in the seven plenteous years. And let them gather all the food of those good years that come, and lay up corn under the hand of Pharaoh, and let them keep food in the cities. And that food shall be for store to the land against the seven years of famine, which shall be in the land of Egypt; that the land perish not through the famine.
>
> — GENESIS 41: 34–36

◀ ◀ ◀

Canadians have entered the twenty-first century with reason to celebrate. The year 2000 saw the size of our economy surpass the $1 trillion mark. After stagnating through much of the 1990s, the real incomes of Canadian families are on the rise. After years of painful restructuring, Canadian companies have been reporting strong profits, record exports, growing investment in new machinery and equipment, and rising productivity. And after decades of deficits, the federal and most provincial governments are reaping the rewards of sacrifice and hard work on the part of Canadians and racking up large surpluses. Across our land there is a renewed sense of possibility, of the belief that, if we put our minds to it, there is no limit to what we can achieve as a country.

We believe that Canada has a real opportunity to make the prosperity of the past couple of years the norm rather than a frustratingly infrequent exception. At the same time, we must remember that prosperity is never guaranteed, that the business cycle is not dead. As Joseph reminded

Egypt's pharaoh thousands of years ago and Maynard Keynes echoed in the last century, the best time to prepare for hard times is when the economy is hot.

The challenge for Canada at the beginning of the new millennium is more complex than worries about famine. But, one way or another, there will be potholes and worse in the economic road ahead. We have the resources now to prepare ourselves, to ensure that a rough ride does not send us into the ditch. More positively, we have the means to make sure that Canadians move steadily and safely towards sustainable growth both in our economic standard of living and in our quality of life.

These two goals are inextricably linked. As the members of the Business Council on National Issues (BCNI) put it in their statement at the CEO Summit 2000 in Toronto in April 2000: "Our goal is not to undermine Canadian values, but to ensure their triumph in a competitive world. Nor is the debate ahead one that should pit an economic agenda against social goals. Rather, this is a debate about how to make economic means serve social ends, about how to foster the economic growth we need to achieve our social vision."[1]

The great disappointment of the federal election campaign of 2000 was that it raised the issue of values, but barely touched the question of how to express and sustain those values effectively through economic and social policy. Now that the heated and divisive rhetoric of the campaign trail is past, it is important to go back to the basics. We must consider how Canadians can build a country that is able both to generate greater prosperity and to ensure that the benefits of that prosperity are broadly shared. As the members of the BCNI continued in their April 2000 statement: "We can and should aspire to build communities free of deprivation and brimming with optimism and opportunity. We can create a country that offers its citizens both a high standard of living and matchless quality of life. But we cannot achieve such ambitious goals through wishful thinking."[2]

Canada's efforts to date to work towards that vision have been hampered by the deep fiscal pit created by governments that converted Keynes' doctrine of using public spending to offset the economic cycle into one of borrowing money during the fat years and borrowing even more during the lean ones. Jack Mintz of the C.D. Howe Institute has calculated that, if we include the interest costs associated with largely unfunded public liabilities such as the Canada Pension Plan, total public debt charges in

INTRODUCTION

Canada rose to 9.1 percent of Canada's gross domestic product by 1994. This figure was more than double the share of the economy they absorbed in 1970. By the time Canadian governments began serious efforts to balance their books, total public debt charges in this country were more than five percentage points higher as a share of GDP than in the United States.[3] This gap was larger than the difference between personal income tax rates in the two countries. In other words, if we were not paying for the sins of our profligate past, we could have lower income taxes today than Americans and still be in a position to add to the superior range of social programs Canadians enjoy.

Still, we have made real progress. In the landmark study of Canadian competitiveness carried out in 1990 on behalf of the BCNI and the Canadian government, Harvard professor Michael Porter warned that we had to pull up our socks, and Canadians proceeded to do just that. Having made the leap of faith into free trade with the United States, we expanded the concept to include Mexico. Thanks to the discipline of the Bank of Canada, we broke the back of inflation, albeit at significant cost. Equally dramatic initiatives followed on the fiscal front, the most significant being the commitment of Liberal Finance Minister Paul Martin to wage war on the public deficit and to achieve his deficit reduction targets "come hell or high water."

When the members of the BCNI committed themselves in 1992 to the goal that Canada should be the best performing economy among the G-7 countries in the year 2000, we were seen as wildly optimistic. Yet, by the end of the 1990s, Canada's rate of job growth was in fact the best in the G-7, and trade, investment, and incomes were all rising strongly. In a few short years Canada had gone from having the highest deficit-to-GDP ratio among G-7 countries to the strongest surplus. By 1997, *The Economist* was praising Canada as a "fiscal virtuoso," and Canadians were rewarded with falling interest rates and improved balance sheets. The fight against national deficits was joined at the provincial level by one government after another. Fiscal responsibility had once again become respectable. Canadians had made clear what they wanted and common sense had triumphed. Today's abundant government surpluses are eating away at the mountain of public debt at an impressive pace.

Canadian business also underwent a profound transformation in the 1990s. The relatively comfortable, complacent, and protected business community of the sixties and seventies had been energized by the free-trade debate of the eighties. The effects of globalization forced Canadian companies to become increasingly outward oriented. The value-added of exports began to improve. Deregulation served as a catalyst as businesses became less reliant on subsidies and protective tariffs. Investments in technology accelerated, and a notable number of Canadian firms began to transform themselves into North American and global players.

Today, Canadians can rightly take pride in having stared down disaster and marshalled the will and consensus necessary to put Canada back on track. The lessons to be learned from this experience are seminal to helping us chart the future. The first lesson, exemplified by the painful struggle against deficits and debt, is that the wrong policy choice can be enormously costly and may carry consequences over many years. The second lesson is that having the vision and courage to do what is right for the country can deliver huge dividends. The best examples here are the determination of the Mulroney government to pursue free trade with the United States, even though there was strong opposition to the idea, and the decision of the Chrétien government to roll back disastrous public deficits. The third lesson is that choices are necessary and that sacrifices pay off. To prove this point, we need go no further than to compare the Canada of 1990 with the Canada of 2000.

Given the prosperity many Canadians are enjoying today, it is tempting to sit back and assume that the hardest work is done. However, it is important to resist the urge to fritter away the returns on our past investments. Although it is true that a healthy portion of our recent gains flows from the structural improvements we have wrought, we have also been the beneficiaries of the longest period of economic expansion in the history of our southern neighbour. The United States has been the engine driving the expansion of the global economy and, as its closest and most integrated partner, Canada has been given a major boost. What we have to remember is that the United States will not keep growing forever at the pace of the past decade. The integration that is so beneficial to us during America's good times will have a comparable impact on the downside whenever the United States economy falters.

The volatility of stock prices in the high technology sector during 2000 was a pointed reminder that all booms come to an end. By November, economist David Hale was warning that the United States faces three major vulnerabilities during the next few years. The first is that productivity growth could falter, leading to higher inflation. The second is that

INTRODUCTION

inflation could re-ignite globally, setting the stage for higher interest rates, slower growth, and a squeeze on corporate profits that would depress both stock markets and investment. And the third is the huge size of the American current account deficit, which is expected to rise from $345 billion (U.S.) in 1999 to $460 billion in 2000 and $510 billion or more in 2001. This figure would exceed 5 percent of that country's gross domestic product. In short, said Hale, the United States has become heavily dependent on a continuing flow of new investment from abroad: "Any interruption of capital flows could set the stage for a large dollar devaluation and rise in the level of interest rates which might then puncture the boom in the equity markets."[4] For all its strengths, the United States has not discovered the ultimate formula for perpetual growth.

Over the past decade, the fervent embrace by Americans of Joseph Schumpeter's doctrine of creative destruction has produced stunning results. But in a world driven by relentless innovation, the best policy choices today may well prove unequal to the challenges of tomorrow. Remember, for instance, the veneration accorded to the Japanese model of industrial development throughout the 1980s, and then consider that country's subsequent misery throughout the 1990s. No one — no person, no company, and no country — gets all the answers right all the time.

The key for Canada, therefore, is to assemble a model that includes enough of the right answers and sufficient flexibility to let us sustain solid progress through good times and bad.

■ A Precarious Perch

The precarious nature of our comfortable perch was illustrated starkly by the 2000 ranking of competitiveness by the World Economic Forum (WEF). Canada's rank improved dramatically during our economic rejuvenation of the mid-1990s, hitting a high of fourth place in 1997 and 1998. But over the past two years, our overall rank has slipped, to fifth in 1999 and to seventh in 2000.

What is worrying about this performance is that the WEF rankings emphasize the factors that contribute to future growth. Canada's ranking is particularly poor within what the WEF calls its "economic creativity index," which measures the pace of effective innovation, technology transfers, and new business start-ups, the keys to success in the knowledge economy. Here, Canada now ranks fifteenth. While the United States

5

stands in first place, Canada's performance lags behind that of many other small economies, including Finland, Sweden, Israel, Ireland, the Netherlands, Switzerland, Hong Kong, and Denmark.

When we talk about economic growth and its impact on the standard of living and quality of life of Canadians, it is important to consider both our relative and our absolute performance. Canada's economic growth in recent years has been impressive, but in spite of our relatively strong competitiveness rankings during the mid-1990s our performance relative to many other countries was lacklustre over the course of the decade.

The most telling of our shortfalls is how poorly we have done as a country in achieving the most basic measure of economic progress — increases in gross domestic product per capita, or the size of the economy per person — as the key marker of the standard of living of our citizens. The cumulative gain in real per capita GDP of Canadians was a meagre 5 percent between 1988 and 1998. The real per capita incomes of the French rose three times as fast; of Americans, almost four times; of the Dutch, five times; of Norwegians, six times; and of the Irish, an astounding eighteen times, almost doubling in a decade (see fig. 1). By 1998, the per capita GDP of Ireland had moved ahead of Canada's.[5] Viewed in the context of our most important trading partner, the United States, the comparisons are sobering. "When GDP is valued at purchasing power parity exchange rates, the income difference in 2000 is about U.S. $8,000 per person *and shows no signs of narrowing*. The gap is even larger when GDP is valued at the market exchange rate," the Conference Board of Canada noted in its report *Performance and Potential, 2000–2001*.[6]

The story in after-tax incomes is even more depressing. According to Standard & Poor's DRI Canada, real disposable incomes per capita in Canada were 20 percent greater than the average in all industrialized countries in 1989; by 1998, they were merely average, and incomes in seven out of ten provinces had fallen below the average. In comparison with the United States, "the richest Canadian province is below the poorest U.S. state in terms of real disposable income per capita . . . And it's not even close; Alberta's real per-capita disposable income is 10 percent below that in Mississippi, the poorest U.S. state."[7]

To some, especially those Canadians who do not travel outside the country, these comparisons may have little meaning. By 2000 the signs of prosperity were everywhere: consumers were buying, construction was robust, the housing market was tight, automobile sales were strong, and

INTRODUCTION

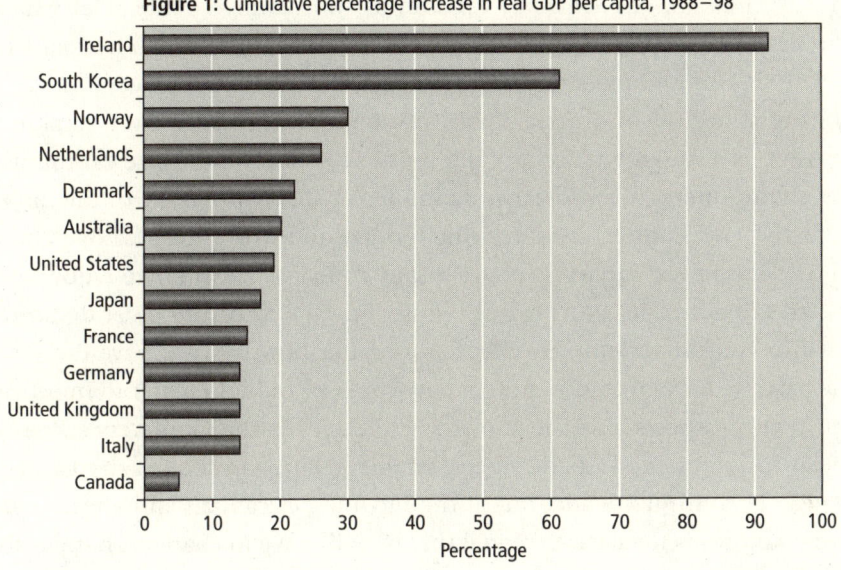

Figure 1: Cumulative percentage increase in real GDP per capita, 1988–98

the Canadian stock market suddenly became one of the hottest in the world. Canada's standard of living remains impressively high. But the fact that other countries are passing us by means that their citizens enjoy higher incomes personally, while, at the same time, their governments can afford to provide a more impressive range of public services.

As Canadians we have long prided ourselves on the quality of our public goods — our social safety net, education, health care, and all the other services we receive for the taxes we pay. Between 1970 and 1994 public spending on health care in Canada rose from 4.5 percent to 6.1 percent of GDP, effectively boosting its share of the total economy by one-third. Yet in the United States, the share of GDP devoted to public spending on health care more than doubled, from 2.7 percent to 6.3 percent.[8] And the more rapid growth of the United States economy means that, while its share of public spending on health care is now equivalent to our own, it actually spends far more public money per person on health care than we do in Canada.

Around the world, societies that have built their advantage on economic grounds are using the returns on their investment to catch up on quality of life. Hong Kong, for instance, is renowned for its laissez-faire economic policies, an approach that helped it generate real GDP growth of 7 percent a year over the past two decades. This growth drove incomes up as well, giving Hong Kong a per capita GDP that now exceeds the level in Australia and the United Kingdom as well as in Canada.⁹ Yet when chief executive Tung Chee Hwa visited Canada in April 2000, he made it clear that Hong Kong is far from satisfied. Having first succeeded in generating superb economic growth, the region's government is making massive investments in improving public education and in cleaning up the environment. "I am determined to make Hong Kong one of the most attractive cities in the world in which to live and work," he said.¹⁰

The lesson for Canada is obvious: any country that wants to enjoy sustained growth in its standard of living and quality of life must dedicate itself to continuous improvement. No matter how well we have done in the past, we have to consider every day what we could do better to improve our own prospects and those of our children. As the Conference Board put it in discussing Canada's performance relative to that of the United States: "A continued widening of the income per capita gap between the two countries is the clearest signal that we will have to change what we do and how we do it. If we cannot or choose not to change, we face the very real risk of long-term deterioration, which in due course could lead to an absolute decline in our quality of life . . . It is important to emphasize that it is necessary to have a high-income society to afford high quality public social programs and income redistribution."¹¹

In seeking to foster higher incomes in our society, we have to acknowledge that the defining characteristic of the knowledge-based economy is the speed with which new ideas emerge that turn yesterday's brilliant innovations into today's buggy whips. In discussing his own company's relentless search for new markets, Bombardier Inc. chairman Laurent Beaudoin has put it this way: "You can never be stagnant. If you think you're pleased with a plateau you've reached, by the time you stop to think about it, somebody's ahead of you."¹² In addition to embracing the principle of continuous improvement, we must be prepared to think and act more quickly than ever before. Let us have no illusions. Change is an exhilarating process, but to many people it is scary. Innovation means doing things differently, challenging the status quo, undermining entrenched attitudes, and upsetting established apple carts. Change is disruptive, but the alternative is stagnation leading to decline. For all Canadians to get ahead, for us to build a better and stronger country, we cannot be satisfied with what we have achieved to date.

The search for ways to accelerate Canada's pace of growth begins with the concept of productivity — a subject both feared and little understood.

INTRODUCTION

Reduced to its basics, productivity is the amount of goods and services produced from each hour of a Canadian worker's time. In countries where workers produce a large quantity of goods and services per unit of time, most people enjoy a high standard of living. Similarly, the growth rate of a country's productivity determines the growth rate of its average income.[13] While economists often dispute how best to measure productivity growth, one thing is clear: Canada's productivity, as reflected in per capita incomes, is simply not growing fast enough.

To boost that rate of growth, the basic recipe is simple: invest, invest, invest. Business investment in machinery and equipment is the most basic activity linked to productivity, and Canadian companies large and small must be more aggressive in adopting new technologies and putting them to use. But the precursor to investment in innovative equipment and processes is investment in knowledge. Canadian governments, companies, and academic institutions must both engage more heavily in research and ensure that new ideas are able to take root and produce an abundant harvest of innovation in our offices and factories. And the prerequisite for investment in both machinery and knowledge is effective investment in people. We must invest in the development of Canada's human capital, from early childhood through retirement from the labour force. This threefold approach of investment in people, knowledge, and capital goods is the key to large and sustained gains in productivity and incomes.

Governments clearly have an important role to play in this process, but direct public investment in human capital and in research is not enough. Governments also need to create an environment that encourages productive private sector investment. Canada has already put in place many of the right macroeconomic conditions, and the time has come to shift the emphasis of policy innovation to the microeconomic level, to address the factors that affect the behaviour of individual people and companies. How do we persuade more young people to complete their basic education, to enable them to move on to post-secondary achievements? How do we encourage more employees and employers to develop true cultures of learning in the workplace? How can we motivate more people to develop new ideas, to invest in those ideas, and to build them into successful global businesses? How do social and economic factors come together in the battle to attract the investment and the people that drive innovation and economic growth?

In this book, we examine such questions from both the theoretical and the practical perspective. We test the findings of leading academics within Canada and abroad against the actual strategies being pursued by major Canadian corporations as they expand in the global market. We see many examples of Canadian individuals and companies succeeding on the global stage, but our concern focuses on the future of our country as a whole. Although we offer criticisms of many current practices, our intention is not to cast blame or to point fingers. Rather, we seek to provoke an honest dialogue that will generate the momentum for change: how all of us can do better; how Canada's diverse parts can work together more effectively to improve the welfare of the whole country.

■ *The Search for Distinction*

As authors, we might be strongly identified with the business community through our association with the Business Council on National Issues, but this book does not press Canadians to embrace unbridled capitalism or to make themselves more like Americans. Continued economic integration and rapid technological change are inevitable and can contribute to human progress around the world, but human progress within Canada depends on how well we are able, as a country, to anticipate, adapt to, and channel those forces. In this new era, we can achieve our aspirations only by innovation, not by imitation. We must look to our strengths and reinforce them; we must examine our weaknesses and deal with them.

But to achieve a superior standard of living and quality of life, we must strive for unparalleled excellence. That goal requires us not only to learn from the successes and failures of others but to forge our own distinct model of economic and social progress. In this struggle for distinction, our small size can be an advantage. The fastest-growing companies in any industry are almost always the smaller, nimbler players more eager to expand. So, too, it is with countries: smaller players take more chances because they can and because they must.

Taking chances and building a new Canadian model of economic and social development do not mean abandoning our values or weakening our established strengths. At the macroeconomic level, we must maintain our commitment to low inflation and fiscal prudence in order to boost confidence in our currency and in our country as a place to invest. We have to continue to support and strengthen the multilateral trading framework to ensure access for Canadians to the export markets that are the lifeblood of our economy. Equally important, we have to maintain the strengths that reflect our fundamental values: our commitment to human rights and global peace; our honest and professional public service; our independent judiciary; our clean environment; our comprehensive systems of public health care and education; our generous social safety net; and, above all, our tolerant and multicultural communities.

What we have to recognize, however, is that none of these strengths by itself is unique. In today's competition for investment and people, many countries offer sound currencies and prudent fiscal policies. Many communities offer a clean environment, good health care and education, safe streets, and income support for the less fortunate. To make ourselves distinct, we must ensure that we can offer a compelling combination of social and economic virtues — while making sure that we do not lag significantly behind our competitors on any of the factors that affect choices about where money flows and where people prefer to live.

■ The Need for Smart Choices

We begin our examination by looking at the concept of globalization. The forces of economic integration and technological change are opening up vast new possibilities for improving human welfare. These forces are empowering consumers in their dealings with companies, skilled employees in their negotiations with employers, and citizens in their relationships with governments. Powerful multinational corporations cannot despoil the environment or exploit workers anywhere in the world without severe risk to their global reputation and their bottom line. And governments can no more prevent the flow of people and investment than they can restrain the flow of information that is renewing grassroots democracy. The forces of integration and technology and the speed of change are fundamentally altering the terms of competition for companies and for countries alike.

For many in the developing world, growing flows of trade and investment have been the keys opening the door to rapidly rising incomes. For others, however, the downside of rapid change and global integration is driving a dangerous backlash that threatens continued human progress within Canada and around the world. The global challenge is to make sure that the vast benefits of technology and integration become more visible and more broadly shared. The challenge for Canada is to shape a new economic and social model that will enable us to make the most of globalization's opportunities.

Our next chapter turns to this domestic challenge. We cannot achieve our goals as a country without making smart choices that recognize the links between economic and social policy. We focus on public health care in particular as an example of one of Canada's great strengths — but we show how meeting the expectations of Canadians for improving service will require faster growth than the current projections for our economy. If we wish to improve public medicare while avoiding wholesale cancellations of other programs or a return to rising taxes, we will need economic policies that add to the growth of our economy. We believe that comprehensive, high-quality, accessible, and publicly funded health care is one of the core elements of the Canadian vision — but even preserving what we have will require some tough choices between current consumption and investment in future growth.

In the meantime, to make room for the public programs that matter to us the most, we will have to discard or diminish those that have proven to be ineffective — Canada's regional development policies being a prime example. We also need to spend existing resources more effectively by trying new approaches to age-old problems. In addressing our social safety net, for instance, we must focus additional resources on helping lower-income Canadians to acquire skills and knowledge — to earn higher real incomes and leave poverty behind — rather than on making people less uncomfortable in their poverty. For the past couple of years, the cyclical strength of our economy has allowed us the luxury of avoiding tough choices on the spending front, but continued procrastination will eventually do the greatest damage to those who need the most help.

■ The Competition for People

International competition is more than ever about people. What people know and can do determines whether a company can earn profits and expand and whether a country can attract investment and grow its economy. What people want for themselves and their families in turn is driving what companies and countries must do to develop, attract, and retain the people they need. As the most crucial element in both corporate and national success, talented people have become far more precious

INTRODUCTION

— and more hotly sought — than the gold, oil, or other natural resources that drove national wealth in the past. As *Fast Company* magazine described it vividly in 1998, what management consultants McKinsey & Co. dubbed the war for talent is raging in earnest:

> In the boardroom bunkers and in the cubicle-filled trenches, the early skirmishes of the next war are being fought. For the moment, most of the action is guerrilla warfare — aerial raids in which the companies under attack are often unaware that they've been hit. Ultimately, though, the war will be global, and for businesses, the stakes will be success and perhaps our survival . . . The most important corporate resource over the next 20 years will be talent: smart, sophisticated business people who are technologically literate, globally astute, and operationally agile. And even as the demand for talent goes up, the supply of it will be going down.[14]

It is impossible to talk about human capital without reference to its principal incubator — the education system. Canadians have long appreciated the value of education. We continue to invest more in the education of our citizens than most industrialized countries. The proportion of young people staying in school longer and moving on to post-secondary studies is on the rise. By 1995 almost half of Canada's working-age population held post-secondary credentials, more than double the average for all industrialized countries.

Considering the extent of our public investment in education, the performance of Canadian students in key subjects such as mathematics and science leaves much to be desired. Noting that Canadian grade 8 students ranked just fourteenth in mathematics and fourteenth in science in international testing, federal Finance Minister Paul Martin warned in September 2000: "These are not sterile statistics; they are flashing red lights and we ignore them at our peril." And beyond such test results, he asked a Toronto business audience, "Do all young Canadians, regardless of income, have a basic knowledge of the Web and how to navigate it, an understanding of its potential and how to exploit it, a grasp of its power and how to employ it?"[15] The results of international math and science tests released in December 2000 showed considerable improvement in Canada, but too often, children still seem to emerge from high school lacking in basic skills such as literacy, numeracy, and the ability to communicate effectively. Most serious, too many young people in Canada still fail to graduate from high school, a deplorable fact and one that, in all likelihood, condemns them to a lifetime of dependency and deprives our society and economy of an essential reservoir of talent.

Beyond the economic implications for these people and for the country, Lester Thurow has warned of the broader danger of allowing an underskilled underclass to grow. "To do nothing, effectively returning skill investments to the vagaries of individual decision-making, is essentially to abandon the skill level of the wealth pyramid to the economic jungle. The ensuing neglect will eventually bring the American wealth pyramid down — just as the real jungle brought down the real Mayan pyramids in Central America or the real Cambodian pyramids at Angkor Wat."[16]

The evolution of the knowledge-based economy means that we have to help all children achieve steadily higher standards of performance. We are starting from a solid base, but for their sake and for our country's we cannot afford to stand still. We must do better, much better, and the depth of the challenge requires a fundamental re-examination of the way we run our public schools.

With the children in our schools today coming from many cultural and economic backgrounds and facing a wide range of family-related stresses all but unknown in our parents' generation, the challenge of ensuring equality of opportunity is more daunting than ever. We have to commit the resources necessary for all children to achieve their potential. At the same time, we must make the most effective possible use of our money. To enable our schools to meet the diverse needs of communities and children across the country, we have to start running our schools like other modern, knowledge-based enterprises rather than industrial-era production lines. We need to set ambitious standards for achievement to ensure that all Canadians are equipped for rewarding lives as citizens of the world. And, to achieve this goal, we must empower parents, teachers, and principals at individual schools to help students from all backgrounds meet our challenging expectations for achievement.

Beyond high school lies another broad range of challenges for the country. Lifelong learning is a concept widely touted, but is far from ingrained either within our post-secondary institutions or within the workplace. Canada needs to develop a framework for lifelong learning that cuts across the public and private sectors and that ensures access to opportunities for learning to all Canadians regardless of their circumstances.

Surveys of BCNI member companies and large employers generally

Introduction

reveal that they are enthusiastic investors in people. Most are active participants in the North American and global economies. All are highly dependent on the skills of their employees and compete actively for talent. As a result, they can readily see significant returns on their investments in training. Too many small and medium-sized enterprises, in contrast, seem to be much more reluctant to invest in training. Some of this hesitation reflects the problem of measuring less formal training delivered on the job in smaller enterprises. But smaller businesses also tend to be less productive, and that lag suggests a need for greater attention to building human capital in the small business sector. This necessity is particularly relevant for the growing number of self-employed. And, within the ranks of the unemployed, access to opportunities for learning and training is both uncertain and uneven.

While Canada must address its shortcomings in improving the supply and quality of human capital, we must also deal with a growing problem flowing from our success. As a country, we are producing an increasing number of talented individuals in a wide variety of disciplines — knowledge workers with globally transferable skills. There is increasing evidence that many of the most talented of these individuals — bright young graduates and globally experienced veterans alike — are being drawn inexorably into the American orbit. They are taking advantage of compelling opportunities to work on the leading edge while enjoying higher pay, lower taxes, and a higher overall quality of life than they can find in Canada.

Canada has suffered "brain drain" scares in the past and has always been able to rely on significant inward flows of immigration to make up for losses. Today, in the face of clear proof that Canada is losing some of our brightest citizens, primarily to the United States, immigration is again being touted to downplay concerns. Citing Statistics Canada surveys, some political leaders are saying that Canada is, in fact, experiencing a "brain gain" — that Canada receives far more highly educated people from abroad than it loses to the United States. Statistically this is true, but the evidence from the corporate front lines of the talent wars suggests that the people we lose represent the guts of our future leadership.

What is more, these skilled emigrants are often taking their jobs with them when they leave Canada. Immigrants cannot step into their shoes because the jobs, their functions within transnational companies, have left as well. Canada is losing the struggle for top workers, for highly skilled work, and, ultimately, its role as home base to successful global enterprises.

In the global war for talent, it is not enough for Canada to invest in developing its human advantage. First, of course, we have to make sure that the Canadian economy is generating enough opportunities for talented Canadians to put their skills to work within Canada. Given the shortage of skills in many sectors, however, we must also ensure that we make the most of the talent we have through more effective recognition of skills developed in different circumstances. We have to work harder to attract talent from abroad, and we must make certain that immigrants are able to integrate quickly and fully into our job market. Even as the private sector scrambles for skills, we must remember that achieving our economic and social aspirations as a country will depend on the ability of the public sector as well to attract and retain its share of talented Canadians.

■ Fostering Innovation

Next we shift our attention from people to ideas. Perhaps only the invention of the printing press can rival the new communications technologies, which are transforming the way we live and work, in their impact on the flow of ideas. In the resulting global ferment, even the winners are running scared.

The United States is the unquestioned champion of the Internet age, yet in a presentation to members of the BCNI in 1999, Council on Competitiveness president John Yochelson expressed great concern about his own country's future prospects. Despite its large market, world-class universities, established clusters of innovation, and entrepreneurial culture, he worries that America is losing ground to other countries. Why? American investment in basic research is declining as a share of the economy even as it rises in most other industrialized countries. The pool of scientists and engineers engaged in research is falling as a percentage of the American labour force, and is now smaller than in most other OECD countries. The number of students earning bachelor's degrees in information technology is actually falling. And the regulatory environment, he suggested, is even more inhibiting to innovation in the United States than in Canada.[17] Is it any wonder that the council warned in its 1999 report on innovation that "America's current innovation leadership is increasingly rooted in past investment and that the long run basis for our future strength is being eroded — all while other nations are accelerating their own efforts."[18]

INTRODUCTION

Canada's research performance is improving, but from a much lower base. Despite the most generous tax treatment of R&D in the world, research as a percentage of the economy is the second lowest in the G-7. The research gap can be seen equally in the public and the private sectors, and it augurs badly for the prospects of future innovation and the creation of breakthrough processes by Canadian companies.

Canada's deficiencies in R&D are a recurring theme in the statements of government and private sector leaders alike. In his 2000 budget speech, Paul Martin noted that the strength of any country in the new economy is measured not by weapons but by patents; not by territory but by ideas; not by resources but by people. "In such a world, successful nations will only be those that foster a culture of innovation. They will be those that create new knowledge and bring the product of that knowledge quickly to market."[19] Governments have begun to respond with improved funding for research. But research on its own, without the benefit of transformation into new products, processes, and services, is of little value. Canada's challenge is to turn more of the ideas flowing from its research into successful global businesses. Too few of the ideas born in Canada lead to patents, and too few of those patents lead to successful commercialization of products, processes, and services.

Some critics suggest that Canada's poor record of innovation reflects a weak commitment to entrepreneurship among the country's business class. In fact, the 2000 Executive Report of the Global Entrepreneurship Monitor (GEM) rated Canada as one of the highly entrepreneurial countries among the twenty-one it studied. But while 7.9 percent of Canadians are involved in entrepreneurial activities, only 2.7 percent are willing to invest personally in start-up ventures, and just one person in forty-five is actually managing a new business — a much lower level than in most other countries (see fig. 2). Despite the dramatic growth in the pool of venture capital over the past five years, the report says access to seed capital is a continuing problem. It noted the wide variations among provinces in policies and programs affecting entrepreneurs, with multiple layers of government creating duplicated costs and incompatible regulations. And it warned that "the allure of lower taxes and strong infrastructure in places such as Silicon Valley attracts entrepreneurial talent out of the country."[20]

The result is that not enough of our new businesses are achieving critical mass as public companies and global players. The January 2000 report of the Canadian E-Business Opportunities Roundtable, "Fast Forward:

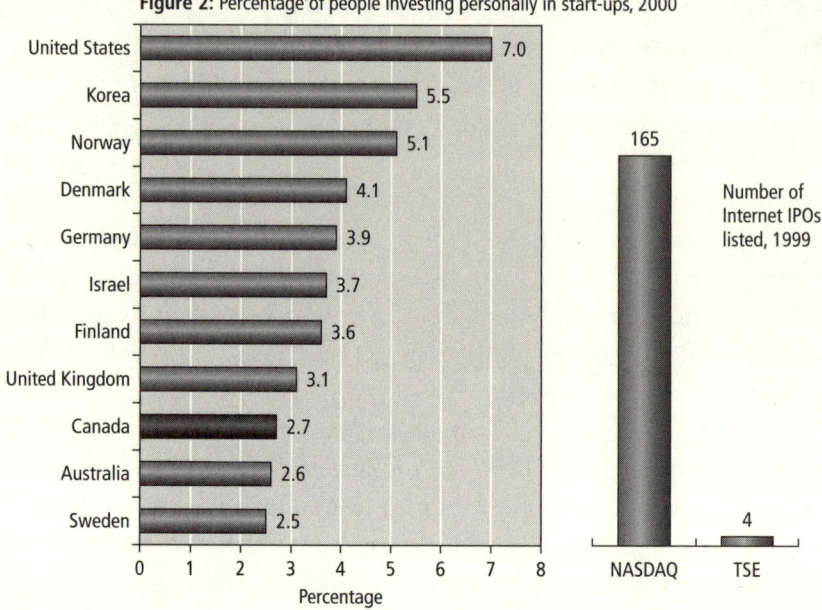

Figure 2: Percentage of people investing personally in start-ups, 2000

Accelerating Canada's Leadership in the Internet Economy," noted that only four Internet companies launched initial public offerings on the Toronto Stock Exchange in 1999. In the same year, 165 IPOs were completed on the NASDAQ exchange in the United States.[21] Clearly, Canada is falling short of capitalizing on its potential to be a leader in the Internet economy.

At both the federal and the provincial levels, governments are taking steps to create an environment more conducive to entrepreneurial initiative and business investment. But the innovation imperative extends well beyond the private sector. If we want to develop a true culture of innovation in Canada, that theme must resonate through the activities of our governments and across all sectors of our society. Governments must become more innovative in the way they administer programs and deliver services. They must find new and better ways of working with one another within the context of the Canadian federation. More fundamentally, they must seize the opportunities being created by new technologies to re-invigorate citizen participation and rebuild public confidence in our democratic institutions.

Citizens, communities, and the private sector must do their part to contribute to such a process. Neither the private sector nor governments working alone can deliver the kind of cohesive and prosperous communities that Canadians desire. The public, private, and non-profit sectors

INTRODUCTION

must draw on each other's strengths as we seek innovative ways to reshape Canadian communities for shared success in a world of change.

■ Building the Canadian Brand

Turning innovative entrepreneurial firms into global leaders requires plenty of smart people with good ideas, but it also means that Canadians must have access to global markets and global capital. Despite being the most trade-dependent country in the industrialized world, Canada, by 1999, was home to just two of the top 150 companies in the world as measured by market capitalization. We have many successful companies that are actively engaged in global markets, yet our exports remain heavily concentrated. Despite our integration with the larger North American market, Canada has fallen behind Belgium, Sweden, and the Netherlands as a host for foreign investment — and is home to fewer multinational corporations than Denmark, Sweden, Switzerland, or South Korea.

Even as foreign investors rediscovered the merits of Canadian-based firms in 2000, Canadians seemed to lose faith in the ability of companies based here to deliver competitive returns. The past decade has seen a steady and growing outflow of Canadian capital into foreign securities — $135 billion during the 1990s, and $39.1 billion more in the first eight months of 2000 alone.

Canadian and foreign-owned companies face the same pressures beyond our borders, and their strategic responses have many similarities. Companies are re-organizing along functional rather than geographic lines. The traditional full-service country subsidiary is dying; in its place, countries must compete to be the preferred location for factories and offices serving customers across an entire continent or even around the world. Canada has important strengths in attracting such investments, but it remains weak on some of the factors that matter most. In particular, a reputation as a country with excessive taxes or unfriendly regulations can be devastating in a world in which money flits across borders in the blink of an eye. Building a more effective Canadian brand does not mean that we must be best at everything — but we have to eliminate the most serious negatives while strengthening our positives. As a truly multicultural country in an era of increasingly multicultural enterprises, Canada is well positioned to attract high-value global functions and well-paid jobs if we coordinate our efforts and aggressively market our virtues.

INTRODUCTION

Success in attracting investment and in building the Canadian brand is just part of a broader challenge. Canadians can and must be a powerful and constructive force among nations. In a global environment where country brands matter more than ever, selling our products and ideas is easier if we are well known and respected, just as attracting investment and people to Canada depends in large measure on how desirable it is to live and work here. What is more, we have both an economic interest and a moral responsibility to engage in the global commons.

Economically, we remain a relatively small country heavily dependent on free flows of trade and investment. That gives us a huge stake in maintaining and improving the multilateral rule of law. Precisely because of the growing integration of our economy with that of the United States, a strong multilateral trade system and an effective World Trade Organization should be one of Canada's highest strategic priorities. Given the stalled progress at the multilateral level, we have to focus on expanding our network of bilateral agreements in Asia, Europe, and Latin America. The time has also come to look seriously at the potential benefits of another quantum leap forward in our relationship with the United States and Mexico. Ten years of extraordinary economic progress have led to a sense of complacency in our relationship with the United States. Yet many serious issues remain to be addressed, including customs and border administration, tariffs, standards, trade in services, government procurement, trade remedies, competition policy, and investment. The key question is whether to deal with these issues piecemeal and incrementally or to pursue a further effort at sweeping and far-reaching change.

As we consider the best approach to defending our economic interests in the world, we must not forget our responsibilities to our fellow global citizens. We must give much higher priority to fighting global poverty and disease, and once again aspire to make Canada a leader in championing the cause of development assistance. We are respected and trusted around the world, and we know how to engage in effective economic development as well as humanitarian aid. As individuals and as a country, we have a duty to contribute our knowledge and experience.

Similarly, our engagement in promoting global economic development will be incomplete if we do not at the same time make a clean and healthy environment one of our core goals. Sustainability is intimately connected with quality of life. Quality of life depends in part on economic prosperity, but also on the quality of our air, water, and natural spaces. The ultimate productivity challenge — within Canada and globally — is to respond to the material needs of a growing population by greatly increasing the value and usefulness that we extract from every barrel of oil, tonne of steel, and litre of water. The challenge to global sustainability is great, but Canada and Canadian businesses should lead. As an energy-intensive economy and a major exporter of resource-based products, aspiring to leadership will be costly. But the very intensity of our energy and resource use presents a clear incentive for Canadian companies to pursue strategies geared to environmental innovation. Canadian companies are taking their environmental responsibilities seriously, but we can and must do more. This is our duty as global citizens — but, as managers, doing the right thing for the global ecosystem is also a necessary element in any successful strategy for sustainable growth in shareholder value.

By marrying smart economic policies with core Canadian values, we can ensure that Canada makes a real contribution to the well-being of people around the world and within our own borders. In taking this approach, we speak directly against those who suggest that the solution to Canada's problems is to be more like Americans. We have much to learn from Americans and others around the world, but to maximize progress in our efforts to improve the standard of living and quality of life of Canadians our country must pursue its own distinctive course in world affairs.

■ Honing Our Edge

Several common themes run through our examination of all these issues. The first deals with the need for more effective government. Much has been written by others about the optimum size of government. Vito Tanzi and Ludger Shuknecht, for instance, have concluded in their landmark study *Public Spending in the Twentieth Century* that the past thirty-five years of growth in government spending has added little to social and economic welfare. They suggest that governments in most industrialized countries could be much smaller, without sacrificing important policy objectives.[22]

How much governments should do in Canada is a question that will be debated and re-evaluated constantly. We focus, instead, on the argument that whatever governments do, they must do well. This means that, in delivering services, forming policies, administering regulations, and competing for human resources, the public sector in Canada needs to undergo transformational change at least as comprehensive as the change many private sector enterprises have already endured. As Jack Mintz puts it: "The key point is that globalization requires governments themselves to be 'competitive,' by spending wisely and with smart tax policies. This is the path for governments to achieve better economic growth in today's global economy."[23]

We all have to pay for what we ask governments to do on our behalf, and Canada's overall tax burden is close to average for the industrialized world. We suffer a particular problem because our burden is out of line with that of our largest trading partner, market, and competitor, the United States. More damaging than our tax rates, however, is our tax structure. Our tax system imposes its heaviest burdens on the most mobile factors of production. This approach is out of touch with the realities of the information age. Canada still has remarkable scope to choose how large and how extensive a range of services it wants governments to provide. What globalization means is that we must be more careful than ever not to impose excessive taxes on the activities we want to encourage, and to lean more heavily instead on those we want less of.

In discussing the role of government, we also emphasize the broader context of governance. New technologies and global integration are empowering consumers and citizens alike to question and challenge the actions of multinational companies and of national and subnational governments. If we want the concept of Canada to remain meaningful, we must rethink the relationships between citizens and governments. We must ensure that all corners of society are engaged in the process of deciding our collective goals and in making progress towards them. Perhaps the most troubling dilemma here is that consensus rarely challenges the status quo. We must seek to be inclusive, yet also foster innovative policies and behaviour in every sector of society.

This point leads to another theme — the need for leadership. As the members of the BCNI put it at the CEO Summit 2000: "In the technology-driven economy, the biggest returns go to leaders rather than followers. Creating new products and finding ways to do business that overturn existing models is always risky. But companies that create new technologies appear to dominate the new markets those technologies create. Companies that wait to see what works and what does not are left to pick up crumbs."[24]

In addition to leadership, we need a winning attitude. We can nurture our core Canadian values of fairness, sharing, generosity, and tolerance and still celebrate both personal and collective achievement. If we waste our energy tearing down anyone who gets ahead of the crowd, if we concentrate our attention on dividing the pie into precisely equal slices instead of making the pie bigger, we will all end up poorer. If we are going to share prosperity instead of poverty, we have to work together to generate more wealth to share.

Our final theme is sustainability. It is easy for governments to be all things to all people at the peak of an economic cycle. But if we take the easy route, using cyclical resources to achieve temporary progress in improving the lives of Canadians, we will fail in the greater challenge. If our society truly believes in achieving certain goals, it must embrace the most effective means of achieving those goals and sustaining that achievement through good times and bad.

One criticism that has been raised of our work and that of the BCNI in the past has been the focus on government policy rather than private sector action. Chief executives, interviewed as part of the Canada Global Leadership Initiative, voiced a common concern about the past shortcomings of Canadian business — notably, the willingness to hide behind trade barriers and to lean on the protective crutches of government subsidies and a weak currency. As the BCNI stated at the CEO Summit 2000, "We have been too conservative in evaluating opportunities, too slow to expand abroad and too defensive in our strategies at home."[25]

We suggest that many talented Canadians and their enterprises understand all too well the imperatives of the global economy. As individuals and companies, they are forging ahead, expanding abroad, and making their mark. As a country, however, we face two challenges. The first is one of equality of opportunity, of providing the environment and motivation for more Canadians to understand and participate effectively in the global economy. The second is one of collective benefit, of making sure that the individual and corporate success we foster rebounds to the advantage of all Canadians. As a country we gain little if we equip our citizens and our enterprises for global success, only to see them flee for climes more hospitable to the very ambitions we have given them the tools to realize.

We cannot stress strongly enough the importance of a strong, stable, and healthy community as the pre-eminent condition for reinforcing and sustaining economic development. This fundamental linkage and interdependence between economic means and social ends is as old as history itself and has been admirably analyzed by Harvard University professor David S. Landes in *The Wealth and Poverty of Nations*.[26] Restructuring government and cutting taxes are the means of achieving our goals, not ends in themselves. Our goal is not to redesign Canada in neo-conservative terms, or to seek to create a carbon copy version of the United States. We are convinced that Canadians can and must develop a better approach — but to achieve sustainable and continuing improvements in the quality of life of all Canadians, we have to make the right moves on economic as well as social policy.

We conclude our book by offering our vision of the goals to which Canadians realistically can aspire, and our thoughts on the actions Canadians must take if we hope to fulfil that vision. Our list of proposals is not intended to be comprehensive, but it does identify concrete steps we can take as a country within the next few years. These steps involve commitments by the public, private, and non-profit sectors, and above all a willingness to set narrow interests aside in order to work for the benefit of our country and of all Canadians. We do not pretend that progress on all the fronts we suggest will be easy — but we believe meaningful progress is possible and that we owe it to our children to try.

Canada's people and economy remain concentrated in a narrow band across the northern edge of North America. Our location has blessed us with resources and imposed disadvantages of distance and climate. We cannot change our geography or weather. We can talk plainly about our potential as a country and how to give Canadians a powerful Northern Edge that will drive our progress together within the global economy.

As we plunge into the excitement and uncertainty of the new millennium, Canada indeed stands on the edge. Perhaps it is on the edge of greatness, perhaps on the edge of precipitous decline. Either result is possible, but neither is inevitable. In today's fast-paced world, disaster is never far away. Ultimately, however, we are optimists. One way or another, many Canadians have the right stuff to succeed globally. For us, the issue is how to make sure that all Canadians emerge as winners in the tumultuous times that lie ahead.

1

RIDING THE GLOBALIZATION WAVE

Whatever cause you champion, the cure does not lie in protesting against globalization itself. I believe that the poor are not poor because of too much globalization, but because of too little.[1]

— KOFI ANNAN, SECRETARY GENERAL OF THE UNITED NATIONS, MAY 22, 2000

◄ ◄ ◄

A passion for discovery, a readiness to adapt to change, and a desire for opportunity motivated our ancestors as they conquered the vast Canadian wilderness. So, too, contemporary generations of Canadians must face the challenge of globalization and embrace the opportunities of the new age, the defining characteristic of which is the borderless integration of technology, capital, information, ideas, and aspirations. Our success in meeting the challenge will be the decisive factor in our drive to create a prosperous, vibrant, and distinctive society in the northern half of the North American continent — to create the winning conditions for Canadians to triumph in the global economy.

To make globalization work to our advantage, we must first understand what it is. We must recognize its powerful and all-encompassing reach and appreciate how, in a few short years, it has transformed the world. Little more than a decade ago the Berlin Wall still seemed impenetrable, the Cold War was very much alive, two great nuclear powers exercised an uneasy hegemony, and democratic capitalism and open societies were the hallmark of only a minority of the countries of the world. In this world defined by blocs and proxy states, technology had not stood still. In the advanced, democratic countries, the pace of change picked up and, by the 1980s, we began to get a glimpse of what was to come. Information technology took hold and the promise of a wired world began to emerge. But the genie was still half in the bottle until we witnessed the unexpected break-up of the Soviet Union and the collapse of the Eastern bloc. Suddenly, central planning was out and the market was in. Overnight, formerly oppressed citizens began to taste basic freedoms and to test the meaning of an open society. Just as quickly, the state began to take on a different role, seen through the eyes of newly empowered individuals.

Against this backdrop of profound and historic change, the forces of globalization began to pick up speed. To most, it was a new phenomenon described in exalted terms such as the "new economy" or the "borderless world." In reality, it was an advanced reincarnation of a previous experience in globalization from a century ago, when capital flows and profits moved freely, governments did little to interfere with wealth creation, and people crossed borders with remarkable ease.

As we delve into the meaning of globalization and what it has in store for Canadians and people throughout the world, it is worth reminding ourselves that this seemingly unstoppable force, which ushered in the twentieth century and now defines the twenty-first, was halted in its tracks some seventy years ago. A stock-market crash, rampant protectionism, a precipitous fall in world trade, soaring unemployment, the spread of communism and fascism, and a catastrophic world war all signalled the demise of what had been heralded as a new golden age of commerce. Only in the 1990s has the legacy of this destructive period begun to be overcome — a legacy we are well advised to keep in mind as we debate the future of globalization. U.S. Federal Reserve Board chairman Alan Greenspan reminds us of our history: "In many important respects, the past half century has represented an uneven struggle to repair the close linkages among national economies that existed before the First World War. The hostilities bred of war, the substantial disruption to established trading patterns associated with that conflict, and the subsequent poor economic performance over the next few decades triggered the erection of trade barriers around the world that have taken even longer to dismantle. To repeat that error would be a tragic act of foolishness and waste."[2]

At one of our seminars a young woman asked us a simple question: "To succeed in a globalized world, what are the subjects I should study?"

"Languages, international affairs, philosophy, politics, economics, and the sciences," we replied. *New York Times* journalist Thomas L. Friedman emphasizes this holistic approach. To succeed in a globalized world, he says, one must learn to think in six dimensions all at once. "Today, more than ever, the traditional boundaries between politics, culture, technology, finance, national security and ecology are disappearing. You often cannot explain one without referring to the others, and you cannot explain the whole without reference to them all."[3]

We begin with this comment on globalization to emphasize that rapidly falling boundaries are not simply geographic but intellectual as well. We must therefore think in an integrated global context. Canadian public policy must be seen and understood in this all-encompassing way. So must the planning and decision-making of corporate leaders. In our research through the BCNI's Canada Global Leadership Initiative, it became clear that Canadian chief executives identified as one of their sharpest challenges the need to think in a global context and to apply solutions in a multidisciplinary way.

■ Forces Shaping Globalization

Understanding globalization is made easier if we are able to identify the important forces that have shaped it. Technology is the most significant of these influences. Beginning two decades ago, we began to witness giant leaps forward in telecommunications, computerization, miniaturization, and digitization. The world as a result has shrunk dramatically in time and space, and hundreds of millions of people in rapidly growing numbers are now connected to one another. Advances in microchip technology have resulted in computing power doubling every eighteen months on average over the past thirty years, while advances in compression technology mean that the amount of data that can be stored on a square inch of disc surface has increased by 60 percent every year since 1991.[4]

Digitization allows us to turn vast quantities of data into computer bits, which can then be transferred by telephone lines, satellites, and fibre optic cables around the world. *The Economist* offers some vivid examples of the new technology at work. "Number-crunching tasks that once took a week can now be done in seconds. Today a Ford Taurus car contains more computing power than the multimillion-dollar mainframe computers used in the Apollo space programme . . . In 1985, it cost $60,000 each

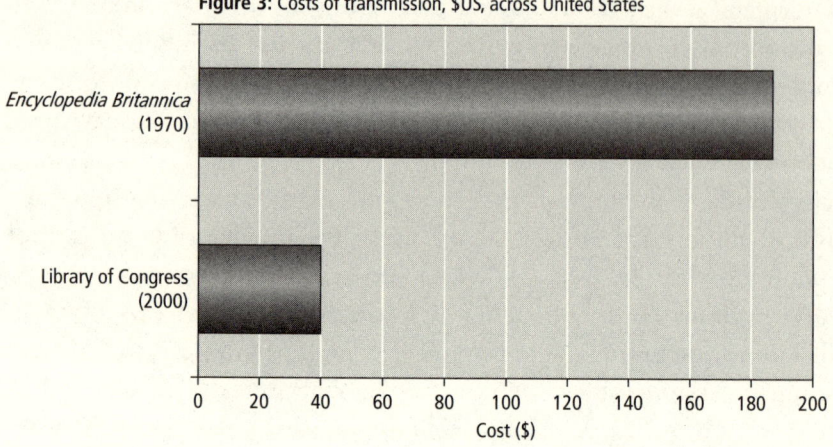

Figure 3: Costs of transmission, $US, across United States

time it crashed a car into a wall to find out what would happen in an accident. Now a collision can be simulated by computer for around $100 ... In 1970 it would have cost $187 to transmit *Encyclopedia Britannica* as an electronic file coast to coast in America. Today the entire content of the Library of Congress could be sent across America for just $40."[5]

The economic impact of these technological advances has been stunning. In the United States, the market capitalization of the technology sector soared to $4.5 trillion from $300 billion in the early 1990s. The market value of the technology companies that went public during the period 1990–99 was $4.2 trillion in January 2000, compared with an aggregate value of $403 billion at the time of their initial public offerings.[6]

The significance of these advances in technology changes the old economics of development. Quickly disappearing are the days when certain countries are limited to being exporters of raw materials. Today, thanks to technology, many countries have the opportunity to assemble the know-how, resources, and funding to become producers. In the words of Alcan chief executive Jacques Bougie, these countries need three essential ingredients to make it happen: "knowledge, organization, and a will to succeed."

A second force that has shaped globalization is the exponential spread of information offering virtually unlimited reach via satellite dishes, television, facsimile, and the Internet. Of these, the Internet is the most transforming of technologies. It is owned by no one, it can potentially reach into every household in the world, and today over 300 million people are using it. Only a decade ago, the Internet was almost unheard of. It offers, at the click of a key, access to a staggering inventory of information from almost anywhere in the world. But in the words of Nortel Networks chief executive John Roth, "this is just the beginning." The Internet is fundamentally changing the way the world is doing business and the way we will live. It is only a matter of time before citizens will have access to broadband Internet communications in their homes, offices, or elsewhere via handheld notepads or wireless telephony.

The information revolution has had a profound impact on governance. It has made it virtually impossible for governments to seal their borders and prevent their citizens from seeing what is beyond. People throughout the world learn more about each other and the way they live. Freedom of information, combined with technology, has been a powerful democratizing force, with the potential for knocking down even the most determined dictatorial regimes.

A third force that has shaped globalization is the increasing integration of global capital markets. The volume of capital in circulation is greater than ever: it moves with extraordinary speed and occupies a much larger share in relation to traded goods than ever before. While capital to some extent has always been mobile, technology has given it a bionic capability. Billions can be moved around the world at the touch of a button.

Faced with this reality, governments and regulators have progressively dismantled barriers to the flow of capital. As a general rule, those countries that have dropped their barriers most quickly have prospered the most. Another instigator has been the growth in the number of individual investors, especially in developed countries. Holders of equities continue to multiply. In the United States, the ratio of stock market capitalization to GDP has climbed to 160 percent from a sixty-year moving average of 49 percent. Close to 50 percent of Americans now own equities either directly or through defined contribution pension plans. In the 1950s it was less than 5 percent. The mutual fund industry now has about $7 trillion of assets, compared with $5.6 trillion for the banking system. In the early 1980s mutual fund assets were equal to 10 percent of bank deposits.[7]

No aspect of globalization has prompted a fiercer debate than the role of capital markets. Canadian prime minister Jean Chrétien has denounced more than once the mischief of "the guys in the red suspenders." Malaysia's prime minister, Dr. Mahathir bin Muhammad, has been the most vocal and persistent critic of irresponsible financial speculators and "morons" who trade in currencies. At the first ever APEC CEO Summit hosted by the Business Council on National Issues (BCNI) in November 1997, Dr. Mahathir expressed his indignation at "the destructive forces that heartlessly plunge hard-working citizens into poverty overnight through no fault of their own." Yet the power of what Friedman calls "the electronic herd" is real and must be reckoned with, whether they are short-term traders of stocks, bonds, and currencies or long-term direct investors. More connected and better informed than ever, these capital market actors are uncompromising arbiters of country or corporate strengths and weaknesses, a reality that no nation can escape. Canada is not an exception.

The most concerted multilateral response to the challenges posed by the globalization of capital markets has been the formation of the Group of Twenty (G-20). Chaired by finance minister Paul Martin, it brings together finance ministers and central bank governors from a diverse group of countries representing 87 percent of the world gross domestic product and 65 percent of world population.

In an address to the House of Commons Standing Committee on Foreign Affairs and International Trade on May 18, 2000, Mr. Martin defined the G-20's sweeping mandate: "to explore virtually every area of international finance . . . and some of the most visible and troubling aspects of today's integrated world economy — including the devastating effects of financial crises, the growing gap between rich and poor, and a system of governance that has not kept pace with the sweeping changes taking place in the global economy." The G-20's progress so far has been limited but it has staked its ground. It is facing formidable forces that will not be easily influenced.

■ The Elixir of Democratic Capitalism

In this new world shaped by technology, information, and capital flows, ideology has become increasingly irrelevant. Labels of left and right resonate less than they once did. In large measure this change is due to the emergence of democratic capitalism as the "winning" system — one that has proven its capability both to generate wealth and to share it broadly. But democratic capitalism's triumph was not an easy one. From the time of the Bolshevik Revolution of 1917 to the collapse of the Berlin Wall in 1989, the world experienced the profoundly inadequate alternatives offered by communism and fascism. Statism and authoritarianism did not deliver on their promises.

Even in Western democratic countries, the twenty-five years following the Second World War did not result in an unconditional embrace of market capitalism. There was still a common view among political elites that markets were prone to excess and to failure, and that "mixed" economies with a healthy dose of government intervention served the public interest best. The economics of John Maynard Keynes were still very fashionable, while the views of Friedrich von Hayek were generally thought of as heretical. In this period, particularly in Europe and North America, political elites, convinced that government knows best in the management of economic affairs, delivered a succession of policy failures, as evidenced by sclerotic growth, stagflation, rising unemployment, and sluggish innovation. World Trade Organization (WTO) director general Mike Moore offers a stark reminder of where things stood in the immediate aftermath of the Second World War. "In 1949, when I was born, trade barriers were still at their post-Depression highs, few currencies were convertible, rationing was commonplace, huge swaths of industry were nationalised, and Soviet communism threatened to crush liberal democracy."[8]

The advent of the Thatcher government in the United Kingdom and the Reagan administration in the United States launched a revolution that began the rollback of the state as the dominant actor in the economy. As the United Kingdom and the United States began to liberalize their economies, so did other countries. The world economy responded in kind. The value of imported and exported manufactured goods, which had been $2 trillion in 1986, ballooned to $5.2 trillion a decade later.[9] And by the early 1990s, the number of transnational corporations, as measured by the United Nations Conference on Trade and Development, had increased to about 37,000, from 7,000 in the 1960s.[10]

During this period, free trade agreements began to flourish. Impatient

Figure 4: Increase since 1950

GDP/person in less developed countries	370%
Global output	700%
Global trade	1,600%
Foreign direct investment	2,500%

with the slowness and uncertainty of the multilateral process, regional free trade agreements became the vogue, championed by business people anxious to have governments help pave the way for the expansion of trade and investment. In Canada, in the autumn of 1981, the Business Council on National Issues began to explore among its member chief executives the idea of a bilateral free trade agreement with the United States. By 1988, after several years of intense debate culminating in a hotly contested election, the Canada–United States Free Trade Agreement was born. Mercosur, a treaty encompassing Argentina, Brazil, Paraguay, and Uruguay, followed in 1991, and in 1992 the European Union adopted its single market initiative. The Asian Free Trade Area was launched in 1993, and the North American Free Trade Agreement, embracing Mexico, was implemented in 1994. These regional agreements, close to one hundred in number in the year 2000, form a network that has helped advance global economic integration and the rule of law.

■ Full Speed Ahead

Concerns about the speed of things is a widespread phenomenon in contemporary society as well. "The world is in a rush, and is getting close to its end" — thus spoke Archbishop Wulfstan, in a sermon delivered in York in the year 1014.[11] Today, the speed of change is blinding, posing severe challenges even for well-educated workers, agile companies, and efficient governments. For the better part of the twentieth century, these demands did not exist. International trade and investment represented a much smaller percentage of the world economy. Capital, constrained by controls, moved more slowly across borders. Corporations, protected by tariffs and other barriers to entry, operated in a less competitive environment. Workers, sheltered by generous safety nets, had little need or incentive to upgrade their skills. And governments, less accountable and transparent, were not on the cutting edge of change.

Everything changed dramatically with the arrival of the information revolution. The barriers to entry in a vast number of businesses were lowered, as were their costs. We witnessed an unprecedented acceleration of product development. In this new environment of stepped-up competition and falling prices, the consumer became empowered as never before. Companies moved much closer to their customers, and consumers faced an unprecedented abundance of choice.

When the Business Council on National Issues launched the Canada Global Leadership Initiative in 1999, David O'Brien, council chairman and chief executive officer of Canadian Pacific, emphasized that the "need for speed" was a powerful catalyst. "Companies, individuals, and governments can no longer measure change in years or months. We are now on Internet time, which means that, to be global leaders, we must be better and faster than the competition day in and day out." Friedman also explains the shrinking of time and space in the new age economy:

> In the walled-up Cold War system this process of going from innovation to commoditization happened at ten miles per hour because the barriers of entry into business were generally much higher and the barriers countries could erect around their economies were much higher. In the globalization world, with the barriers now lowered or removed, this process is happening at 110 miles per hour. And as we evolve into an economy that will be increasingly defined by the Internet, the move from innovation to commoditization is going to reach Net speed, which is as fast as the speed of light.[12]

■ Winning in a Globalized World

Faced with a globalized system that imposes increasingly similar rules and expectations on countries, corporations, and individuals alike, a system that is operating at faster and faster speeds, what are the ingredients of success? What are the formulas for winning and for staying ahead of the pack? We will deal with these issues in detail in a Canadian context in subsequent chapters, but we outline them here as a set of principles, as the six imperatives of success in a globalized world.

The first of these imperatives is effective social organization, the ability of a community or a country to marshal its resources in a disciplined way. This requires a sense of common purpose, an efficient, honest, and accountable government, an education system that is advanced and open to all, an entrepreneurially driven economy that is productive and agile, and a social identity defined by high levels of health and public safety and a fair distribution of income.

Professor Charles P. Kindleberger of the Massachusetts Institute of Technology speaks of "social capability" when describing why countries and societies rise and fall.[13] He emphasizes that the ability to excel relies on the influence of complex historical, social, and cultural factors.

Harvard professor David S. Landes reinforces the point in seeking to answer the question why some nations are rich and others are poor. In explaining the ascendancy of Great Britain in the eighteenth century, he points out that it was "not God-given, not happenstance, but the result of hard work, ingenuity, imagination and enterprise."[14] Professor Lester Thurow addresses the centrality of social organization to the creation of wealth and its linkage to the ability to change:

> Social organization is the starting point at the bottom of the wealth pyramid, but it is also an essential building block at every stage of wealth creation. All successful societies periodically confront new problems that their old institutions cannot solve. If they are to remain successful, they have to reinvent themselves. Yet social systems are very resistant to change and have an enormous ability to tolerate, rather than solve, problems. The path of least resistance — simply allowing problems to fester — all too often ends up pulling down even the greatest of societies.[15]

There can be no doubt that Canada's high level of social capability is a source of strength and competitive advantage. But are we slipping in relation to other countries around the world? We believe this to be the case, in part because we are resting on our laurels, and also because we are not embracing change nearly quickly enough.

The second imperative for success in a globalized world is speed of adaptation — the facility with which countries, governments, businesses, and workers must respond to change. Until relatively recently, in most parts of the world, rapid change was feared and resisted. Those countries that embraced change most willingly, and were buttressed by an effective social organization, generally prospered the most.

The role of governments is crucial. Indeed, as a result of globalization, governments matter more than ever. Small government, efficient government, focused government, honest government — these are powerful sources of competitive advantage. It is often said that the principal responsibility of government is to prepare the citizenry for the future. Yet how many national governments around the world are genuinely visionary? By our count, very few. A case can be made that Hong Kong, Singapore, the United Kingdom, the Netherlands, Finland, Ireland, and the United States qualify. In an address to the Business Council on National Issues in April 2000, Hong Kong chief executive Tung Chee Hwa captured the essence of government's role in advancing and preparing for change. "The priority for our government is to lay the groundwork for prosperity in the twenty-first century by having leading-edge people skills and a technological infrastructure second to none. In Hong Kong, we always have had to confront change face to face. Change is our friend; it is not our enemy."

A similar theme was echoed at a meeting of BCNI members with Mexico's then president-elect, Vicente Fox, in August 2000. "One of my principal missions," he said, "is to make Mexico a first-world country. To get there, we must have a strong consensus around a vision for my country in 2025 — a vision that is shaped by change and fuelled by socially responsible growth."

If the role of governments is to help create the climate for change, the role of business is to be the engine of change. Companies today more than ever before operate in a Schumpeterian environment where the virtues of creative destruction can be seen at work. New ideas, new companies, new products, new skills, and an ever-accelerating cycle of innovation are revolutionizing the way we work and live. Bill Gates has neatly summed up the importance of speed: "If the 1980s were about quality and the 1990s were about reengineering, then the 2000s will be about velocity. About how quickly the nature of business will change. About how quickly business itself will be transacted. About how information access will alter the lifestyle of consumers and their expectations of business. Quality improvements and business process improvements will occur far faster."[16]

The speed of change has become unsettling to some who run businesses, driving them to support protectionism and regulation and to seek out subsidies. If any, the relief is temporary, the benefit fleeting, and the ultimate damage possibly irreparable. Business leaders around the world increasingly understand this danger.

If the acceptance of rapid and relentless change is becoming the dominant global corporate culture, the same cannot be said of organized labour. Resistance is evident and, in some cases, growing in various parts of the world. Jay Mazur, president of the Union of Needletrades, Industrial, and Textile Employees, sums up his concerns as follows:

> The future is a contested terrain of very public choices that will shape the world economy of the 21st century. The forces behind global economic change — which exalt deregulation, cater to corporations, undermine social structures, and ignore popular concerns — cannot be sustained. Globalization is leaving

perilous instability and rising inequality in its wake. It is hurting too many and helping too few.[17]

The Canadian Labour Congress makes the same point even more forcefully. "Amidst the disastrous effects of global economics and global politics, Canadian workers call for global solidarity. We join with working women and men around the world to demand an end to unconstrained capital and the self-serving absolutist doctrine of so-called free markets and free trade."[18]

How then do Canadians stack up in our willingness to embrace ever-accelerating change? We have to do better, considerably better. BCE chief executive Jean Monty offers this opinion on the collective responsibility of Canadians: "Technology has revolutionized how we govern, how we run our businesses, how we work and with what skills. The constant factor at play here is change and the speed of change. Whether we like it or not, we have to do everything smarter and faster or increasingly fall behind and see our relative standard of living fall."

The third imperative for success in a globalized world is the need to be open to ideas and to competition from beyond a country's borders. "In an open system, we compete with our imagination, not with a lock and key," observes Nicholas Negroponte. "The result is not only a larger number of successful companies, but a wider variety of choice for the consumer and an even more nimble commercial sector, one capable of rapid change and growth."[19]

Not long ago, the hallmark of product development was one of secrecy. Business people believed that market share was won by shutting competitors out. That world has been turned topsy-turvy. Monopoly businesses are doomed, and a lock on information is impossible. Today the dominant standard is the open standard. The ability to succeed in a wide-open race is the measure of true competition.

Countries are now being judged to a degree in the same way. There is a direct correlation between a country's degree of openness and its level of prosperity. Friedman warns that globalization will continue to drive the need for openness:

In the future, the virtues of keeping your economy as open as possible will only multiply, because in the era of globalization, knowledge is the key to economic growth, and if you close your country off in any way to either the best brains in the world or the best technologies in the world, you will fall behind faster and faster. That's why the most open-minded, tolerant, creative and diverse societies will have the easiest time with globalization, while the most closed, rigid, uptight, self-absorbed and traditional companies and countries, which are just not comfortable with openness, will struggle.[20]

By world standards, Canada is an open country. Is it sufficiently open? We do not believe so, as we will elaborate in later chapters. Foreign ownership restrictions and outdated regulations still affect significant areas of enterprise. According to the Economic Freedom of the World 2000 Annual Report sponsored by the Fraser Institute, the Hong Kong Centre for Economic Research, and the Cato Institute, Canada is trailing extraordinary country performers such as Hong Kong, Singapore, Ireland, New Zealand, the United Kingdom, and the United States.[21]

The fourth imperative for success in a globalized world is the need for openness *within* national borders. Countries that aspire to be leaders in a global arena increasingly characterized by disappearing walls cannot afford to live with walls at home. Internal barriers to the unfettered movement of people, goods, services, and capital within a defined state make no sense whatsoever. They stifle development and are a powerful disincentive to the achievement of economies of scale on the part of homegrown enterprises seeking to bulk up for global competition.

Canada fails severely in this area. While as a country we have made some progress in knocking down internal barriers, they persist in significant numbers. In part this fragmentation is due to the fact that Canada is a large, federated country with a relatively small population. The challenge of eliminating internal barriers falls squarely on the shoulders of the country's premiers and their respective governments. Repeated appeals over several decades by Canadian business leaders for a totally open domestic market have gone unanswered.

The Business Council on National Issues has summed up the contradiction in this state of affairs: "We consider it nigh on unbelievable that Canada, which takes pride in its openness as an international trader and which aspires to be a global player, should still harbour an array of barriers to the free movement of people, goods, services and capital within our borders. In some cases, it is much easier to do business abroad than within our own country. This is intolerable and costly. It reflects a failure of political will. Worse yet, it demonstrates a parochialism which hampers

Canadians from competing from a position of maximum strength in the global marketplace."[22]

The fifth imperative for success in a globalized world is an entrepreneurial culture and the ability to manage well. Given that competition for ideas, talent, and market share is increasingly a global exercise, the bar for testing the quality of entrepreneurs and managers is ever higher. At the heart of entrepreneurialism is the willingness to take risks, to test the unknown, to weather adversity. In the words of Lester Thurow, "Societies dominated by the fearful are never wealthy societies. Wealthy societies allow individuals with explorer mentalities to flourish. No one ever knows what is possible or whether monsters really exist unless they are willing to take risks, venture out, and explore."[23]

But entrepreneurs are like rare flowers that will flourish only in the most welcoming of environments. Societies, in Kindleberger's words, that lack "social capability," that cannot organize themselves, that do not value hard work, that begrudge success, that protect vested interests and refuse to change are societies that will create few entrepreneurs, and will drive those they do have away. John Roth of Nortel Networks speaks of the need for societies to "nurture their most creative minds and to reward builders and bold thinkers not just financially, but also through respect and recognition." Robert Brown, chief executive of Bombardier, says that "Canada must work much harder at celebrating entrepreneurial achievement and at promoting Canadian success stories around the world." Israel Asper, chairman of CanWest Global Communications, is blunter: "Bad attitudes on the part of politicians, bureaucratic red tape and a culture of envy is a deadly cocktail that kills entrepreneurship in the bud!"

The climate in Canada for entrepreneurialism is at best lukewarm. Success in business is still regarded by too many with scepticism and suspicion. A thin veil barely conceals a broadly based culture of envy. We seem to take much greater satisfaction in taxing our economic heroes than in celebrating and rewarding them. Some politicians and writers openly revel in promoting outdated images of rich versus poor and in attacking the demons of "big business." Attitudes are beginning to change for the better, especially as a young and outwardly oriented generation rises. But do we have time to wait? We do not think so.

The sixth imperative of success in a globalized world is perhaps the most important: people must be empowered with knowledge and skills in a never-ending process of renewal. The more knowledge and the greater the skills, the more creative and productive a society will be. This reality places a solemn responsibility on the shoulders of society as a whole. We must foster knowledge and succeed in imparting it to our young and to future generations. In our mission, universal and publicly funded systems of education are crucial to success.

Effective skill acquisition in a knowledge-centred world will be the defining factor of individual empowerment. The skills that will be needed will grow ever more demanding. Lifelong learning will become the norm, and countries as well as companies will compete for talent in a global marketplace.

Canada's "education credentials" are quite impressive if one measures how much of the country's resources are applied to preparing our young for the future. But we are not maximizing our potential, and in a number of crucial areas we are falling behind. Part of the reason, according to Professor Thomas Courchene, is that we are not placing sufficient emphasis on a human capital strategy for Canada. In an attempt to galvanize a national consensus, Courchene throws out a challenge. He invites Canadians "to design a sustainable, socially inclusive and internationally competitive infrastructure that ensures equality of access for all Canadians, so that they may develop, enhance and employ their skills and human capital in Canada, thereby enabling them to become full citizens in the information-era Canadian and global societies."[24]

Boiled down to its bare essentials, Courchene is saying that a supreme national effort is required to ensure that Canadian attitudes, policies, and infrastructures are geared to produce excellence in human capital and skills. To this he adds a thinly veiled appeal to Canadian nationalism. This achievement will help ensure that new generations of globally empowered Canadians will choose to apply their knowledge and skills from a Canadian base.

We have identified six imperatives of success in a globalized world. Without any one of them, countries, companies, and individuals would be handicapped. All six imperatives are driving forces in Canada, and, in this sense, we have a competitive advantage over most countries. At the individual level, most Canadians are participating well in the new economy, putting to work an excellent education and advanced skills. But not all Canadians are benefiting from globalization, especially those who, for one reason or another, have not been able to meet the ever-higher education requirements or to renew their skills. With commitment, this failure can be remedied in Canada. In the global context, it is an affliction with far-reaching consequences.

■ Globalization on Trial

Globalization has produced both winners and losers. We will make the case that the positive impact of globalization has resulted in a much better world overall, and a significantly improved human condition. But the costs have been significant as well, and in some cases terrible. To ignore them would be immoral and foolish.

Canadian journalist William Thorsell, a former editor-in-chief of the *Globe and Mail*, has poignantly captured the concerns and fears about globalization:

> Globalization generates enormous wealth, but it is also about the supermarket, where the superior thrive because they are the super-men. The cruelty of excellence oppresses the rest, though successful people are also disabled by lack of empathy, insight and compassion. The globalized world is too hard, too tough, too perfect, too demanding for most people. The Internet is too virtual, too immaterial, too imaginary to create real meaning and happiness. Human experience is the measure of man. Our fragility, rather than perfection, should be the central point of reference.[25]

Thorsell's evocation of fear and fragility is a sober reflection of how tens of millions of people view globalization. The same liberating and enriching process that has yielded so much in the way of good has, in some cases, also destroyed jobs, poisoned the environment, and created a divide between those empowered by knowledge and those too incapable or too poor to catch the wave.

As individuals, regions, and countries leap briskly ahead, the plight of the world's disadvantaged becomes all the more apparent. The facts are sobering. About one-quarter of the world's population lives on less than one dollar a day; one in five is illiterate; the top 20 percent consume roughly 85 percent of the world's goods and services. In 1960 the world's richest countries had thirty times more income than the poorest 20 percent. Today, the wealth gap has grown significantly wider. Children rank high among the casualties: eight million die each year because of polluted water or dirty air; some six million die from malnutrition. Of the 27 substantial armed conflicts that raged throughout the world in 1999, 25 were civil wars. Of the 40 poorest countries, 24 are either in the midst of war or have recently emerged from civil conflicts. In the rush for economic development, the environment is often ignored. Frequently, the justification for environmental despoliation is that there is no choice — we must pollute or be poor.

As hard and frightful as these realities are, the fact is that in most parts of the world, with the notable exception of Africa, standards of living rose enormously in the last half of the twentieth century. GDP per head in less-developed countries has tripled since 1950, life expectancy has risen by more than twenty years, and adult literacy rates have increased by more than thirty percentage points. Many countries, including China and India, which are home to the greatest number of the world's poor, are making important progress in defeating the scourge of poverty. Significant middle classes have emerged where none before existed. Infant mortality on a worldwide basis has fallen dramatically. Education is much more widely available than ever before. Respect for human rights has seen vast improvement, as the majority of the world today is home to democratically elected governments.

In a recent study David Dollar and Aart Kraay of the World Bank have shown that the benefits of growth are more inclusive than imagined to date. The study, entitled *Growth Is Good for the Poor*, covered eighty countries over a period of four decades. It establishes that the income of the poor has risen one-for-one with overall growth — through good times and bad and within developing and industrialized countries alike.[26]

In many cases, poverty and misery are man-made creations — the results of corrupt and incompetent governments, of protectionism, of failed public policies such as those that provide subsidies in ways that undermine sustainability, of cronyism, of ruling classes with no sense of social responsibility, of tribalism. Again to invoke Kindleberger, poverty and misery are most rampant where there is an absence of social capability.

■ Globalization under Attack

Klaus Schwab, president and founder of the World Economic Forum, is a worried man. At the annual meeting in Davos in 2000, he urged world political and business leaders to use every ounce of creativity to respond to the growing backlash against globalization or to risk seeing many of its benefits rolled back. Financier George Soros has warned of the dangers to world order in the workings of unbridled market capitalism. "If we care about universal principles such as freedom, democracy, and the rule of law, we cannot leave them to the care of market forces; we must establish some other institutions to safeguard them."[27] Federal Reserve Bank Chairman Alan Greenspan has also voiced his concerns. "While recognizing the efficacy of capitalism to produce wealth, there remains considerable unease among some segments about the way markets distribute that wealth and about the effects of raw competition on the civility of society. Thus should recent positive trends in economic growth falter, it is quite imaginable that support for market-oriented resource allocation will wane and the latent forces of protectionism and state intervention will begin to reassert themselves in many countries including the United States."[28]

Their sentiments are being echoed by a growing number of world leaders from both developed and developing countries. Pope John Paul II, who played a critical role in helping to dismantle the communist Eastern bloc, the most massive barrier to globalization in this century, has weighed in with dire warnings. "If globalization is ruled merely by the laws of the market applied to suit the powerful, the consequences cannot but be negative," he said in his apostolic exhortation to the Catholic Church in the Americas in January 1999.

In *The Lexus and the Olive Tree*, Friedman has captured the tension that is inherent in globalization:

> The challenge in this era of globalization — for countries and individuals — is to find a better balance between preserving a sense of identity, home and community and doing what it takes to survive within the globalization system. Any society that wants to thrive economically today must constantly be trying to build a better system. Any society that wants to thrive economically today must constantly be trying to build a better Lexus and driving it out into the world. But no one should have any illusions that merely participating in this global economy will make a society healthy. If that participation comes at the price of a country's identity, if individuals feel their olive tree roots crushed, or washed out, by this global system, those olive tree roots will rebel. They will rise up and strangle the process.[29]

The image of olive tree roots rebelling brings to mind the protests in Seattle in November 1999 against the World Trade Organization. Some 50,000 demonstrators surged through the streets representing a staggering multiplicity of causes — some serious, some bizarre, some comic — but seemingly united in one purpose: to express their anger at the effects of globalization and of its dangerous handmaiden, the World Trade Organization. The drama that ensued with outbreaks of vandalism and violence, and the eventual calling in of the National Guard, drew a focused and unprecedented level of attention to the issue of globalization.

The meeting of international trade ministers and WTO officials in Seattle failed to launch a new round of multilateral negotiations, a development that was unique in the history of the postwar global trading system. Never before had countries come together to start a negotiation and failed to do so. The protesters were quick to claim credit for the scuttling of the talks. In reality, the WTO meeting collapsed because of the failure of governments, developed and developing, to reach agreement over the agenda for a new multilateral round of talks. In the words of international economist Jeffrey J. Schott, the "key damage to the WTO was self-inflicted."[30]

There are some important lessons to be learned from the Seattle fiasco. John Micklethwait and Adrian Wooldridge suggest that the anti-globalization protests "could have been an early insight into the official politics of the next century: a continuing battle between a technocratic commercial elite with a minimal grasp of politics and a disenfranchised, angry minority with a minimal grasp of economics."[31] Certainly, Seattle showed that the forces against globalization are newly empowered and, ironically, the source of their strength is the very system that many of them condemn. The protests were carefully planned months in advance and were largely facilitated by the Internet. Similarly, wireless telephony enabled the protestors to marshall their forces on Seattle's streets.

Canada's minister for international trade, Pierre Pettigrew, participated in the failed ministerial talks and expressed his dismay at the contradiction in the position of the protesters — a number of Canadians prominent among them. "The real world of globalization has created or at least greatly empowered the very players who were decrying globalization, and they emerged in Seattle for the first time in a very forceful way. The irony is that they came to decry the very movement that brought them there."[32]

There is another sobering lesson in the events of Seattle. In a world in which decision-making still resides predominantly in the hands of nation states, global public policy will continue to be determined in the main by national governments. It was the absence of consensus leading to the Seattle trade meetings that led to failure: the unresolved disputes across the North-South divide, and the collision between the countries of the developed world on issues such as farm subsidies. The lukewarm support at best in the United States for a new multilateral round of negotiations was a major negative factor at work in Seattle, a situation not helped by President Bill Clinton's failure to gain fast-track authority from the United States Congress. The message we learn from this fiasco is that global rules and global order continue to depend heavily on the collective commitment of the world's political leadership. A failure of vision, courage, and political will is a recipe for stalemate and risks retreat to protectionism, conflict, and chaos.

A third lesson emerging from Seattle is that global institutions such as the WTO are badly in need of shoring up. Granted, part of the WTO's problems are self-inflicted. It had been startlingly inept at explaining what it does, at rebutting its critics, and at implementing badly needed changes to its structure and operations. In addition, governments and business leaders have done little to assist. Their advocacy of the benefits of a rules-based multilateral system has been weak and defensive. More often than not, they have run for cover in the face of determined and aggressive protesters committed to direct action. The result has been a form of paralysis, a dangerous stalemate in policy terms. In the meantime, critical reforms in areas such as agriculture, services, tariffs, anti-dumping, investment, competition policy, electronic commerce, the environment, and labour remain stalled.

The malaise gripping the WTO is part of a broader affliction touching other key global institutions such as the International Monetary Fund, the World Bank, the International Labour Organization, and the United Nations itself. The weaknesses of these institutions does not augur well for the prospects of global governance, which remains the goal of those hoping to harness the growing power and reach of globalization. In the face of such uncertainty, the role of the nation state remains pivotal, a point emphasized by political scientists David Cameron and Janice Gross Stein:

> *Democratic states, constitutionally governed by the rule of law, will continue to be the venue where the exercise of power is best held accountable and where*

> legitimate and representative governance is most likely. Indeed, it is likely that demands for representation and accountability will grow if globalization deepens, as citizens seek to assert control over important areas of public policy that directly affect their lives.[33]

The fourth lesson of Seattle is that private actors in growing numbers are becoming influential players in the global public policy process. In addition to transnational corporations, private individuals and a huge number of non-governmental organizations have embraced a new form of activism largely enhanced by the Internet. In principle, this is an immensely positive outcome that demonstrates the empowering effect of globalization. The goals of openness, transparency, and accountability are well served by their presence and activism.

But there is also a danger — a danger that some of the private actors will rely increasingly on direct action in the streets to attain their goals and, in so doing, will ignore or subvert democratically elected institutions. Justifying their role on the ground that governments do not speak for the people, but only for corporate interests, is a challenge that must not go unanswered. Governments must respond by ensuring that the political process is open, and by encouraging dialogue with those genuinely committed to reform. At the same time, governments must not buckle under the intimidation of the extremists. To do so would undermine years of hard-won progress that has raised the level and the effectiveness of democratic governance worldwide.

The Economist challenges governments to do more: "Governments are apologizing for globalization and promising to civilize it. Instead, if they had any regard for the plight of the poor, they would be accelerating it, celebrating it, exalting in it — and if all that were too much for the public they would at least be trying to explain it."[34] WTO director general Mike Moore has this to say of the anti-globalization extremists: "We shall never convince such zealots of the case for economic liberalism. But we must not allow the zealots and self-serving privileged people to discredit liberalism among the wider public. We need to make the case for freedom, economic, political, and social, again and again.[35]

Canadian political commentator Rex Murphy is even more blunt in his condemnation of the activists who reject the legitimacy of the democratic process in favour of direct action in the streets. In the December 9, 2000, edition of the *Globe and Mail* he vents his rage:

> The contradictions inherent in this global anti-global messianism are multiple. The activists — a vague term — are against the WTO because it is not democratic, it steals the sovereignty of nations. Canada sends its delegates to the WTO because Canadian citizens elected a government to act on their behalf to make such choices. There's more democracy in that one sentence than in all the movement's manifestoes and press releases.

■ Globalization and Responsibility

As tensions rise over the effects of globalization, there are some who argue that the process itself will solve the problem — that the market, over time, will work its beneficial magic on the poor and the oppressed. We do not subscribe to this point of view. As Micklethwait and Wooldridge argue, globalization "needs to be fought, politicked and argued for. Things rarely change of their own accord; somebody has to change them."

As we have already pointed out, and will reinforce in subsequent chapters, governments have a crucial responsibility in preparing their electorates for the effects of globalization. The policy environment can be a decisive factor in winning in a global environment. But corporations, too, have far-reaching responsibilities, particularly those who lead them. Business chiefs would be wise not to take globalization for granted. They would be equally wise to embrace a broader notion of corporate responsibility which not only respects the primacy of shareholder value but, at the same time, recognizes the importance of human capital and of environmental and community values.

Hostility towards the so-called corporate agenda is growing around the world and big business is seen as having too much power. Pollster Daniel Yankelovitch, in a poll conducted for *BusinessWeek*, says: "There's an increased readiness to believe negative things about corporations today, which makes it a dangerous time for companies . . . Executives haven't had to worry about social issues for a generation, but there is a yellow light flashing now, and they had better pay attention."[36]

One way to counter this rising tide of anti-business sentiment is to practise responsible corporate leadership. Progress on this front has been significant and momentum is growing. In a special report on global capitalism, *BusinessWeek* points to "a new era of corporate responsibility. Multinationals are hiring human rights advisors, drafting and enforcing codes of conduct, appointing monitors, and improving operating practices."[37]

Effective corporate governance procedures are an essential element of responsible business conduct, but the exercise of such governance is still alien to many companies throughout the world. Transnational corporations in general are setting a good example, but more needs to be done. The Organisation for Economic Co-operation and Development is advancing the cause through its work on the development of the *OECD Principles of Corporate Governance*. These principles are intended to assist governments throughout the world in their efforts "to evaluate and improve the legal, institutional and regulatory framework for corporate governance in their countries, and to provide guidance and suggestions for stock exchanges, investors, corporations, and other parties that have a role in the process of developing good corporate governance."[38]

Business leaders must not only run model companies but have a broader responsibility in helping to explain the basics of democratic capitalism. Accordingly, they should engage much more actively in the policy debate on globalization. They must demonstrate that they can do their homework and deliver a convincing message. We have seen ample evidence of this role in the free trade debates in Canada in the 1980s, in the single-currency debates in Europe in the 1990s, and, more recently, in the pro-China accession to the WTO debates in the United States.

But effective advocacy must be sustained. It must not be an on-again, off-again commitment. This point was reinforced at a roundtable discussion on global issues with Canadian chief executives in November 2000. "The business communities of the world, and in particular the business leadership of the developed world, face a huge task. Yes, we must do what is important — run our enterprises well, grow them, create jobs and value, innovate and carry our products and services and ideas to the world. But we must do more, much more. We have to become global citizens, agents of change, articulate spokespersons for a vision of enterprise and democracy that will bring immense benefits to the world at large. We will have to learn how to understand global issues and to work with the reality that local issues and national issues are invariably connected to global issues."[39]

In summing up the case for globalization, Micklethwait and Wooldridge offer a concise and balanced assessment:

> *Globalization ... does increase inequality, but it does not create a winner-take-all society, and the winners hugely outnumber the losers. Yes, it leaves some people behind, but it helps millions more to leap ahead. Yes, it can make bad*

governments worse, but the onus should be on crafting better government, not blaming globalization. Yes, it curtails some of the power of nation-states, but they remain the fundamental unit of modern politics. Globalization is not destroying geography, merely enhancing it . . . The simple fact is that globalization makes us richer — or makes enough of us richer to make the whole process worthwhile. Globalization clearly benefits producers by giving them greater choice over their raw materials, production techniques, the markets where they sell their goods. Equally clearly, globalization benefits consumers by providing them with better goods at better prices. Globalization increases efficiency and thus prosperity.[40]

■ Globalization and the Canadian Challenge

Canadians are well positioned to triumph in the global economy. We have an ideal geographic location, with three oceans on our coasts and a common border with the most dynamic market in the world. We have a diverse, multicultural, and multilingual population. We have one of the most effective federations in the world, with an honest legal and regulatory environment. We invest heavily in human capital. We welcome large numbers of new immigrants every year. We have vast open spaces, a beautiful landscape, and massive resources, including a large percentage of the world's water supply. We have relatively secure borders.

We have, in other words, all the basic ingredients for success in a world in which knowledge, stability, societal discipline, tolerance, and natural endowments are considered vital assets. What is it, then, that stands in our way? In a simple word, it is complacency: complacency in assuming that prosperity and security are part of our birthright; complacency in believing that our high standard of living somehow will sustain itself without having to embrace a vibrant entrepreneurial culture; complacency in the lip service we give to the importance of embracing innovation; complacency in our expectations of our political leadership; complacency in our readiness to reach out to the world with our ideas, our products and services, and our influence.

The good news is that our shortcomings can be addressed and remedied. But they cannot be fixed without vision, leadership, and the courage to make difficult choices.

2

MAKING SMART CHOICES

We must never eliminate frugality from government. There will be no rewind to the reckless spending of other people's money . . . We must never shy away from the need to make choices. A government with too many priorities is a government that has none.

— FINANCE MINISTER PAUL MARTIN, FEBRUARY 16, 1999

◀ ◀ ◀

We have looked at how global economic integration is transforming the way people live and work and the way organizations and countries compete and cooperate. The rapidly growing flow of people, capital, goods, and services across national borders has made many traditional recipes for growth suspect at best, and, at worst, destructive. The intense pace of global change has also put a premium on anticipating events rather than reacting to them, on setting trends rather than following them. Countries face new limits to their options, but the choices their governments make are more important now than ever.

■ Balancing Act: Debt, Taxes, and Spending

As individuals, all of us make decisions about the kind of work we want to do and the proportion of our time to devote to earning a paycheque. How much can we spend today? How much do we need to borrow? How much should we save for the future? We make choices between competing priorities (earning more money or spending more time with our children), between ways of meeting our needs (taking the bus or buying a car), and among features and prices within our chosen courses of action (which model of car to buy and what options to add).

Governments go through a similar process on our behalf. They make decisions about how much money to raise through taxation and what forms of activity to tax. They save through surpluses or borrow through deficits. They make decisions between current consumption (public pensions and social assistance) and investment in expanding future capacity (debt reduction or investment incentives). Whether spending for the short-term or long-term benefit of citizens, they still have to choose between competing priorities (such as health care or education). And for each goal they choose as a priority, they have to figure out what combination of policies and programs can have the greatest impact. If the goal is to maximize participation in lifelong learning, for instance, what share of resources should they allocate to early childhood development, primary and secondary schooling, colleges and universities, and adult training programs? They must also ask which level of government can provide a given service most effectively — assuming that any government can do so more effectively than providers in the private or non-profit sectors.

Governments never have enough money to meet all the possible demands for their services — any more than they can ever charge too little in the way of taxes. The key to good government is making careful choices, choices that focus limited resources on the needs that are most urgent, on the forms of intervention that are most effective, and on the roles that governments are best equipped to play.

Decision-making can be simplified when a country has few options left. When Canada faced imminent collision with the debt wall during the early 1990s, Canadians achieved a remarkable degree of consensus on the need to rein in inflation and runaway deficits. That decision made, governments were forced both to raise taxes and to cut spending until the books balanced. These choices were not without challenges of their own, but contention was muted by the fact that everyone shared the pain. Objections from public sector employees and the clients of government programs were offset by the even greater misery that private sector employees and taxpayers were swallowing.

This remarkable show of unity — in which the minister of finance, whose job it was to say no, became the most popular and respected figure in his government — came to an end before the first dabs of black ink in the pages of the federal budget had even dried. As soon as it became clear that Canada could look forward to spiralling surpluses rather than deficits, all the hard-nosed resolve evaporated. Saying no stopped being the road to political popularity.

The current treatment of the public debt is symbolic of this fundamental shift in attitude. Two decades of federal deficits have left Canada with one of the highest bills for debt service in the industrialized world (see fig. 5). At 4.7 percent of GDP in 1999, the cost of servicing the public debt was almost two percentage points higher than the average for all OECD countries.[1] That 2 percent of GDP may not sound like much, but over a five-year period its impact is roughly equal to that of the $100 billion in tax cut plans announced by the federal government during 2000. In other words, if Canada had entered 2000 with just an average debt load, the government could have doubled its tax relief. Our high debt cost is also one reason that Canada recorded the third-largest decline in government program spending by industrialized countries during the 1990s. As governments in Canada rake in surpluses, paying down public debt remains the simplest and most effective long-term choice they can make.

In a September 2000 paper, Royal Bank of Canada chief economist John McCallum (shortly before deciding to run — successfully — as a Liberal candidate in the autumn federal election) laid out five good reasons for accelerating the repayment of public debt. First, governments should focus on stimulating the economy through tax cuts and new spending when the economy is weak, not when it is strong. Second, stimulating the economy when it is strong adds to the danger of rising prices

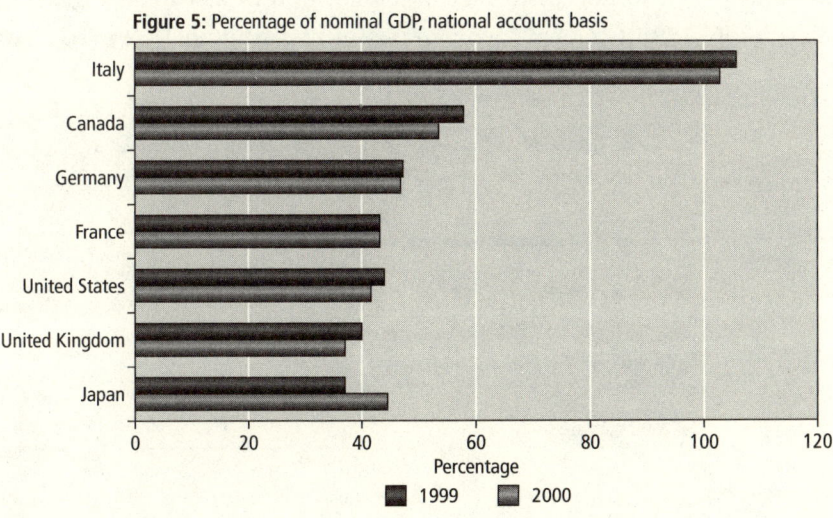

Figure 5: Percentage of nominal GDP, national accounts basis

and therefore could lead the Bank of Canada to raise interest rates. Third, Canada needs to bring its total debt down to more internationally competitive levels. Fourth, the current level of debt is still too high for comfort, potentially undermining the stability of Canada's currency and our ability to attract investment. And fifth, if we do not pay off a substantial portion of the public debt before the baby-boom generation retires, the less numerous next generation will be hard pressed to support the social programs on which its parents are counting.[2]

Despite its best efforts to come up with last-minute ways of spending year-end surpluses, the federal government will in fact have paid off at least $28.7 billion in debt in the four years ending March 31, 2001. This makes a noticeable dent even in the immense mountain of debt built up over decades of deficits. The immediate benefit amounts to $1.7 billion every year thereafter in savings on debt interest, savings that add to the government's flexibility in meeting the future needs of Canadians. As a result of these substantial early payments on our collective mortgage, the government estimates that the debt-to-GDP ratio will fall to just 40 percent by 2005/6 from a high of 71 percent in 1995/96.[3]

In the meantime, however, interest on the debt still gobbles up one dollar out of every four the government collects in taxes. The need to pay all that interest while striving to eliminate the huge deficits of the early 1990s pushed tax rates — especially on personal incomes — to dangerous levels. Between 1993 and 1998 federal revenue from personal income tax grew by 43 percent — almost twice as fast as the economy as a whole over the same period and close to two and a half times faster than wages and salaries.[4] By 1998 personal income taxes were eating up 14.2 percent of

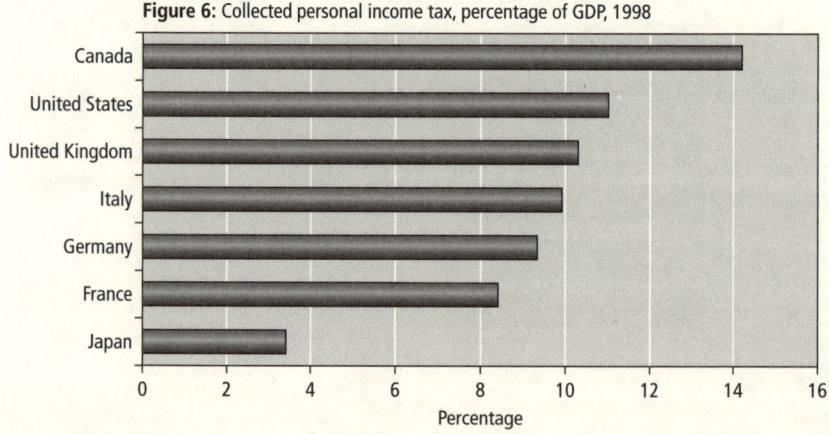

Figure 6: Collected personal income tax, percentage of GDP, 1998

GDP. That represents a bigger slice of the economic pie in Canada than in any other G-7 country — 29 percent bigger than in the United States, and 50 percent bigger than the G-7 average (see fig. 6).[5]

Defenders of big government say Canadians are willing to pay more in taxes because they want more public services. This is true to a point. No one likes to pay taxes, but people do not mind as long as they feel they are getting good value for their money. Canadians are not seeing that value today. For instance, even though we profess to believe more strongly in public health care than Americans do, governments in the United States spend just as large a share of their economic pie on public health care as ours do here, despite their lower taxes. In fact, there is remarkably little variation across the industrialized world in public spending on health care as a share of the economy.

As Caroline Tuohy, Colleen Flood, and Mark Stabile of the University of Toronto showed in a review of twenty-four OECD countries, only three (France, Germany, and Sweden) spent more than 7 percent of GDP on public health care in 1999. At the same time, just four countries (Greece, Ireland, Portugal, and Turkey) spent less than 5 percent of GDP on public health care. At 6.4 percent, Canada's public health care spending was marginally lower than that in the United States and barely above the twenty-four-country average of 6 percent.[6] We can take pride in the fact that our health care system is both more efficient and more equitable than that of the United States, but our current level of public spending on health neither causes nor justifies our higher rates of taxation.

What has emerged as a result is a remarkable degree of political and public consensus on the need to make Canada's tax rates more competitive. In October 1998, the BCNI proposed a detailed tax reduction strategy that focused on the need to bring down Canada's excessive rates of personal income tax. It recommended substantial increases in the basic and spousal credits that would remove a million low-income Canadians from the tax rolls, and achieve a cut in the middle tax rate from 26 to 21 percent and a cut in the upper tax rate from 29 to 26 percent on incomes from $60,000 to $150,000, as well as eliminating the upper-income surtaxes and fully re-indexing tax brackets to inflation.[7] At the time, this combination was seen as highly ambitious, but by the autumn of 2000, rapid economic growth had brought cuts on this scale well within reach.

In the course of its 1999 and 2000 budgets, along with its Economic Statement and Budget Update in October 2000, the federal government added substantially to the basic and spousal deductions and cut the lower-income rate from 17 to 16 percent. It chopped the middle rate to 22 percent and the top rate to 26 percent on incomes from $60,000 to $100,000. Both surtaxes have been eliminated, and the tax system has been re-indexed.

As Canadians went to the polls in the autumn of 2000, the governing Liberals had proposed $100 billion in tax relief over the next five years. The Canadian Alliance had put forward a more aggressive plan with some $125 billion in tax cuts. And the Progressive Conservatives were coming up the middle with a $114-billion package.

The parties differed in significant details. The Canadian Alliance, for instance, proposed bigger increases in the basic and spousal exemptions instead of the one percentage-point cut in the low-income tax rate introduced in the October mini-budget. The Alliance's proposal for the personal tax structure had two brackets, the Conservatives' three, and the Liberals' four. The Conservatives did not propose cutting personal tax rates or brackets, but did call for complete elimination of the capital gains tax. What is significant is that all three parties (the New Democratic Party being the notable exception at the national level) are committed to significant reductions in both the personal and the corporate tax burden.

Nor has the trend toward more competitive tax rates been confined to the federal government. Alberta has not only cut tax bills but has transformed its personal tax structure to include much bigger basic exemptions as well as a single flat rate on remaining income. Ontario has made tax cuts the centrepiece of its strategy for growth, slashing taxes even before balancing its books. Across the country, governments of all political stripes have come to understand the importance of competitive tax rates in attracting investment and encouraging growth in employment and incomes.

But we see two remaining problems, both of them major. The first relates to the speed of global change. As we have already discussed, economic integration and technological innovation have made capital and people more mobile than ever. This mobility makes them increasingly sensitive to differences in tax rates between countries. We will look at the implications of this sensitivity in greater detail later, but the fact is that other countries, our competitors for investment and skilled people, are cutting taxes too — and in many cases faster than in Canada.

Our second major concern is about the gaping chasm between economic logic and political decision-making. All taxes have some impact on economic growth. Canada's biggest problem is not so much its overall tax burden as its structure of taxation. According to a 1997 estimate supplied to the OECD by Canada's Department of Finance, an extra dollar in sales tax causes a loss in real economic output of just 17 cents. A dollar in payroll taxes cuts output by 27 cents, and a dollar in personal income taxes, by 56 cents. The greatest damage of all is done by corporate income tax, where an extra dollar in tax reduces economic output by $1.55 — hardly a healthy trade-off by any standard.[8] In other words, paying for public spending by increasing taxes on corporations hurts future growth by nine times as much as raising the same revenue through higher sales taxes — and cutting corporate taxes would be nine times more effective in creating more jobs and higher incomes than cutting the GST (see fig. 7).

Logic dictates that the most effective way to stimulate economic growth and encourage investment is to cut corporate taxes. Public opinion, however, continues to regard corporations as undeserving milk-cows rather than as investments whose returns are central to the well-being and incomes of Canadians. Political support for corporate tax cuts therefore ranges from lukewarm to non-existent, and the result is that corporate tax cuts account for barely 10 percent of the tax relief announced at the federal level over the next five years, and less than 6 percent of the relief in the first three years. By the same token, the least economically damaging form of taxation is a tax on consumption. Yet public antipathy for the GST remains intense, and the political appetite for increased reliance on this source of revenue is nil. Indeed, in the run-up to the autumn 2000

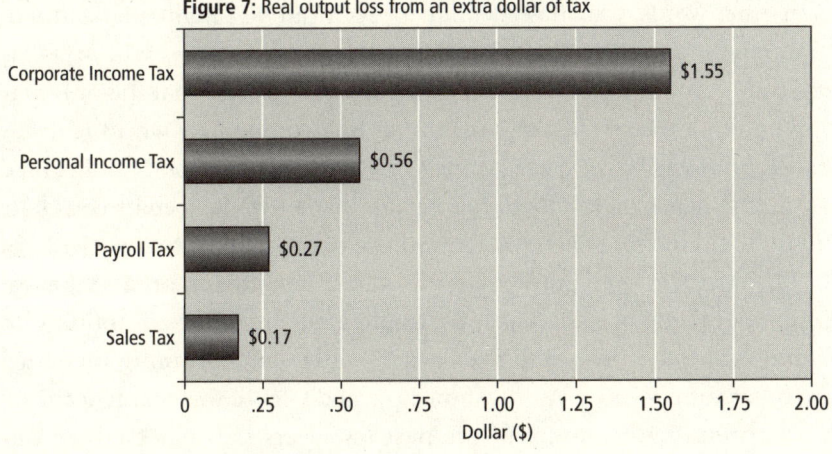

Figure 7: Real output loss from an extra dollar of tax

election, the Canadian Alliance even toyed with the idea of campaigning on a promise to cut the GST.

Tom Courchene, a professor of economics at Queen's University, has suggested that Canada can choose to keep its tax rates relatively high in order to fund bigger governments and more public services only if it gears the structure of its tax system to the realities of a competitive world.

> *Maintaining a high-tax economy relative to the Americans would require a significant shift in taxes away from mobile factors (human capital and corporations) and towards residence-based and export-neutral taxes such as the GST. I believe that many Canadians, perhaps a majority, would opt for a high-wage, high-transfer, high-tax economy . . . But this is where a huge disconnect exists. I have yet to see social activists amongst us embrace the requisite shift in instruments in order to achieve the goal of a high-wage, high-transfer, high-tax economy. Specifically, I have yet to see a prominent social group embrace the notion that the export-import neutral value-added tax (the GST) represents one of the key instruments in maintaining a high-tax, high-transfer economy. Yet clearly it is.[9]*

Jonathan Kesselman echoed these sentiments in a November 2000 study for the Institute for Research on Public Policy. "Canada and the U.S. stand out from their European counterparts as being relatively much more reliant on income taxes and much less reliant on the lower-distorting payroll and goods and services taxes. This may help to explain why some of the heavily taxed European countries have nevertheless surpassed both Canada and the U.S. in their longer-run growth."[10]

In other words, Canada can still choose: it can be a high-tax country or it can rely heavily on personal and corporate income taxes within its tax mix, but it cannot do both. What Courchene suggests is that the only way to maintain a relatively high tax burden in a competitive world is to tax what cannot easily get away. Money can leave in an instant, and skilled people are increasingly able to follow. If Canada tries to keep its corporate and personal income tax rates above those of other countries, we will not be able to sustain our competitiveness, attract investment, or raise the real standard of living of Canadians. We would argue that the best option is to continue cutting our overall tax burden while also reforming the structure of taxation — and we will show how and why in the chapters ahead.

The booming economy of the past few years that has enabled our governments to cut taxes as fast as they have has bred a dangerous complacency about the need for fundamental tax reform. At the same time, surging revenues have enabled governments to re-open the spending taps with a vengeance. At the federal level, the biggest single increase was the five-year, $23.4-billion deal in September 2000 to boost transfers to provincial governments for health care. But the October 2000 economic statement included plans for rapid spending hikes in all kinds of federal programs. It projected that total program spending would reach $129.6 billion in 2002/3. This represents a jump of $17.8 billion in just three years, a compound annual growth rate of more than 5 percent, more than double the expected rate of inflation. Furthermore, the pre-election statement admitted that the government was holding in reserve an additional $8.8 billion over three years on top of the usual prudence factors and contingency funds, money that "will allow the government in the future to consider other priority measures."[11] In this atmosphere of plenty, public servants and elected officials alike are insisting, first, that there is no waste left to cut and, second, that there is a desperate need to restore funding to get back to where we were before.

This fixation with restoring old spending patterns is a big mistake. The pattern of public spending should change over time. People's needs change, and private sector companies seeking to meet those needs have to change. So should governments. Instead, governments once again are making choices only about where to add. The notion of cutting existing expenditures has all but disappeared from political discourse. If we want to be able to afford the goals that matter most to us as a society, we have to make more effective choices between competing priorities. As new priorities arise, governments must remain willing to provide for them by taking money away from areas of concern that have become relatively less urgent and from existing programs that have proven to be less effective.

Globally, there is convincing evidence that governments can shrink substantially without hurting their citizens. Vito Tanzi and Ludger Shuknecht, for instance, have argued persuasively that while government spending grew enormously throughout the twentieth century, the increases of the most recent thirty-five years have not brought about much additional social and economic welfare. This, they suggest, means that governments across the industrialized world should be shrinking. What is more, the forces of globalization will increasingly put pressure on government spending both by making it more difficult for countries to impose uncompetitive taxes and by giving consumers greater ability to get around their home governments in seeking the services they want.

> Spending will not decline to the levels seen 100 or 70 years ago, but it can be rolled back to levels closer to those experienced around 1960. With this, we are not advocating a return to the "Hobbesian jungle" as some critics may claim. We suggest, rather, a more modest and more focused role for the state and for public spending with which countries are likely to experience much invigorated economies and a growth in social well-being. This will allow the citizens of these countries to lead more balanced lives, enjoying the choice and invigorating effects of markets, the benefits from public goods, and security of social safety nets.[12]

For now, however, the momentum for public spending in Canada is clearly in the other direction, driven primarily by worries about the deterioration of the public health care system. In an examination of public opinion surveys on health care undertaken in 2000, the Conference Board of Canada found that health care became the public's number one worry not when governments were slashing budgets in the early 1990s, but after fears of unemployment faded in 1998. Even as the strengthening economy enabled governments to resume boosting health care spending, confidence in the system has dropped, with 80 percent of Canadians believing that the health care system is in crisis.[13] It was these perceptions that drove the massive increase in federal transfers agreed to in September 2000.

But health care is not the only sector competing for increased public spending. While health outcomes have an impact on economic growth and social cohesion, health care spending is mostly current consumption. Other activities, particularly in education, training, and research, are more clearly investments in the future capacity of the country. When new jobs in every industry require higher levels of knowledge and skills, improving access to learning is essential both to the equality of economic opportunity for individual citizens and to the country's ability to compete globally for investment and jobs. Allocating more money for health care now at the expense of investment in education could reduce our ability to finance the health care needs of Canadians down the road.

While governments will always have roles involving current consumption, the priority for funding increases should be on measures that will help the economic pie to grow. Our pie is already bigger today because of key choices that Canada made in the past. The decision to embrace freer trade with the United States and then with Mexico accelerated the process of North American economic integration. This integration, combined with steadfast support for multilateral trade liberalization, has enabled Canadian companies to participate fully in the global economy, multiplying the value of the goods and services we sell to the world and shifting our production towards higher-value goods. The decision to strangle inflation was costly in the short term, but it laid the foundation for lower interest rates and today's robust yet non-inflationary growth in jobs and incomes. Reining in spiralling deficits during tough economic times might have delayed the cyclical recovery, but it has opened up a whole new world of flexibility for governments as they contemplate the challenges of the future.

Canada has changed a great deal, and for the better. At the same time, our future prospects remain overshadowed by the consequences of poorer choices in the past. In particular, the mountain of debt built up by decades of deficits continues to drain a huge share of our tax dollars and leaves us exposed to considerable risk in the event of rising inflation and high interest rates or a global economic downturn. And the steady decline of the Canadian dollar over the past decade has persuaded too many Canadian businesses to rely on a weak currency for competitiveness instead of boosting their productivity through investment in employee skills and new technologies.

For better and for worse, Canada has changed, but it cannot escape the need to make choices. Just as the right choices made in tough times led to the prosperity we enjoy today, the wrong choices made today could push us back towards leaner times in the future.

■ The Consequences of Complacency

Kevin Lynch, now deputy minister of finance, has been a relentless crusader on the subject of productivity and its role in expanding the economic pie. Throughout his years as deputy minister of Industry Canada, he made frequent presentations about the difference between competitiveness and productivity. During the 1990s Canadian companies became more competitive — but less productive. American productivity growth outstripped Canada's, and only the falling dollar and smaller pay hikes kept Canadian costs looking attractive.

Lynch had a favourite gimmick to illustrate the consequences — the large and growing gap between the standard of living of Canadians and Americans. After laying out the traditional bar graphs showing the gap growing to $9,000 a year per person by 1998, two cars would scoot onto the bottom of the screen to the sound of revving engines. The one with the Canadian flag was a two-door subcompact; the one with the stars and stripes was a full-size, four-door family sedan. The matching price tags illustrated just how much less Canadians can afford to buy today because our economy has failed to keep pace with that of our dynamic neighbour to the south.[14] This is not to suggest that the greater relative wealth in the United States is well distributed. But saying that Canada's way is better just because our relative poverty is more equitably shared is simply not good enough. The lagging pace of our wealth creation means that our capacity for improving social performance has been eroded as well. Governments in the United States already spend more public money per person than their Canadian counterparts on health care. The same is true of their spending on other public goods: education, infrastructure, and research. The United States will keep extending its advantage as long as Canada extends its underperformance.

Canada's performance has perked up recently, but the 1990s were not kind to Canadian incomes. Real GDP per capita grew just 0.7 percent a year between 1989 and 1998 — less than half its average rate of 1.7 percent from 1979 to 1989, and less than a quarter of the 3.3 percent average growth recorded from 1961 to 1979.[15]

Our failure to act to re-invigorate growth in Canadian incomes through good times and bad will have consequences that go well beyond the amount of money Canadians have to spend. In a February 2000 lecture to the University of Waterloo, the Royal Bank of Canada's John McCallum suggested that, in the absence of significant action, Canada could become irrelevant as a country within a generation:

While anything can happen over a twenty-year time span, barring some very major crisis, it seems likely that Canadians in 2020 will continue to send elected representatives to the House of Commons and the provincial legislatures. The question is whether these elected representatives will have anything substantive to do. If decision-making powers have shifted out of the country to the degree that Canadians, through their elected representatives, have negligible power to shape their own destiny, then we may say that the country no longer matters, in the same sense that the monarchy in Canada and the Bundesbank in Germany no longer matter today.[16]

Over the past decade, the real disposable income of each Canadian has dropped by 2 percent. For Americans, by the same measure, the standard of living rose by 18 percent. In 1989 Canadians enjoyed a living standard equal to 74 percent of that of Americans. Ten years later, that figure had dropped to 61 percent. If this trend continues, McCallum pointed out, Canadian living standards will drop to just half of the American level by 2010. McCallum saw two reasons why the underperformance is likely to continue. One is the likelihood of further widening in the Canada–United States tax gap. Canadian governments are cutting taxes, to be sure, but the American government is running huge surpluses as well, and both major political parties are committed to significant tax cuts in the years ahead. The tax gap has grown significantly over the past three decades, and current policies seem unlikely to change the trend. The second factor contributing to Canadian economic underperformance, in McCallum's view, is the lower rate of our productivity growth. "Continuing poor productivity performance at a time of accelerating employment growth means that something other than cyclical factors were at work."

McCallum added that, even in politics, complacency will not be a viable option for much longer. Any government that cooperates in this continuing relative decline will soon pay a heavy price. "While some citizens vote with their feet and move south to greener pastures, others would vote with their ballots in favour of political parties promising an end to long-term economic decline." As they watch Americans boosting public investment in education, paying down public debt, shoring up social security, and improving their health care system, Canadians will at some point lose their cool and demand radical action. The status quo may look comfortable, but it is not sustainable.

McCallum suggested that Canada has two alternatives to the status quo. The first is to be more like the Americans. The argument for this point of view is that Canada can only maintain a distinct national identity if it can ensure an adequate level of wealth creation. Economic integration with the United States has had a powerful positive impact on wealth creation. The question is whether even closer integration — adopting American currency and harmonizing everything from external tariffs and taxation to immigration and social policies — would help to accelerate economic growth in Canada.

We see two major problems with this strategy. The first is that broad integration on so many fronts would limit Canada's ability to maintain a distinct identity. How can Canada matter in the world if it is simply a shadow of its southern neighbour? The second is that, while copying American policies could help Canada to match American growth rates, it cannot logically be a successful strategy for outperforming them. Even if our policies were identical, we would remain the smaller economy, the northern suburb, the second choice for new investment.

Rather, in line with McCallum's second alternative, we believe that Canada must pursue a strategy based on distinctiveness, one that builds on our strengths to cultivate Canadian advantage. In their statement at the CEO Summit 2000, the member chief executives of the BCNI put it this way: "Seeking to catch up and surpass the standard of living of others does not mean that we need to imitate their lifestyles, values or policy choices. We certainly should be prepared to learn from others, to adopt and improve those aspects of their models that work for us. But we can and must do better, and create our own uniquely successful model of economic and social development."[17] To achieve that level of performance, we need to take a hard look at what our governments do, where they tax and spend, and how to make them a more effective force for sustainable growth in the quality of life of Canadians.

■ *Spending More: The Health Care Challenge*

Nothing illustrates the folly of complacency more effectively than the Canadian health care system. Universally accessible, publicly funded health care is central to our vision of a caring and sharing society and provides an important competitive advantage for Canadian companies. Whatever its faults, the system as it stands achieves economies of scale by covering everyone, saves administrative costs by avoiding insurance rating and multi-stage billing, and cuts financing expenses by collecting its revenue through taxation. While public health care spending in the United States is about the same as in Canada as a share of the economy, the American system as a whole is much more expensive, depending on private insurance and personal spending to make up the difference. As Robert D. Brown, former chief executive officer of Price Waterhouse, has put it, "the difference is that Canada gets a comprehensive health care system — slightly frayed around the edges — for its public money, while the less efficient U.S. system provides only a patch-work quilt, with lots of holes, for the same relative cost."[18]

At the same time, health care is seen to be in a state of crisis. There is palpable anguish in the air, a sense that years of government cutbacks are hurting the quality of care, causing overworked and underpaid doctors and nurses to flee the profession, and leaving patients fuming over waiting lists for treatment and lineups in emergency rooms. Today's worry and frustration are captured well in the following letter to the editor published in the *Ottawa Citizen*:

> My husband, a terminal cancer patient, died earlier this year. During his last months, he suffered unspeakable horrors of pain. As a result of the Ontario government's cutbacks his condition was exacerbated by overcrowding, substandard care, shortages of supplies and breakdown of equipment... On his floor there was obvious need for twice the nursing staff... Cutbacks have contributed to a decline in both patient and staff morale to the extent that there was a hopelessness throughout that hospital.
>
> Personally, I saw and my husband experienced some of the effects — wrong diagnosis, both at the onset and after remission of his particular cancer, a six-hour wait in an emergency room before being admitted to the intensive care unit, breakdown of communication between patients, family and doctors.[19]

This letter, however, was published more than twenty years ago, on December 29, 1979, long before the budget squeezing of the 1990s. It shows that health care, by its very nature, is and always will be an emotional topic. If we truly value publicly funded and universally accessible health care, we need to bring some logical detachment to the debate.

Consider the recurring nightmare faced by patients in hospital emergency rooms each winter. They can wait for hours just to see a doctor and, if admitted, they may languish for days in hospital corridors. But, as reported in a 1999 study for the Manitoba Centre for Health Policy and Evaluation (MCHPE), the problem is to a great extent predictable. Almost every year, Winnipeg hospitals experience a high-pressure period of one to three weeks, always in the winter and always linked to waves of elderly patients coming into emergency rooms with flu-related illnesses. "Periods of high pressure during the winter months were apparent before 1991/92 when there were about 700 more beds in the system than in 1997/98, and in every year since 1991/92. High-pressure periods, therefore, can be expected to recur, regardless of the absolute number of beds in the system."[20]

The government of Manitoba has since demonstrated that such problems are not insoluble. By June 2000 the chief executive of the Winnipeg Regional Health Authority, Dr. Brian Postl, was able to report that the number of patients waiting in hallways for treatment in Winnipeg hospitals had dropped by 75 percent. With political will, a commitment to good management, and a willingness to modify many parts of the health care system simultaneously, he said, the same results could be achieved across the country within six months and at little cost. "There's no reason this can't be done in every jurisdiction in Canada."[21]

Across the health care system, there is plenty of room to do a better job with as much or less money. Take acute care, for instance. As health budgets came under pressure in the early 1990s, closings of acute-care beds in hospitals — the most expensive form of care — became common across the country. The shortage of acute-care beds was then blamed for much of the subsequent frustration over emergency room overcrowding and surgery waiting lists. But an extensive study of the consequences of hospital cutbacks in Winnipeg suggested that this perception is mistaken. Hospitals in that city closed 731 acute-care beds between 1991/92 and 1996/97. In just six years, 24 percent of the city's acute-care beds were eliminated. In a 1999 study, however, the MCHPE found that closing even one in four acute-care beds had little or no impact on access to hospital care, on the quality of care, or on the health of the population. Just as many people received care in Winnipeg hospitals in 1997 as before the cuts, but they stayed in hospital for shorter periods. Surgery increased by 5 percent overall, but inpatient surgery fell by 21 percent, while outpatient surgery, in which the patient goes home on the day of the operation, increased by 33 percent. There certainly was no resulting rationing of surgical care. In some cases the number of procedures in fact jumped dramatically. Knee surgery, for instance, rose by 118 percent.[22]

The shift to outpatient care has had no apparent impact on the subsequent health of patients. There was no increase in the number of deaths, visits to emergency rooms, or visits to doctors' offices within the month following discharge from hospital. Nor, except for one of the thirteen surgical categories, was there any increase in the number of people being re-admitted to hospital after their initial procedure. And the overall mortality rate for Winnipeg residents has not changed. Differences in health between socio-economic groups persist, but the access of poorer people to hospitals has remained unchanged. Bed closures cannot be blamed. As the MCHPE summary of the study concluded:

> Hospitals have responded remarkably well to the challenges of downsizing by adopting new ways of delivering care. They also are delivering many more of those procedures known to have clear impacts on the quality of patients' lives: knee replacements, cataract surgery and heart bypass. Readmission and mortality rates have generally held steady. Our results demonstrate that on a system-wide basis, the closure of 24 percent of Winnipeg's hospital beds has not resulted in fewer patients treated, poorer quality of care or poorer health for Winnipeg residents.[23]

Similarly, a 2000 study at the University of British Columbia found that despite a 30 percent drop in the number of staffed acute-care beds in that province between 1991 and 1996, changes in overall health care use by elderly people were small. "This implies that the changes in capacity were absorbed by decreasing the amount of care received by each individual. In other words, the differences were not in getting through the hospital door but, rather, in the length of stay once through it."[24]

In a commentary on the UBC study, Noralou Roos of the University of Manitoba suggested that there is a huge disconnect between "doom and gloom" media headlines and the objective reality portrayed by health care system data. "Were there more deaths after bed closures? No — the overall death rate was unchanged. Were fewer people getting into hospital? Not really — despite the sizeable bed closures, there were 'only minor changes' in the proportion of elderly people who received no facility care or acute care . . . Bed closures have not made it tougher for sick elderly patients to get into hospital. Claims to the contrary are false."[25] Necessity, as the old saying goes, is the mother of invention. People — and Canadians are certainly no exception — somehow manage to come up with creative ideas when they must. When hospital administrators had to trim budgets, they and their colleagues found more efficient ways to meet the needs of Canadians.

The ability to find greater efficiencies within hospitals has not been helped by the piecemeal approach often taken to health care reform. Michael Decter, a former deputy minister of health in Ontario and chairman of the Canadian Institute for Health Information, has suggested that governments have too often failed to invest in new and cheaper alternatives before shutting down the old and expensive. Imagine, he has said, if Canada's banks had closed thousands of branches several years before setting up a comprehensive network of automated teller machines. The result would have been intolerable — yet this short-sighted approach has too often been applied in managing health care.

Decter suggests that the strain on hospitals has been compounded by a failure to keep the provision of basic medical services in line with the needs of our changing society. "Many services and stores operate on a 24-hours-per-day, seven-days-per-week basis. This has shaped our expectations as consumers. The pizza comes in 30 minutes. Why not home care? In health care, there is a sharp divide between the 24/7 health system and the rest. The 24/7 world consists of ambulances, hospital emergencies, a few pharmacies and some home care. But the 9–5 world embraces doctors' offices, clinics, most pharmacies, and most home care. The consequence of this divide is an overuse of the 24/7 services."[26]

Forcing people to turn excessively to expensive hospital treatment for lack of more efficient primary or home care is both frustrating for patients and bad for taxpayers. Across the country, cash-strapped provincial governments have begun to take action, scrambling to improve health care and save money at the same time. In a June 2000 report on the sustainability of health care, the provincial and territorial premiers noted that every government is trying to reform the way health care is run, improve accountability, and achieve better integration of health services. They are shifting resources from acute-care hospital beds to less expensive long-term care beds and personal care homes, to meet the needs of their aging population. All provinces are developing some form of home care and pharmacare, another means of diverting treatment from high-cost hospitals. All have developed strategies for reducing the need for treatment by promoting greater public health. All jurisdictions have projects in place looking for better ways to deliver primary health care around the clock at the community level, from group practices and alternative means of paying doctors to ways of making better use of the skills of registered nurses and nurse practitioners. And all provinces are trying to find better ways to measure and evaluate the performance of the health care system to ensure that public policy and administrative decisions are based on solid evidence about their impact on costs and health outcomes.[27]

Despite all such intense efforts at reform and efficiency, health care costs have continued to rise inexorably. As Brian Lee Crowley, David Zitner, and Nancy Faraday Smith commented in a 1999 study:

> The rise in health spending has been one of the key reasons why other forms of provincial spending, notably education, have been severely squeezed in recent years. Yet the apparent popularity of health care spending has made it almost impossible to bring spending more in line with other kinds of public spending. Political rhetoric notwithstanding, since medicare's inception, there has been only one year in which total public sector health care spending declined on a year over year basis: 1994, when spending was down 0.3 percent (or $1.75 per capita in constant dollars) relative to 1993. Current angst over health care "cuts" is really a reaction to a slowdown in the rate of increase in medicare spending.[28]

Even staunch defenders of public health care worry that not enough attention is being paid to getting better value for money. In a 1999 speech, A. Charles Baillie, the chairman and chief executive officer of TD Bank Financial Group, said Canadians have to find ways to make the system work better if we want to maintain universal access to a broad range of high-quality health care services:

> Health care, no matter what form it takes, will consume an ever-increasing proportion of our GDP. The best we can do is manage the increased costs and ensure that funds are intelligently invested. And so, the issue is not only how much we spend, but rather how we spend it. Health care is no different than any other activity. There can be waste. There can be misplaced priorities and poor allocation of resources.
>
> The fiscal crisis of the past decade put decision-makers at all levels in a very difficult situation. Very significant savings in health care were demanded in short order. This, almost inevitably, resulted in decisions that were often taken in isolation and taken too quickly. But a bad movie does not become a good one when it is played in reverse. I believe we are in very real danger of repeating the errors of the past.[29]

The premiers confirmed in mid-2000 that, despite all the efforts of provincial governments to increase efficiency, costs will keep rising dramatically (see fig. 8). Just sustaining health care systems across Canada

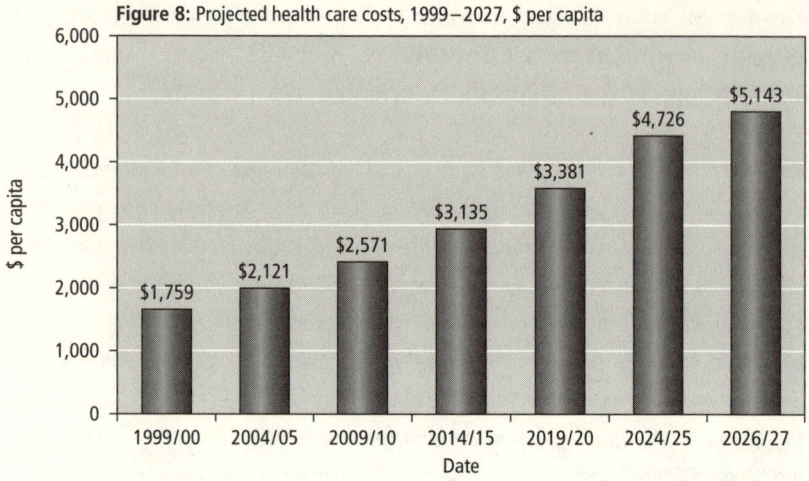

Figure 8: Projected health care costs, 1999–2027, $ per capita

will cost $85 billion within ten years, a 57 percent increase from the current level of $54 billion (and almost ten times the $9 billion spent in 1975). Reforms and improvements they consider to be indispensable would add another $19 billion to the annual tab, for a total of $104 billion. As Ontario premier Mike Harris noted when the June report was released, the $4.2 billion a year the premiers were demanding as a starting point for discussions with the federal government was merely "a drop in the bucket."[30]

The premiers predicted that costs would rise by a minimum of 5 percent a year for the indefinite future. Base operating expenditures will likely rise by two percentage points a year faster than population growth plus consumer inflation. About half of the extra would be due to the aging of the population; the remaining half to other factors. And their report suggests that the actual growth in spending is likely to be much higher because of a series of "cost accelerators" that have the potential to increase health spending far more quickly. "Examples of accelerators include: emerging and new technologies (such as major joint surgery, neonatal and fetal technologies, dialysis, organ transplantation, genetic testing and therapy), and increased incidence of chronic and new diseases such as heart disease, diabetes, tuberculosis, hepatitis C, HIV and AIDS. In addition, new pharmaceuticals, declining productivity gains and changing expectations will also impact on costs."[31]

Another cost accelerator, one not highlighted in the report, is likely to be the salary bill for the specialized doctors, nurses, and technicians needed to deliver all these new technologies and meet growing needs.

Health care is very much part of the knowledge economy and, just as in any other knowledge-based industry, highly skilled people are in short supply and operate increasingly within a continental labour market. Doctors and nurses have been disproportionately the largest stream of the Canada–United States brain drain. According to Statistics Canada, nineteen doctors moved to the United States from Canada during the 1990s for every one that moved north. For nurses, the ratio was fifteen to one. At the same time, annual immigration from all countries was falling in these professions. Between 1990 and 1997 the annual immigration of doctors fell by 40 percent and that of nurses by 70 percent.[32]

The result has been a widely publicized shortage of medical personnel, especially in rural regions and smaller towns, and within narrow medical specialties. A partial solution is to educate more doctors and nurses and make it easier for trained immigrants to get accreditation. But Canada cannot expect to eliminate its shortage of health care professionals unless it follows the example of the private sector and comes to terms with the realities of a continental market for skilled labour. Medicine is a high technology business and, like all Canadian high-technology companies, Canadian health institutions face competition from the United States for their best minds. They will be forced to offer significantly greater financial incentives to these specialized employees, along with improved working conditions and better opportunities for continuing skills development. Limiting the compensation of doctors, nurses, and technicians may have been a necessary short-term response to budget pressures, but it is not a sustainable strategy. In the global knowledge economy, employers must treat people well and pay them what they are worth or lose their services. This is one more pressure that will continue to push up the costs of the Canadian health care system significantly in the years ahead.

David Dodge, the former federal deputy minister of health, agrees that health costs are destined to grow as a share of the total economy despite everything that can be done to improve efficiency and effectiveness. Seniors consume much more health care than younger people, and they are rising as a proportion of the population. The per capita cost of treating seniors is rising faster than that for people under sixty-five. New technologies, on balance, are also adding to cost pressures. "We keep inventing new procedures to treat illnesses heretofore untreatable," Dodge reminds us. "While the unit cost of existing treatments has been falling, many more acute care services are available, and we want to consume them. So, just as in the case of consumer electronics (where increased expenditure on new products outweighs lower expenditures on existing ones) we have been rationally choosing to allocate more to health care and less to other goods and services."[33]

Many others have come to similar conclusions. The 1998 report of the auditor general of Canada compared alternative projections of public spending on health care as a share of the economy. If per capita public spending on health care rose no faster than consumer inflation, its share of GDP would remain constant. If, on the other hand, it continued to grow at the same pace as in the previous two decades — by two percentage points a year faster than the inflation rate — the share of the economy gobbled up by public health care would nearly double by 2031. It would rise from 6.4 percent of GDP in 1996 to 12.5 percent in 2031.[34]

This additional 6 percent of GDP is equivalent to an increase of $60 billion in today's government health budgets. While health spending falls largely under provincial jurisdiction, the problem would be national. To put it in context, compare this amount to the current spending and revenue of the federal government. If an increase in health care spending of this magnitude were to be funded at the federal level by chopping other programs, it would mean cutting the equivalent of all old age pensions ($23.3 billion in the 1999/2000 fiscal year), all Employment Insurance benefits ($11.7 billion), *and* all direct federal subsidies and transfers, including those for agriculture, international development aid, human resources development, industry and regional development, Indian Affairs and Northern Development, and Veterans Affairs ($20.2 billion). A good portion of the federal bureaucracy administering those subsidies and transfers would have to go as well. If the government wanted to raise an additional $60 billion in tax revenue, it would require the equivalent of boosting personal income taxes by more than 75 percent or almost tripling the GST from 7 percent to 19 percent. Even these comparisons require the unlikely assumption that people's earnings and spending habits would be unaffected by such a huge tax hike.

The auditor general's projection is not the most pessimistic estimate in circulation. The Canadian Medical Association reviewed a wide range of projections in a paper prepared for its 2000 annual general meeting. Among other studies, it cited the 1992 *Federal-Provincial Study on the Cost of Government and Expenditure Management*, which warned that public health spending could only be kept constant as a share of GDP if real per capita spending growth were cut to zero by 2005 and grew thereafter in line with population and inflation. If all costs grew in line with historical experience, however, public health care costs would rise to 17.3 percent of GDP by 2025. (By way of comparison, the total tax revenue of the federal government in 1999/2000 came to 16.9 percent of GDP.)

Also mentioned by the CMA paper was a 1996 projection by the OECD suggesting that public health care costs could only be kept constant if the cost of health treatments grew by one percentage point slower than the economy as a whole. If they grew by one percentage point faster than the economy, the share of GDP going to health care would almost double by 2030, to 13.8 percent. And the CMA cited a 1998 study by David Baxter and Andrew Ramlo of the British Columbia–based Urban Futures Institute said that, assuming no change in the pattern of spending by age and product or service, health expenditures are likely to grow twice as fast as the population. "To keep the amount spent on health per Canadian constant at its 1994 level, in spite of an aging population, would mean that every Canadian's consumption of health goods and services would have to be reduced by one-third."[35]

Similarly, a projection of health care costs in Ontario by the Conference Board of Canada suggested that real provincial health care costs would more than double by 2020. Even on a per capita basis, health care costs would rise by almost 60 percent faster than inflation. This in turn would boost health care's share of the total provincial budget from 35.5 percent to 46.6 percent. With almost half of the budget being eaten up by health care, "other expenditures such as education, welfare, infrastructure, and administration will not get as great a dollar share of provincial revenues as they do today, setting the stage for considerable tension in budget making debates."[36]

Projections over such a long period are far from reliable. A bad estimate on even one element can change results dramatically over periods of two or three decades. Advances in information technology, for instance, have the potential for vast improvements in the efficiency of managing records and preventing errors in patient care. But the field of biotechnology is rich with the promise of new treatments, ranging from gene mapping and testing and gene therapy to new vaccines, artificial blood, and tissue and organ transplants from animals to humans. Other developing technologies will lead to miniaturized devices that will enable minimally invasive surgery in fields such as neurosurgery, cardiology, and radiology. Some developments will replace less effective and more expensive treatments, but others will create demand for additional costly services.

Some experts believe that health care costs can be kept affordable. Statistics that people are living longer, healthier lives can be cited as evidence for future cost reductions. But, human nature being what it is, people will want even longer and healthier lives as new treatments become available. As the World Bank put it in its *World Health Report 2000*:

> If a car worth $10,000 would cost $15,000 to repair after an accident, an insurer would only pay $10,000. The impossibility of replacing the body, and the consequent absence of a market value for it, precludes any such ceiling in health costs.
>
> Since the poor are condemned to live in their bodies just as the rich are, they need protection against health risks fully as much . . . This basic biological difference between health and other assets even exaggerates forms of market failure, such as moral hazard and imperfect and asymmetric information, that occur for other goods and services. Directly or indirectly, it explains much of the reason why markets work less well for health than for other things, why there is a need for a more active and also more complicated role for the state, and in general why good performance cannot be taken for granted.[37]

Other experts believe that gains in efficiency from new procedures will keep future costs from exploding. Yet, as we have already discussed, the efficiency gains made to date have failed to stop spending from growing, and provincial governments believe that the easy gains have already been made. Additional savings will be harder to achieve and less spectacular in their impact on budgets, they say, and demand for health services will continue to rise. "There is rapidly diminishing capacity of the Canadian health care system to absorb this increased demand through improved productivity. Further reduction in hospital utilization is unlikely and the health care inflation rate will likely exceed the general inflation rate," the premiers concluded in making their pitch for more money to the federal government last summer.[38] And by December 2000, the Canadian Institute for Health Information confirmed that costs were already rising sharply again. As provincial governments opened their coffers once more, public spending on health care rose 6.7 percent in 1999 and was on track to grow by a further 7.7 percent in 2000.[39]

Canada's doctors think that drastic remedies will be needed. As Dr.

Hugh Scully, then president of the Canadian Medical Association (CMA), wrote in May 2000: "The Canadian health care system, as currently structured, cannot survive. Simply put, if we do not make substantial changes to the system, it may not be there when we need it the most . . . There will need to be a balancing act between the driving forces of demography, technology and consumer demand and a three-pronged strategy that comprises rapid adaptability, innovation and a focus on excellence throughout the health care system."[40]

The CMA, which represents Canada's 46,000 doctors, maintains that, to keep essential services free to all patients, Canada will have to narrow the range of services that would be covered. In a June 2000 interview with the *Ottawa Citizen*, Dr. Scully was blunt. Without clearer limits on what should be included in medicare coverage, the system cannot survive. "We believe the playing field should be level and that access to services without barriers should be essentially the same for everybody. But people should also recognize that not everybody can have everything." He noted that the World Health Organization (WHO) has adopted the term "the new universalism" to describe the principle that health coverage should apply to all patients, but not necessarily to all services. Choosing which services not to cover becomes a risky political exercise. "Understandably, today's political leaders are loath to enter into a discussion where painful choices will be unavoidable. However, continuing to avoid this discussion will only hasten the deterioration of the system."[41] The fact that Canadians already pay for such a high percentage of the medical services they consume accounts for Canada's low ranking in the WHO's 2000 report. Canada was ranked thirtieth overall because it spends too much money for the health outcomes it achieves and allows too many health care costs to slip outside the public health care system. Canadian patients, it noted, pay 17 percent of all health care bills out of their own pockets at the point of service — compared with just 3 percent in the United Kingdom. And the annual health care tab in Canada comes to $1,800 (U.S.) per person, an amount that is 50 percent higher than in Britain, but offers no corresponding advantage in health outcomes.[42]

There are plenty of examples of other ways to finance health care. As Tuohy, Flood, and Stabile have described, other industrialized countries tend to use one of three other models. The first is to allow parallel public and private systems. In Britain, for instance, public health care is essentially rationed by waiting lists, but those who can afford it can seek private care as well. The second approach is to offer a broad range of publicly subsidized health care services, but to require patients to pay some portion of the cost. The degree of co-payment may be scaled according to the patient's income. Some countries, such as Australia, combine co-payments with parallel systems. The third alternative is to offer publicly funded health care only to certain groups. The groups covered may be narrow or broad. In the United States, public coverage is effectively limited to the elderly and those on welfare, while in the Netherlands, compulsory social insurance financed by employers and employees covers 62 percent of the population, leaving only higher income earners to fend for themselves.[43]

Canada's model of public health care is unique in covering the full cost of some services for all citizens and requiring full private payment for all other services. While it ensures that no Canadian need worry about the cost of what are defined as medically necessary services, this all-or-nothing division into public and private services causes problems of its own. For instance, given an alternative between a course of drug treatment administered at home and treatment through hospitalization, patients have a financial incentive to seek the more expensive hospital care because their personal cost is lower. What is more, Tuohy, Flood, and Stabile have pointed out that, in the mind of the patient, public and private costs are bundled together. A trip to the doctor is free, but the drug that may be prescribed is not. The result is that despite all the best intentions of the Canada Health Act, poorer people are less likely to visit the doctor if they cannot afford the probable treatment.

This is one reason other countries have opted instead for explicit co-payments. While even visiting the doctor may involve a fee, the poor may be better off if the total cost of the visit plus any resulting prescription is included in a single, known, and reasonable fee. Certainly if Canada wants to broaden the range of health services that are publicly subsidized, it will have to consider the idea of cost-sharing both for newly covered services and for those that are now completely publicly funded.

The other argument for shifting towards some form of co-payment is to reduce waste and unnecessary use of public services by making patients more aware of the costs involved. As Tom Kent put it in a paper for the Caledon Institute, "the ideologues of market economies are right, in the sense that pressure to exceed reasonable needs is inherent in tax-financed health care. Medicare does require a way to contain its costs without breaching the principle of universal access."[44]

Kent's recommendation is to require patients to pay a small share of their health care costs in a progressive way through the tax system. The value of the public health care services they consumed would be reported annually on the equivalent of a T4 slip, and a portion of that cost, no more than 10 percent, would be added to taxable income. This means that upper-income Canadians (those with higher marginal tax rates) would pay a greater share. To keep the burden reasonable for all families, Kent proposes a ceiling on the clawback, so that consumption of health care services could never boost taxable income by more than 10 percent. This would result in maximum additional federal tax, even in the top tax bracket, of 2.9 percent of income.

Another means of increasing patient awareness of and responsibility for health care costs is the Medical Savings Account proposed by author and doctor David Gratzer. This scheme would provide complete public insurance against major costs, but only after a big deductible. A smaller annual allowance would fill the gap and act as both carrot and stick. Patients who used a lot of services would have to pay the difference between the allowance and the beginning of catastrophic coverage. Those who used services sparingly could take all or part of the leftover allowance and either accumulate it to provide more coverage in future years or use it to pay for items that would not normally be publicly insured.[45]

We support strongly the five principles of the Canada Health Act: that health care should be universal, accessible, portable, comprehensive, and publicly administered. To put the first four of those principles in simpler terms, we believe that all Canadians should be able to get all the health care they need when they need it and where they need it. The final principle, that of public administration, is one we support not out of any ideological bias, but because of its demonstrated efficiency relative to the fragmented system used in the United States. For all its faults, single-payer public coverage has been a key element in making Canada's health care system a competitive advantage for our country.

The existing financing and administration of public health care does not live up to these five principles, primarily because so many health costs are not covered. As even federal Health Minister Allan Rock was forced to admit during the autumn 2000 election campaign, Canadians already live with a two-tier health care system. In particular, while Canadians strongly support the principles of the Canada Health Act, a 1999 Angus Reid poll found that only 50 percent believe that the system is living up to the principle of comprehensiveness.[46] All of us recognize that we are spending our own money on health services that, while not addressing life-threatening conditions, are still necessary. We have to pay for the drugs our doctors prescribe, fill cavities in our teeth, correct failing vision, and, increasingly, access new techniques from laser eye surgery to in vitro fertilization. Canada's public health care system is not as comprehensive as it should be.

The challenge, of course, is how to pay for more comprehensive public coverage — in addition to meeting the rising costs flowing from population aging, new technologies and treatments, and growing salaries for health professionals. Meeting this challenge will require intensive efforts if we are to deliver services more efficiently across the full spectrum of care, from doctors' offices and emergency wards to long-term facilities and home care. This need in itself is an argument in favour of more comprehensive and consistent coverage of different forms of health care delivery.

At the same time, the trade-off for public coverage of new services such as pharmacare and home care must be some degree of private contribution to the cost of all services. As Kent, Gratzer, and others have shown, there are ways to introduce co-payments without jeopardizing access to care for those with low incomes and without putting any family in danger of catastrophic losses. But only by introducing some form of cost sharing can we hope to afford the range as well as the quality of services that Canadians clearly want.

Even with a significant degree of co-payment, Canada will have to expect health care costs to rise in real terms in the decades ahead. This inexorable growth in health care costs as a share of our economy will force governments to take action on two other fronts. The first is to make sure that our economy grows faster than currently projected in order to generate a larger tax base. The second, as health care eats up a growing share of their budgets, is to decide where to spend less on other services and how to spend more effectively on those that remain.

Spending smarter and fostering economic growth are critical to Canada's ability to sustain universal, timely, comprehensive, and high-quality public health care. They are equally important in addressing other major public policy issues. We look next at ways in which Canada could improve its performance in dealing with two other key goals of public policy: the elimination of poverty and the reduction of economic disparities between regions.

▪ Spending Less: Regional Development

Redistribution of income is a primary function of governments. They take money from those who have created wealth — either individually through their work and investment or collectively through profit-making enterprises. They then spend money to meet the needs of society as a whole, with much of their activity geared towards improving the quality of life of lower-income citizens, either through direct income support or through equalization of access to public services and infrastructure.

Global integration has been accompanied by a general polarization of incomes. The gap between the earning power of those with advanced skills and those without has widened, in Canada and elsewhere. Canada, however, has succeeded in reducing the impact of this trend and has avoided a widening of the gap between rich and poor. In this country, the rich (relatively speaking) have been getting richer before tax, while the earned income of the poor has been declining. But after taxes and government transfers, the top 20 percent of Canadians are left with about five times as much money as the 20 percent of those at the bottom end of the income scale. This ratio has remained roughly constant, through good times and bad, for more than two decades. In short, Canada's emphasis on sharing the benefits of growth has worked. To the extent that Canada's economy has expanded, Canadians at both ends of the income scale have benefited at about the same rate.

On the other hand, measures to counter inequalities in income have both limits and costs, and, as former Price Waterhouse chairman Robert D. Brown has pointed out, these costs can include a lower average standard of living. "Redistributing incomes through the tax system involves three layers of costs: reduced incentives for those paying higher taxes; lower incentives for those receiving income subsidies; and transaction costs in handling the flows. In the long run we may need to consider a greater emphasis on positive and dynamic responses that emphasize training, labour market flexibility and personal incentives, including lower marginal tax rates."[47]

Canada needs to rethink the way it redistributes income among individuals, but even more urgent is a review of our efforts to redistribute income on the basis of where people live. As enshrined in section 36 of the Constitution Act of 1982, "Parliament and the government of Canada are committed to the principle of making equalization payments to ensure that provincial governments have sufficient revenues to provide reasonably comparable levels of public services at reasonably comparable levels of taxation."[48]

There is nothing wrong with this principle of equalization. Access to equivalent government services is critical to equality of opportunity within our society, and equalization payments for this purpose should be maintained. Where Canada has gone wrong is in its incessant efforts to dole out layers of additional grants to people and corporations solely on the basis of where they live and operate. Instead of treating all Canadians equally, the Employment Insurance system has tended to make qualification easier and benefits more generous in regions of high unemployment. Instead of offering tax incentives to encourage viable businesses equally across the country, programs have subsidized companies in certain locations, regardless of their ability to compete. And instead of making investments in infrastructure according to their impact on productivity and competitiveness, governments too often seem to calculate the returns on public works in terms of potential votes.

The mania for persuading Canadians to do certain things in specific places is not limited to the federal government. In Montreal, the government of Quebec has created a $1.5 billion, ten-year program to subsidize e-commerce and multimedia companies that set up shop in two specific real estate developments. The program prompted huge protests from other real estate developers and building owners faced with competition from 4 million square feet of new subsidized office space. They suggested that the subsidy amounted to $500 a square foot, more than the $300 per square foot cost of building the new E-Commerce Place, and contended that, by draining tenants away from existing buildings, the subsidies would cut the value of other Montreal office towers by $400 million.[49]

Across the country, the alphabet soup of programs trotted out over the years in the name of regional development stands as an example of government spending at its worst — not because the intentions are bad, but because the results have been so pitiful. The federal government has thrown money in all directions, to the East, West, and North as well as specifically into Quebec — almost anywhere, it seems, more than a few hours' drive from Toronto. But with the possible exception of the repeated efforts to subsidize farmers in western Canada, nowhere is the lack of a positive return on such spending more evident than in Atlantic Canada.

At times, for example, the net inflow of wealth to Atlantic Canada during the 1960s and 1970s from transfers to individuals, payments to governments, and large federal projects came to more than a third of that region's gross domestic product.

As documented by Fred McMahon in a study for the Atlantic Institute for Market Studies entitled *Retreat from Growth: Atlantic Canada and the Negative Sum Economy*, many of these attempts to close the economic gap made the problem worse. For example, the introduction of extended unemployment insurance benefits made so many people unwilling to seek full-time jobs that wages rose faster in Atlantic Canada than in other parts of the country. High wages relative to productivity made investment so unattractive that even economic development subsidies had little effect. Governments became the biggest customers of their regional businesses and showed little concern for cost and quality, thereby reinforcing their lack of competitiveness abroad. The cost-shared nature of many programs encouraged governments to raise taxes, so that Atlantic Canada became a high-tax as well as a high-cost region. Politics trumped sensible investment in infrastructure. Monies flowed into excess fish plants and secondary roads, but allowed the region's primary road link with central Canada to deteriorate. Uneconomic coal mines and an antiquated steel industry were propped up by billions in subsidies. And the huge flow of subsidies into the fishery more than doubled the number of people working in that industry over a thirty-year period, diverting people from education to seasonal work, devastating fish stocks, and driving the industry towards low-quality and low-priced products. "Regional development policies in Atlantic Canada inflated wages, dampening investment; politicized the economy, weakening business activity; discouraged educational achievement; and froze in place declining economic activities. It also likely had an effect on the regional psyche. People came to expect government to support them."[50]

If this approach to regional development had lived up to its expectations, Atlantic Canada should long ago have closed the economic gap between its residents and those of central Canada. It has not. Other geographically marginal and economically depressed jurisdictions — from the Netherlands and Ireland in Europe to American states including Michigan, Massachusetts, and Georgia — have used very different strategies. Over the same period they have made labour markets more flexible, cut taxes, stopped protecting outmoded activities, invested in human capital, and cut back political influence on economic decisions. And they have recorded remarkable resurgence in economic activities and incomes.

Atlantic Canada does not need regional development programs in order to become powerfully attractive to skilled people and leading-edge companies. The distance from major markets that might have discouraged manufacturers is of little consequence to companies dealing in data passing through optical fibres. At the same time, the region offers people an unbeatable combination of a low cost of living and excellent quality of life. As the City of St. John's claims in its economic development literature, newcomers can expect the same high-quality health care and education they would elsewhere in Canada (thanks to equalization). At the same time, they gain access to cheap housing, wonderful scenery, terrific recreation opportunities, safe streets, clean air, an energetic artistic community, and (we speak from experience) a lot of warm and friendly people. These factors, not government grants, are what matter most in the high technology era.

Already Newfoundland is home to some two hundred information technology companies that do business in forty countries. By 2000, the province's IT sector employed 4,000 professionals, a number that has been growing by 25 percent a year.[51] But, in government, old habits and attitudes die hard. One entrepreneur told us that he accepted a small subsidy for preparing a business plan that he was going to do anyway, but astonished the government official who reviewed it by not including as one of his objectives the goal of "leveraging government money." Instead, like other forward-looking Canadian entrepreneurs, he was intent on using local opportunities as a springboard for the global growth, an ambition he went on to realize.

Expensive and ineffective corporate handouts are not the only way governments have held back economic growth in the very regions they are trying to help. The evolution of the unemployment insurance system during the 1970s offers an even starker example of perverse outcomes to well-meaning policies. By allowing recipients to collect forty-two weeks of benefits after ten weeks of work, governments actively encouraged people to stay in, and even to seek out, low-skill seasonal work. As McMahon puts it in *Retreat from Growth*:

> This program quickly exceeded all policy bounds and became a central fact of life in Atlantic Canada. In some areas, it became common for 80 percent or more of two-income households to draw Unemployment Insurance (UI) each

year. Both levels of government, federal and provincial, paid for make-work projects primarily intended to enable individuals to draw UI. Cycles of 10-week job sharing developed, while employers offering full-time jobs were unable to fill them.

An unfortunate side effect of this pattern was to discourage educational achievement and skill advancement. Collecting UI required no skills, and payments were not available to those furthering their education. The program thus reduced the incentive to obtain education while creating incentives to leave educational and skill-enhancing institutions. This is a true human tragedy.[52]

Subsequent reforms to what is now called Employment Insurance reduced the scope of this problem, but the run-up to the 2000 federal election led the government to repeal the so-called intensity rule, which reduced benefits slightly to people who made repeated claims. As Dale Orr, senior vice-president of economic consulting firm WEFA Inc., has noted, Canada's EI system remains a convoluted mix of insurance and income support. And because it provides income support to many families less needy than others who are not eligible for EI benefits, it is inequitable and persuades people not to move in search of work — two outcomes that are costly to all Canadians. "One of the leading barriers to a lower level of unemployment in Canada is geographical immobility. This will sound surprising to the thousands of Newfoundlanders who move to Alberta and Toronto seeking work. However, the statistics are blatantly obvious. Too many people stay in regions of persistently high levels of unemployment in Canada." He has noted that in the United States, which does not have the same degree of entrenched rigidity, only four of the ten states with the highest levels of unemployment in 1990 were still in the top-ten list by 1999.[53]

In a foreword to McMahon's book, Nobel laureate economist Robert Mundell points out that regional policies always involve government intervention and often interfere with the market. "The case for intervention must be based on the need for public goods or market failure. But it is not always easy to distinguish between market failure and often-painful-but-necessary adjustment processes. A region becomes poor for a variety of reasons that might include a collapse of demand for its export products, unstable monetary or fiscal policies in the currency area of which it is a part, inefficient taxation or regulation, and demographic factors. Quite often, government is the problem, not the solution."[54]

This can be true even when governments are targeting support, not at specific parts of the country, but more generally at creating jobs. Human Resources Development Canada spends some $3 billion a year on grants and contributions for such purposes. In his extensive 2000 audit of four programs covering $570 million a year, federal auditor general Denis Desautels issued a devastating critique. "We found a widespread lack of due regard to probity in spending public funds and to achieving desired results. Several practices in the four programs we examined were unacceptable. These included lack of adherence to program terms and conditions, inadequate project selection processes, breaches of authority, payments made improperly, and inadequate monitoring. We were particularly concerned about the pervasiveness of the deficiencies we found."[55]

On the eve of the autumn 2000 election, opposition parties seized on both the auditor general's report and the internal HRDC audit that had preceded it in 1999, primarily as evidence of government mismanagement. But in practical terms, the design and administration of these two programs were hardly unique. They were simply two of many examples of the political need for fast responses to cyclical unemployment problems. As economics professor Rick Szostak of the University of Alberta has pointed out, the desire for quick fixes tends to result in programs that reward those who can come up with promises to create jobs as soon as possible. "Civil servants are placed under severe time pressure and are unable to evaluate proposals properly. A related difficulty is that much of the funding goes to projects that would have been undertaken anyway. When firms are asked to bring forward proposals for new initiatives, they often find it easiest to request a subsidy for what they were planning to do anyway. What results is a mere transfer of funds to certain businesses, with only the appearance of job creation."[56]

In concentrating on supposed mismanagement, opposition politicians missed the main point — that this was a program designed to meet political needs and bypass detailed scrutiny. When the political heat became too intense, the federal government cancelled the program, only to shuffle the money immediately into the regional development envelope.

As the auditor general pointed out, the problems with the HRDC grants and contributions go far beyond the issue of mismanagement. He extended his audit to the core question of whether such programs actually achieve their stated objective of creating jobs. What he found was that governments' claims that they created jobs were both dubious and overstated. "Project officers did not properly monitor the number of jobs created, even when it was the basis for the payment of the contribution. In most cases, officers obtained information from the employer without making a site visit. To determine the number of jobs created, project officers often relied on lists of employees working at the end of the project, without recourse to information on the jobs that had existed at its beginning. In some cases, project officers relied on lists of people hired, without information on either turnover or the duration of their employment."[57]

What is more, the auditor general reported, the department attributed all jobs created by a project to its contribution, no matter how small or large that contribution might have been. And he found widespread double-counting of jobs created, because when both HRDC and a regional development agency made contributions to a project, each would claim full credit for all the jobs created by the project.

The auditor general also took a broader look at the economic impact of such job creation programs. He turned to Statistics Canada's labour force data to see if the areas targeted for spending actually ended up any better off. While acknowledging some problems with data quality, he concluded that "the estimated $3 billion in total project spending over three years — if it occurred to the extent claimed by sponsors in project applications — should have been of identifiable benefit to local economies and their labour markets. However, we could find no evidence that the leveraged spending estimated was associated with longer-term improvements in general employment and in unemployment conditions in the areas targeted by the program."[58]

In a 2000 report for the C.D. Howe Institute, Ben Cherniavsky made the point that distorting the labour market through taxation may be justified to fund essential public goods such as education or defence. For job creation, however, cutting the tax wedge — the difference between the amount an employer pays out and the amount the employee receives after taxes — is far more efficient. "Although publicly financed employment programs are generally based on altruism, good intentions do not necessarily produce economic efficiencies. Administrative costs, indirect effects, deadweight losses, stigmatization effects, and lack of demand stimulants associated with past employment subsidies suggest that tax cuts of the same cost would, in fact, have produced better net employment results. Assisting the disadvantaged is a worthy goal, but governments need to choose their tools carefully if they hope to produce meaningful results."[59]

We do not question the goal of wanting people in all regions of Canada to be able to earn higher incomes. What we find terribly disappointing is the inability of governments, year after year, to recognize that some approaches just don't work. The real flaw in federal policies intended to spur regional development is that they have lost sight of the goal — which is to help people get ahead, no matter where they live. By propping up traditional industries and work patterns, they have made people more comfortable in their relative poverty, but held back their ability to adapt to economic change and raise their market incomes. The result is a perpetuation of wide disparities rather than a convergence of living standards across Canada. If we want to help people get ahead, we should invest in people and their skills rather than handing out subsidies to businesses just because of where they set up shop. We need to spend less on propping up our past and invest more in helping Canadians prepare for a better future.

■ Spending Better: Attacking the Scourge of Poverty

Perhaps no challenge is more closely tied to the caring and compassionate values we consider the essence of Canadian society than the elimination of poverty. Yet here, too, badly designed policies can end up hurting the very people they are intended to help most. Decades of determined effort by governments and others have failed to eradicate hunger, homelessness, and deprivation of the minimum necessities for an acceptable quality of life.

Efforts to get at the roots of poverty are frustrated from the beginning by disputes over definition. At the global level, the United Nations uses two measures of basic poverty: about 1 billion people around the world "cannot meet their basic consumption requirements," and about 1.3 billion live on incomes of less than one American dollar a day. Neither of these definitions is particularly useful in Canada. Even the poorest Canadians have access to public services and cash transfers that would make them well off by the standards of much of the less-developed world. Yet, clearly, Canada has people who live in conditions that are unacceptable by the standards of our own society.

The basic disagreement on the issue of poverty in Canada is whether to measure it by absolute or relative standards. The absolute, or "basic needs," approach considers what goods and services are necessary to sustain a decent standard of living. A person without sufficient income to pay for these goods and services is considered poor. The relative approach looks at the median income in a society and defines as poor anyone with an income lower than a defined percentage of that median. Following the "basic needs" approach tends to reduce estimates of poverty levels. It exempts from classification as poor such people as university students, who may temporarily have low incomes but have access to other resources and an enjoyable lifestyle, as well as elderly citizens, who may be living on modest pensions but have substantial assets such as a mortgage-free home. On the basis of this kind of calculation, Christopher Sarlo, in his 1994 Fraser Institute study *Poverty in Canada*, concluded that poverty is not a major problem in Canada. "It is almost certain that less than 2 percent of Canada's population lives in poverty. Of those all but employable persons or those with substantial assets qualify for programs that would lift them above the poverty line. So, while poverty has not been entirely eradicated, there is no reason for anyone in Canada to be permanently poor. Everyone is able to acquire all of the basic necessities of life."[60]

Such statements fly in the face of everyday experience — the experience of single mothers trying to raise children on social assistance, of homeless panhandlers, of residents of overcrowded shelters, and of the growing numbers who must rely on food banks. There are people in Canadian society who need help, and not all of them are getting the help they need.

On the other hand, there is a fundamental problem with using relative measures to define poverty. If the wealth of the Canadian economy doubled and the distribution of income did not change, a relative measure would declare that there had been no reduction in the level of poverty. Yet the standard of living of all citizens would be twice as high as before. If we use this approach, poverty can, by definition, never be eliminated except through higher taxation that leads to greater redistribution of income.

The most commonly cited measure of poverty in Canada is Statistics Canada's Low Income Cut-Off (LICO). By its calculations, people are considered poor if they and others at their income level spend 20 percentage points more than average of their income on necessities. As a measurement, it is both complex and arbitrary, and Statistics Canada itself explicitly rejects its use to define a poverty line — but in the absence of other official measures, this is the measure commonly used to ascertain the number of poor people in Canada.

No matter how we define poverty, what should matter is not the number of people in poverty at any given moment. In our view, the key measure of Canada's success in dealing with poverty should be the absolute increase in the real standard of living of the worst-off in our country. We should focus on whether our poorest people are getting ahead and, if so, how fast.

As mentioned earlier, Canada's existing combination of social supports and progressive taxation has been quite effective in preventing the poor from getting poorer, whether in absolute or in relative terms. What is disturbing, however, is a distinct shift in the mix of income received by the most disadvantaged families. Rather than being dominated by market income, their incomes are increasingly made up of transfers from governments. This redistribution of money through taxes and social programs is the only reason that Canada has avoided a sharp decline in the standard of living of its lowest-income families.

While Canada's social safety net has worked to stabilize the incomes of the poorest, many of them have been successful in leaving poverty behind. Episodes of poverty are widespread, but often short-lived. In 1998 an estimated 752,000 Canadian families, 9.1 percent of the total, had incomes lower than the LICO. That total was down from 852,000 families in 1997, a net drop of 100,000 families. But fully one-third of those who were living in poverty in 1997 had moved above the LICO a year later, and 26 percent of those in poverty in 1998 had not been there in 1997.[61]

When analyzed over longer periods, the dynamics of poverty are even more striking. Between 1993 and 1998 almost one in four Canadians experienced life below the LICO at some point. But only 3.3 percent of the population stayed in the low-income range for the entire six years. For most individuals and families, poverty is a temporary state, and Canada's existing system of redistribution through taxes and transfers has held the depth of poverty fairly stable.[62]

That is all very well, but now we must focus on moving the floor up, on improving the real incomes of the worst-off over time. Work by Ross Finnie of the School of Policy Studies at Queen's University has shown that the poor in Canada fall into two distinct groups. He found that about half of those who fell into poverty at some point between 1992 and 1996 stayed there only briefly. The other half remained in poverty most of the time, and made up three-quarters of those in poverty at any given moment. These long-run poor clearly represent the most difficult and urgent policy challenge.

Finnie suggests that three elements are necessary: carrots, sticks, and an economy strong enough to generate the jobs that poor people will need to move into the economic mainstream. The "carrots" he proposes include "opportunities for developing marketable skills, learning about job search, and making work feasible and worthwhile through the provision of child care, help with transportation, aid in the purchase of necessary clothes, [and] assistance with other work-related costs." Financial incentives to work are equally important, however: "allowing welfare recipients to keep a greater share of their benefits as their labour market earnings rise, providing direct wage subsidies, increasing earned-income tax credits, and so on." Also necessary, he suggests, are "sticks," penalties to discourage people from refusing to participate in available programs, and "to help prod those who have lost (or never learned) the ability, willingness, or hope required to better their lives into participating in the programs that offer — on a good day — the promise of improving their lot in life."[63]

After the autumn 2000 election, there was a burst of speculation that the federal government was interested in reviving the decades-old idea of a Guaranteed Annual Income. On the surface, this concept has appeal even for fiscal conservatives. Wrapping together the gamut of social supports from Employment Insurance and welfare to public pensions and workers' compensation benefits into a single income-support program offers the potential for huge administrative savings. But no industrialized country has managed to crack the problem of designing a GAI plan that works.

The major problems are cost and marginal tax rates. If the minimum income is high enough to keep people out of poverty, keeping the cost affordable requires scaling back the benefit quickly as income rises, creating a giant welfare trap that makes it difficult for lower-income people to get ahead. In a country like Canada, two further problems arise. The first is that many existing programs that support incomes and relieve poverty are within provincial jurisdiction. The second is that the cost of living varies widely by region. If the minimum income is set only high enough to keep people out of poverty in St. John's or Regina, families trying to live on that income in Toronto or Vancouver will still be sorely in need.

In attacking poverty, one size does not fit all, and we think that the focus of policy innovation should be on finding ways to help more people earn higher incomes.

We would argue in particular that helping people to learn is critical to the ability of poorer Canadians to move into the economic mainstream. Only by investing more in education and training can we improve the ability of all Canadians to earn higher market incomes and free them from dependence on state transfers.

The trend in labour markets is clear. Fewer and fewer jobs in our economy are available to people with a high school education or less. Many of the jobs formerly requiring little education have disappeared, and the vast majority of jobs being created require knowledge and skills that go beyond secondary education. Even more important, the knowledge and skills needed for new jobs change over time. The process of lifelong learning has become critical to the continued ability to earn high and rising market incomes. Only by increasing the ability of more Canadians to adapt to changing labour markets can we sustain and improve the quality of life of those who otherwise would be left behind.

Increasing direct income support is the most immediate way to reduce the depth of poverty. It is the only way to create an immediate increase in the real disposable incomes of those below some defined threshold. Measures designed to enable and encourage people to earn higher market incomes may not alleviate the depth of poverty in the short term, but they are more effective in reducing the duration of poverty. Any given dollar of government spending cannot do both — and the decision to focus on targeted income support can prolong rather than shorten the period of dependency. There is clearly some minimum standard of living that Canadians are prepared to accept as decent and respectable. Beyond that, merely settling for improvements in the quality of poverty is not good enough. We need to give people a more meaningful shot at a better future. This does not mean abandoning the idea of an effective social safety net. Like equalization, the safety net is an embedded part of the Canada's definition of itself. But as the design of social support programs unfolds, we do need to address the huge disincentives to progress that are created by our obsession with targeting stop-gap help to the most needy.

The proliferation of income-tested transfers and tax credits has pushed marginal tax rates to ridiculous heights. We think it is appalling that people trying to move from poverty-level incomes into the middle class are faced with the highest marginal tax rates in the country. For example, two parents trying to raise a family on modest incomes can lose 70 cents of each extra dollar they make by putting in more hours or earning a raise after upgrading their skills. As the BCNI put it in 1998: "Efforts to channel resources to low-income Canadians have given short-term relief to those most in need. But in the process, they have mired families with modest incomes in a quicksand of disincentives, a trap in which the harder they try to pull themselves toward the security of a higher after-tax income, the more they feel the futility of their efforts. The huge marginal tax rates that flow from tightly targeted incentives are simply unfair to those they are intended to help."[64]

In our search for better ways to reduce the depth and duration of poverty, it is important that different levels of government work together. Many elements of the poverty challenge cross jurisdictional boundaries. For instance, education is clearly within provincial jurisdiction, but access to high-quality lifelong learning is an issue combining economic competitiveness and social equity at the national level. In another example, the federal government has felt obliged to create both a minister and a budget to attack homelessness. A shortage of affordable housing, however, is a problem predominantly associated with rapidly growing cities where rising population and incomes push up rents and reduce vacancy rates. Federal action on this front therefore requires putting more money into the richer regions where the fastest-growing cities are located — a policy that runs counter to its usual bias.

Decades of constitutional conflict have made it clear that formal changes to powers between levels of government are difficult to achieve even when they seem logical. But experience also has shown the flexibility of Canadian federalism. Where there has been a will, Canadians have found ways. Regardless of jurisdiction, the key is to ensure that all governments are committed to the principle that public action should be taken by the level of government best equipped to create a desired impact at the lowest cost.

The war against poverty within our society must also be waged beyond the corridors of government. Canadians have learned the hard way that governments are not the answer to all of society's problems. It is critical that our governments become more innovative in building partnerships with organizations in the private and voluntary sectors if they want to be more effective in delivering solutions to Canadians who need help. Contracting out to the private sector and providing funding to non-profit organizations may be ways of improving the efficiency and effectiveness of some programs. Whatever goals governments adopt, they must be willing to seek out the best means of getting the job done.

■ Choosing a Better Future

The issues we have discussed here — health care, regional development, and poverty — hardly do justice to the huge range of challenges we face globally and locally. As citizens of the world, we see that too many people are still deprived of opportunities for development; efforts to ensure that economic development remains environmentally sustainable continue to be fragmented; and progress towards greater sharing of opportunity through clear rules for trade and investment have been stalled. Closer to home, we must acknowledge that key elements of public infrastructures and highways are crumbling; economic and social outcomes for Aboriginal people are appalling; the military wage structure has sent soldiers to food banks to make ends meet, and our military equipment is falling apart. We could go on.

But the issues of health, regional development, and poverty illustrate our key themes about the choices facing governments in Canada. In some areas, more public spending will be needed, and we have to plan for those needs. In other areas of government spending, we need to let go of what does not work. And finally, we need to find ways of doing a better job with the resources we have.

We think Canadians are remarkably united about our goals as a society. The business community is not in the habit of quoting the leader of the New Democratic Party, but as members of that community we have to agree fully with a recent declaration made by Alexa McDonough in the *Ottawa Citizen*: "I believe it is not credible to talk about values without also talking about a commitment to putting those values into action. If you believe in social justice, than you must end the national shame of poverty. If you believe in opportunity, then you must ensure that every Canadian has access to education and training. If you believe in caring for others, then you must fund our universal public health-care system so it does not die of neglect."[65]

Our disagreement is not over ends but over means. We share goals such as eliminating poverty, ensuring access to education, and providing better public health care. But our ability to achieve those goals as a society depends on our progress as an economy. As the Standing Committee on Finance of the House of Commons put it in its 1999 report "Productivity with a Purpose: Improving the Standard of Living of Canadians": "Social cohesion results from productivity enhancement and economic growth, and does not cause it. In other words, we must first bake the pie before we cut it up and distribute the slices. The bigger the pie, the more slices we can cut, or the larger the slices might be."[66] There are ways to fix what's wrong with Canada. There are ways to take what we already do well and do it better. There are ways to ensure a strong and distinct Canadian society within an integrated global economy. But to achieve the kind of progress we all want, we have to break away from our emotional attachment to outdated labels and focus on ideas, not ideology. As we discuss more fully in the chapters ahead, the approaches that will be most useful in attaining our shared goals require us to break with the past and embrace fundamental change. We can choose to build a better tomorrow for all Canadians, but, to do so, we have to invest in our future instead of in our past.

3

DEVELOPING HUMAN ADVANTAGE

Education is now the main barometer of competitiveness among countries — more than capital, and more than technology. More than ever, learning is intimately linked with the wealth and well-being of nations. Our environment is making new demands on all of us, especially in the way we think about education. It has become a linchpin in planning for Canada's future.[1]

— JEAN MONTY, PRESIDENT AND CHIEF EXECUTIVE OFFICER, BCE INC.,
MAY 2, 2000

◀ ◀ ◀

Despite the pressures of technological change and global economic integration, Canada can and must develop its own distinctive recipe for economic and social progress. No strategy for investing in the future can hope to succeed, however, without a primary focus on the development and retention of human capital. People's knowledge and skills determine the prosperity of their families, the competitiveness of their employers, and ultimately the quality of their lives within their communities and their countries.

As a share of its economy, Canada already invests more in the education of its citizens than most other industrialized countries — and as a result enjoys the benefits of a highly educated workforce. The Council of Ministers of Education, Canada (CMEC), in its 1999 report on Education Indicators in Canada, noted that fully 48 percent of our working-age population (25 to 64) had a post-secondary education by 1995, more than double the average for all industrialized countries. What is more, Canada has made important progress in education levels over the past decade. The proportion of 25-to-29-year-old Canadians with less than a high school education dropped by a third between 1990 and 1998, from 20 percent to just 13 percent; and the percentage of university graduates jumped over the same period from 17 percent to 26 percent.[2] Our country's well-educated workforce already gives us a major competitive advantage, and Canada's young people clearly are preparing themselves to use that advantage in the new millennium (see fig. 9).

Daunting challenges still remain, however. Although more young people than ever are graduating from high school, too many of them still lack the basic functional skills for the knowledge economy. An OECD study of literacy skills in twenty countries found significant weaknesses in Canada's performance. Overall, Canadians ranked fifth in their ability to understand texts such as news stories, eighth in accessing information in formats such as maps, forms, and schedules, and ninth in applying math skills to chores such as balancing a chequebook. But the study, which assigned people to one of five levels of literacy, found that four out of ten Canadian adults aged 16 to 65 were at the lowest two levels of literacy in all three categories.[3] Lagging in literacy has huge costs for society as well as individuals. A 1997 Conference Board of Canada study estimated that a male with high document literacy skills would earn $585,000 more than one with low literacy skills over the course of his lifetime. The lifetime earnings gap for women was even higher, an estimated $683,000.[4]

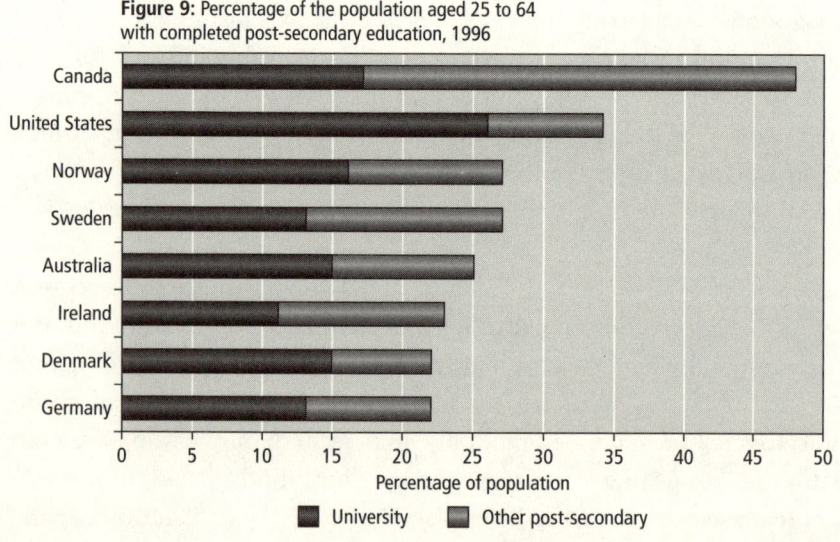

Figure 9: Percentage of the population aged 25 to 64 with completed post-secondary education, 1996

Developing Human Advantage

There also appears to be a growing gap between the achievements of boys and girls within our schools, and it is the boys who are falling behind. In a 1998 nationwide test of reading ability, for instance, 55 percent of 13-year-old girls were at an advanced level, in comparison with just 33 percent of boys. In British Columbia, 30 percent of boys do not finish high school, whereas 20 percent of girls do not. Males now make up just 44 percent of undergraduates at Canadian universities.[5] In a world in which most of the jobs being created require post-secondary qualifications, this widening achievement gap in our secondary schools has ominous implications. Even though the proportion of post-secondary graduates in Canada's workforce may be greater than that of any other industrialized country, we have to do a better job of helping boys and girls alike get the education they need for success in a world of rapid change. Developing our human capital from earliest childhood right through to each person's retirement from the labour force also matters to our country. It is the most effective strategy we can pursue both to hone Canada's competitive edge and to foster a stronger, more cohesive society.

■ *Off to a Fast Start*

If it is to be effective as a strategy for developing human capital through lifelong learning, education must start early in life. As all new parents quickly discover, babies are intellectual sponges; they soak up every sight, sound, taste, touch, and smell. Each new experience triggers new connections in the brain, laying the foundation for a lifetime of learning. A wide range of research has established that the way infants are nurtured and stimulated has a major impact on their ability to succeed in school and in life. Improving early childhood development opportunities has therefore become a high priority for governments and communities alike.

There are two caveats to consider in discussing early child development. First, children need help in getting off to a good start no matter what their families' income level is. It is well known that a higher proportion of children in low-income families than in higher income families fail to do well academically or socially. However, as the Honourable Margaret McCain and Dr. Fraser Mustard noted in their landmark *Early Years Study* for the government of Ontario: "There is no economic cut-off point above which all children do well. Because of the size of the middle class, the number of children not doing as well as they might is greater in the middle socio-economic group than in the bottom 20 percent of the scale."[6] In other words, there are actually more troubled kids living in middle-class households than in poor ones — and even rich families can be dysfunctional. Whatever approaches Canada adopts to help children must be extended to all who need it, regardless of the income level of their parents.

Second, investing in early development should not mean that we focus on the early years to the exclusion of interventions later in life. This is the fear that Dr. John Bruer expressed in *The Myth of the First Three Years*: "It seems to follow that if we can't help children by age 3, then we can't help them at all . . . A strong and beguiling neural-environmental determinist argument for the importance of the first three years weakens the policy case for supporting programs and interventions to assist older children and citizens[7] Dr. Bruer and Dr. Mustard agree that, while helping children to develop when very young may be easier and cheaper than turning their lives around at a later date, we should not give up on helping people to achieve their potential at any age. If the theories are right, more effective programs for early development should lead to a reduced demand for other public services down the road, but services for continuing education are still needed now — and will be needed to some extent in the future.

Given these caveats, how can Canada do a better job of getting all children off to a better start in life? The simplest approach for governments to support parents of young children is to use the tax system. The most significant change in child support in recent years has been the development of the Canada Child Tax Benefit and its low-income National Child Benefit supplement, which was introduced in 1997. This support mechanism includes two notable elements. First, the amount of child tax benefit is determined by family income rather than individual income and is scaled back as income rises. Second, the low-income supplement was introduced specifically to let provincial governments redirect some of their spending and extend to low-income working parents a range of services and benefits for children that once were available only to families on welfare.[8]

The major flaw in the existing structure of the child tax benefit system flows from its attempt to provide relatively generous benefits while at the same time limiting the overall cost by reducing benefits sharply as incomes rise. Targeting of benefits may have been unavoidable in the money-tight 1990s, but circumstances have changed. Canada is now almost alone in the industrialized world in not providing some financial recognition of the fact that families with children spend more money on necessities than families with no children — at any level of income. The income-testing of child benefits also has resulted in extremely high marginal tax rates for families with modest incomes. In some provinces, the combination of income taxes and clawbacks in the child tax benefit and other credits can cause parents trying to raise a family on very modest incomes to forfeit 70 cents out of every extra dollar they manage to earn. As the Business Council on National Issues noted in its 1998 proposal for a Canadian tax reduction strategy, the highest marginal tax rates in the country are being paid by families whose incomes may fall below Statistics Canada's Low Income Cut-Off. Subsequent increases in the Canada Child Benefit have boosted federal tax support for children, but done little to improve either horizontal equity or the high marginal rates faced by families with modest incomes.[9]

In addition, Canada's income tax system is biased in two ways against families in which one spouse chooses to stay home with the children. First, Canada's progressive tax brackets mean that one-income families suffer horizontal inequity. In other words, a single-earner family with an income of $60,000 pays more tax than a two-earner family with the same total income. The United States, France, and Germany deal with this problem by treating the family rather than the individual as the basic unit of taxation. Canada does not.

A second bias is created by the child care expense deduction, which allows families to deduct up to $7,000 a year in child care expenses. This deduction, however, can be applied only to the lower of two incomes in a family. A mother in a dual-income family who chooses to earn even a part-time income can deduct expenses for child care that is provided at any time of the day or night and on any day of the week. A mother in a single-income family, on the other hand (and it usually is the mother who chooses to stay at home), is expected by government to remain on duty at home for twenty-four hours a day, seven days a week, with no right to assistance for respite. Any parent knows that raising children is one of the toughest jobs around. The discrimination built into our tax rules shows not merely disrespect but outright contempt for the contribution that parents make to the healthy development of their children.

In a 1998 C.D. Howe Institute study, Kenneth Boessenkool and James Davies noted that allowing joint tax filing would have some significant advantages. It would improve horizontal equity, redistribute income towards lower and middle-income families, and improve the integration of the "give" and "take" portions of the tax and transfer system. While pointing out that joint filing also would have some major drawbacks, Boessenkool and Davies spoke strongly in favour of re-introducing universal deductions for children. The current Income Tax Act, they suggested, "treats children as consumer purchases" and unfairly penalizes families that choose to care for their own children instead of paying others to provide that care. Even if the child care expense deduction were to be reduced by a similar amount, "these reforms would allow Ottawa to lower by five to twenty percentage points the prohibitive tax rates faced by families earning between $21,000 and $26,000."[10]

The idea of a universal child care deduction was adopted by the Canadian Alliance in its platform for the 2000 federal election. The party proposed an annual deduction for all families of $3,000 per child up to the age of 16. Parents who work outside the home would then be able to claim an additional deduction for receipted expenses greater than $3,000 up to the current limit of $7,000.[11]

Those who defend the existing bias against families with stay-at-home parents suggest that governments ought to help with the extra costs of going back to work and should also encourage women to stay attached to the workforce as a way of promoting gender equity in the workplace. People who work outside the home, however, generally earn income that more than offsets any additional costs associated with employment. And while gender equity remains a worthy goal and it is undeniable that most spouses who stay home are women, the decision about whether to spend time with children or make additional income is both difficult and personal. The state has no more business in the kitchens and family rooms of the nation than it does in the bedrooms.

There is strong evidence that the quality of attention children get in the early years is vital to our collective success as well as to their individual prospects, and government policy should be driven first and foremost by what is best for children. Unless governments can produce convincing evidence that paid child care is *better* than that provided by a parent, they should at least stay neutral on the question of whether one parent stays at home. No matter how they are structured, however, financial benefits delivered through the tax system are not sufficient to ensure the best possible start in life for all children. There will remain a need for access to a wide range of services at the community level, where flexibility, diversity, and networking are the keys to success.

Take as an example the Parenting and Family Literacy Centres hosted by the Toronto District School Board in lower-income communities since 1981. These centres combine child care with classes to help parents do a better job at home. They work with other agencies in the community, sharing resources and both making and receiving referrals. They identify early signs of learning disabilities and refer children for needed treatment. Parenting centres operate on a drop-in basis and set their schedules on the basis of parents' requests, so that families can attend at their own convenience. Some offer additional services such as English as a Second Language training for immigrants. Mary Gordon, who founded the centres, notes that their location within schools, rather than churches or community centres, creates a vital link for the future: "It is through daily contact with community, parents and school staff that easy communications and trusting relationships grow. When parents are introduced early and positively to the school system, they usually stay involved and increase the likelihood of their child's academic success."[12]

This is precisely the approach recommended by McCain and Mustard in their *Early Years Study*. They propose that comprehensive versions of this network be set up in communities across the province and, presumably, across the country. In their vision, early child development and parenting centres would involve both the public and private sectors. Resources would come from a wide range of partnerships with the community and governments — partnerships that involve not just money but also the exchange of services, use of space, and volunteer labour.

The community centres in turn would be part of a broader set of social supports that would include improved maternity and parental leave benefits, family-friendly workplaces, tax incentives, integrated and independent measurement of human development outcomes, and a network for sharing information within and between communities. What the study did *not* propose was a massive one-size-fits-all government program with a big budget: "These initiatives cannot be considered as a mandated, universal government program. We are proposing that communities build on existing strengths and resources to create a variety of solutions compatible with the goals of the early child development and parenting program, based on public, private and local communities' resources. The role of governments, the private sector and communities is to ensure the centres are available and accessible in all sectors of society."[13]

While some additional public spending would be required, they said, most of the needed resources could be found through "a realignment of existing initiatives." The federal government has already adopted the report's recommendation to extend maternity leave benefits to a full year. To the extent that governments do need to spend more money on early childhood development, Mustard has suggested that there is plenty of room for re-allocation of the resources that are now being used for "repair shop" functions within existing public sector budgets — even within the health care sector.[14] This potential for re-allocation within existing budgets is in addition to any savings that would be generated over the long term through improvements in early child development.

The report also points out the need to share community resources more equitably. Schools, for instance, should be kept open for families to use on evenings and weekends. Traditional bureaucratic boundaries need to be broken down. Ironically, the Toronto child development centres used as a model by McCain and Mustard themselves almost fell victim to rules on what activities could take place on school premises.

Mustard has suggested that governments look in particular to the tax system to encourage greater private sector participation. Corporate tax rules, for instance, could be tilted to encourage investment in building and operating child development and parenting centres in communities — perhaps on employer premises. They might also be used to promote more flexible and family-friendly workplaces that will be able to respond more readily to parents' and children's needs. Even without such incentives, however, employers competing for skilled workers are expanding their efforts to help employees meet the needs of their children. Family-friendly policies are becoming an increasingly important tool for attracting and retaining employees.

McCain and Mustard's fundamental message is one of creativity and innovation. Children have many common characteristics and needs, but each child is different. So are the circumstances of their families and the characteristics of their communities. We should have high expectations for all of our children, but the strength of Canada's current approach is its very diversity. We need to build on that diversity to give more children a solid start in life — and then we need to look onward to the next vital phase of our children's development and breathe some of that spirit of community innovation into our school systems.

■ Learning to Excel

Canada spends a great deal on its schools and gets respectable results. Better still, as we mentioned earlier, the level of achievement of Canadian students is on the rise; more young people are staying in school longer and moving on to higher education. In that narrow sense, our schools are not in crisis. But even as the world shifts into high gear and demands greater levels of learning as a prerequisite for personal success, our systems of education often seem to be revving in neutral. Jennifer Lewington of the *Globe and Mail* makes an intriguing comparison: "Imagine if the health care sector behaved the same way as education. Medical researchers would be guided by ideology and instinct rather than information. Patients would clamour for the same medical procedures they experienced as children. Doctors would ignore the results of testing and other diagnostic data. Yet, all too often, that's exactly the behaviour of those in education. Whether it's early childhood preparation for school, reading methods or high school curriculum reform, there's usually more ideological heat than educational light. In the absence of data, facts and observation, it's difficult to see how to make improvements at the individual or system level."[15]

As in health care, systemic change is frustrated by deep ideological divisions even among the experts within the educational community. The resulting lack of consensus means that, despite the best efforts of many well-intentioned people, the very institutions on which our children are depending to equip them for life as global citizens are themselves dangerously slow to evolve. The current buzzwords of the knowledge economy are flexibility, teamwork, and empowerment. Companies prize independence and creativity, and are fighting to attract and retain top talent. They woo the people they need most with generous salaries and benefits, performance incentives such as bonuses and stock options, and extensive investments in their professional development. They rush from one achievement to the next, striving to generate new ideas that will destroy the status quo of their own businesses before their competitors do it for them. In business, to settle for mediocrity or stagnation is to die.

Contrast that world with the structure of our schools, these engines of the knowledge economy. Rigid contracts define every minute of the working day, often preventing educators and administrators alike from experimenting with promising new practices. Pay scales are confined to narrow bands defined by credentials and seniority. The incompetent and the inspirational are treated much the same way. Despite giving teachers summers free from teaching responsibilities and setting aside numerous days for professional development, the educational sector was, according to a 1996 study for the Conference Board of Canada, the economic sector that invested the least in employee training.[16] There are numerous examples of local success, but every effort to promote systemic change seems to get mired in a quicksand of confusing bureaucracy and confrontational politics.

In a study for the Business Council on National Issues, Helen Raham of the Society for the Advancement of Excellence in Education outlines the problems school systems currently face: "The struggle over core curriculum content and measurable standards and the proper balance between knowledge and skills and learning processes . . . is unresolved. Effective integration of technology into instruction is uneven and insufficient. Professional development is incoherent and idiosyncratic, largely unrelated to provincial, district or school learning objectives. Schools appear to have limited capacity to develop the skills of teachers to adapt to the changes required for teaching and learning in the next century. Comparisons with other highly successful systems suggest Canada must find ways to help all schools do better if our students are to be competitive in the global information economy."[17] We also agree emphatically with the assertion of Penny Milton, executive director of the Canadian Education Association, that building an economy that creates wealth from ideas and sustaining a social environment that is best for human development are no longer separate endeavours. Helping children of all backgrounds to learn more effectively is the key to improving everyone's economic and social prospects. "Schools do make a difference. Public education is the single largest public investment in the development of children and youth. By systematically applying all that we know about effective teaching and learning to the domains of both policy and practice, we can reasonably expect to improve the life chances of children and youth in Canada."[18]

The knowledge that our children need to acquire is changing daily. So too are the attitudes and skills they need for success in the workplace and in society. The most rapid change of all is in the tools now used for learning, both within and beyond our schools, for children and adults alike. William R. Brody, president of Johns Hopkins University, has previewed the schools of the future: "Many people believe that, in the future, everything done in schools today using blackboards and chalk, pen and paper will still be done, only on computers instead. They could not be more mistaken. We are faced with something new and profoundly different. In the next several decades, we will need to use information technology to advance the science of education itself, to make learning more efficient, more effective, more universal, and more easily available. We will need to create entirely new paradigms of learning."[19]

Incremental change is not enough. We need to completely transform our schools, a process that invites the involvement of people in every sector of our society. Such transformational change must go well beyond mere tinkering with curriculum or governance or funding. It must be centred on a clear overriding goal: to broaden the scope of knowledge and skills that our children absorb in school and to instill a love of learning that will serve them well throughout their lives. Only if we achieve that goal can we really claim that all Canadian children have an equally good opportunity to succeed in the knowledge economy and participate fully in our society as informed and engaged citizens.

Canada is not alone in striving to achieve this goal. As the OECD has noted: "At a time when the role of education as an equalizing institution has again come to the forefront, addressing the needs of students with diverse learning abilities has become a major challenge for all education systems."[20] While the problem is complex and schools alone cannot overcome all the barriers to achievement that students without sufficient family resources face, the study found that real improvement for students at risk is possible.

Consider, for example, the transformational approaches being taken in some other industrialized countries. Britain began a major school improvement effort in 1986 by establishing a new national curriculum and instituting annual standard achievement tests to measure student performance. The results on these tests were used to rank schools publicly in order to help parents select better-performing schools.[21] Individual schools gained more control over their own budgets and staffing. Some 1,200 schools opted to become fully independent of local authorities and to deal directly with the national government. More recently, the government has introduced national competency tests for teachers, changes in teacher training and professional development, performance-related pay for teachers and principals, and school-based performance bonuses shared by all staff. The result has been a steady improvement in test scores as well as increased efficiency.[22]

The state of Victoria in Australia launched sweeping reforms in 1993 and, in addition to reporting similar improvement in student learning, has also cut costs. It, too, established a new framework for curriculum and standards and an accountability system for schools, which included annual reports, triennial external assessments, and appraisal of staff performance. The government devolved 90 percent of its education budget directly to schools, allowing it to reduce the size of the state and regional bureaucracies by almost three-quarters.[23]

New Zealand also devolved considerable authority and responsibility to the school level when it abolished its school boards in 1989. Despite the fact that these changes in governance came at a time of fiscal crisis that had left administrators feeling short of money, a 1997 study for the New Zealand Council for Educational Research found that school-based management had provided many benefits. "School self-management brought new energy and focus to primary schools. It increased the local financial and human resources available to schools. Teachers and principals have paid more attention to what they do and why. Many principals and teachers see positive gains for children."[24]

The widest variety of approaches to educational reform in recent years has been undertaken in the United States. There, too, the four dominant trends in reform have been in the direction of more rigorous standards and assessment, more effective accountability, more site-based management, and increased school choice.

What can Canada learn from all these experiments in other countries? First, while there is growing awareness in Canada of the need for more comprehensive and meaningful assessment of student achievement as a precondition for effective change, we have a very long way to go. In any strategy for improving what our children are able to learn, we have to know not just where we want to go but also where we are starting from. Ontario's 1994 Royal Commission on Learning is emphatic on this point: "It seems obvious to us that the public school system is responsible to the public, and owes it to the public to demonstrate how well it's doing with our children. It seems equally obvious that in learning, as in most other endeavours, your family is helpless to assist you to improve yourself unless you and they know the criteria for success and how close you come to meeting them. Finally, what holds for the individual holds for the system: its programs too must be assessed to determine if they're working properly. So we take a stand on behalf of close monitoring of every child's progress right from the earliest years, and of the system itself at every level, in order that both can learn to be even better."[25]

Similar sentiments have been expressed in the United States by education, business, and labour leaders alike. In a statement for a 1996 education summit, Albert Shanker, then president of the American Federation of Teachers, emphasized the need for overall standards: "The first essential element in effective school systems is the existence of academic standards at the national or state level. These specify what students need to learn — and how well they need to learn it — in each subject at each grade level . . . National standards represent a real opportunity for public schools to turn themselves around and win back the confidence of the people we serve . . . Without standards we have no way to determine which reform ideas and programs really work."[26]

Edward B. Rust Jr., chairman of the Business Roundtable Education Task Force, has expanded on Shanker's recommendations. "Can you measure success solely by test results?" he asks. "Of course not. No one suggests that scores on standardized tests are the last word on academic success . . . These new standards are the 'floor' of basic learning, not the ceiling. These tests should be a starting point, and we should provide an educational system that allows students to master these basics and move on . . . Measures of accountability are necessary to make certain that our instructional practices and our students' performance meet the higher academic standards the public supports."[27]

It is difficult for Canadians to get a meaningful nationwide picture of student achievement and school performance. The School Achievement Indicators Program introduced in 1993 by the Council of Ministers of Education, Canada (CMEC), is restricted to random samples of 13- and 16-year-old students, covers only reading, writing, math, and science, and is administered in each subject only once every four years. But even the limited data that are available show significant gaps in performance. The provinces that have consistently done well — Alberta, British Columbia, and Quebec — are also those with the most explicit guidelines for student learning and, until recently, the only provinces with external Grade 12 graduation exams. In addition, Alberta publishes individual school results on its exams and requires rolling three-year business plans that announce targets for improvement against a range of indicators. Quebec has published its exam results by school since 1993, and more recently has told individual school councils to prepare annual improvement plans.[28]

Once Canada develops better ways to assess and compare student achievement, we have to apply what we learn to the way we run our schools. In particular, we must use assessment of student performance to improve the quality of teaching in our classrooms. Our schools already benefit from the efforts of many talented and dedicated teachers. As adults, we all remember the handful of teachers who really made a difference in our lives, helped us break through to new levels of understanding, and inspired us to seek new avenues of learning. Our challenge is to enable such teachers to flourish. As in any knowledge-intensive industry, our school systems must strive to recruit and retain more people with the talents that matter, so that teaching excellence becomes the norm rather than the exception.

The importance of teachers to educational outcomes has been highlighted by the latest techniques of assessment. William Sanders at the University of Tennessee has developed a complex statistical model to determine the value a teacher adds to his or her students over time. This technique compares each student's achievement with his or her own record over a period of several years rather than to an average or a fixed standard. It then applies a complex mathematical formula to factor out potential biases such as socio-economic status. Using this approach, Sanders found that children with weak teachers two years in a row never recovered. A subsequent study in Dallas concluded that students with good teachers three years in a row scored 40 to 50 percentile points higher on standardized math tests than those who had sub-par teachers for three years. Researchers in Massachusetts and Alabama came to similar conclusions.[29]

Value-added studies, in short, have shown convincingly what many of us have always believed intuitively — that the factor most influencing a student's academic growth is the effectiveness of the individual teacher in the classroom. If value-added assessment is broadly adopted, concluded a paper for the Thomas B. Fordham Foundation, it "holds the promise to revolutionize education. The public has been flooded with information about school and teacher quality, but making sense of it has required experts; and most of the experts have been educators who work for or with the schools. Now schools can produce a balance sheet and report an objective bottom line that is understandable to the interested citizen. The next step is to free up the system so that resources and students can flow to the most effective schools and the best teachers."[30]

Many teachers and administrators, however, object to the use of student achievement data in the process of managing schools. They argue that tests do not measure the full spectrum of student learning, that emphasizing assessment just leads teachers to "teach to the test," and that tests are expensive and undermine the confidence and self-esteem of low achievers. It is true that the goals we have for our children are complex and cannot be captured by a morning of multiple-choice questions. We need to take into account a broader range of indicators as well, measures such as attendance rates, ability to set and work towards personal goals, parent and student satisfaction, and community involvement, along with the kind of student learning that is not captured by set-piece exams. But there are ways to measure achievement in so-called soft skills as well as the acquisition of concrete knowledge.

The American Federation of Teachers (AFT) has warned that even sophisticated methodology has limitations in terms of evaluating the performance of individual teachers. The value-added approach, for instance, can reliably identify only the top and bottom 20 percent of performers, and can do that only with a minimum of three years of data per teacher. But the AFT agrees that the impact of each teacher is important; the quality of a teacher can affect subsequent student performance no matter how good or bad later teachers are. As a result, the AFT objects to basing performance pay *only* on individual student test scores, but agrees that test scores do have a role in evaluating teacher performance. "It is frankly not reasonable to suggest that student test scores have no place in teacher evaluation . . . The task before us then is to determine the appropriate weight to place on such scores and the circumstances under which they can and should be used in teacher evaluation."[31]

This willingness to engage in the process of assessment and accountability is still foreign to teacher associations in Canada, however. The British Columbia Teachers Federation, for instance, has refused to cooperate in using standardized tests to measure student achievement. After the province launched a new series of tests of reading comprehension, writing, and numeracy for all Grade 4, 7, and 10 students, with the intention of assessing individual and school results, the union advised its members "to refuse to perform any administrative procedures that would identify individual students or schools."[32] Similarly, the Canadian

Teachers Federation argues that standardized tests lead to educational inequity, and "continues to work on behalf of teachers and students against the rising tide of standardized testing in Canadian schools."[33] Unless we adopt more effective assessment tools that are linked to teacher and school performance, however, stagnation will be inevitable. Other countries have already moved well beyond the debate about more comprehensive assessment and begun to link student achievement directly with teacher pay. In Britain, for example, the government offers performance pay of up to £2,000 per year to individual teachers as well as collective bonuses worth up to £30,000 per school.[34] In the United States, at least fifteen states now offer bonuses and salary increases for meeting or exceeding academic objectives, and half of the states offer cash subsidies and incentives for teachers who become certified through the National Board for Professional Teaching Standards.[35] In Dallas, Texas, teachers and principals at the schools with the highest "value-added" rating share $2.4 million a year in performance rewards — and pass rates in reading and math in that city now exceed those in other Texas cities.[36] To give another example, in 2000 the California Board of Education approved a $677 million package of incentives for schools and teachers, which included bonuses of up to $25,000 each for teachers in schools in the lower half of the rankings that demonstrate exceptional improvement for two years in a row.[37]

Canadian jurisdictions have taken a few tentative steps towards offering institutional incentives for performance. In British Columbia, the Kamloops-Thompson school district signed a pilot agreement with the provincial government that would provide an increase of 10 percent over base funding for Aboriginal programs only if performance targets are met. Targets include reducing the gap between Aboriginal and non-Aboriginal students by 2 percent annually on six key indicators such as attendance and graduation rates. More broadly, Alberta tried introducing a School Performance Incentive Plan in its March 1999 budget, offering $104 million in additional funding to school boards (not even individual schools, much less teachers) that reached provincially set improvement targets for student learning. After objections from a variety of stakeholder groups, the plan was dropped in favour of funding for school improvement initiatives.[38]

Whether at the individual or school level, bigger rewards elsewhere are being balanced by greater risk. Oregon, for instance, has eliminated tenure for both teachers and principals. Other states have taken action to help schools assess, retrain, or dismiss inadequate teachers and help school districts retrain or remove administrators whose schools fail to improve. Twenty-three American states now have "academic bankruptcy" provisions allowing them to intervene directly in persistently low-performing schools, whether by providing more resources, by replacing administrators or teachers, or by closing a school.[39]

There is an important point to note here: we cannot hold people accountable for what they cannot control. We should aspire to ambitious standards of achievement for all Canadian children, and to aid in that quest we must do our best to measure our progress. But to improve the performance of our schools, we need to manage them in a way that empowers teachers and principals, and fosters their creativity and initiative. The prevailing management structures and collective agreements have the opposite effect. Especially during the years of restraint, government negotiators have put too much emphasis on squeezing costs through restrictive formulas on everything from minutes of preparation time per class to the number of square feet of floor space per pupil. Instead of encouraging teachers and administrators to think outside the box, governments have too often simply tightened the screws that are keeping a lid on the box. Frustrated and demoralized, teachers have reacted by clinging more fiercely than ever to seniority-based pay schemes and placement rules that stifle flexibility and discourage innovation.

What is needed is a new approach, one that sets high expectations and then lets teachers and administrators get on with the job they know best. Progressive employers, especially in the high-technology sector, have learned how important it is to empower and invest in employees and to encourage the expression of their innovative and creative skills. We need to infuse our schools with the same sense of shared purpose; revamping the way teachers and administrators are evaluated and rewarded is a critical element in that transformation.

Just as standardized tests cannot be the only means of evaluating teacher performance, performance-based pay is not enough on its own to move our schools into the knowledge economy. The next element is to give more power to parents, primarily by offering them greater choice. Like assessment and pay for performance, the subject of school choice is intensely emotional, as controversial in education as two-tier medicine is in health care.

Yet two-tier education is firmly established. Parents who are not satisfied with the quality of public education can and do send their children to a wide variety of private institutions, if they can afford to do so. Private schools attract parents away from public schools for a variety of reasons — religious affiliation, more rigorous discipline, different teaching styles, or a focus on particular areas of study — but the common element that parents seek is a dedication to academic excellence.

Technology is opening up new avenues to excellence for parents who are unhappy with public schools and are unable to afford private schooling. In particular, virtual schooling appears to be a growing phenomenon in Canada and elsewhere. It is estimated that fifteen times as many parents chose to educate their children at home in 1996 than in 1988, and the range of material, learning tools, and other supports available through the Internet is increasing daily.[40] Parents who care about their children will turn more and more to alternatives if they lose confidence in the public system. There is nothing wrong with enabling families to pursue home schooling as an option within the public education system, but surely our goal as a society should be to make our schools so good that such alternatives become unnecessary.

Some advocates of school choice say the best means of making alternatives available is to give all parents government vouchers that could be exchanged for education at either public or private schools. This approach, already in use in a few jurisdictions in the United States, usually targets disadvantaged families who otherwise would be trapped in underperforming inner-city schools. Vouchers can indeed stimulate choice, but since there is no guarantee that the value of the voucher would be sufficient to pay the full fees of all private schools, they cannot ensure equality of opportunity.

More promising and much more frequently seen around the world are efforts to provide more alternatives within the public school system. Even within Canada, school boards have set up a wide range of schools that offer unique programs or methods, or cater to a particular clientele. Examples that have been identified include "single sex schools, rigorous academies, fine arts, technical schools, schools for street youth, schools for gay youth, Montessori, work experience, science and technology schools, virtual schools, Mandarin immersion, schools for gifted, music or sports schools," as well as a host of traditional back-to-basics schools.[41]

Such schools are intensely popular and usually generate long waiting lists. A 1999 study of three alternative public schools by Daniel Brown of the University of British Columbia found that even though the demographic makeup of their student bodies was similar to the average in their communities, the alternative schools produced higher academic achievement, encouraged greater parental involvement, and demonstrated strong parent and teacher satisfaction rates. By offering such options, Brown concluded, school districts appear to have retained many parents who otherwise would have left the public school system, and they have done so with no major regulatory change or increase in costs. "The evidence gathered strongly suggests parental choice makes an important difference in the lives of children, parents and educators. Parental choice among public schools is associated with a number of very positive attributes that serve our children, their families and our entire society."[42]

Yet Raham notes that school boards often turn down requests for more alternative schools, even when such requests are backed by large numbers of parents. "Requests for alternative learning environments for students are commonly viewed as criticism of the neighbourhood school, and many boards lack policy and procedure to deal with requests for alternative programs with clear and objective criteria."

In other jurisdictions, public alternative schools are just the beginning of the menu being presented to families. Philadelphia, Boston, and Baltimore are experimenting with contract schools designed to meet the needs of under-served and disadvantaged students. The school board issues a request for proposals to manage a contract school and offers considerable autonomy in return for specific performance goals. By exempting such schools from the usual district and union rules, school boards encourage innovation, flexibility, and a focus on improving student performance.

Another approach to increasing choice within public schooling is to create independent public schools, known as grant-maintained schools in Britain and charter schools in North America. Laws permitting charter schools now exist in thirty-eight American states but just one province, Alberta. These laws vary in the extent to which they facilitate setting up new schools and place restrictions on their operation. But, in general, charter laws allow any group to apply for permission to set up a new school. In return for the freedom to operate as a separate legal entity, a charter school must promise to meet agreed performance targets under the same per-pupil funding as all other public schools. They cannot charge extra fees and they must be as open to all students as any public school (so they cannot boost performance by excluding higher-risk and higher-cost students such as those with learning disabilities).

The charter concept also is being used to experiment with new technology-enabled approaches to learning. The state of Ohio, for instance, has awarded a charter to Ecot, a "telecommunity" school that will offer Internet-based distance learning on a statewide basis. It is open to all students between the ages of 4 and 22 who live in Ohio. Each student is given the use of a complete computer system with all the devices needed to complete assigned lessons, and no one has to pay either tuition or fees for the use of equipment.[43] Some jurisdictions use multiple approaches. The city of Milwaukee in Wisconsin has regular public schools, specialized public schools, charter schools (some of which are even run on a for-profit basis), and a voucher system. Its experience shows how providing choices can spur the public school bureaucracy into action. "There is a gathering passion about raising performance. An advertising campaign is pushing a new 'guarantee' that children who attend school regularly will be reading on grade level by the end of the second grade or will get personal tutoring. New curricula in math and science are being introduced, aimed at overturning a record of low test scores in those areas . . . If a few words can sum up all the ferment on the education scene, perhaps they are these: Provide more options. Seek better results. Find proof that we're getting them. Or make more changes in what already exists."[44]

Experience is starting to indicate that school choice will be most effective in improving student achievement if it is combined with greater autonomy in school management. If each school is allowed the flexibility to best meet the needs of its own student body, it will be able to use its initiative to narrow the achievement gaps between rich and poor and deliver on the goal of equality of economic opportunity. As Raham noted: "School improvement is a highly complex and collaborative exercise. No single magic solution or simplistic measure will work for all schools. The task of educating very diverse learners to much higher standards of learning in a world of fast-changing educational demands will require more responsive schools than present bureaucracies allow. High-performance schools require a high level of autonomy and flexibility at the school site."[45]

When all of these elements — assessment, accountability, autonomy, and choice — come together, the results can be impressive. The two American states with the most rapid gains in student achievement in the 1990s were North Carolina and Texas. These are both states with an above-average proportion of minority students and poor students with under-educated parents. Yet students in both states made substantial and sustained achievement gains, with greater improvement against the indicators set out by the National Education Goals Panel than any other state. Neither state increased spending significantly or reduced its class sizes to achieve these gains. Rather, concluded a 1998 RAND Corporation study, "changes in the organizational and incentive structure for educators emerge as the most decisive aspect of the policies." Key elements in both states included clear teaching objectives for each grade and statewide academic standards for all students; annual state assessments linked to those standards; accountability systems with both rewards and sanctions; local flexibility for teachers and administrators; computerized systems that provide continuous feedback; and a shifting of resources to schools with more disadvantaged students.[46]

The result in both these states was that teachers adapted their methods of teaching to produce higher achievement, working together and sharing knowledge more effectively. Principals made more effective decisions on staffing and professional development. Superintendents put more effort into schools with weak performance — giving them more help, but also visibly transferring or retiring administrators of schools that failed to pull up their socks. The state education department was downsized and refocused on assessment and support, while schools gained much more freedom to decide how to spend money and how to teach. By working together with clear and common goals, teachers and administrators were also able to target resources more specifically at those most in need so that outcomes for all students were improved.

As we try to do a better job of helping all Canadians achieve their full potential in the global economy, we have to ensure that schools and postsecondary institutions have the funding they need. But money isn't everything. Through more accurate assessment, greater accountability, and more flexible management, we can create a much-needed culture of continuous improvement within our school systems, one that will prepare all students for success in the new economy. Knowledge and skills evolve constantly and rapidly; so must our educational institutions.

■ Learning for a Living

In the knowledge economy, a high school diploma is a beginning, not an end. Industry Canada has calculated that, from 1990 to 1998, Canada's economy created 2,131,000 net new jobs for people with post-secondary diplomas or degrees. For those with only a high school education, there was no job growth at all. And for those who failed to finish high school, almost one million jobs disappeared (see fig. 10).[47]

Another illustration of the growing importance of post-secondary education was produced by a 1996 survey of employees of companies run by chief executive members of the Business Council on National Issues. In 1995 employees with post-secondary qualifications made up 55 percent of their combined workforce, a proportion that, while higher than the qualifications of the population as a whole, was not far out of line. But during the intense restructuring of the early 1990s, the impact of education was crystal clear. Five out of every six jobs these companies created between 1990 and 1995 required post-secondary qualifications: 58 percent a university degree, and 26 percent a college diploma. Over the same period, almost two-thirds of the jobs restructured out of existence had belonged to people with a high school education or less.[48]

The federal government sees that trend continuing in the years ahead. Human Resources Development Canada has projected that 72 percent of the 1.3 million jobs that will be created between 1999 and 2004 will require some form of post-secondary qualification, whether university

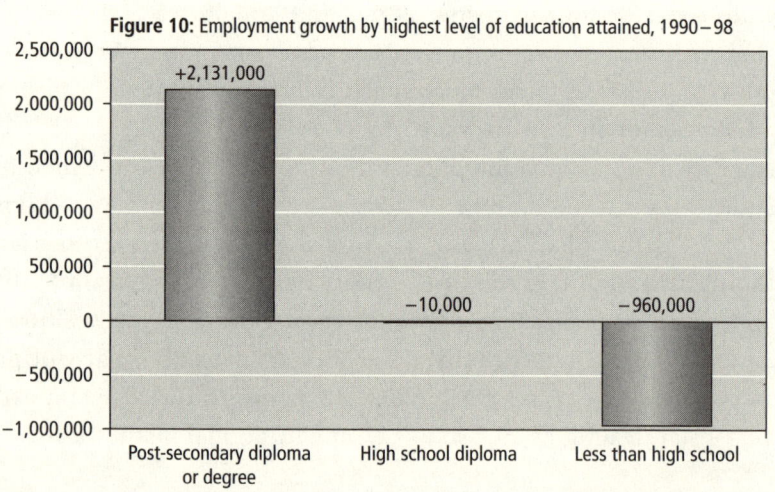

Figure 10: Employment growth by highest level of education attained, 1990–98

degree, college diploma, or trades certificate — up from 60 percent of existing jobs in 1998. Only 5.8 percent of the jobs being created will be open to those who fail to graduate from high school. The share of new jobs requiring a university degree will rise to 23.4 percent in 2004 from 16.7 percent in 1998.[49]

In short, a high school diploma no longer provides the foundation for a stable and well-paid career. It is simply a prerequisite for the continuing studies needed to become and stay employable in the knowledge economy. It is important to note here that the concept of post-secondary education is not limited to immediate attendance at a community college or university. It may involve apprenticeship in a skilled trade or one of a host of other options for continuing studies — and also involves continued learning even for those who have graduated from post-secondary institutions. As Micheline Bouchard, the president and chief executive officer of Motorola Canada Limited, put it in a 1999 speech: "It's estimated that a third of what an electrical engineer learns and half of what a computer scientist studies are out of date within three years of their graduation. Whatever the exact figures, it's clear that skill sets need regular updating no less than do your company's information systems."[50]

The key issues in post-secondary education and lifelong learning in this economy of change are somewhat different from those that have an impact on primary and secondary education — as is the starting point for improvement. The big difference between public schools and publicly funded colleges and universities is that the latter are much more exposed to competition. Potential students have a vast array of alternatives open to them — and both their tuition fees and the even larger per capita government grants go to the institutions they choose to attend. Similarly, government support for research and for capital projects is increasingly linked to an institution's ability to raise contributions from alumni and corporate donors. University governance structures may still be resistant to radical change, but even tenured professors cannot entirely escape the influence of the marketplace.

The tight government budgets of the 1990s have intensified these competitive pressures. According to the Association of Universities and Colleges of Canada, total government grants rose from $3.9 billion in 1986/87 to $4.9 billion in 1997/98, an increase of just 26 percent over 11 years. Over the same period, however, total tuition fees more than tripled, from $768 million to $2.3 billion. This re-allocation means that, by the end of the 1990s, more than 30 percent of the operating revenue of postsecondary institutions was coming from the fees paid by students, up from 16 percent in the late 1980s. Revenue from private research contributions and donations also rose sharply, from $132 million to $376 million.[51]

While excellence in research in any given discipline is likely to be concentrated in a few institutions, we need to foster excellence in teaching in all institutions. In the context of lifelong learning, what is taught in colleges and universities is less important than the way it is taught. The ability to handle pressure, solve problems, and communicate clearly can be developed just as easily in sociology as in computer science. Some of what a student learns in the course of earning a degree or a diploma may be directly relevant to a desired career, but much of the most important learning is transferable to any line of work — and often takes place outside the classroom.

Earning a university degree in any discipline seems to be the factor that determines subsequent success in the job market much more than the specific discipline involved. A 1999 report from the Council of Ontario Universities showed that 91 percent of the 1996 graduating class found jobs within six months, and 97 percent were working two years later. What was striking, however, was that, at 91.8 percent, the proportion of graduates in the humanities who found work within six months was actually higher than that of engineering or computer science graduates — 91.5 and 90.5 percent, respectively.[52]

High technology companies may be salivating for more engineers, but they also need people in sales and marketing, communications, human resources and finance. Even as business leaders talk of the need for relevance of education to the job market, many have been expressing strong public support for the traditional liberal arts, which are at least as relevant today as they were a century ago. That is precisely because they teach young people how to think rather than attempting to instill in them a specific body of soon-to-be-obsolete knowledge. McGill University dean of arts Carman Miller expressed support for this view in a 1999 article: "Taking an arts education demands a greater sense of risk and adventure . . . an arts education seems to provide the skills needed to function in a world where we are bombarded by information. The challenge today is not in finding the information, but in making sense of it."[53]

While the Internet gives students access to a world of data, it does not teach understanding or develop wisdom. As a result, suggests the Corporate–Higher Education Forum (C-HEF), the quality of teaching available through our publicly funded post-secondary institutions will continue to play a vital role in helping our young people grow into effective citizens as well as employees. "With the advent of instantaneous access to information, all attempts at controlling information or containing it in predetermined packages are off. And this means we need to reaffirm the important role teachers will play — not primarily in relaying information, but in setting the context, guiding the process, expanding on the stories so their students can go from isolated pieces of information to a true understanding of what it all means."[54] It is an essential quality of excellent teachers that they are at all times tuned in to the process of individual students' learning.

The need for institutions as well as teachers to be responsive to the needs of their students points to a major shortcoming of Canada's publicly funded post-secondary institutions. Despite the diverse needs of students in today's economy, the programs of colleges and universities still remain primarily geared to the body of students coming directly from high school rather than those in the workplace. Timetables are flexible enough to meet the scheduling needs of part-time students, who make up 30 percent of the more than 800,000 students attending colleges and universities at any given time. But the course offerings themselves are still geared to the completion of traditional degree programs. Employees and employers both need to tap into the vast body of expertise existing in our post-secondary institutions in more flexible ways. As C-HEF put it, the old ideas of courses, semesters, and programs are being called into question: "Learning needs to occur at any time, in any place and at the pace of the individual's choosing — not the institution's or the faculty members'. That means lock-step timetables and limited choices for students will become ideas of the past while the most nimble and forward-thinking institutions will put together just-in-time learning opportunities geared directly to the students' needs."[55]

Whether they like it or not, today's publicly funded colleges and universities are embroiled in the worldwide evolution of communications and information technology. Through virtual learning, students can take courses anywhere in the world without leaving home. This development will not make obsolete the traditional campus and the rich exchange of ideas and personal growth opportunities that go with traditional student life. But it will mean that no one need be excluded from opportunities for post-secondary learning just because they can't afford life on campus.

By 1997/98, total enrolment in post-secondary credit-granting distance learning courses in the United States was over 1.3 million and growing fast. This growth presents both opportunities and challenges to traditional colleges and universities. If they cannot meet the changing needs of students and their appetite for easier access to higher quality courses at convenient times and competitive prices, others will take their place. By 2003 the American market for virtual higher education will be worth an estimated $10 billion (U.S.) a year, in addition to an $11 billion corporate-learning market.[56] Distance education is becoming a big business, and it is the student as consumer who is in charge.

Consider, for example, the growth of the University of Phoenix. It is the largest private accredited university in the United States, with more than 56,000 students at seventy-four campuses and learning centres (including one in Vancouver). In 1989 it launched its Online Campus, which a decade later had more than 4,300 students worldwide. Phoenix targets working adults with an average age of 38, and enables them to work together in virtual classes with an average size of 8.6 students. Courses are sequential, each one taking about five to six weeks, and people can start a course of study in any month of the year. Most of the courses are taught by part-time instructors with full-time jobs in industry. And, in 1998, the university's publicly traded parent company, Apollo Group Inc., launched a joint venture with Hughes Network Systems that will deliver highly specialized courses (such as a course for doctors on how to manage small community practices) anywhere in the world.[57]

All sorts of new models are being tried. In 1998 New York University, already a leader in continuing education, launched a for-profit online subsidiary. This model will offer standard courses and also work in conjunction with private companies to manage their training needs. In 1999 Jones International University, affiliated with a major cable television company, became the first Internet-only school in the United States accredited to grant college degrees. And 2000 saw the launch in Britain of the University for Industry, a government-supported institution that delivers learning materials through a network of franchised learning centres. Its target is to have 210,000 students in more than 1,000 learning centres, and another 300,000 students working from home, by 2003.[58]

Canadian colleges and universities have been experimenting with more flexible offerings and with distance learning options. Examples of institutions with online programs include the University of Waterloo, Royal Roads University, Athabasca University, Southern Alberta Institute of Technology, and Technical University of British Columbia. But the competition for students of distance learning products is global — and that means the offerings of Canadian universities have to be global in quality. The investment required for that level of quality necessitates consortia and partnerships — a degree of collaboration that has become common in the private sector, but remains all too rare in our academic institutions today. The first compilation of all the distance learning offerings in the country was assembled not by colleges and universities, but by Industry Canada. The government department initially created its Campus Connection initiative as a means of encouraging public servants to take advantage of distance learning opportunities. But it also seized the opportunity to help colleges and universities across Canada open up new markets for their online courses by promoting their offerings through private-sector employers as well as provincial and municipal governments.[59]

Whether publicly or privately sponsored, new technologies for learning and the impetus provided by greater competition will give Canadians more options for pursuing lifelong learning. The critical issue is not whether the suppliers of education and training will be in the public or private sector, however. The question remains: How to ensure that all Canadians have access to the resulting opportunities for learning? The current debate over access to post-secondary education tends to focus on tuition fees at publicly supported institutions. Fees have been rising much faster than inflation, raising legitimate concern about whether increasing numbers of Canadians will be prevented from getting a degree or a diploma because they cannot afford it.

One possible intervention that is always popular with students is the elimination of tuition fees. This option sounds attractive, and has become policy in some countries. We need to remember, however, that education is an investment both in the individual and in the economy as a whole. For individuals, the evidence about continuing education is clear: it pays to stay. College and university graduates are more likely to find and keep jobs and to earn considerably higher incomes. It is also true that a strong supply of highly educated people is key to attracting the business investment that leads to more jobs, higher productivity, and rising incomes. Although public policy must enable and encourage more Canadians to keep learning, however, it should also reflect students' obligation to pay something back to the taxpayers who have helped them get ahead.

A case in point is the 1996 study by Randall Kangas at the University of Illinois, which suggested that the public cost of providing a university education is quickly recouped through the tax system. According to Kangas' calculations, the state got $4.31 back in taxes as a result of the higher earnings of college graduates for every dollar it invested in providing their undergraduate education. Over the course of their lifetimes, a male graduate would pay an additional $116,648 in income tax and sales tax and a female graduate would provide a net gain to the state of $59,096. (Kangas put the inflation-adjusted rate of return to Illinois taxpayers at 6 percent.)[60]

Such calculations, however, depend on one critical assumption — that graduates stay for life within the jurisdiction of the government that pays for their education. The increasingly intense competition for skilled workers, however, keeps boosting mobility. In Iowa, for instance, an estimated 59 percent of the graduates from public colleges get their first job out of state.[61]

In Canada we have a further worry. The figures on the Canada–United States brain drain suggest that the more we invest as a country in a given individual, the more likely that individual is to take his or her publicly funded knowledge and leave the country. We will look at the problem of retaining our talented graduates in more detail in the next chapter, but, for now, it suffices to say that chopping tuition fees improves the returns on education for the student, but does not guarantee a high return for taxpayers.

In considering how else to overcome the financial barriers that prevent or discourage access to higher education, we must remember that tuition fees are not the only costs involved. Indeed, despite the sharp increases in tuition in recent years, living costs such as food and accommodation during full-time study remain greater than the direct academic fees. For students in the workforce who perhaps have family obligations, the opportunity cost of time away from paid work can be even more significant.

Grants through bursaries, scholarships, and fellowships can offset some of these costs, as can an effective student loan program. But we have to acknowledge that even if students are allowed to borrow large sums to finance their education, the prospect of assuming huge debts can be intimidating for those of modest means. We would like to propose that

DEVELOPING HUMAN ADVANTAGE

Canada consider a risk-sharing approach that would still provide a substantial portion of student aid through loans, but guarantee forgiveness of some or all of those loans over time providing that the graduate remains a Canadian taxpayer.

The Progressive Conservative Party proposed such a model in its platform for the 2000 federal election. It suggested giving graduates a tax credit worth up to 10 percent of the principal amount of a Canada Student Loan each year for the first ten years after graduation.[62] When combined with the existing ability to deduct interest payments on student loans, this credit would effectively assure students from all socio-economic backgrounds that tuition costs could be written off against future income — as long as they were willing to put their education to work and pay taxes as Canadian residents. This proposal would reverse the incentive faced by graduates today: if they leave Canada, they can earn higher (American dollar) salaries that let them pay down large student loans more quickly.

Governments could also help to reduce the burden of student loans by doing more to encourage people to save for education and training. Registered Education Savings Plans already allow parents to build up a nest egg for post-secondary education for their children, but provide tax relief only on the income earned. Registered Retirement Savings Plans allow deduction of contributions and can be withdrawn before retirement for education or any other purpose, but the contribution limits already are modest in relation to income needs in retirement. One option is to expand contribution limits significantly, and allow contributions to be withdrawn tax free if they or any member of their family uses the money to pay for education or training costs at any accredited institution. The other option is to allow all Canadians to open RESP-style accounts for themselves. As the government does now with the RESPs for children, it could then top up or match contributions to provide a greater incentive. Either approach would have the double virtue of helping more Canadians gain access to lifelong learning and tilting the tax system more generally in favour of savings rather than consumption.

The federal Liberal Party seemed to be leaning in this direction during the autumn 2000 election. Its platform promised to introduce Registered Individual Learning Accounts to help Canadians finance their learning needs. The platform did not specify how such accounts would be treated from a tax point of view, but stipulated that the government would "top up the savings of each contributor and provide additional support for people with low and modest incomes."⁶³

Even in the absence of such public support, the growing competition for skilled employees is likely to galvanize further help for post-secondary students from employers, albeit with strings attached. For instance, the Canadian Armed Forces have for many years used guaranteed summer jobs and free tuition, whether at a military college or other university, as a recruiting tool. Young people have their education costs covered, but agree in turn to serve at least four years in the forces. Similarly, some First Nations have funded university education for Aboriginals in return for promises that they bring their skills back and put them to use in building their communities. More recently, provinces have been offering tuition refunds for medical students who are willing to set up practice for minimum periods in under-served and remote communities. We may see more such targeted deals in future, especially in the public sector, where the federal and provincial public services find themselves competing for skilled employees without being able to offer competitive pay rates. As with the armed forces, there is a logical link between public subsidy and an obligation for public service.

We must be careful not to limit the debate about ways to facilitate access to higher learning to education through colleges and universities. Lifelong learning means just that. If Canada is going to compete effectively and maintain a high standard of living in the knowledge economy, we must set up and maintain a comprehensive framework of accessible opportunities for lifelong learning. For the moment, our framework remains highly fragmented. Young high school graduates have access to one network of support. Parents on social assistance are eligible for other programs aimed at helping them learn and enhance their ability to earn income in future. People who are collecting Employment Insurance benefits are eligible for a set of training programs or support different from those available to unemployed Canadians who do not qualify for benefits. Such disparities have been made worse by the process of devolving full responsibility for active labour market measures to the provinces. Delays and disagreements between governments have created considerable disruption and uncertainty even in core programs such as apprenticeships in skilled trades.

Similar disparities exist within the private sector. Larger companies as a group are heavily committed to investment in employee training and development. BCNI members reported an average investment of $1,074 per employee in formal training, and an additional $757 per employee in other human resource development spending in 1996. This investment, a total of 4.2 percent of payroll, compares with average Canadian expenditures, as measured by the Conference Board of Canada in the same year, of just $842 per employee, or 1.6 percent of payroll.[64]

Extensive investments — at least in formal training — are less evident in the small business sector. This observation may not mean a lack of training, but it suggests that smaller companies are more likely to provide informal and on-the-job training directly related to job requirements than to foster employee access to more transferable knowledge and skills. Future needs for transferable skills indicate that, as a country, we have to do more to make sure that employees of smaller businesses, along with the growing ranks of the self-employed, have the same opportunities as their peers in large companies to develop their skills and update their knowledge.

Whether they are young high school graduates or labourers in their fifties, employed, unemployed, or on welfare, self-employed or employees of large companies, all Canadians now need to have access to opportunities for learning throughout their lives. Canadian governments are already spending large sums of money on training and lifelong learning programs, but as with their investments in our schools, they must do a much better job of coordinating their offerings. Access to lifelong learning is the key not just to equality of economic opportunity for individual Canadians but to the prosperity of our communities and ultimately, perhaps, the survival of the country. As Finance Minister Paul Martin put it in his 2000 budget, "Skills and knowledge join the ambitions of the individual with the potential of the country. They are the meeting place between social and economic policy — the best means available to us to narrow the gap between rich and poor."[65]

■ Honing Our Human Capacities

How can the different sectors of our society best work together to make real progress and do the best job possible to help all Canadians achieve their individual potential and contribute to our country's collective human resources? Governments, employers, employees, parents, and citizens, as well as educators, all have a part to play in building a more flexible and effective framework for lifelong learning.

Consistent with their mandate to ensure equality of opportunity for all citizens, governments will remain the primary spenders on education and training — and will certainly be required to spend even more money in certain key areas. Expanding the number of child development and parenting centres in low-income communities, raising the pay of top performing teachers, increasing investment in the professional development of all teachers, and devoting more resources to schools with a high proportion of disadvantaged and at-risk students are all important measures that would boost government budgets. As we have seen, however, money is not the biggest obstacle. Both within Canada and beyond, there is plenty of evidence that we can achieve more effective results without spending large additional amounts of money.

Where more resources are required, governments have alternatives to greater direct spending. In particular, they can use the tax system to encourage more private investment or individual donations for specific purposes. One possibility is differential treatment of corporate expenses. Federal tax policy already treats expense-account meals as only partially deductible for corporate tax purposes. The same principle could also be applied in reverse to forms of expenditure that governments wanted to encourage. McCain and Mustard have pointed to tax policy as a means of encouraging employer investment in community child development and parenting centres, for example. The tax-incentive approach could be applied even more broadly to employer spending on family-friendly but costly workplace policies, education and training for employees, or community and charitable donations. We remain advocates of keeping the tax system as transparent, simple, and neutral as possible, but suggest that tax incentives may be more efficient in directing resources to desired goals than program spending by governments.

Whatever levers governments use to raise money, the key to achieving the desired results is good management of that money. Our elementary and secondary schools, where the case for transformational change that will affect all members of society is so urgent, offer the best examples of possible change. The primary role in managing our school systems belongs to provincial governments, and the indications for improving management are clear. All provinces need to encourage more comprehensive student assessment, greater accountability, and higher performance-based pay scales for teachers and administrators. They must also encourage greater choice within the public school system and devolve more management authority to individual schools.

The second priority for provincial governments is to do a better job of integrating education with other social and economic services. Schools, especially those with excess space in inner cities, could be hubs of community activities of all kinds. Models for this kind of integration exist, but they need to be explicitly encouraged. Similarly, it is time that post-secondary institutions evolved from being ivory towers to being agoras of knowledge, meeting places between people with a desire to learn and scholars with wisdom and insights to offer. If we want Canada's future to be based on a culture of learning, our institutions of learning must be central to the everyday life of all families.

The third direction for provincial governments is to demonstrate a clear commitment to working together in the interests of all Canadians. The tendency in the past has been to work together primarily as a means of wresting money or jurisdiction from Ottawa. But citizens and taxpayers are more interested in results than turf. If the provincial governments are in fact the ones most capable of delivering opportunities for lifelong learning, they need to do a better job of proving it, and that means collecting and publishing more good information about student achievement across this country.

Parents, students, employers, and post-secondary institutions would all benefit from pan-Canadian benchmarks of achievement. The easiest course would be for the CMEC to expand its national testing dramatically and establish national benchmarks for all students at high school graduation. If all provinces could agree to use such standards for provincial graduation, no separate national standard would be required. If some provinces opted out, CMEC could administer exams for a voluntary national high school leaving certificate, allowing students to opt in to this certification even if their provincial government had opted out. Provinces that refuse to respond more effectively to the need for performance measurement could open the door to federal intervention along the same lines. A third possibility is the creation of an independent agency to set Canada-wide benchmarks for achievement in core subjects, administer voluntary tests, and publish results.

Such an initiative could even come from the private sector. In the state of Washington, for instance, the Bill Gates Foundation has awarded a $1.6 million grant to help develop a more effective school evaluation system. The Washington School Research Center will provide parents, educators, and policy-makers with annual school evaluations published on the Web.

Its reports will measure the percentage of students passing each subject, the pass rate for students who have been at the school for three years or more, and the average pass rate for the top ten schools with similar demographic profiles. They will compare state achievement test results for each school with those of its highest scoring peers, and with schools of equal or greater proportions of poor or minority students.[66] One way or another, we need better measurement of our progress and of our strengths and weaknesses in Canada. We cannot expect to make good choices about how to improve our schools unless we have clear evidence of what works and why.

Greater cooperation among the provinces and with the federal government is also needed at the post-secondary level and through the lifelong learning process. The $2.5 billion Canada Millennium Scholarships Foundation is an example of how a small, flexible organization independent of governments can help young people gain access to learning. But, although the foundation eventually succeeded in striking agreements with provincial governments from coast to coast on how to deliver financial help to 91,000 young Canadians, its path was far from smooth. When it comes to developing Canada's human capital, governments at all levels need to place a higher priority on putting people first.

Another priority for governments should be to encourage a more unified framework for access to training and other learning opportunities. Some companies, especially larger ones, invest heavily in their employees. Others do not. The self-employed are on their own, and unemployed people receive unequal treatment. Equality of economic opportunity depends on equality of access to learning. Progress on this front is unlikely to be quick, but we would like to see all governments agree to the principle of equal opportunity and pursue it vigorously within the context of Canada's social and economic union.

The federal government must recognize provincial jurisdiction in these matters, but has several legitimate avenues for helping Canadians move ahead. We have already mentioned the potential of the tax system, which is a well-accepted vehicle for transferring benefits to individuals. In another venture, Industry Canada has carved out a distinctive role in connecting schools and students to the technologies and potential of the Internet, and in building networks of learning among students across the country. Through the Department of Indian Affairs and Northern Development, the federal government also has a critical role in funding education within Aboriginal communities.

On this front, the results to date leave much to be desired. According to the Council of Ministers of Education, Canada, 42 percent of the Aboriginal working-age population still had less than a high school education in 1996, compared with 22 percent for the non-Aboriginal population. At the other end of the scale, only 35 percent of Aboriginal people had post-secondary qualifications, compared with 52 percent for non-Aboriginals.[67] Work by the Caledon Institute of Social Policy has shown that this education gap is directly linked to high rates of Aboriginal unemployment. "The proportion of the Aboriginal workforce with less than secondary school graduation was found to explain 56 percent of the difference in the relative rate of unemployment."[68] Fully 35 percent of the Aboriginal population was under the age of 15 in 1996, in comparison to 20 percent of the non-Aboriginal population. How well our country meets the needs of Aboriginal youth therefore will have major social and economic implications both for First Nations and for Canada as a whole.

The federal government currently spends about $1 billion a year on the 117,000 Aboriginal students who live on reserves and attend elementary and secondary schools. In a recent review of that spending, the auditor general noted that modest progress is being made. Between 1991 and 1996, the high-school completion rate for Aboriginal students rose from 31 per cent to 37 percent. This, however, compares with a high-school completion rate of 65 percent for the Canadian population as a whole.

The auditor general identified a wide range of areas for action. For instance, he said the federal government must establish indicators of education performance and results to ensure that its spending meets student needs and that it can demonstrate accountability for results. He also criticized the fact that the department has commissioned many studies over the past twenty years — covering everything from governance and management to curriculum, teacher training, and special education services — yet had never even costed out any of the resulting proposals. "Action plans that identify how and by whom action will be taken, the time frames, the costs and the funding responsibilities should be implemented expeditiously," he advised.[69] The need for action in improving education outcomes for Aboriginal youth is clear and pressing. By working to encourage effective innovation in meeting the needs of some of the most at-risk youth in the country, the federal government and the First Nations have a huge opportunity to show leadership in rising to the challenge of human development.

Even working together, however, governments cannot improve education outcomes without the willing participation and support of those on the front lines. Bob Rae, the former New Democratic Party premier of Ontario, has pointed out that if teachers really care about the survival of public education and the equality of opportunity within our society, their associations and federations must shed their narrow attachment to contractual conditions and get engaged in broader issues.

"Over twenty years of political life, I was increasingly struck with the fact that the professional representatives of teachers have been remarkably under-represented in the debate about the quality and performance of the public school system. Issues of compensation, governance as it relates to job tenure, and the broad political issues with the government of the day . . . have been the focus of teacher-union activity. Dealing with poor results, curriculum reform, young kids' performance in science and math, the central questions of how to improve education — here the debate has been filled by parents, by academics, by some politicians, but not so much by the organizations whose job is to advance the point of view of teachers."[70]

Stephen Lawton, a professor emeritus at the University of Toronto, has suggested that teacher unions need to separate the commitment of their members from political ideology to teaching excellence. For now, he says, unions are in favour of big government and oppose free trade, privatization, and changes in the way education is tested, funded, and governed. They seem to stand for little except more money and job security for their members, along with more power for political and labour organizations that share their philosophy. He suggests they should redeploy their energy to more productive activities that would help schools adapt to changing needs and preferences. "If unions recognized that their primary commitment is to children and their parents, they might take more supportive stances toward parental preferences for a clear and well-supported curriculum, fair and constructive assessment, and public disclosure of school-level performance data. A consensus is already evolving in the area of school safety, where parents, children and teachers are of one mind in terms of goals, if not means. Similar agreement is possible in other areas if energy is committed to learning and acting together."[71]

As Raham has pointed out, the outcomes of our past pattern of industrial bargaining are well known. Rigid class size, work schedules, and personnel classifications discourage creative approaches to meeting student needs. Administrators have trouble managing their schools, putting the right teachers where they are needed, and rewarding effort and excellence.

If we want to hold schools accountable for boosting student achievement, we need to rethink the standard contract. In the United States, the American Federation of Teachers has suggested a new two-tier model. It combines a thin master contract at the district or state level that covers basic teacher pay and portable pensions and benefits. Each school would then build on this base in reaching an agreement with its own teachers. This school-level contract would spell out in detail measurable student performance targets, class sizes, instructional time, criteria for hiring and evaluating teachers, and a professional development program that reflects the needs of that school and its students. Teachers would get additional pay based on their responsibilities and demonstrated expertise. Raham notes that enabling schools to adopt such an approach in Canada would require major changes. Labour laws would have to authorize schools to sign contracts augmenting the master agreement. School boards would have to support the individual school as the basic unit of management. Contracts would have to make improved student learning their primary shared objective. To this end, employers would have to agree to invest in their staff, while employees would gain more authority to make workplace-specific decisions and accept responsibility for educational performance. Parents and the community would have to gain access to information in areas such as staffing and contract decisions.[72]

In short, reshaping the management of our schools to enable them to meet the evolving needs of our children will require a profound change in attitude on the part of governments, administrators, and teacher associations alike. In particular, governments and school boards have to stop treating and paying teachers as if they were interchangeable cogs on an educational assembly line. Teachers deserve compensation and respect as key players in the knowledge economy. They should receive commensurately larger paycheques. Why shouldn't an outstanding teacher make a six-figure salary? Really good teachers are worth their weight in gold. Can teachers in Canada be persuaded to accept greater accountability and reduced job security in return for higher pay, more training, more autonomy, and greater respect? Given the current state of relations between governments and teacher unions in Canada, this will be no easy negotiation. But it should be possible, and we must try.

In this context, it is important to remember the demographics of the teaching profession. Across the country, we face a massive wave of retirements and a projected shortage of educators in the years ahead. On the one hand, our schools, colleges, and universities will have to offer higher pay and better working conditions to recruit the huge numbers of talented knowledge workers they will need. On the other, the influx of new blood represents a unique opportunity to reshape both the structure and the culture of our institutions of learning.

In the meantime, an excellent way to encourage effective change in education is to create more opportunities for parents to become involved. More frequent and more public assessment of student achievement is one vehicle to spur their interest and engagement. Another is to increase the education choices available to children within the public system. Choice drives change, and systemic change and improvement will prevent Canada's public education system from suffering massive defections and becoming an education of last resort for those people unable to afford better alternatives.

Expanding the range of choices available within the public system is also essential to the evolution of curriculum and teaching methods within a fast-changing world. Parents may not themselves know which option is best for their children, but giving them options and then measuring the outcomes of different choices over time can help our system itself learn and grow. Parents trying to make the best decisions for their children deserve all the input that can be generated, but ultimately they should be trusted to make their own decisions about where their children will flourish best.

We can teach children in different ways without giving up our commitment to high expectations for all. To meet that commitment, we have to be ready to provide more money and support to schools and programs serving the particular needs of students who might otherwise be at high risk of failure or dropping out. But it is precisely because children learn in different ways that we must provide multiple paths to achievement within our public schools.

Some Canadian provinces have already been experimenting with grassroots-driven change. Quebec, for example, has engaged the whole community in its effort to boost its high school graduation rate from 65 percent to 85 percent by 2010. The province has re-assigned powers from school boards to individual schools, revised its Education Act to allow schools to be different, and established the Quebec School Improvement

Network to support and share school-level ideas for projects that boost student success. Membership in the network requires a two- to three-year commitment to participate in a process of systemic change that is supported by at least 80 percent of faculty in a secret ballot vote.[73]

The Quebec network follows in the footsteps of the Manitoba School Improvement Program Inc. This independent, non-profit organization was set up in 1991 with support from the Walter and Duncan Gordon Foundation. Its network now includes about thirty schools dedicated to improving learning opportunities for youth, and it has produced some impressive results. At Glenlawn Collegiate, for instance, teachers identified three key skills — team-building, problem-solving, and lifelong learning — and built them into their curriculum for all students. The percentage of students graduating rose by 15 percent. Ashern Central School, serving a rural community, went in a different direction. It re-ordered its teaching schedule so that students could take two complete courses every nine weeks, making it easier for students with work responsibilities to stay focused. The number of students earning A marks doubled, and discipline visits fell by 50 percent.[74]

Studies of school improvement consistently show the importance of parental involvement, but our current school systems are often hostile towards parents who are critical or who press for change. Parents are always welcomed when supporting teachers' and administrators' fight against funding cuts or when raising money, but in too many other instances they seem not to be wanted.

One of the most egregious examples occurred in 1999 in Surrey, British Columbia. As described by columnist Margaret Wente of the *Globe and Mail*, the Canadian Union of Public Employees set about to systematically remove thousands of parent volunteers from schools on the basis that they were unqualified to help and, more to the point, were taking away union jobs. This decision made it impossible for parent volunteers to come into the school each morning to call back other parents of children who failed to show up at school. Then the union banned the breakfast club, which used volunteers and corporate sponsors to offer hot breakfasts to children from low-income families. At one school, the union would not even let parents spruce up the school by planting flowers.

Parents are partners in the education of children and should be encouraged to participate fully in our schools in any way they are willing.

That does not mean that school boards should see them as a source of cheap labour to be exploited, but, as Surrey parent Reggi Balabanov told Wente: "There's mountains of research that says when parents are involved, kids do better. The children see the parents in the school, and they realize — this is our school. We get to know the teachers. It creates mutual respect and teamwork . . . It's sad. Kids will go hungry. Kids won't get read to. Kids won't get called back to make sure they're safe. Surely, as adults, we should be able to avoid this."[75]

Parents are not the only people who need to feel more welcome in our schools. Many business people would like to be constructively engaged in improving the process of learning, yet they often face an atmosphere of suspicion, if not outright hostility. In their book *Class Warfare: The Assault on Canada's Schools*, Maude Barlow of the Council of Canadians and Heather-jane Robertson of the Canadian Teachers Federation assert that every effort at school reform, from assessment of student achievement to greater choice for parents, is part of an ideological battle for control of Canada's minds.

In the Barlow/Robertson view of the world, multinational corporations and right-wing ideologues are trying to force schools to produce consumer drones and obedient workers programmed to deliver standardized answers to standardized questions. "Under the guise of 'reforming' or even 'supporting' schools, there is a great deal of activity in education advancing the interests of the competitive-corporate ideology of the right wing . . . Whether directed to children or policy makers, these efforts have common goals, all of which are self-serving, all of which are designed to increase the 'market share' of corporations in the lives of our children, in the conduct of public policy and in the shape of our future."[76]

This industrial-era conspiracy theory is completely out of touch with the realities of the knowledge-based economy. Today's employers need people with broad knowledge, flexible skills, innovative instincts, and an attitude geared to challenging the status quo at every opportunity. Indeed, the portfolio of competencies needed to function effectively in today's workplace is the same set of skills needed to exercise a citizen's responsibilities in a modern democratic society. In our schools, as in any vibrant democratic society, some conflict is inevitable. The challenge, as Ben Levin, Manitoba's deputy minister of education and training, has observed, is to manage the conflicts within our education system in a way that maximizes constructive potential and minimizes destructive force. "While democracy is something all of us say we believe in, its practice stretches us in ways that are often uncomfortable and difficult. At the same time, a real commitment to democracy in schooling will push all of us to do things that are important and potentially very positive."[77]

The business community has no interest in meddling in curriculum or teaching methods. As members of that community, we would no more presume to offer advice to teachers on how they should do their jobs in the classroom than we would to the surgeon in the operating theatre. That is not our expertise. What matters to employers is not how students are taught, but how effectively they are learning. Are they emerging from our schools with the knowledge and skills to enable them to earn good incomes, help our companies compete in the world, and engage effectively as citizens in a cohesive democratic society? These are the essential questions.

Business leaders want to be involved in ways that make a difference, and are not prepared to wash their hands of the problem and leave everything to government. As John Mayberry, president and chief executive officer of Dofasco Inc., expressed the role of business leaders, "We have got to stop pointing the finger at governments and do more ourselves as business people. Business has to do a better job of investing in the schools and stimulating research and creating an environment in which good professors want to work. We've got to create exciting places for kids to work, where there is opportunity for growth. If we don't, we are going to get more and more entrenched with those who are left, the people who don't want to change, who like the status quo, who like rigidity. Government has a role to play, especially in tax policy, but business has a role too."[78]

In accepting an award from the Collegium of Work and Learning, BCE's Jean Monty suggested four ways that businesses could do more to support education. First, they can provide funding and expertise to help schools do a better job, for instance by providing computers and Internet access. Second, business executives must show leadership, speaking up frequently for public education and helping to build a genuine consensus for changes that will improve it. Third, large and small businesses alike can provide guidance and experience to young people through programs such as mentoring, cooperative work terms, and internships. And, fourth, businesses can get involved in a wide range of partnerships with governments and educators. "At pivotal moments in the life of our country, educational reform has been an arena for debating the shape of our society's future. Such a debate is a broad, civil enterprise in which all citizens are stakeholders. And so it must be with our efforts to re-envision education and work."[79]

Education partnerships pay direct and immediate returns to employers competing for talent in the knowledge economy. A recent study by the Conference Board of Canada found that augmenting student programs through vehicles such as partnerships and cooperative work placements was the most important predictor of a company's success in recruiting the graduates it needed. "Such a finding underlines the importance of enhancing partnerships with educational institutions, further developing co-op opportunities and developing a better understanding of the needs and values of the new generation of employees." Reinforcing this point, the second most significant predictor of success was the sincerity of a company's commitment to a culture of lifelong learning and substantial investment in training and employee development.[80] It is not surprising that corporate community involvement has become more strongly linked to human resource goals, to the ability to recruit, retain, develop, and motivate employees. A 1996 survey of BCNI member companies found that support for education was the fastest-growing community activity of large Canadian companies.[81]

In addition to their extensive relationships with schools, colleges, and universities, major employers have been developing creative new approaches to partnership, especially those involving the school-to-work transition. Perhaps the most notable was the creation in 1996 of Career Edge, a Canada-wide internship program conceived, established, and funded entirely by the private sector. In addition to creating internal positions, some corporations have used Career Edge to enhance their external relationships by funding internships in non-profit organizations and among small business customers and suppliers. A group of major banks also used Career Edge as the base for a project creating internships for people with disabilities.

The program's employer-funded and Internet-based structure enabled the federal government to make more effective use of its resources as well. Freed of the need to fund a bureaucratic infrastructure, the government devoted its money fully to hiring interns. But it also concentrated its hiring on at-risk youth, those less likely to be hired by private sector participants. And in seeking to prepare such young people for effective transitions to the workplace, it created another partnership, drawing on the proven expertise of YMCA Canada in preparing at-risk youth for effective integration into the workplace.[82]

Companies large and small have considerable experience in improving the school-to-work transition and have been active innovators on that front. They also engage in a broad range of partnerships with individual schools and boards, contributing equipment, learning materials, and support for activities. But the experience of the United States in pulling up the achievement of its students shows that business also can contribute its expertise in managing change.

In North Carolina and Texas, for instance, the business community played an active role in encouraging the school reforms that gave those states the fastest progress in the country in improving student achievement. Business leaders were motivated by their belief that long-term economic development depended on higher-quality elementary and secondary schooling. While coalitions of education organizations initially opposed reform, business leaders lobbied for legislative changes and were able to build local and state task forces to offer support and develop consensus at the community level. In her 1999 report for the BCNI, Raham suggested that business could make a similarly valuable contribution to education reform in Canada:

> *To meet the challenges of the 21st century, education in Canada needs to quickly reach a higher plateau of student performance and school productivity. Incremental school improvements are a slower and therefore less preferable option than powerful systemic reforms which have elsewhere demonstrated potential to cause powerful change ... The business community has a wealth of technical and change management experience to offer schools and local education authorities. This expertise in designing and implementing performance measurement, goal setting, incentives, and allocation of resources to support priority goals could provide powerful assistance to restructuring schools and districts.*[83]

Sound management practices and an entrepreneurial spirit are the keys to continuous improvement in school systems. Effective assessment, accountability, school choice, and local school autonomy are all powerful tools that could improve management and build a spirit of entrepreneurship and innovation in the world of education. Business people, as parents, as employers, and as members of the community, should contribute what they can to that quest to make better education available to Canadians at every age.

We have focused here on reform of our elementary and secondary schools, but in every phase of lifelong learning, a similar approach seems to offer the best opportunities for progress. We need to set ambitious goals as a country and work together to measure our progress and to ensure equality of access to learning. But the emphasis of our national efforts should be to encourage innovation and creativity at the local level. And within our communities, we must look to governments not as the sole provider of services but as an anchor for a web of relationships that ranges across the public, private, and non-profit sectors.

Developing our human capacity is the most important challenge Canada faces in honing its competitive edge in the twenty-first century. It is vital to our economic health and to our social development that all Canadians are equipped with the skills to survive and prosper in the global economy. They must also have access to lifelong opportunities to improve their skills and to keep them up to date. Federal and provincial governments, educators and administrators, parents and business people have essential roles to play. Expanding our pool of human capital, however, is just the beginning. Our next task is to discover how to persuade Canadians to put their skills and knowledge to work more effectively within Canada.

4

COMPETING FOR TALENT

Humans, their brainpower and know-how constitute a form of capital that in many ways surpasses the value of cash and other traditional capital assets. Regardless of whether we measure it on balance sheets, managers should rethink how to attract and retain human capital . . . Giving people the high status of capital doesn't dehumanize them — it implies that knowledge workers, more than money or factories, drive wealth creation and prosperity.[1]

— DON TAPSCOTT, DAVID TICOLL, AND ALEX LOWY,
DIGITAL CAPITAL, *2000*

◀ ◀ ◀

E-business guru Don Tapscott and his colleagues at consulting firm Digital 4Sight suggest that knowledge workers are no longer a variable cost, an expense to be minimized by their employers. They suggest, rather, that such employees are in fact investors in their employers. Just as traditional shareholders commit financial capital to an enterprise, employees invest their human capital, or, as Tapscott calls it, their digital capital, in the enterprises they choose. He notes that the growing popularity of equity and stock options as core compensation means that companies like Microsoft have sold fewer than half of their shares to stock market investors for cash — the majority have been bought by employees with their brainpower.

As Canadians increase their personal stock of knowledge and skills, they gain more human capital to invest and more power to decide where they will invest it. Companies that want to attract and retain skilled people are being forced to rethink their relationships with their employees. They are facing a human resource challenge that extends to countries trying to build and maintain competitive advantage in the global economy. To meet that broader challenge, Canada must ensure that all Canadians get access to opportunities for lifelong learning. The implications of this challenge for our country were brought into sharp relief in the autumn of 1999, when John Roth, president and chief executive officer of Nortel Networks, agreed to an interview with the *Ivey Business Journal*. In the resulting article — quickly cited across the country — he noted that only 28 of Nortel's top 400 executives still lived in Canada.

Nortel is the flagship of Canada's ambitions in high technology and the most highly valued company in the country. It routinely hires a quarter of Canada's engineering and computer science graduates and has been adding thousands of jobs a year at its Canadian research laboratories and manufacturing plants. It performs 25 percent of all private sector research and development in the country. Unquestionably a global champion, it is making more than 90 percent of its sales beyond Canada's border. The news that less than 7 percent of Nortel's top executives were still living, working, and paying taxes in Canada came as an abrupt shock to those who had been suggesting blithely that anyone who didn't like Canada's high taxes should leave.

That, said Roth, was precisely what many of Canada's top brains were doing. About nine in ten of the company's top managers are still Canadian, but now live and work beyond Canada's borders. It was not the global requirements of the company's business that spurred their exodus. Rather, one by one, individual executives had looked at their personal options and decided that they and their families would be better off if they worked elsewhere. "It's pretty much a Canadian management team, but living outside Canada, mainly in the States. They moved themselves to the United States. Each one came in and said, 'You know, John, I think I should be located in the U.S. because . . .' and they make up a story. The interpretation is, 'I want more take-home pay.'"[2]

Roth admitted that the human resource policies of Canadian employers are responsible for some of the exodus. During the 1990s Canadian salaries did not grow as fast as American salaries, and the widening gap was compounded by the devaluation of the Canadian dollar. Too many Canadian companies, Nortel included, continued for too long to benchmark their pay rates against those of their Canadian competitors, even as their highly skilled employees began to realize that they were working in a North American market. In recent years, Canadian pay rates in the high technology sector have been rising quickly, but for people with the right skills, moving south can mean keeping the same salary figure but in the much more valuable U.S. dollar — and that is before tax.

In a subsequent discussion with us, Roth said that at least 150 of the 372 executives outside Canada by late 1999 could just as easily have kept doing their jobs north of the 49th parallel. But given their desire to move and Nortel's desire to keep their services, most of the top leadership jobs in the company have left Canada. "What hasn't been put on the table is that when these people go, they take their jobs with them. When I say I have to follow talent, I don't mean that I can't get people. I can get people. But they don't want to work from here. They want to work from there, so they take their jobs there. This is about an exodus of high-paying jobs."[3]

The major struggle for Canadian employers today is to hang on to talented people, the leaders with the ability to steer their organizations through a rapidly changing and highly competitive landscape. It is a struggle for quality over quantity. "You can't find these leaders in the brain drain statistics," Roth added. "They're such a small percentage. Small in numbers but large in impact and multiplier effect. Large in their ability to create high-value jobs and career opportunities with a future. The 400 executives I talked about represent one half of one percent of Nortel. Would you notice half of one percent? You couldn't find that in the statistics we're talking about."[4]

In today's global economy, money flows to locations where it can find the right people — but people increasingly flow to places where someone is willing to show them the money. We've talked about what Canada can do to develop its human potential, but once we have invested successfully in leading-edge education and built a world-beating workforce, we have to hang on to it. Given the intense competition for talented people everywhere, we're bound to have some losses, but we must do our utmost to attract other people capable of replacing those we lose. In both in the public and the private sector, the war is on, and it is a struggle that our society cannot afford to lose.

■ Down the Drain

At first glance, immigration statistics might appear to allay our concerns about our human resource losses. On the whole, Canada continues to attract far more people from other countries than it loses to its southern neighbour. The ratio of total Canadian immigration to emigration to the United States has risen steadily and now exceeds ten to one. And university graduates entering Canada outnumber those who leave for the United States by four to one. Canadian emigration to the United States remains at very low levels compared with the 1950s and 1960s: only 1.5 percent of all Canadian university graduates choose to move south.

Within these totals, however, lie disturbing trends with ominous implications for Canada's future. A 2000 review by Statistics Canada confirmed that while "the magnitude of these losses is relatively small," our country is suffering a net loss of workers in a variety of key knowledge-based occupations. "The composition of emigrants . . . is weighted towards the better-educated, high-income earners and people of prime working age. Further, they are drawn from sectors that are thought to be important to Canada's economy and society."[5] The number of managers and professionals moving south has been accelerating dramatically. Their numbers more than doubled between 1986 and 1996, according to a 1998 study by Don DeVoretz and Samuel Laryea for the C.D. Howe Institute. Of greater concern is that the flow is increasingly one way. Northbound flows declined over the same period, and Canada's net loss of managers and professionals almost quadrupled.[6]

Statistics Canada cites three sources of data all pointing to roughly similar rates of southbound migration: the Canadian Reverse Record Check (part of the census), the U.S. Current Population Survey, and Canadian income tax returns. The Reverse Record Check shows that the total number of permanent emigrants to the United States between 1991 and 1996 reached 126,000, a 15 percent increase over the previous five-year period. The number of temporary emigrants, however, almost doubled, to 52,000 from 28,000 over the same time span. The American population survey data are less precise, but indicate "a significant increase in the number of the Canadian-born who were living in the United States in 1998 and 1999 and who entered during the 1990s." Canadian data on tax filers who left Canada suggest an even steeper rise. In 1997, 28,870 tax filers ceased to reside in Canada, an increase of 88 percent from the 15,360 who left in 1991.[7]

One reason for the explosion in temporary emigration is the ease with which Canadians can obtain NAFTA work permits covering a wide range of professional occupations. For instance, a survey by Human Resources and Development Canada (HRDC) of Canadian university graduates of the class of 1995 who moved to the United States found that over half of them initially did so through NAFTA permits. These temporary permits are increasingly becoming precursors to permanent emigration. By 1999, 36 percent of the graduates who had moved to the United States in 1995 already had permanent resident status. And 44 percent of those still living on temporary permits in the United States said they planned to become permanent residents within two years.[8]

The same trend can be seen across all forms of temporary permits. In 1991 less than 8 percent of all Canadians who moved to the United States as a result of an intra-company transfer changed their status to that of permanent resident. Five years later, that proportion had more than quadrupled. Fully 37 percent of all professionals who had taken temporary corporate transfers to the United States opted not to come home in 1996. Over the same period, the proportion of Canadian visitors for pleasure to the United States who opted for permanent residency almost tripled, from 11 percent to 32 percent. And the proportion of Canadians with temporary work permits who converted to permanent residency doubled from 6 percent to 12 percent.[9]

Even if Canada more than replaces its losses to the United States with immigration from other countries, turnover is costly. DeVoretz and Laryea estimated the "churning costs" of replacing the managers, scientists, and health science professionals who left between 1989 and 1996 at $11.5 billion.[10] The costs at the company level are easier to measure and appear to be growing. According to *Fortune* magazine, "When all factors are considered — not only the headhunter's fee but also the defector's lost leads and contacts, the new employee's depressed productivity while he's learning, and the time co-workers spend guiding him — replacement costs can be as much as 150 percent of the departing person's salary."[11]

More worrying for Canada is the extent to which emigration to the United States seems to be concentrated in high-value occupational groups and within high achievers at all levels of experience. The HRDC survey of 1995 graduates found that more than half (54 percent) of those who moved to the United States were concentrated in health, engineering, mathematics, and the physical and biological sciences. These disciplines accounted for just 27 percent of the graduates remaining in Canada, half the proportion among emigrants. At the other extreme, only 33 percent of emigrants had taken degrees in social sciences, humanities, or education, but these fields accounted for 54 percent of graduates who remained in Canada.[12]

Within the fields heavily in demand in the United States, most Canadian students are ready and willing to move. A 1999 survey by Personnel Systems and National Public Relations found that 88 percent of computer science and engineering graduates in Canada were willing to relocate within Canada — but 78 percent were also ready to move to the United States.[13] These results are consistent with an earlier survey by the Canadian Advanced Technology Association of electrical and computer engineering students at the University of Waterloo, which found that more than three-quarters of the fourth-year students were willing to move to the United States for their first job.[14]

Emigrating students are far more likely to be highly qualified and have achieved excellent marks. Fully 44 percent of the 1995 graduates who moved south ranked themselves in the top 10 percent of their class. While the accuracy of such self-ranking may be suspect, graduates with advanced degrees were significantly over-represented among the departures. Master's and doctoral graduates accounted for only 8 percent of all graduates who remained in Canada, but 23 percent of those who left — almost one in four. Those leaving made up only 1.5 percent of the total number of Canadian graduates, but 12 percent of doctoral graduates.[15]

Wherever we go across Canada, we certainly hear anecdotal evidence of emigration by a large proportion of the best students at Canada's top academic programs. Patrick Monahan of Osgoode Law School in Toronto has suggested that American firms take about 5 percent of the school's graduates, but half of the graduating "A" students. At McGill University's law school, first-year students are told by the university's placement office that the top ten will get offers from New York; the next rung can expect to be recruited by the top Canadian firms in Toronto and Montreal. Graduates in 2000 from a specialized MBA program at Queen's University for science and technology students — a prime recruiting source of high-technology management talent — told us that the vast majority of them planned to accept offers from American employers. Although members of the Association of Universities and Colleges of Canada do not share data on where their graduates go, the stories from all quarters are both pervasive and consistent: too many of our best and brightest see better opportunities abroad.

David Graham, a Canadian graduate of the Harvard Business School and a successful entrepreneur, has monitored a similar pattern affecting that institution's Canadian graduates. A review of Canadian HBS graduates from the classes of 1986 through 1999 found that only 40 percent are still living and working in Canada. The proportion of graduates who return to Canada is dropping steadily: of those who graduated from 1986 through 1989, fully 59 percent came back and are still here; by the early 1990s, that proportion had dropped below 40 percent. And of Canadians in the four HBS graduating classes from 1996 through 1999, only 29 percent had returned to Canada and were still here in 2000.[16]

The American Current Population Survey confirms that, as a group, recent migrants from Canada to the United States are highly educated. Between 1994 and 1999 almost half (49 percent) of immigrants from Canada aged 16 and over had a university degree. According to the Canadian 1996 census, that is four times the proportion of native-born Canadians with a degree and more than double the proportion of immigrants to Canada with such qualifications.[17]

Statistics of the Canada Customs and Revenue Agency show a pattern of migration clearly linked to the tax burden shouldered by high-income earners in Canada. People with transferable skills and upper-end incomes are generally very mobile, and those who leave the country certainly are much more likely to be top earners. In 1996, for example, professionals who earned in excess of $150,000 were seven times more likely than the average income earner to have left Canada in 1996. For those earning between $100,000 and $150,000, the likelihood of departure was five times the average, and for those in the $75,000 to $100,000 range, departure was more than three times as likely (see fig. 11).[18] A tally of all emigrants to the United States in the last five years indicates that rates of exodus are accelerating sharply. From just 24,206 in 1995/96, the overall number of people leaving leaped to 58,787 in 1998/99 and 62,131 in 1999/00.[19] Assuming that the income profiles of emigrants has remained the same, Canada may now be losing more than 1 percent and possibly close to 2 percent of its upper income earners every year.

Even small numbers of departures of higher-income Canadians can have a powerful impact on our tax base. According to a Canada Customs and Revenue Agency count, taxpayers who ceased to reside in Canada in

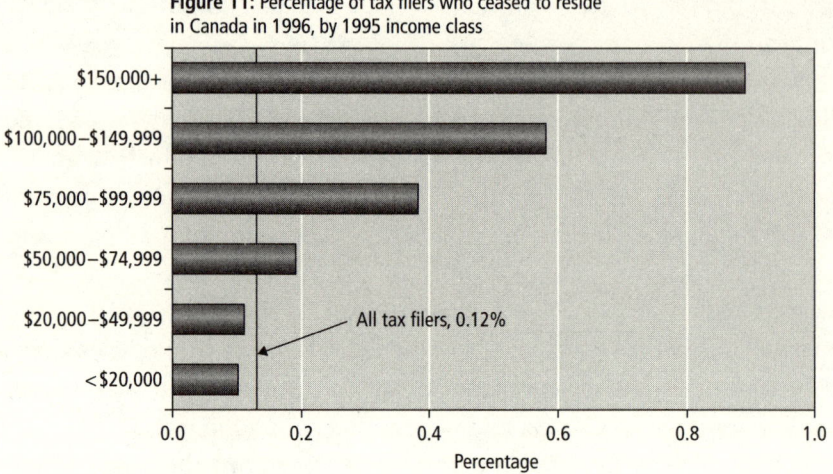

Figure 11: Percentage of tax filers who ceased to reside in Canada in 1996, by 1995 income class

1996 represented an *annual* loss of more than $350 million in federal and provincial income tax revenue alone. Almost two-thirds of that loss, 62 per cent, was due to the departure of people who had earned $75,000 or more in 1995. And while taxpayers who earned more than $150,000 represented only 4 percent of those who left in 1996, they account for more than 40 per cent of the income tax revenue lost in subsequent years. Put another way, the loss of 1,020 such individuals in 1996 cost federal and provincial governments more than $140 million in annual income tax revenue.[20]

The total forgone tax revenue is obviously much higher. First, the low-income departures include young graduates moving into the workforce abroad from full-time education in Canada. Second, this estimate does not begin to count all the other taxes such individuals would have paid — sales taxes, GST, fuel taxes, real estate taxes, payroll taxes, and so on. And, finally, this single-year snapshot does not capture the cumulative effect of losing 1 percent each year of Canada's high-income workforce. As the top people in business, education, and health care head for what they see as greener pastures, they take with them not only their own jobs but the other purchasing and employment that flows from their activities — and the critical element of leadership.

Canada still attracts far more people from the rest of the world than it loses to the United States. Furthermore, immigrants as a group are also highly educated and concentrated in knowledge-intensive professions. As Statistics Canada analyses the situation: "Because of the much larger number of Canadian immigrants, university graduates migrating to Canada from all countries of the world outnumber those leaving for the United States (permanent and temporary) by a ratio of approximately 4 to 1. There are as many immigrants entering Canada with a master's or doctorate as the number of university graduates at all levels leaving for the United States."[21]

Between 1986 and 1997 permanent immigration increased fifteen-fold among computer scientists, ten-fold among engineers, eight-fold among natural scientists, and four-fold among managerial workers. More than 20,000 engineers, computer scientists, and natural scientists moved to Canada in 1997 alone. The health and education sectors, in contrast, saw a sharp drop in immigrants in the 1990s. By 1997 Canada recruited from abroad 30 percent fewer university and college professors, 50 percent fewer elementary and secondary teachers, 40 percent fewer doctors, and 70 percent fewer nurses than it had in 1990.[22]

Although as a country we are receiving great numbers of technically qualified professionals, we seem to have trouble making full use of the education and experience many immigrants bring with them. Statistics Canada has noted that even though the education levels of immigrants rose sharply between 1986 and 1996, fewer immigrants were able to find work. In that ten-year period, among immigrants who had arrived in the previous five years, the percentage of males between the ages of 25 and 44 who were able to find jobs fell from 81 percent to 71 percent, and the percentage of women immigrants in jobs slipped from 58 percent to 51 percent.[23]

A 1999 study by the province of Ontario, where almost half of all immigrants choose to settle, found that even though 61 percent of immigrants arrive highly educated and trained, they are three times less likely to find jobs than highly educated Canadians. Less than a quarter of immigrating professionals found work in the exact profession to which their education and training apply, and 27.6 percent were employed in subsistence jobs that had no relationship to their background. Over time, the unemployment rate among newcomers and the proportion of people finding work in their chosen profession converge with the Ontario average. The transition costs, however, are clearly significant and suggest that the large numbers of highly skilled people entering the country are not necessarily filling the positions of the Canadians who leave.[24]

While Canada is suffering a net loss of workers in key knowledge-based occupations, it is true that the number of people Canada is losing remains small, especially in comparison with our always steady immigration flow. The issue goes beyond numbers, however. Jean Monty, president and chief executive officer of BCE Inc., put the statistics in another light: "Some studies say we should not worry about the brain drain because our immigration offsets our losses. I find it unbelievable that our country would say that it is okay to lose my sons, after we have been in this country for 250 years . . . That to me is taking the heart out of Canada."[25] Brain drain also has an emotional quotient.

Small though the net number of emigrants may be, the brain drain to the United States is having a real impact on the growth strategies of Canadian companies. It is also affecting Canada's ability to foster research and innovation, to ensure equality of opportunity through education and training, and to deliver high-quality health care and social services. As Tony Fell, chairman of the board of RBC Dominion Securities, sums it up: "It's not as if everyone is picking up and moving, but unfortunately, it's the best that are leaving. You don't judge it by the numbers. A lot of people could leave this country and it wouldn't matter. But when you lose your best scientists or your best surgeons or your best entrepreneurs, then it can have a huge impact."[26]

How are the human resource challenge and the war for talent affecting Canadian companies' strategies for growth in the global economy? And what impact are they having on Canada's public sector? After looking at these questions, perhaps it will become clear what Canada can do to improve its performance in attracting, keeping, and making better use of its human capital.

■ The Private Sector Impact

NOVA Chemicals Corporation was created when NOVA Corporation merged with TransCanada PipeLines Limited in 1998 and decided to spin off its chemicals division. NOVA Chemicals now ranks as one of the top producers in North America of ethylene, polyethylene, styrene, and polystyrene, operating eighteen plants in Canada, the United States, France, the Netherlands, and the United Kingdom. Its experience has become a vivid symbol of the challenge facing Canada in the war for talent. NOVA's operations have expanded rapidly, and the southern and eastern United States have become the central focus of both its operations and its customer base. When it needed investment capital for expansion, it raised its profile with American investors. The expansion south of the border in turn necessitated additional management talent, and in NOVA's business, much of the experienced talent is American.

NOVA's president and chief executive officer, Jeff Lipton, told us that the company did succeed in recruiting the key executives it needed in order to grow. Only one of the senior people it hired, however, was willing to move to NOVA's Calgary head office, and the single exception agreed to come only on a temporary basis. These new executives were willing to work for NOVA only if they could be based at the company's American office in Pittsburgh. The company agreed, and the Pittsburgh office developed into a significant centre of expertise and decision-making.

At the same time, Lipton told us, travel was becoming a serious issue for many of the company's Calgary-based executives. "You have to think about what a head office does. Senior management has to be able to build relationships with employees, make an impression on customers, and sell stock to investors. Two-thirds of our employees work within one hour's air time from Pittsburgh. More than 60 percent of our customers are based within a similar radius. So are 95 percent of our investors. To get from Calgary to the centre of this circle by corporate jet is three and a half to four hours. To travel there commercially takes a full day." By mid-1999 the combination of the growing pool of executives in Pittsburgh and the demands on the time of those based in Calgary prompted a wholesale shift. While the company retained a corporate office presence in Calgary, sixty-five members of its head office staff, including all the senior vice-presidents, moved to Pittsburgh.

The move of NOVA's core head office functions out of Calgary has not prevented the company from continuing to expand its operations in Canada. Lipton noted that its Joffre, Alberta, plant has just completed a $1 billion (U.S.) expansion, and its Calgary-based research centre continues to grow. "We do most of our research in Canada. We are going to continue to build our research effort here, because it has been very fruitful for us. We have found it easy to recruit talented chemists and engineers from Canadian schools. We have been able to build excellent relations with Canadian universities. Some of our best technology comes from our work with Canadian professors."[27]

NOVA Chemicals is not alone in feeling a southward pull driven by the growth of its investments and customer base south of the border. Another company experiencing a similar shift is Regina-based IPSCO Inc., which decided in 1999 to establish its operational headquarters in Chicago. "IPSCO has, and will continue to have, a long-standing commitment to Saskatchewan," said Roger Phillips, its president and chief executive officer. "This change was driven by the increasing scale and maturity of our operations in the United States." With facilities in five provinces and seven states, and with about three-quarters of its assets south of the border, Chicago became the logical nexus for the steelmaker's operations. Also, as at NOVA, quick access by scheduled air carriers to its plants, customers, and relevant government centres was a critical factor in IPSCO's decision.[28]

For today's much-travelled executives, distance does matter, and there is little Canada can do to change its geography. But objections to distance can be overcome if enough people with the necessary skills want to live in a particular location. The real problem, as Nortel discovered, is that skilled employees and managers have more power than lower-ranking workers to choose where they want to live and work. And across corporate Canada, there is a growing sense that too many Canadians see a better quality of life for their families somewhere beyond our borders. This tendency has serious implications both for corporate strategy and for the welfare of our country.

On the surface, Canada has been doing very well. Across the economy, companies have been growing and creating jobs. In the high technology sector, Canada has actually been creating jobs at a faster pace than in the United States. A more disturbing picture emerges, however, when we look at what kinds of jobs are being created. In a study for the C.D. Howe Institute, Daniel Schwanen divided the overall job creation record within the high-technology manufacturing sector into production and non-production functions. The non-production work — research, management, marketing, finance, and so on — pays far higher salaries, an average of $58,000 a year compared with $41,300 for employees doing factory assembly work. He found that, in the United States, the ratio of non-production to production work in the high technology sector has changed little in recent years.

In Canada, however, non-production jobs have been plummeting as a share of total employment in this sector (see fig. 12): "The predominance of the production side of high-tech industries in Canada (relative to the U.S. situation) suggests that global decision-making functions in knowledge-intensive industries are not locating here to the extent warranted by the

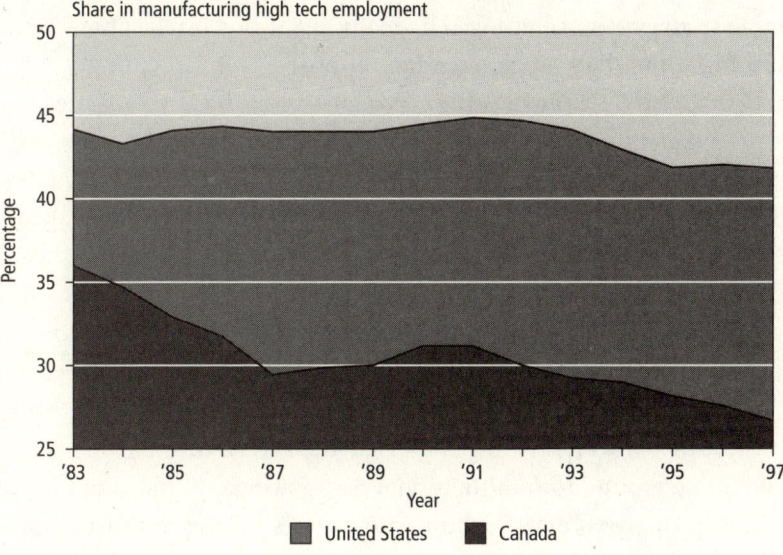

Figure 12: Non-production workers, Canada and United States: Share in manufacturing high tech employment

size of the Canadian economy and Canada's access to the North American market. The economic impact of these differences is real . . . Canada's specialization in production activities represented a payroll shortfall in 1997 of $1.37 billion in these industries."[29]

Schwanen's picture is certainly consistent with Nortel's experience. The combination of available skilled labour, relatively lower wages for production-level employees, and a cheap dollar have kept the company's overall job totals growing in Canada. But the more vibrant competitive environment and the higher after-tax salaries south of the border are pulling more and more of the top jobs out. The rapidly growing technology giant continued to add thousands of jobs a year at its Canadian operations even as the vast majority of its top leadership positions were leaving the country.

Nortel is not unique. In industry after industry, Canada is losing future leaders — and is increasingly at risk of losing the leadership jobs as well. Paul Hill, a former vice-president at Ottawa-based Cognos Inc. who moved to Minneapolis to join Adaytum Software Inc., said Canada's very future is at risk: "I am part of an alarming trend that threatens to define Canada's role in the New Economy — a subordinate role. Is Canada becoming a high-tech body shop for the United States? With increasing frequency, U.S. companies are outsourcing product development to Canadians . . . While our politicians continue to congratulate themselves with every new

Canadian engineering job created, they fail to understand that the outsourcing strategy being employed by many U.S. firms is relegating Canada to nothing more than an engineering outpost . . . By accepting a role as engineers for hire, Canada is only serving to assist the United States in its mission to become the global leader of the new economy."[30]

Rapid economic growth in the United States has created tight labour markets there and forced major American companies to look abroad. Canadian companies are favourably positioned. As former NOVA Corporation chief executive Edward Newall comments: "There was a time, as recently as five years ago, that almost no U.S. corporation looked at recruiting in Canada. Now they are having to recruit all over the world, and Canada is a very easy place to come to first."[31] Youssef Nasr, former chief executive officer of HSBC Bank Canada, agreed that Canada is a fertile recruiting ground for multinational corporations. "Canada has proven to be a great place to develop human resources for the rest of our group worldwide. This is a fantastic country for finding young people. We have hired Canadians who have moved into positions of senior responsibilities in our operations around the world, including the United Kingdom, the United States and Brazil. We have found that Canadian executives travel well, that they are much more capable of adapting to different cultures."[32]

Although Canadian companies are seeing some employees picked off by foreign competitors, their larger challenge flows from their need to expand abroad. As Canadian companies grow globally, they need to help existing employees develop global experience, and they need to hire people from other countries. They are consistently finding, however, that Canadians who have experienced life abroad are reluctant to come home. And as they attempt to tap the broader North American talent pool, they are finding a great unwillingness to move north.

Lipton at NOVA recalled his experience with an employee who moved first to Dallas and then to Vancouver with an affiliated company. "After working in Vancouver for two years and becoming one of the top executives there, he asked to go back to Dallas even though doing so would require a two-level demotion. He was a Canadian and very ambitious, but he felt that even with the demotion, he and his family would be better off in Dallas. It shook this company up tremendously."[33] David Kerr, president and chief executive officer of Noranda Inc., has seen a similar attitude emerge in his company: "Canada does on balance have a high quality of life for our employees. There's no question about that. But when people get a chance to move from here to Nashville, they leap at it. When they get a chance to move from Nashville to Toronto, it's harder, a lot harder."[34]

"It's very hard to repatriate," agreed Gwyn Morgan, president and chief executive officer of Alberta Energy Company Ltd. "What a global company should do is send its people around the world, offer them the best in training and other support, and then bring them home to help run the company." But his company has found that even when senior employees are sent to developing countries such as Ecuador, they are reluctant to come home. "Once they get a taste of life elsewhere, they don't want to come back. They want to stay as global employees being paid in U.S. dollars and they don't want to come near the Canadian tax system again."[35]

"Tax rates are very worrisome," said Michael Phelps, chairman and chief executive officer of Westcoast Energy Inc. "We can't hire people. We can't get them here, and some of our best people are being lured away to the States . . . And the younger they are, the more they won't have anything to do with the costs and the taxes here. There isn't a company based in Vancouver that hasn't done the head-office-move study."[36] Raymond McFeetors, president and chief executive officer of the Great-West Life Assurance Company and London Life Insurance Company, suggested that tax concerns trump patriotism: "There's no question that the tax burden is much too heavy in Canada relative to our ability to support it and certainly relative to the Americans . . . The longer you live and travel around, the more you value a country like Canada, and there's a lot to be said for Canada. Taxes are not one of those things, and I think we've gotten way out of line."[37]

Americans are just as reluctant to move north of the border, even when doing so would bring them into the centre of corporate action, as John Willson, former chief executive officer of mining giant Placer Dome Inc., discovered. "We consolidated our U.S. head office and our Canadian head office into one entity here in Vancouver, and we brought up some of our American talent. They have all gone back. The brain drain is real. I see it happening in this company. We really have to find a way to retain our talent."[38]

A recent study by Industry Canada suggested optimistically that cross-border migration could be of benefit to both countries by boosting the two-way flow of trade and knowledge. As long as the moves are temporary, migrating managers and skilled workers can gain knowledge about American customer needs and ways to operate there more effectively, so they can help Canadian companies in their efforts to design, produce, and market goods for export. "To the extent that Canadians improve their productivity in the U.S. labour market and return to Canada with enhanced skills, there is again likely to be a net 'spillover' benefit to the Canadian economy."[39]

John Van Brunt, president and chief executive officer of Agrium Inc., found, however, that the two-way flow is difficult to achieve. "We don't have too much trouble moving Canadians down to the United States. But even though we tell them they're down there only for two or three years, usually we have trouble getting them back. Sometimes they will just quit because there is such a big difference in their quality of life. So we don't do it as much as we would like, and that inhibits a company like ours with a head office here that is trying to develop its people for the future."[40]

The inability to move employees back and forth detracts from a company's ability to grow globally. "To me, the real problem is the free movement of people within a global multinational enterprise," said Robert Brown, president and chief executive officer of Bombardier Inc. "The pool of talent in Canada is not big enough to let us grow as fast as we must in order to stay competitive on a global basis. And yet because of the tax structure and the exchange rate, bringing people here from Europe or the United States is all but impossible."[41]

John Cleghorn, chairman and chief executive officer of the Royal Bank of Canada, says:

> We have no choice. We have to have North American competency. We have to have the networks of people who don't just think of life north of the forty-ninth parallel but actually look at challenges from a North American and global perspective. We have to have the talent and we'll do whatever we must to get that talent, but it is an incredible cost for us, because you have to make up for the tax load and the currency.
>
> Canada cannot be cavalier about this at all. There are not enough people to go around. The inducements for people to go to the e-commerce centres in the United States are real. It is hard just to persuade experienced people to stay with you, let alone to get them to move to your company. And the situation will continue to get worse as we move forward.[42]

In a 1999 BCNI survey of member chief executive officers, 82 percent said foreign competition for skilled employees was having some impact on their ability to maintain and expand critical operations in Canada. More than one in four, 27 percent, rated that impact as significant. As Canadians take their jobs south and refuse to come home, and as Canadian companies unable to persuade foreigners to move to Canada hire them instead to work abroad, new centres of corporate activity have sprung up elsewhere, especially south of the border. This growth is leading to a significant shift not just of individuals but of major corporate functions and, as we have seen already, even entire head offices.

When asked how likely their own job functions were to leave Canada within a decade, 40 percent of the responding chief executives put the probability at 50/50 or higher. In total, those who thought the chances of the departure of the CEO function would be even money or higher headed companies in every sector of the Canadian economy, with total assets of more than half a trillion dollars and annual revenues of more than $160 billion.[43]

To be sure, the departure of the chief executive's job does not put at risk all of a company's presence in Canada or even necessarily its entire head office function. But to the extent that Canadian companies become run from abroad, they risk losing important connections with the Canadian political and social agenda — and the economic as well as social consequences could be profound. "Think of it in terms of hockey teams," suggested David O'Brien, chairman, president, and chief executive officer of Canadian Pacific Limited. "It just takes a few of the best hockey players going to the United States to make the difference, so that our franchises are losing all the time. Well, that's what is going on in business. There are franchise players, and if you start losing all your franchise players, it has a huge impact."[44]

■ The Public Sector Challenge

Top talent is just as important in the public sector as it is in the private sector. If governments are unable to recruit and retain talented leaders — both at the political level and within the public service — they will not be able to provide the competitive base Canadian companies need to succeed in the global economy. If our hospitals cannot find and keep enough doctors, nurses, and technicians, they will not be able to deliver the quality of health care that Canadians want and expect. And if our schools, colleges, and universities cannot make themselves attractive places to teach and to carry out research, our ability as a nation to innovate and to succeed in the knowledge economy will be in jeopardy.

In the postwar era, the public sector had little trouble attracting the best and brightest. It was an era of prosperity in which public policy was driven by a determination never to put Canadians through a repeat of the Great Depression. "We remembered what it was like when people of 70 years of age who didn't have savings or a pension from their employers had to prove they were absolutely destitute — had nothing — in order to qualify for a provincial payment of $25 a month: the hated means test," recalled former public servant and cabinet minister Mitchell Sharp in a 1998 speech. "We remembered when people who lost their jobs had to apply to municipalities for relief. We remembered how doctors had looked after penniless patients. There was political agitation and steady support among the voters for social security measures to prevent a repetition of that kind of privation, humiliation, and suffering." That support led to a major expansion of government. That expansion, combined with a sense of mission and a belief in great possibilities, brought many of Canada's most talented individuals into public service at the federal and provincial levels. "In those days, particularly in the 50s and 60s, a job as a senior official in the federal government was highly regarded, not because the salaries were better than in the private sector — they weren't — but because of the prestige attached to government service during one of the greatest periods of economic expansion in Canadian history. Morale was high. Officials took pride in their profession."[45]

Government was the place to be, for people who wanted to change the world. As a result, there was a surge of enrolment in liberal arts, social science, and education programs at universities during the 1960s. By 1973 the Highly Qualified Manpower survey showed that 53 percent of all Canadians with university degrees were working in the public sector, including health and welfare, public administration, and teaching. Those with the highest credentials were even more likely to be on the public payroll. Among scientists and engineers with doctoral degrees, 80 percent were employed in the public sector.[46] Decades of deficits subsequently proved that there is a limit to what governments can do effectively. The resulting retrenchment in the 1990s froze pay rates, slowed recruitment and promotions and, above all, took away much of the excitement and prestige of public service. The new focus was not on what governments could do, but on how to save money and where to cut. The cuts were necessary, but the impact on public sector pay and morale was enduring.

We do not propose to spend time rehashing how public sector restructuring might have been better handled. Suffice it to say that, in our view, the degree of restructuring in the public sector pales in comparison to the restructuring the private sector endured. As Canadian companies adapted to the realities of freer trade and technological change, they launched new businesses and got out of ones in which they could no longer compete. They acquired other companies and they were bought, merged, and formed into new alliances at a furious pace. Many employees lost their jobs. Many more were hired. In the public sector, by contrast, most activities and organizations remained in place. To minimize layoffs, the workforce was subjected to prolonged periods of frozen wages and limited advancement. As potential employers, government organizations vanished from campus recruitment centres, and public service no longer presented an attractive career choice for many young graduates. Simultaneously, the conditions within the public service were prompting a growing number of talented people to seek better opportunities in the restructured and blossoming private sector.

By the end of the 1990s Canada had fewer public servants. Treasury Board figures show that the federal public service had been reduced from 242,958 employees in 1992 to just 187,187 in 1998. Much of the reduction was achieved not by layoffs or elimination of jobs, but by their transfer outside the public service through privatization or creation of independent organizations such as local airport authorities. But the smaller public service was also older. The lack of new hiring in the 1990s meant that only 7 percent of federal public servants were under the age of 30, and 42 percent were over the age of 45 years. By 2005, 70 percent of the executive ranks of the public service will be eligible to retire.[47]

Public sector paycheques appear to have weathered the decade relatively well compared with those in the private sector. Despite the extended wage freeze, a study for the Canadian Policy Research Networks Inc. showed that public sector workers on average were still getting paid 9 percent more in 1996 than employees in the private sector with equivalent skills. What is more, the pay premium for government workers has grown over the years, from 4.6 percent in 1971 to 5.5 percent a decade later and to 8.5 percent in 1991. Even the fierce budget pressures of the early 1990s did nothing to erode the premium.

That said, the pay structure of the public service is markedly different from that of the private sector. The public sector pay premium is very high for relatively low-skilled workers in service jobs such as protective services or food preparation. Within this group, the premium is especially large for women. For clerical workers, the premiums are modest. And at the top of the scale, the premiums go negative. Senior managers in the public service get paid considerably less than their counterparts in industry. Employees in management, administrative, and professional jobs in the private sector get paid an average of 41 percent more than workers in service jobs; in the public sector, the pay spread is just 10 percent. "In other words, the spread between the top and the bottom of the scale is less in government than in the private sector, likely a result of political, public and collective bargaining pressures."[48]

The study suggested a number of factors in particular. Pay equity policies in government clearly have had an impact in reducing the differentials between job categories dominated by men and those dominated by women, and seem to be particularly important in driving up relative wages for low-status service jobs. The much higher degree of unionization also has contributed to the pay differential between the public and private sectors, and to the relatively high premium for lower-skilled work. The government pay premium is about 50 percent higher for unionized workers than for non-union employees — and the public sector is much more heavily unionized than the private sector. Overall, governments have faced greater public and political pressure to be "model employers" and have established pay scales that emphasize equity over market value. Whatever its merits in terms of social justice, the public sector approach to compensation faces a severe challenge in the context of the global war for talent. As within the private sector, changing technology has led to a significant shift in the makeup of the public sector workforce. Within the federal public service, there has been a substantial shift towards jobs held by knowledge workers. The number of clerical positions has shrunk, while the number of employees in the executive, scientific, professional, administrative, and foreign service categories grew from 43 percent of the total to 53 percent in just five years, between 1993 and 1998.[49]

The challenge is formidable: the government's pay scales are least competitive for the positions that are in greatest demand and for the people and skill sets that are most likely to retire from the public service in the next few years. The government has taken some major steps to address the challenge already, notably by setting up an external advisory committee on senior level retention and compensation chaired by then

Unilever Canada Limited president and chief executive officer Lawrence Strong. Many of the committee's early recommendations on issues such as inadequate differentials between senior management levels and the failure to pay managers for performance have been addressed. In its second report in March 2000, however, the committee warned that further improvements in public service compensation will be needed. "The new ways of doing things must be reinforced and improved, and a more concrete plan must be developed to address the significant turnover anticipated during the coming decade. The loss of experience and know-how implicit in this turnover remains the most significant long term Public Service issue facing the government."[50]

The human resource challenge in the public sector is faced not only by government bureaucracies but also by many other activities crucial to Canada's economic success and social cohesion. Indeed, the challenge facing deputy ministers in the public service pales in comparison with the obstacles facing most administrators and managers in the health care system. Public service managers are at least competing for talent primarily with Canadian companies. In health care and education, however, Canadian institutions have to attract and retain employees whose skills are in demand around the world and who can move easily to take advantage of opportunities abroad. And while Canadian high technology firms have been able to respond to the competition for engineers and computer scientists by boosting pay, hospitals and universities have been constrained by budgetary pressures at the same time that their competitors for talent have been upping the ante.

Take, for example, the experience of Canadian nurses. Between 1985 and 1997 the number of full-time registered nurses working in Canada stagnated, falling from 123,808 to 119,503. Over the same period, the number of part-time nurses grew by more than 50 percent, from 70,553 to 110,310. Health care institutions coped with budget constraints essentially by limiting the growth of full-time positions. New nurses moving into the profession were shunted into part-time positions with inferior compensation, working conditions, and job security.[51]

Limited opportunity and deteriorating compensation in Canada, coupled with a strong demand for health care professionals in the United States, has been a poisonous cocktail for Canadian health care. It has accelerated the exodus of health care professionals and reduced the supply of skilled people in Canada at a moment when they will be most needed by our growing and aging population. The number of registered nurses moving to other countries (of which about nine in ten have been going to the United States) rose from 1,032 in 1988 to 4,789 in 1997. As a percentage of the new graduates entering the nursing profession from Canadian schools, the exodus grew from 12.3 percent to 70.9 percent (see fig. 13).[52]

Health care represents the most lopsided sector in the Canada–United States brain drain. Statistics Canada says the combination of falling immigration and rising emigration means that nineteen doctors left Canada for the United States in the 1990s for every one that came north. Among nurses, the ratio was fifteen to one. The actual number of doctors moving to the United States tripled between the late 1980s and the late 1990s.[53] And amid newspaper headlines dominated by growing shortages of family physicians and specialists in rural areas, the Canadian Medical Association said the number of doctors leaving for the United States each year is equivalent to the output of five of the country's medical schools.[54]

As in public administration, the restrictions on health care hiring have produced an aging workforce. According to the Canadian Nurses Association, the number of registered nurses between the ages of 25 and 29 dropped by a quarter in just five years, between 1994 and 1999. Over the same period, the number of nurses between the ages of 55 and 59 grew by 26 percent.[55] A full one-quarter of the nurses working in 2000 are slated for retirement in the next decade.[56]

In a 1997 paper the CNA estimated that, by 2011, Canada's population would grow by 23 percent, at the same time as the rising average age of

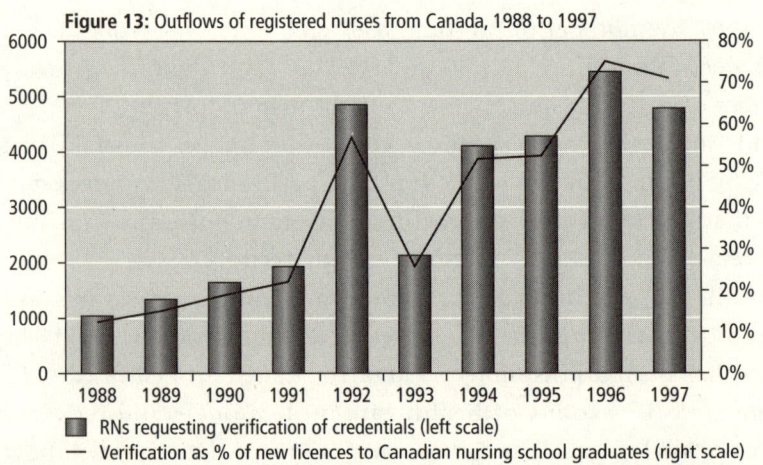

Figure 13: Outflows of registered nurses from Canada, 1988 to 1997

■ RNs requesting verification of credentials (left scale)
— Verification as % of new licences to Canadian nursing school graduates (right scale)

that population boosts the demand for health care services even further. Meanwhile, the number of nurses graduating from nursing schools has fallen from a high of about 10,000 a year in the 1970s to as low as 5,200 by 2001. The result could be a shortfall of between 59,000 and 113,000 nurses by 2011. "The impending situation is much more than a labour market shortfall. It is a serious public safety issue," the report warned.[57]

Canada's education system faces a similar challenge, and although the danger to individual Canadians is less acute the consequences of inaction could be even more serious for the country over the long run. In this sector also, the combination of budgetary restraints, growing competition for talent, and institutional rigidities is leaving Canada at a disadvantage. A 1997 study for the Association of Universities and Colleges of Canada found, for example, that Canadian universities were losing 1,350 professors a year in the mid-1990s, of which 1,000 were retiring or taking buyout packages and 350 were leaving for other jobs. Of those moving to other jobs, half left the country and two-thirds were mid-career or senior academics. Furthermore, only about 70 percent of those retiring and leaving were being replaced; the result was an overall shrinkage of university faculties.[58]

In the coming decade, university enrolment is expected to rise by 20 percent for three reasons. First, the number of university-aged Canadians is increasing. Second, more jobs now require post-secondary education, so the economic incentive to attend universities keeps getting stronger. And third, the chances of young people going to university are influenced by their parents' education level — and today's youth have the best-educated parents ever, with almost three times as many 45- to 54-year-olds holding university degrees today than there were fifteen years ago.[59]

Universities will have to hire between 1,200 and 1,400 faculty members a year over the next six years to meet enrolment growth and make up for the shortfall in hiring over the past few years. On top of that, with the average age of professors up to 49 by 2000, universities will need to hire between 1,300 and 1,600 professors to replace departing and retiring faculty members. The resulting requirement to hire 2,500 to 3,000 professors a year represents a potential pace of hiring triple that of the mid-1990s.[60]

Many academics question whether there will be enough talent to keep Canadian universities and colleges at the forefront of research and teaching. Some are already pointing out signs of deterioration. For instance, Paul Beamish of the Ivey Business School has noted that the research productivity of Canadian business schools was flat in the 1990s — but that contributions to scholarly journals became heavily concentrated. In the second half of the decade, three business schools (Ivey, Rotman, and UBC) made up over one-third of the total contributions to thirty-two journals. Six schools made up half the total. Over half of all Canadian universities contributed only one or fewer articles in total to the thirty-two journals over the most recent three-year period. If the top three schools are removed from the sample, research productivity drops 9 percent, even though the proportion of professors with PhDs has grown, the number of Canadian universities with business programs has increased, and many scholarly journals have increased their frequency of publication, creating more opportunities to publish. "With a handful of exceptions, the overall contribution of Canada-based business schools to major academic and practitioner business journals is low or declining. For students or managers this should be disturbing because it means one's instructor is increasingly only retailing someone else's thinking/research. Research talent is mobile. It will migrate (or emigrate) to those places where support can be found."[61]

In research and education, in health care, and in public administration, there are still opportunities for Canadians to break new ground and enjoy stimulating and rewarding careers. But to attract people to those opportunities, public sector employers must address the same challenges that Canadian companies face in a labour market in which talented people have global options. What is more, public institutions face far more constraints — in their missions, their mandates, and their governance — than private corporations do in adapting to this changing market for talent. There may be many disagreements within our society about how large a role governments ought to play in our economy and society. But whatever governments do — directly and indirectly — they must do well if Canada as a whole is to succeed. Governments as employers must compete just as vigorously as industry for the people they need if they are to continue meeting the high expectations of Canadians.

■ Winning Moves

The challenges facing Canadian employers in both the public and the private sectors are daunting, but they are not insurmountable. Every employer can take steps to offer a more enticing workplace. And, as a country, we have considerable room to attract more skilled people from abroad, make better use of all the talent we already have, and persuade Canadians to keep putting their skills to work within our borders.

▼ Attract More Talent to Canada

The most obvious way to counter the brain drain to the United States is to accelerate Canada's brain gain, the flow of immigration from the rest of the world. Immigration has always been a major source of strength for Canada. And within a highly integrated global economy, immigrants bring with them not just vital knowledge and skills but the diverse perspectives and worldwide contacts that are critical to Canada's growth as a multicultural base for global enterprise.

Canada has a solid record in attracting skilled immigrants. We mentioned earlier the more than 20,000 computer scientists, engineers, and natural scientists who moved to Canada in 1997 alone and the rapid growth in immigration in such categories. The points system that is used to evaluate applicants for independent immigration helps to facilitate entry by highly skilled people. Still, the growing global competition for talent means that we cannot afford to remain passive recipients of skilled people; as a country, we have to take more active measures to attract and keep the people we need. The Expert Panel on Skills of the Prime Minister's Advisory Council on Science and Technology made three recommendations in early 2000 that we would support.

First, as the current list of occupations in demand does not evolve quickly enough to meet the needs of Canadian employers, the federal government should pay more attention to the changing needs of employers in developing a new system for evaluating skilled prospective immigrants. The model for temporary recruitment that has been tested in the software industry should be expanded to other sectors.

Second, it is pointless to keep searching abroad for talent while we maintain barriers to labour mobility within Canada. As part of the Agreement on Internal Trade (AIT), the Forum of Labour Market Ministers is supposed to eliminate all such barriers by mid-2001. Given the low political priority assigned to the AIT generally, we are not optimistic about the prospects for complete success on this front. We cannot emphasize strongly enough, however, how important it is for Canada to stop letting scarce talent languish in one part of the country while jobs go begging in other provinces. Some self-regulating professions have made important progress, but more remains to be done. And beyond lifting the direct restrictions on mobility, we need to eliminate policies that act against mobility — policies that support incomes to such an extent that people are encouraged to stay where they are, in seasonal jobs or jobs that under-employ their talents.[62] In the mid-1990s, for instance, Finning International Inc. ran into a severe shortage of mechanics qualified to work on the heavy-duty industrial equipment it sells and services to resource companies in western Canada. Former chairman and chief executive officer James Shepard told us that at one point the company had as many as fifty openings for highly skilled workers. The company was not allowed to recruit immigrants because heavy-duty mechanics were not on the government's list of skills in short supply, yet Finning was unable to persuade Canadians from other parts of the country to move and take its well-paid jobs.[63]

The third set of recommendations from the Expert Panel on Skills that we would emphasize relates to the role of the education system in attracting talent to Canada. The first requirement is to recruit more faculty from abroad to help meet the looming shortage of teachers and researchers and to help bring more global perspectives to Canadian students. The second need is to persuade more of the 100,000 international students who attend Canadian colleges and universities to stay here permanently. Some of these students have scholarship obligations to their home governments, but Canada should, like Australia, offer permanent resident status to foreign students within six months after graduation.

▼ Make Better Use of the Talent We Have

It often takes even highly skilled immigrants years before they are able to practise their chosen profession in Canada. Some of the lag time occurs because they need to improve their language skills and make up the sometimes significant gaps between foreign training and practices and Canadian standards. However, like the Expert Panel on Skills, we are convinced that Canada must do a better job of recognizing the skills and experience that immigrants bring with them to Canada, and we concur with its recommendation that we speed up this process. "We are concerned . . . that many highly trained professionals and technically skilled immigrants, who have been welcomed to Canada, find provincially legislated licensing bodies slow or reluctant to recognize their credentials. In our view, this reticence — which varies among professions and provinces

— often cannot be justified on the basis of protecting standards, and amounts to a restriction of the supply of skills and a waste of human potential."[64]

The problem of recognizing the equivalency of the skills, knowledge, and experience gained in diverse settings is not limited to the evaluation of immigrants. Prior Learning Assessment and Recognition (PLAR) has been the subject of a great deal of work within Canada, notably by the former Canadian Labour Force Development Board (CLFDB). Here, too, the Expert Panel on Skills has made important recommendations. In particular, it said that governments should force self-regulating professions to fast-track assessments of immigrant competency and that the PLAR process should begin as part of the immigration procedure abroad, so that immigrants will be able to put their skills to work faster after their arrival.[65]

More effective assessment and recognition of diverse education and training experiences also has to become routine within Canada. As the CLFDB noted: "PLAR should give equal value to learning and skills whether these skills come from school, community work, on-the-job training or other life experience . . . PLAR can make it easier for individuals to find out where they stand and what they need to do to get a job or reach a career goal. It can help schools and training institutions place students in the right courses. It can help employers improve their workplace by making the best use of a person's skills."[66] It is a waste of time, money, and talent for companies to invest in training employees in skills or knowledge they already possess and for governments to subsidize training or fund postsecondary education when the only benefit gained by students is a stamp on a piece of paper. Especially as companies and individuals invest in a broader range of lifelong learning experiences, we must develop better ways to recognize achievement and avoid duplication of effort.

▼ Offer Competitive Compensation

It is just as important to retain as to recruit. Once an employer — and a country — has succeeded in developing or attracting the people it needs, it has to ensure that they want to stick around. Among the means of attracting and keeping employees, the most obvious is to pay them what they are worth. Canadian professional hockey teams have been the highest-profile examples of what happens when companies with primarily Canadian revenues have to compete for talent within a North American marketplace.

Given that they have to match American pay rates in American dollars, Canadian clubs have argued that they must have support, such as tax breaks, to cut their other costs — or must consider moving to the United States to shift their revenue base to American dollars. Winnipeg and Quebec City have already lost their teams to such moves; others seem continually threatened. The only managerial difference between Canada's hockey teams and its high technology sector is that technology companies have the flexibility of moving individual players instead of the whole team. When conditions get attractive enough, however, whole teams of people do choose to move.

The major advantage that Canadian technology firms have over hockey teams in the war for talent is that most of their revenues are global. They can in many cases afford to pay North American wages in U.S. dollars, and have indeed been raising their pay rates. It is important to acknowledge, however, that the primary motivation for many skilled people is not pay, but the opportunity to work with leaders in a field, to be part of an industry's cutting edge. Why have more such leading-edge opportunities not emerged in Canada? Compensation does matter, but it involves more than money. Competitive salaries and benefits must mesh with a healthy work environment, an attractive corporate culture, and a commitment to ongoing training and professional development. Don Tapscott acknowledges that the "employee as investor" model does not work for everybody. "In the digital economy, where new business models and structures destroy entire companies and industries, job security has become a relic of a brief moment in human history. But managers must rethink the contract between firms and independents. Whether part-time, mobile, teleworking, contingent, contract, or all of the above, new working relationships based on ability to add value to the task at hand, clear expectations, mutual support, trust and commitment will need to be forged."[67]

Graham Lowe of the University of Alberta has suggested that too many Canadian companies continue to follow internal policies that prevent them from offering optimum work opportunities for their employees. According to his book *The Quality of Work: A People Centred Agenda*, many employees still find themselves under-utilized, unable to apply all of the knowledge and skills they have. In addition, few organizations have made the leap from a commitment to training to a culture of continuous learning. And growing numbers of workers feel over-stressed and under-appreciated. The psychologically unhealthy work environments that result contribute to absenteeism and disability claims, and detract from performance and productivity. "Leaders must champion the involvement of workers in their jobs, empowering individuals to take risks and contribute their ideas. Work structures must become more flexible with wider job descriptions. Teams are a good idea, but to perform at their best, they need to be self-managing. Organizations' cultures must value people and their potential by supporting work-life balance, providing opportunities to actively learn and paying decent wages."[68]

For many employers, the need to attract and retain talent is leading to more than improved pay, benefits, and working conditions. It is driving a renewed emphasis on good corporate citizenship and community involvement. While Canadian business leaders have always understood the importance of good corporate citizenship and its links to the success of their enterprises, a 1996 BCNI survey revealed a growing awareness in companies of more specific links between community investment and shareholder value.

The traditional justifications for community activities — impact on corporate image and on relations with customers and governments — remain significant. But the most frequently cited reason for community involvement by Canadian companies was people management. Canadian CEOs said helping their communities was an important tool for meeting a wide range of human resource goals, from recruiting and retaining skilled people and raising employee morale and loyalty to building employee skills, motivation, and productivity. Community investments are increasingly driven by employee interests, concerns, and values precisely because being seen as an employer of choice is an important competitive advantage in the war for talent.[69]

This trend highlights the importance of the outstanding quality of life available in communities across Canada. In comparison to centres in many other parts of the world, Canada can offer vibrant multicultural communities, clean air and water, safe streets, good schools, and a robust social as well as economic infrastructure. That is the good news. What has received relatively little attention in Canada, however, is the extent to which our social infrastructure depends on mobile talent. On one level, ensuring that Canada generates plenty of well-paid jobs is crucial for maintaining the tax base that a healthy social infrastructure requires. At the same time, we have to make sure that our public institutions are able to compete effectively on North American and global markets for the talent that they need.

Paul Beamish of the Ivey Business School has suggested, for instance, that if Canadian business schools are going to stay competitive, they will need a larger number of fully funded research chairs, each with an endowment of $2.5 million or more. Currently, the number of such chairs in all Canadian business schools combined is lower than the number at a single business school at a well-funded American institution such as the University of Texas at Austin. Such chairs are critical to offering competitive salaries to the academic stars who can drive research performance. "Retention or loss of a single star researcher in a particular area can directly affect an institution's rank in that area."

The same argument could be made for any other university faculty. Beamish has said that, in addition to lower salaries for top performers, the handicaps suffered by Canadian universities in the competition for talent include relatively low levels of funding for general research, a lack of support for doctoral programs, Canada's higher taxes, and the low Canadian dollar. "A low dollar may be great for exports, but it is terrible on the import side, where Canada is importing (or, more typically, trying to retain) productive faculty members."[70]

The exodus of doctors and nurses from Canada's health care system represents another face of the compensation challenge. Canadians in effect are paying for health care through taxes on Canadian incomes and in Canadian dollars, but health care institutions are competing for talent in a North American marketplace where the benchmarks are in American dollars. We cannot expect hospitals to compete effectively for doctors or nurses while ignoring the competitive realities of the United States market any more than we should expect our high technology companies to survive without boosting the pay of their key employees. This is one more reason that we must plan for substantial increases in the costs of public health care — and focus on how to make Canada a more attractive location for talented people able to do high-value work.

▼ *Offer Competitive Taxation*

Canadian employers in both the public and the private sectors have a lot further to go in offering competitive compensation and more effective working environments. But even if companies do try to match the pre-tax compensation available outside Canada, they are hobbled by the rates and structure of taxation in Canada. Some of the disadvantage, we shall see, flows from corporate income tax and other forms of taxation that affect business investment. Here we want to illustrate the impact of Canada's highly uncompetitive taxation on personal incomes.

As a share of GDP, personal income taxes in Canada gobble up more of what people earn than they do in any other major industrialized country, and about 30 percent more than in the United States. Because it is easier for Canadians to move to the United States than to any other jurisdiction, it is this comparison that is most relevant. And Canada's disadvantage goes beyond its tax rates. By applying our highest tax rate to much lower levels of income than in the United States, we put our country at a particular disadvantage for many of the people being lured south by the enticements of the brain drain.[71]

Consider two examples measured by Industry Canada in 1998. For an entry-level engineer in the information technology sector, moving from Ontario to North Carolina would have resulted in an effective pre-tax salary increase of more than 50 percent, even when converting currencies at purchasing power parity of 85 American cents to the Canadian dollar. Taxes at this level made very little difference. The impact of taxation became much more important for senior executives and other high-income earners. Industry Canada calculated that a vice-president in the same industry would have earned the equivalent of US$170,000 in Ottawa and 32 percent more, $225,000, in Raleigh. But, after tax, the compensation gap widened to 64 percent, leaving the American executive $61,300 better off. The higher American salary and currency still had a big impact, but taxes accounted for 36 percent of the differential.[72]

Canada's higher tax rates force Canadian companies trying to persuade people to move here to offer competitive pay before tax and then additional pay (also taxable) to offset the greater tax burden. These amounts, when combined with the impact of a weak dollar, can more than double the cost of a foreign hire. "The need to gross up salaries for recruits from the United States to offset both the low Canadian dollar and the higher tax rates in Canada is extremely costly," said Kerry Hawkins, president and chief executive officer of Cargill Limited in 1999. "On a $100,000 (U.S.) salary, you would have to give an employee $222,000 (Canadian) or more for tax equalization. For a single employee, $94,000 would go toward increased taxes. The Canadian who was doing that same job probably will be getting $140,000 and . . . would be a top performer."[73] "It's very hard for us if we want to get non-Canadians to relocate in Canada," agreed Jacques Lamarre, president and chief executive officer of SNC-Lavalin Group Inc. "Every time we move an American here, we have to give him tax equalization, which means you have to give him twice the difference in the taxes, because he has to pay tax on that too. The result is that we have very few non-Canadians in our Canadian operations."[74]

The year 2000 saw considerable progress on the tax front, especially in the tax treatment of stock options, the compensation fuel of choice for the fast-growing technology sector. The measures announced in the February 2000 federal budget and October Economic Statement and Budget Update, along with moves in provinces such as Ontario and Alberta, mean that Canadians now can even get better tax treatment of stock options than Americans, a huge shift from just a year earlier. The elimination of the high-income surtaxes and the creation of a new 26 percent tax bracket on incomes of $60,000 to $100,000 mark a significant narrowing of the Canada–United States tax gap for many of those most likely to be tempted south in search of higher after-tax incomes.

Tax cuts alone, whether corporate or personal, will not eliminate the pressures that are drawing Canadian individuals and companies south. Any Canadian strategy for making this country the preferred location for head offices and high-value functions must do more than continue to narrow the tax gap. But whether Canada takes a passive approach that simply narrows the tax gap or whether it chooses to use tax policy more aggressively as a tool for attracting people and investment, we will need both lower taxes and better value for our taxes if we want to emerge as winners in the war for talent. We need a robust tax base to support our shared aspirations as a society. The ability to attract and retain skilled people and to put their skills to work within our borders in turn holds the key to building that tax base.

■ The Need to Lead

In business as in politics, leadership matters. The ability of a company or a country to develop and carry out successful strategies depends not on the numbers of its employees or citizens but on the quality of its leaders. The observation has been made many times that our democratic process — and in particular the level of exposure and possible abuse that elected officials undergo — keeps many talented people out of public office. The quality of our national leaders depends on the degree of trust and respect we accord them and on how well we treat their jobs. We get the leaders we deserve. The private sector is no different. Leadership makes all the difference between success and failure, between excellence and mediocrity.

"I believe in the Queen Bee theory that one really talented leader, particularly an entrepreneurial one, can create all kinds of enterprise and wealth," said Jeff Lipton of NOVA Chemicals. "If you lose that one person or that small group of people, to places where they would rather be, they're not going to come back, and you're going to lose a tremendous amount of wealth creation."[75] Gwyn Morgan of Alberta Energy Company Ltd. agreed: "Leadership is the key — leadership in every area, in politics, in business, in every profession, and every technical field . . . It's our leaders that we need to develop and nurture and grab hold of and hang on to. Our success or failure, our ability to compete domestically or internationally, is tied to relatively few high-quality people who can pull things off and really make it happen."[76]

Canada offers many attractions to people with valuable skills in the knowledge economy. Since we are a small country we will inevitably lose some of our talent to global opportunities. Indeed, as long as some of those people choose to return over time, we should welcome such forays into the international arena as a means of enriching our stock of human capital. At the same time, we have to get better at attracting new talent into our economy and, in doing so, we must recognize that the environment we provide for our human capital must compare very favourably with what our larger competitors can offer. "Just being good enough is going backwards," said Hartley Richardson, president and chief executive officer of James Richardson & Sons, Limited. "We've got to get back in line and then be better at, not everything, but enough things to give us an edge. Maybe I'm not being a realist, but I do think that we can turn the tide and attract people back. Sure, not everybody is going to stay, but this is not an issue of everybody leaving or everybody staying. This is an issue of competitiveness, of keeping more than we lose."[77]

The human resource challenge facing Canada is to develop, recruit, and retain the leaders we need to succeed in every sector of society, from business and public service to education and health care. We need to cultivate our future leaders and ensure that all Canadians are encouraged to achieve their full potential. We need to make the most of the pool of talent we enjoy today, and we must persuade others to join us. As Finance

Minister Paul Martin emphasized in a speech to the Toronto Board of Trade in September 2000, this course requires a national dedication to excellence: "Ours must be an economy that attracts talent like a magnet attracts metal; a society where our people feel that there is nowhere else they would rather be than here, because there is no place else they can achieve so much."[78]

5

CREATING AN INNOVATION SOCIETY

If innovation were simply a matter of inspired genius occasionally fertilized by government funding, the challenge of building a national innovation infrastructure would be relatively simple and straightforward. Yet, executives from industry, universities and government describe a far richer and more complex system of innovation-enablers. The availability of human talent and cutting-edge research, the regulatory, legal and capital conditions that facilitate the transition from ideas into wealth-creating products and services, the access to international markets and protection for intellectual property that enable innovators to capture the returns on their investments are all essential parts of the process. Weakness in any of these elements diminishes the others and, indeed, the entire platform for innovation.[1]

— COUNCIL ON COMPETITIVENESS, "GOING GLOBAL," SEPTEMBER 1998

◄ ◄ ◄

Smart people generate ideas, ideas drive innovation, innovation is the key to greater productivity, and productivity growth leads to higher incomes. Canada has plenty of well-educated people and generates its share of good ideas — but it is failing to turn enough of those ideas into innovative products and processes. As a result, productivity growth is lagging behind that of our competitors, and the real incomes of Canadians stagnated through most of the 1990s.

What are the reasons for our lagging productivity growth? What is the chain of innovation from public and private research through to entrepreneurship and business growth? Government certainly has a role to play in enabling innovation through taxation and other policies, and in encouraging more innovation within our public sector institutions. But to create a country that thrives on change, every sector — business, education, labour, to name but three — must seek out the potential for accelerating innovation within the Canadian economy and within our society as a whole.

■ Innovation and Productivity

Canadian companies have been able to cut production costs over the past decade, but not by becoming more productive. According to Industry Canada calculations, Canada's unit labour costs in manufacturing fell by 12.4 percent between 1989 and 1998, while those in the United States rose by 5.5 percent, both measured in American dollars, a net gain in cost competitiveness of almost 18 percent. But Canadian workers actually became 7.8 percent less productive over the period. Costs fell only because Canadians' wages grew 3.1 percent more slowly than in the United States, while the Canadian dollar plunged 22.6 percent. Those lower costs made Canadian exporters more competitive — but did nothing to boost the standard of living of Canadian workers.[2]

As Gerry Schwartz, chief executive officer of Onex Corporation, put it in an interview with the *Ivey Business Journal*, the depreciation of the Canadian dollar has been an easy way to make the country look more productive and to keep more people employed: "But how are we doing it? We're doing it by paying them less. If I hire a plumber in my house in Florida and pay him $50 an hour, and I hire a plumber in my house in Toronto and pay him $50 an hour, I'm paying the guy in the U.S. 50 percent more than I'm paying the plumber in Canada. And that's exactly what we're doing. We're selling our labour cheaper. Keep it employed but at an ever cheaper price — which eventually leads to an ever worsening standard of living. So we're selling out tomorrow's standard of living for today's jobs" (see fig. 14).[3]

The Canadian economy as a whole has consistently been about 15 to 20 percent less productive than that of our major competitor over the past two decades. But in the manufacturing sector, the gap has been widening, reaching more than 25 percent in 1998. Comparisons with

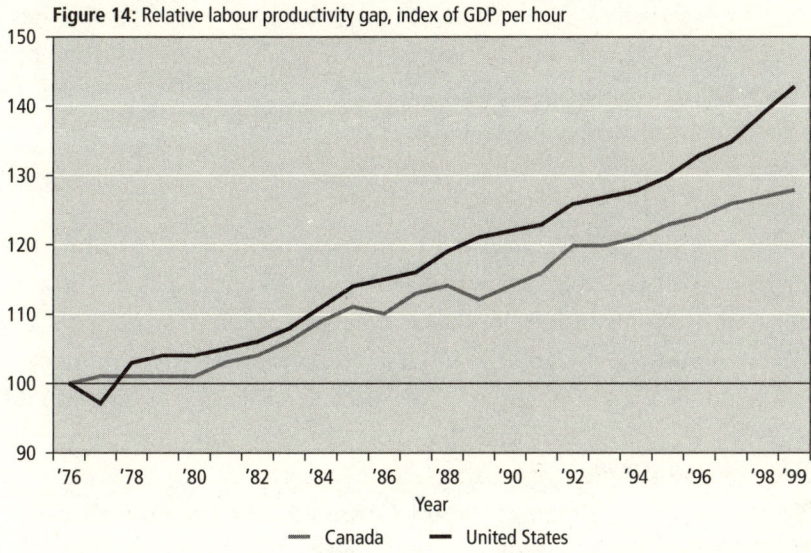

Figure 14: Relative labour productivity gap, index of GDP per hour

other countries are not much more encouraging. Canada's labour productivity was second only to the United States in 1976, but has since dropped to fifth within the G-7 countries, ahead of only Britain and Japan.[4]

Part of the explanation for what is happening in Canada and the United States is the difference in structure of the two economies. Much of the growth in productivity driven by technology is occurring in the two sectors of the economy most directly affected — electronics and industrial machinery. According to Andrew Sharpe at the Centre for the Study of Living Standards, productivity in the American electrical and electronic products sector grew by 13.8 percent a year between 1989 and 1997. Productivity in the industrial machinery and equipment sector grew at an 8.5 percent annual pace. Canada's productivity growth in these two sectors was much more modest — just 3.7 percent and 2.5 percent, respectively.

These two sectors have also been a big part of the American economic growth story. They accounted for 18.5 percent of American manufacturing in 1989, but almost doubled their share to 34.8 percent in 1997 — and this huge growth in output was accomplished with very few additional jobs. In Canada, the electronics and industrial machinery sectors not only accounted for a more modest 11.9 percent of manufacturing in 1989 but barely budged over the next decade, increasing their share to just 13.5 percent by 1997. So overpowering was the performance of these two sectors in the United States that it masks a stagnation of productivity in other American industries. Taking out the contribution of these two sectors would cut the overall productivity growth rate in American manufacturing from 3.3 percent to 0.2 percent. In twelve out of nineteen manufacturing sectors, Canada actually outperformed the United States in productivity growth.[5]

Industry Canada has suggested that many of Canada's productivity gains have been realized in mature sectors and by cutting costs and jobs rather than through innovation. That said, workers in Canada's oil and gas, lumber and paper, and primary metal sectors are all more productive than their American counterparts. Resource industries may be symbolic of the "old economy," but Canadian companies in this sector are active developers and adopters of leading-edge technologies.[6]

Peter Bentley, chairman of Canfor Corporation, talks enthusiastically about the way his company has applied research to innovative practices in every phase of its business, from forest management to sales and service. "We are probably at the leading edge of forestry computer technology. We know far more about what goes on in our forest than the government. We also are hooked up electronically with our biggest customers in the United States. We replenish their shelves because we know what has gone through their checkout counters. We have to carry a large inventory to do that, but we get a premium for the service we give and we get a premium for the quality we supply."[7]

Examples such as these bring up another important divergence in productivity performance. Large companies have done a lot better at improving their productivity than small ones. Small and medium-sized businesses have been Canada's job creation champions over the past decade, but their productivity record is dismal. Smaller businesses have been creating more jobs, but it is larger companies that have been creating better jobs. Don Daly of the Schulich School of Business at York University has shown that the productivity gap between large and small plants has widened dramatically since the mid-1970s. Relative to the United States, large Canadian plants have registered greater gains in productivity than the American average, while smaller Canadian plants have been falling further behind. Because small businesses account for a bigger share of manufacturing in Canada than in the United States, Canada's overall performance has suffered. "Small business has been an important source of employment growth in Canadian manufacturing, but the contributions of small plants to real and money wage income, to profits and to productivity per employee, have been to pull down the national totals."[8]

Size is not the only factor that seems to affect productivity growth and innovative behaviour. A 1999 study by Surendra Gera, Wulong Gu, and Frank Lee at Industry Canada found that inward flows of foreign direct investment (FDI) help to cut production costs and increase productivity in most Canadian industries. "Inward FDI appears to act as an important channel for the diffusion of ideas and innovations. While Canada's inward FDI stock has been increasing over the past decade, its share of FDI in North America and worldwide has been declining since the Free Trade Agreement. A key challenge for policy makers is how to attract more FDI into Canada."[9] The link between foreign ownership and productivity has been thoroughly documented. Foreign-owned plants of all sizes have increased productivity faster than comparable Canadian-owned plants. As Daly noted: "There is only a small difference in relative productivity levels of large and small foreign establishments, but small domestic establishments had productivity levels only half [that of] the foreign establishments with under 100 employees in the 1985–90 period. It is clearly in the small domestically owned plants where the relative productivity levels have experienced the greatest relative declines."[10]

Ownership also has a direct impact on the process of innovation. John Baldwin and Petr Hanel of Statistics Canada have shown that foreign subsidiaries in Canada perform more research and development than domestically owned firms. They are also more likely to take part in joint ventures and partnerships for research and to collaborate with Canadian universities. As a result, they surpass Canadian companies in introducing world-first and Canada-first innovations. What is more, innovations developed by foreign affiliates tend to be used to boost exports and to increase foreign market share. Innovations introduced by Canadian-owned companies are more often used to win domestic market share. In short, they concluded, the research activities of multinationals in Canada defy the branch-plant stereotype. "Multinational firms not only exploit their proprietary advantages in Canada, but they also increasingly develop their own innovation initiatives and tap local sources of technology and scientific research."[11]

Nestlé Canada Inc. provides one example of innovative behaviour by a multinational subsidiary. Frank Cella, former chairman and chief executive officer of the Canadian unit and now a senior executive at world headquarters, notes that Canada has become a hotbed of innovation within the Swiss-based multinational. "Canada has highly sophisticated consumers, and yet a population base that allows us to experiment without breaking the bank. We made a case for allowing us to be an experimental lab, and that has given us a uniqueness in the Nestlé world that we would not have otherwise. We add value by innovation, by trying new ideas, and by getting them to market faster. We are so innovative that the worldwide group is sending people here to learn about how we are doing it."[12]

This accent on innovation has allowed jobs to flourish here even in the face of global restructuring. For instance, a plant in Trenton, Ontario, which made mass-market frozen dinners, was scheduled to close to allow consolidation of production at a more efficient location in the United States. Nestlé Canada kept the plant open and used it as a test-bed for a whole new line of business. The Canadian subsidiary came up with the idea of selling restaurant-quality frozen food prepared in custom batches to food-service operators in areas such as hospitals, hotels, and airlines. The Trenton plant today employs more people than ever, with much of its output being exported to the United States.

Similarly, the global banking group HSBC sees its Canadian subsidiary as a centre for global innovation. Youssef Nasr, a former president and chief executive officer of HSBC Canada who went on to head the bank's American operations, said Canada has proven to be a great place to develop new ideas and to test new products before their launch worldwide:

> With any new invention, the take-up in Canada is faster than almost anywhere else, particularly in the banking industry. The highest pickup rate for ATM cards and for debit cards was in this country. Internet banking is heavily used here. So it is a place where you can test new products three to seven years ahead of the rest of the world. The United States is sometimes faster, but if you make a mistake in that market, it is a lot more damaging than if you make a mistake in Canada. And if our products prove themselves here, then we offer them to consumers elsewhere, in places like Brazil and Singapore.[13]

Canada's role as a test market led to the creation of a software development centre in Burnaby, British Columbia, with some 400 programmers. It is one of only four such centres the bank maintains worldwide, with the others in Buffalo, London (England), and Hong Kong. "The most productive, the lowest cost per line of code and the one that has the best record in terms of delivering on time and under budget, is in Burnaby," Mr. Nasr concluded.

Why are foreign-owned firms on average more innovative? The answer, according to Baldwin and Hanel, lies not in their ownership, but in their intense links to the global economy. When they compared the performance of foreign multinationals with that of Canadian-based global companies, the picture changed dramatically. "Comparisons to Canadian multinationals show that the two groups of multinationals are quite similar, both with regards to the likelihood that they conduct R&D and that they introduce innovations. It is the international orientation of both foreign and domestically controlled firms that is related to their degree of innovativeness."[14]

In other words, Canadian companies that are actively engaged and competing in world markets are matching the global pace of change and innovation. This comment may seem obvious when considering Canada's star players in high technology such as Nortel Networks and JDS Uniphase. But even in traditional manufacturing businesses, Canadian companies that have made the move into global markets also demonstrate a penchant for innovation.

Consider steel-maker Dofasco Inc. President and chief executive officer John Mayberry says his company has done much more than use technology to become one of the most efficient steel producers in the world. It has also formed partnerships with other steel-makers to create a combined ability to deliver consistent quality to customers worldwide. It has invested in research leading to patents on new products. And it has formed Internet-based multidisciplinary teams to help customers design future generations of automobiles. By using computer-aided design techniques, Dofasco has been redesigning steel-based components in ways that would save car-makers millions of dollars in production costs. "This is a modest effort, but it has helped us to create some interdependence with a major customer. We believe very strongly in that, and we think it is a real key to our success."[15]

The problem is not that Canadian-owned companies are incapable of being innovative; it is that too few Canadian companies are globally oriented. Too much of the Canadian economy is still made up of smaller businesses focused on the domestic market. As a whole, therefore, the Canadian private sector is not keeping up with the rapid pace of global change, from investing in new machinery and equipment in manufacturing to exploiting the potential of e-commerce in services.

Andrei Sulzenko, assistant deputy minister of industry and science policy, Industry Canada, told a conference on productivity in January 2000 that Canada is not growing quickly enough into the new high-growth, high-value, high-wage, and high-productivity sectors that increasingly define the knowledge-based economy. "The issue for policymakers is not only what can be done to put the right incentives in place to increase investment in physical capital, in innovation and in human capital, but perhaps as importantly or maybe even more importantly, what can be done to remove the constraints from the creative destruction process that goes on in an economy, so that business decision-makers, from entrepreneurs right through to pension plan managers, have the right sets of incentives to invest in dynamic, high-growth pursuits as compared to lower return pursuits."

Sulzenko noted that his department has been working to improve those incentives on three fronts: modernizing the business framework laws such as the Canada Business Corporations Act and intellectual property rules; promoting innovation, both by funding more research and encouraging commercialization; and promoting the development and use of critical enabling technologies. But the real challenge, he concluded, comes back to the need to increase the pace of adjustment in Canada's economy, through social policy as well as macro- and microeconomic policies. "My concern, and this is very much a personal view, is that if we don't look at our policy choices through that kind of prism, over time, as Canada's economy integrates increasingly with that of the United States, Canada will be heavily invested in lower-growth, lower-wage activities compared to the United State's high-growth, high-value, high-wage activities. Now these would make wonderfully complementary economies, but is that where we want to be down the road . . . increasingly as the farm team for the big leagues?"[16]

■ Innovation and Research

The conventional wisdom is that strong and growing investment in research and development (R&D) is critical to any strategy for growth in the New Economy. In 1999, for instance, the Council on Competitiveness in the United States warned that declining investment in research was undermining that country's capacity for innovation. United States research and development as a percentage of GDP has been falling since 1985. The share of the total committed to basic research is in decline. The government share of all forms of research has been falling steadily for three decades. All real increases in R&D have come from private industry, but these activities have been heavily concentrated in product development rather than basic research. And even as American research intensity has fallen, the council lamented, other industrialized countries have been increasing their commitment to R&D.[17]

Canada's problem is somewhat different. According to the Organisation for Economic Co-operation and Development (OECD), our research spending has been growing faster than that in the United States, but we are starting from a lower base. Canada's spending as a share of the economy remains weak in both the public and the private sectors — the second lowest among the G-7 nations. The United States still invests almost twice as large a share of its economy, 2.8 percent of GDP compared with 1.6 percent in Canada.[18] Paul Davenport, president of the University of Western Ontario, has noted that, despite its low level of research spending, Canada accounts for a respectable 5 percent of scientific citations among the top fifteen countries worldwide. That number represents almost twice as many citations per dollar of spending as in the United States.[19]

Canada's record is less inspiring when it comes to turning new discoveries into patents, the pieces of intellectual property that are the building blocks for new businesses in the knowledge economy. As Manuel Trajtenberg of Tel Aviv University noted, Canada has a mid-range performance in terms of patents per capita and patents per dollar of R&D, but it is being overtaken by a group of smaller countries — notably Finland, Israel, Taiwan, and South Korea. He also points out that in both research spending and patents, the absolute numbers are at least as important as relative measures such as research as a percentage of GDP or patents per capita: "In order to establish a viable, self-sustaining high-tech sector, a country has to achieve a critical mass in terms of pertinent infrastructure, skills development, managerial experience, testing facilities, marketing and communications channels, financial institutions, etc. . . . Thus, the medium to poor showing in the relative measures mean[s] a very poor standing in absolute terms and carr[ies] potentially serious implications for economic performance."[20]

Trajtenberg cites a variety of other worrying trends. The makeup of

Canadian patents is out of step with the rest of the world. We do reasonably well in traditional fields, but lag badly in sectors such as computers. There is an ownership gap, with less than half of all patents filed in Canada owned by Canadian assignees. The quality of Canadian patents, as measured by how frequently they are cited in other patent applications, also lags far behind the United States.

To improve Canada's record, governments have been pouring more research money into colleges and universities. New efforts to boost public support for university research include the creation of the networks of Centres of Excellence, the Canada Foundation for Innovation, the 21st Century Research Chairs, the Canadian Institutes of Health Research, and a range of provincial initiatives such as Ontario's R&D Challenge Fund.

Universities already play a particularly strong role within the Canadian innovation process. According to OECD figures, the share of total research and development performed by Canadian universities is second highest in the G-7. Links to the private sector are especially strong. Canada tops the major industrialized world when it comes to the share of industry-funded R&D performed by universities.[21]

In addition to putting more public money into university research, governments have been trying to make sure that the money is used more effectively. The Canada Foundation for Innovation, for instance, has helped to move both colleges and universities towards a broader strategy for building excellence in their faculties. CFI president David Strangway says that in handing out grants, the foundation has introduced a new focus on documenting and reporting back on the results of funded research, and has shifted proposal assessment away from the traditionally narrow and conservative peer-review process towards a more multidisciplinary approach. "By crossing all discipline boundaries we have caused institutional planning to take on new significance. Institutions are making strategic plans that link capital plans, other funding partners and their own faculty recruiting, renewal plans and fundraising campaigns for the coming years."[22]

One further policy reform that is having a significant impact on Canada's research capacity is the change in tax rules making large individual donations of shares in publicly traded companies more attractive. The Honourable Henry Jackman, chairman and president of E-L Financial Corporation Limited, noted that the resulting growth in private donations has not been evenly spread, but focused on support for world-class centres of excellence within the university system. "As long as they rely exclusively on per capita government funding, everybody is simply guaranteed mediocrity. You have to have really great universities, or you don't have a great country."[23]

The experience of the United States in building clusters of new industries shows just how important really great universities can be. As described by Robert Berdahl, chancellor of the University of California, Berkeley: "The United States created the model of how to cultivate innovation through quality education connected to research. Take, for example, biotechnology, a field synonymous with both innovation and entrepreneurship. Universities, by nurturing scientific discovery and producing a highly educated workforce, have been the catalyst for this growing industry. Today, one in three U.S. biotech companies are located within 35 miles of a University of California campus. Six of the ten best-selling biotech drugs stem from University of California research, and 85 percent of California's biotechnology companies employ alumni with graduate degrees from the University of California."[24]

Investing public money in research plays a vital role in stimulating innovation and the growth of new industries, but it is only the beginning of Canada's challenge. Work on behalf of the Business Council on National Issues by McKinsey & Co. suggests that Canada in fact produces plenty of good ideas, but it fails to turn enough of them into business success stories.

It is interesting to compare the record of Canadian and American universities when it comes to generating licensing revenues from their research. Canada's top five universities in terms of licensing revenue carried out an average of $101.6 million in sponsored research in 1997, less than one-third the average $320.3 million at each of the top five American universities. Those five American universities, however, received an average of twenty times as much in gross licensing revenue, $34.3 million compared with $1.7 million (see fig. 15). In both countries, the top 10 percent of schools accounted for about three-quarters of all sponsored research dollars, but the gap in total performance was staggering. While the value of sponsored research in the United States was almost fourteen times the Canadian total, American universities reaped forty-two times as much licensing revenue. Only three Canadian universities — Alberta, Calgary, and Waterloo — exceeded the *average* American ratio of licensing income to total research.

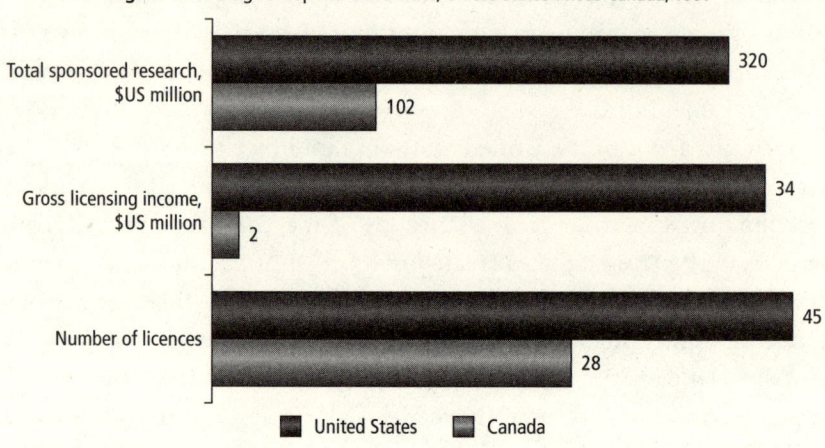

Figure 15: Average of top five universities, United States versus Canada, 1997

One striking observation about American success is the extent to which licensing revenues have been fuelled by a relatively small number of "home runs." Stanford reaps $23 million a year from the results of its recombinant DNA research; Michigan State derives more than $17 million from cancer treatment drugs; and Florida receives 92 percent of its $18 million a year in licensing revenue from just three patents, one of them for Gatorade.[25]

In seeking to improve the performance of Canadian universities and colleges, Canada must address both the general barriers to commercialization of research and the specific challenges involved in trying to hit more "home runs." The easy but incomplete answer is that leading American universities are better funded and therefore more able to attract the leading-edge researchers who are most likely to produce new breakthrough discoveries. But the staggering gap in performance points to a range of other problems, including less effective treatment of intellectual property; lack of capacity within universities for commercializing research; too much emphasis on areas of research with less commercial potential; and a shortage of expertise and capital for new ventures.

The federal Liberal government has acknowledged the importance of some of these factors, including tax policy and the commercialization of university research, but the centrepiece of its strategy for accelerating innovation is increased public investment in research. During the autumn 2000 election campaign, the Liberal Party promised to move Canada from fifteenth in the OECD in spending on research and development into the top five by at least doubling federal R&D spending by 2010.[26] We would suggest, however, that in seeking to improve Canada's performance, greater public investment in basic research by itself is far from enough. Investment in research is just one step in the chain of innovation, and how much is invested in basic research is less important than how effectively companies and countries make use of its results.

The OECD found that public investment in basic research stagnated in much of the industrialized world during the 1990s, while competitive pressures pushed businesses to put more emphasis on market-driven research. At the same time, companies became more innovative in their efforts to make use of the knowledge base that emerged from research laboratories:

> Networking has become a key factor in innovation. Interactions between the science system and the business sector have become more prominent than in the past, as key technologies such as biotechnology and information technology are closely linked to scientific research. In addition, while firms have cut down on long-term research expenditures, they have developed new ways of linking to the science base and absorbing available technologies. Networking and collaboration between firms, at national and international levels, has increased partly because firms can no longer bear all the costs and risks of innovation alone, and because the required knowledge is often multidisciplinary and emerges from a wider range of firms and institutions.[27]

The Conference Board of Canada agrees that innovative companies are far more likely to report collaboration with other firms and with public institutions such as universities and government laboratories. Those that collaborate tend, in turn, to get more of their revenue from the sale of new products and are more likely to introduce world-first innovations. "We strongly believe that collaboration and the ability to build linkages among all players in the economy are critical to building a high-performing and innovative nation." Yet the Conference Board found that only one in four Canadian manufacturers engaged in such collaboration between 1997 and 1999. Although large firms are well advanced in the process of collaboration, the board stated that "there is definitely room for improvement" in fostering more collaboration among smaller enterprises.[28]

Canada has to continue fostering new ideas, but good ideas are not enough. As a country, we must become far more effective at using those ideas to stimulate investment and build growing businesses within the global economy. A culture of innovation depends not just on research but on a dynamic process of entrepreneurial investment that turns new ideas into growing businesses, new jobs, and higher incomes. As the OECD has suggested, to succeed in turning more of Canada's research into growing businesses and rising incomes, we have to do a better job of bringing ideas and money together.

■ Innovation and Entrepreneurship

California was the world's hub for movie-making long before Silicon Valley came along. Screenwriters there learned early on that their success in winning backing for a multimillion-dollar movie could depend on their ability to sell their concept to a studio executive in the time it took an elevator to go from the ground floor to the penthouse. That combination of relentless networking and highly focused marketing is also driving California's success in technology. Venture capitalists sponsor an annual "elevator pitch" contest for students at Stanford University. While students elsewhere engage in extended debate during case study competitions, those at Stanford get two minutes to lay out a business plan and pitch an idea. They learn quickly how important communications skills have become to success in high technology.

Nor are the opportunities limited to campus. A company called MoneyHunt sets up cameras at venture capital conferences around the United States. Its contests provide a screen test for would-be entrepreneurs, judging both the potential of their ideas and their ability to handle the spotlight. The prize for winning is recognition of their ideas on a Web site, but, more important, access to opportunities to meet and pitch to venture capitalists.

All these strategies are part of a vast web of relationship-building among venture capital investors, existing businesses, universities, new business incubators, individual mentors, entrepreneurs, and researchers. For people with ideas and for those with money, the search for partners is high-speed and non-stop, the competition intense and relentless. Opportunities may appear in thirty-second windows, but no good idea gets overlooked. As a 1999 report to the Joint Economic Committee of the United States Senate concluded: "One important factor in U.S. high-tech success has been the efficiency with which innovation inputs are employed. High levels of entrepreneurship and competition ensure that R&D, education and investment capital are used to maximum advantage."[29]

The OECD agrees on the importance of venture capital to a country's growth in a knowledge-based economy. "Venture capital is only a small component of total investment, but plays an important role in stimulating innovation and in the emergence of new technology-based firms. Such firms play a growing role in innovation, job creation and the commercialization of public R&D."[30] Venture capital seems to have a key role not just in moving research from academia to the marketplace but in stimulating innovation within industry. A 1998 study by Samuel Kortum of Boston University and Josh Lerner of Harvard Business School looked at research in twenty industries over the past three decades. It found that success in filing patents for new discoveries had less to do with the scale of research than the company's success in tapping venture capital markets for funding. "The results suggest that venture funding does have a strong positive impact on innovation . . . a dollar of venture capital could be up to ten times more effective in stimulating patenting than a dollar of traditional corporate R&D."[31]

The Global Entrepreneurship Monitor has found that the level of entrepreneurial activity in a country may account for as much as half of the variations in overall economic growth among industrialized countries. By some measures of such activity, Canada ranks well. According to GEM's 2000 Executive Report, 7.9 percent of adult Canadians are involved in entrepreneurial activity, one of the highest participation rates in the twenty-one countries it studied. However, just 2.5 percent put their own money directly into start-up ventures. And only one person in forty-five is active in managing a new business — lower than average for the group studied.

Despite a dramatic increase in the supply of venture capital in Canada over the past five years, the authors suggest, the industry is still seen as risk averse. The availability of financing remains the dominant issue and is made worse by insufficient tax incentives and support networks for private entrepreneurs. The report also notes that there are major differences in government policies and programs among provinces, with multiple layers of government creating duplicated costs and incompatible regulations. It suggests that Canadians do not appreciate the potential for entrepreneurial activity to create wealth.[32]

While Canadians start up a large number of companies, very few of these firms grow to any significant size. Gordon Sharwood, chairman of venture catalyst Sharwood and Company, noted that only 1.1 percent of

Canadian companies with fewer than five employees in 1985 had grown to more than twenty employees by 1993. "We have a system that provides a lot of incentives for the creation of small businesses," he says, "but it is biased against growth."[33]

Jeff Lipton, president and chief executive of NOVA Chemicals, sees a world of difference between the environment for entrepreneurs in Canada and in the United States. "It starts with people willing to take ideas and run with them and then be able to get funding for those ideas. There isn't an adequate infrastructure in Canada to make this happen. That's not to say entrepreneurs can't flourish here, but there is a tremendous infrastructure for venture capitalism in the U.S. that doesn't exist in Canada. The issue is how to create an environment that is positive and nurtures entrepreneurs and business growth as opposed to one that is basically negative. What we need in Canada is a revolution."[34] According to the Canadian Venture Capital Association, half of the $12 billion in assets under administration by all venture capital companies in Canada in 1999 was held in just twenty-one funds. These funds, known as Labour-Sponsored Venture Capital Corporations, exist only because federal and provincial governments give individual investors generous tax credits for putting their savings into these vehicles. These tax credits have succeeded in expanding the pool of available venture capital, but only by having taxpayers absorb much of the risk (see fig. 16).

Dedicated venture capital firms are beginning to flourish in Canada, but, as Mary Macdonald, president of Macdonald & Associates, has noted, some real challenges remain. "We aren't close to developing the critical

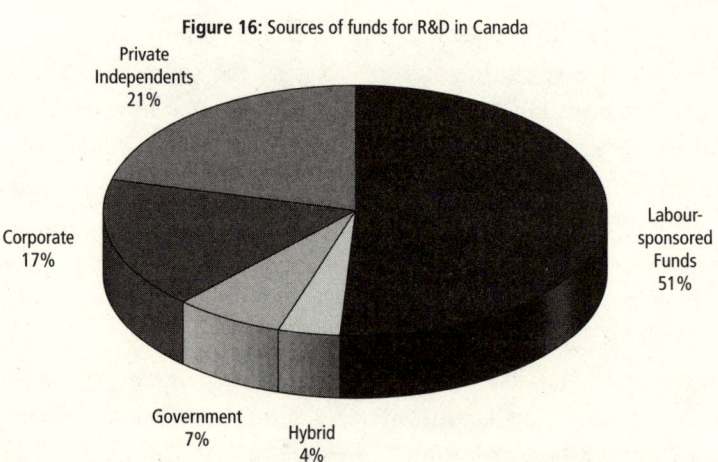

Figure 16: Sources of funds for R&D in Canada

Private Independents 21%
Corporate 17%
Government 7%
Hybrid 4%
Labour-sponsored Funds 51%

mass in the venture industry that has evolved in the United States, even on a per-capita basis. There is a much broader commitment among the pension fund community to this asset class in the United States, with public and private pension funds committing about $15 billion (U.S.) a year to venture funds in that country. By contrast, pension funds here commit $200 million (Canadian) or less to fund managers (excluding their direct investments)."[35] The Canadian Labour and Business Centre has estimated that Canadian pension funds contribute less than 7 percent of the total pool of venture capital in this country, representing less than 0.2 percent of total pension fund assets.[36]

The most critical problem in Canada, however, seems to be the relative shortage of so-called angel investors. These individuals are experienced in a specific field and understand the challenge of starting a business, usually because they have done so successfully themselves. In addition to ploughing their money into other people's new ideas, they usually sit on the boards of companies in which they invest and provide valuable insight and advice.

The OECD has reported that Canada actually surpasses the United States in terms of the relative availability of formal venture capital. However, it acknowledges that, in the United States, informal capital (angel investors) provides about twice as much money to new ventures as all formal sources of venture capital combined. This is a pattern unmatched in any other country.[37] The injection of proven management experience from angels appears to make a huge difference to the probability of success. The personal involvement of a successful entrepreneur is worlds apart from the relationship the owners of a start-up company are likely to have with revolving account managers at an institutional venture capital investor. The fact that angels tend to invest close to home also contributes to the growth of new industry clusters.

A 1999 study for the Expert Panel on the Commercialization of University Research identified a range of barriers to greater angel financing in Canada. Aside from the high level of risk, experts pointed to a fragmented and inefficient market, unrealistic expectations on the part of entrepreneurs, constraints on the amount of time angels were able to devote to their investments, and high capital gains tax rates. In addition, they said venture capital financing was inhibited by the weak potential returns available in Canadian markets; under-resourced and inexperienced technology transfer offices at universities, which also had unrealistic expectations; and a lack of management talent with the ability to turn good ideas into successful commercial ventures.[38]

As a result, American investors have access not only to a far larger pool of venture capital but one that has been growing about 10 percent a year faster than in Canada. According to figures compiled by the Boston Consulting Group for the 2000 report of the Canadian E-Business Opportunities Roundtable, Canadian venture capital investments grew to an estimated $2.1 billion in 1999. That was three times their level in 1995. But American investment in 1999 hit $37.7 billion, four and a half times its 1995 total, and eighteen times the total investment made in Canada.

What is more, the American venture capital industry seems to have maintained angel attitudes and tactics even as it has grown, providing entrepreneurs with advice and resources as well as money. "Leading venture capital firms often install experienced, Internet-savvy management in those new companies in which they invest. They are able to provide new companies with introductions to support service agencies that have e-business expertise and to potential business partners and customers. Some early stage capital providers 'incubate' companies by providing access to shared space and facilities, in addition to funding and management expertise. All of these activities combine to accelerate the start-up's growth."[39]

A 2000 study by the Conference Board of Canada compared both the direct and the indirect costs of going public on the Toronto Stock Exchange, the New York Stock Exchange, and NASDAQ. It concluded that, in terms of direct costs and the pricing of new offerings, growing companies were better off making their initial public offerings in Canada.[40] The E-Business Roundtable, however, noted that just four Internet-related companies went public on the Toronto Stock Exchange in 1999, and two of those were cross-listed on American exchanges. In the same year, 165 Internet-related companies made initial public offerings on NASDAQ.[41]

Roger Martin, dean of the Rotman School of Management at the University of Toronto, has suggested it would be a mistake to focus on the number of new listings that end up on the TSE. In Silicon Valley, he points out, the process of raising and allocating capital is the most efficient in the world — even though its favoured stock market, NASDAQ, along with the headquarters of all the major investment banking and securities law firms, is on the other side of the continent. "In Silicon Valley, the capital market epicentre is Sand Hill Road, home of a whole new breed of venture capital. Firms such as Kleiner Perkins, Benchmark, Sequoia and scores of others have taken the financing of start-ups to a level of sophistication not yet seen anywhere else in the world." He suggests that Canada needs to do more than foster a robust pool of angel investors and sophisticated venture capital firms. "While we now have a growing number of venture capital funding sources," he says, "we need them to generate a level of competition that matches the intensity in Silicon Valley, to ensure that entrepreneurs have sufficient choice and bargaining power. Currently, they're obliged to give up too much in the early rounds of financing, which leaves too little room for investors in later rounds when start-ups are close to going public."[42]

This conclusion is consistent with earlier work for the Business Council on National Issues by McKinsey & Company, which noted that Canadian high technology companies tend to go public earlier in their life cycles and at much lower market capitalization. As a result, they face the rigours of the public marketplace much faster, before they may have developed the experience and history to weather difficult market bounces. Furthermore, with average market capitalization of less than half their American counterparts, Canadian companies then find that their shares tend to be less liquid, less likely to attract analyst coverage, and more likely to fall in value after the initial public offering.[43]

Martin is suggesting that many of these later-stage problems have their roots in the shortage of early stage investors. In this, he agrees with the conclusions of the United States Senate Joint Economic Committee report that called early-stage angel investors the key to a "virtuous circle" of wealth creation, especially in the high technology sector: "The success of the U.S. high-tech sector illustrates America's mutually reinforcing strengths of entrepreneurship, open markets, and diversity. Entrepreneurs have flooded into dynamic and competitive high-tech industries because of the huge opportunities and rewards available to successful innovators. Diverse sources of financial and human capital have ensured that good ideas don't get overlooked, and that many paths to innovation and economic growth are pursued."[44]

The report links the existence of the unparalleled network of venture capital in the United States directly to that country's ability to generate more wealthy households. "The U.S. had at least 3.5 million households with net worth of more than $1 million in 1996. By comparison, a 1997 study found just 965,000 millionaires (in ECUs, or European Currency

Units) in seven large European economies . . . It appears that the United States has at least three times the density of millionaires as Europe."[45] Only someone with at least a million or two in the bank can afford to risk $100,000 or more on somebody else's wild idea. Yet people willing and able to make such investments consistently play a critical role in fostering more entrepreneurial innovation. In essence, former finance minister Michael Wilson had it right when he said that Canada needs more rich people — though his statement met with little but derision. Encouraging people to get rich and celebrating their success is too often seen as un-Canadian.

John Roth, president and chief executive officer of Nortel Networks Corporation, suggests that Canadians need to put this attitude behind them if they want to maintain a caring society. "Why isn't it honourable for somebody to become a millionaire in Canada by working for a living as opposed to playing a sport or winning a lottery? Our system is very much based on taxing the rich and giving to the poor and I don't argue with that. On the other hand, we have to build wealth if we want to continue to support the poor. If we continue to drive the rich out, then who will we tax in the future?"[46] Riches don't come without risk. Harvard University professor William Sahlman suggested in the *Harvard Business Review* that American entrepreneurs are honoured in their own society not because they get rich, but because they are willing to risk everything. "The American love affair with entrepreneurs couldn't happen if we didn't have such a high tolerance for failure. Americans admire people just for trying — the harder, the better. We find something honorable — gutsy, even — in a businessperson starting company after company until he or she gets it right."[47]

The 2000 GEM study confirmed that social and cultural values can be at least as important as the economic environment in stimulating entrepreneurial investment. "Opportunity alone does not result in entrepreneurship. As noted, individuals need to feel motivated to take advantage of opportunity. The extent to which they do will reflect their belief that being an entrepreneur, irrespective of whether one is successful or not, is socially valued. The conviction that success will not be resented or failure stigmatized is fundamental."[48]

Royal Bank chairman and chief executive officer John Cleghorn sees signs of an important shift in attitude among younger and older Canadians alike. "A generation ago, young people aspired to careers in the professions or in large companies. Today, I see people in their twenties coming out of business school eager to build companies from the ground up, especially in high technology. At the same time, much of the entrepreneurial growth is being driven by experienced managers in their late thirties and forties who have left government or major companies and are using their knowledge and networks to help young companies grow."[49] On the whole, though, Canadian National president and chief executive officer Paul Tellier says that Canadians still have less taste than their American neighbours for risk or for people who take chances and win big. "In Canada, we don't recognize, appreciate, encourage, or support success. In the United States, the saying 'nothing succeeds like success' is true in every sense of the term. You feel it. It's much more vibrant. There's much more eagerness to compete to be the best."[50]

Some degree of income inequality is clearly needed to stimulate innovative behaviour, entrepreneurial risk-taking, and overall economic growth. As the *National Post* noted in an August 2000 editorial: "Despite the connotations that an unequal distribution brings with it, there are good reasons to worry about uniformity in incomes. Those inhabiting the upper income [band] are the wealth creators of any economy. They earn more, invest more, save more, provide the entrepreneurial drive that powers a growing economy and tend to be more philanthropic than the rest of the nation. And these things, while done in self-interest, are a great benefit to all citizens, rich and poor."[51]

In the 2000 report of its Expert Panel on Skills, the Prime Minister's Advisory Council on Science and Technology noted that Canadians acquired their "admirable image" as fair and caring people during a period in which our major industries were protected from competition and much of our wealth flowed from the sale of resources. The result, however, is that we remain risk averse at a time when only innovation and risk-taking can build the wealth we need to sustain and improve our national lifestyle. What is more, the panel agreed, we remain ambivalent in our attitude towards individual success. "We generally wish people well (but not too well) and feel compassion for those who fail (but are stingy in extending our grace for them to try again). We are uncomfortable with the notion of conspicuous wealth or success, and have difficulty with the notion that equal access to opportunities does not necessarily lead to equal outcomes." The panel recommended that Canada's first ministers discuss the challenge of building a more innovative culture at their 2001 meeting and consider "articulating a clear national vision of an economy and society in which innovation and entrepreneurship are broadly accepted as Canadian values."[52]

We certainly see no conflict between the desire to live in a society that shares resources fairly and the need for incentives that encourage people to take risks and get rich. We are convinced that it is possible to emulate the virtuous circle of entrepreneurial investment and wealth creation that has fuelled growth in the American high technology sector without adopting that country's huge disparities between rich and poor. But if we truly want to help disadvantaged Canadians to enjoy a growing quality of life, we have to encourage our most talented citizens to achieve their full potential as well. It is time for Canadians to focus on sharing success instead of sharing only misery.

■ Innovation and Taxation

If Canada wants to experience the vibrant growth in jobs and incomes that flows from dynamic new investments in leading-edge ideas, it has to come to terms with what motivates people to put their time and money on the line. Diving into the unknown is both expensive and stressful. The ability to reap rewards commensurate with the risks involved is directly related to how often people take the plunge and how much money they are prepared to invest. We will look more broadly at the impact of taxation on corporate investment decisions in the next chapter, but taxes have a particularly direct impact on entrepreneurial activity. Because business start-ups involve the assets and income of individuals, personal as well as corporate taxation comes into play.

The impact of personal taxes on investment and hiring by small businesses was shown conclusively in two 1998 papers by American tax economists Robert Carroll, Douglas Holtz-Eakin, Mark Rider, and Harvey Rosen. Based on the behaviour of entrepreneurs before and after the substantial changes to American individual income tax rates in the 1986 Tax Reform Act, they reached two important conclusions. First, raising the marginal income tax rates faced by entrepreneurs has a significant impact on both the likelihood of new capital investment and the amount invested. An increase in marginal rates of just 5 percent made small business owners 10.4 percent less likely to make an investment, and cut the average amount invested by 9.9 percent. "Do high income tax rates discourage entrepreneurs from making capital outlays? On the basis of tax return data for sole proprietors before and after the Tax Reform Act of 1986, we conclude the answer is yes. When a sole proprietor's marginal tax rate goes up, the probability that he or she buys capital assets goes down, as does the expected amount of investment expenditure."[53] In their second paper they found that higher marginal rates on entrepreneurs reduced the likelihood that they would hire additional employees and cut the wages they paid. A 10 percent reduction in the marginal tax rate on entrepreneurs made them 12 percent more likely to hire employees. "Given that an entrepreneur chooses to employ workers, lower taxes also raise the total wage payments made to those workers."[54]

As we have shown earlier in this chapter, Canadian small businesses have been major creators of jobs, but have persistently lower productivity. The American findings suggest that Canada's higher personal tax rates could be contributing significantly to the poor productivity performance of Canadian small businesses by inhibiting their investment in new machinery and equipment and their adoption of new technologies.

It is true that Canada offers some of the most generous tax incentives in the industrialized world for research and development. But as economist Pierre Fortin has warned, there may be an inconsistency between having generous tax provisions for R&D while maintaining a heavy overall corporate tax burden. "My worry is that Canada may have become an attractive location for *producing* R&D, but an unattractive place for *using* R&D. The consequence of the high corporate tax burden would be either that Canada attracts R&D activity purely for re-export or that Canada does not attract it at all (despite the advantageous tax provisions) because it is more profitable to use it elsewhere."[55]

The federal budget of February 2000 and the pre-election budget update of October made significant progress in reducing both the corporate and the personal income tax burden. The corporate income tax rate is scheduled to fall by seven percentage points over four years, and Canadians at all income levels are already enjoying significant cuts in their personal tax burden. But even more important to the stimulation of entrepreneurial activity is the progress being made in reducing taxation of capital gains.

Lower tax rates on capital gains encourage more people with ideas to risk their time, and more people with money to risk their capital. They also enable successful entrepreneurs and investors to build capital faster, thereby speeding up the cycle of success that is so important to the development of new clusters of activity in rapidly evolving industries. In the words of Paul J. Hill, president and chief executive officer of Harvard Developments Inc. — A Hill Company: "Eighty to ninety percent of start-ups are going to be in some technologically related industry. Give people the opportunity to start their company in Canada and the incentive to keep and grow it in this country. Ultimately these companies will become larger, compete in world markets, and be taxed in this country as opposed to other jurisdictions."[56]

Other countries have jumped ahead of Canada in choosing to reduce taxation of capital gains. The United States lowered its capital gains tax from a single rate of 28 percent to 20 percent for assets held by individuals for at least a year and a half. In the United Kingdom, the Labour government announced plans to cut its rate on capital gains to just 10 percent on assets held for five years or more. In Germany, a coalition of Social Democrats and Greens eliminated capital gains taxes on equities held by the corporate sector as a means of facilitating restructuring. And Australia unveiled a tax overhaul that will cut the top capital gains tax rate to 24.25 percent from 50 percent on assets held longer than a year.

In 2000 the compelling logic of such policies finally became clear to political leaders in Canada. In May 2000, for instance, the Standing Senate Committee on Banking, Trade and Commerce headed by Liberal senator Leo Kolber recommended that Canada quickly cut its capital gains tax to match the rate in the United States. Furthermore, it said, international competitiveness should be the criterion guiding the choice of a capital gains tax regime, and the federal government should be prepared to lower the tax until that criterion is met.

While a lower capital gains tax could make the tax system slightly less progressive and lead to minor losses in revenues, the committee concluded that it would improve Canada's international competitiveness, enhance the mobility of investments, create more wealth, accelerate business and job creation, and enhance economic activity and productivity. More to the point, it added, Canada has no choice if it wants to flourish in the New Economy. "It is the future prosperity of all Canadians that is at stake. By maintaining a policy of high taxation of capital gains, Canada is running the risk of falling behind and declining in economic terms — a situation where everybody is economically worse off. This Committee believes that reducing the tax rate on capital gains will result in a richer society that will make all Canadians better off."[57]

The federal government already had made some moves in this direction in the February 2000 budget, cutting the percentage of capital gains included in taxable income from 75 percent to 67 percent, improving the tax treatment of stock options, and allowing limited deferral of tax on capital gains that were rolled over into new ventures. But it was the province of Ontario that pushed the envelope that spring by using its 2000 budget to chop the capital-gains inclusion rate provincially from two-thirds to one-half. By changing the definition of taxable income within the province, this unilateral move threatened to lead to more paperwork for taxpayers and a balkanization of Canadian definitions and policies. In the end, the federal government decided to follow suit and match the 50 percent capital-gains inclusion rate in its October budget update.

The changes Canada has made on this front do not remove all the impediments to entrepreneurial investment and growth. New business owners enjoy better treatment of their gains, and stock options have become more attractive for employees of public companies. But the very speed of progress in reducing taxation of capital gains has widened existing disparities in the treatment of employees of businesses that choose to continue growing as private companies. Such companies often try to provide compensation equivalent to equity or stock options through so-called phantom shares. This form of compensation helps private companies avoid complications that may be caused by expanding the ranks of shareholders, but gains on phantom shares are taxed as regular employment income, which is now double the tax rate on gains from real shares or options.

One of those affected is Howard Mann, president and chief executive officer of McCain Foods Limited. He suggests that private companies competing on the global stage have the same need to recruit and retain talent as public companies. "Do Canada's many excellent privately owned businesses need or deserve less able, less motivated and less well-rewarded non-owner, 'outside' executives than do public companies? I suggest not. If that is so, this is neither a wise or fair tax on non-owner executives."[58]

Although considerable progress has been made, the process of tax reduction and tax reform is far from over. First, we have to be aware that our competitors for people and capital understand the same economic logic, and we should expect their rates of taxation on capital gains to continue falling as well. Even within Canada, the Progressive Conservative

Party made the complete elimination of capital gains tax part of its election platform for the autumn 2000 election. To the extent that Canada wants to stimulate innovation and entrepreneurial activity, it makes sense to continue reducing taxes on personal and corporate incomes generally, and on investment and savings in particular.

■ Innovation in Government

Taxation is not the only way for governments to affect, for better or for worse, the process of innovation. Government policies, programs, and regulations can all have a powerful impact on what people and companies choose to do with their capital. The behaviour of governments as customers, as suppliers, and as employers is also critical to the country's success or failure in creating a culture of innovation within Canada, as is the way that different levels of government work together in the national interest. Finally, the use of new technologies could become a catalyst for innovation not just in the delivery of public services but in the very nature of the relationship between governments and citizens.

We looked earlier at the abysmal record of Canadian governments in their efforts to use grants, loans, and other subsidies to reduce regional disparities and promote industrial development. Success in the global economy depends on attacking rather than preserving the status quo. If governments want Canadians to put their money into innovative new ventures, they must ensure that rewards flow from market success, not bureaucratic approval. Incentives must encourage risk-taking, not grant-taking. They must help capital shift from less productive uses to more productive ones.

To its credit, the federal government has slashed business subsidies dramatically over the past decade. It should continue to do so — as long as it improves the incentives for success at the same time. As with tax policy, the driving principle behind any Canadian subsidy that remains should be the need to ensure a competitive base for Canadian companies, not to protect existing jobs under all circumstances.

In seeking to build a society based on innovation, governments must do more than curtail ineffective corporate handouts. They must also ensure that the management of their own activities lives up to their professed support for innovation. Nothing illustrates the gap between rhetoric and practice better than health care. We have already talked about the importance of seeking greater efficiency in health care in our efforts to preserve a wide range of universally accessible and high-quality public services. Yet the way public health care is run today tends to discourage innovation.

Canada's Research-Based Pharmaceutical Companies (Rx&D) have documented numerous examples of the value of new medicines. For example, clinical trials show that new cholesterol-reducing drugs cut death rates from coronary heart disease by 42 percent and reduce hospitalizations by 30 percent. To take another example, schizophrenia affects 300,000 Canadians between the ages of 16 and 30, and nearly one-third of the nation's homeless. These Canadians occupy one in twelve hospital beds at an annual cost of $2.3 billion. About 30 percent of these patients could benefit from drug therapies that would reduce the annual cost per person to $4,500 in drugs from $39,000 in hospitalization.[59] From cardiovascular diseases and cholesterol to osteoporosis and ulcers, pharmaceutical companies have been able to develop advances in treatment that both improve health outcomes and reduce the overall cost to the health system. Governments, however, have failed to ensure that cost-effective innovations are adopted quickly and used effectively to improve the health of Canadians and the efficiency of the public health care system.

Drug budgets are often managed separately from hospital budgets. Even when a new drug could replace much more expensive hospital treatment of a given condition, the bureaucrats in charge of the drug budget resist providing public coverage because their costs would rise. As a result, patients faced with a choice between a drug they must pay for personally and hospital care they can receive at no charge will choose the treatment that costs them less — but is more expensive for taxpayers. To ensure that governments reap the full economic benefits of innovative treatments and technologies, they must do a better job of managing health care across the full spectrum of services.

The gaps in Canada's current approach translate into two troubling results: public health care costs more than it should, and lower-income Canadians get inferior care. As Statistics Canada noted in a 1999 study, only 61 percent of Canadians aged 15 or older had insurance coverage for prescription drugs in 1996/97. That figure dropped to 52 percent for people who were not working. "Only 38 percent of lower income groups had insurance compared with 74 percent of the highest income group.

Regardless of the number of chronic diseases individuals had, those with drug insurance were more likely to report taking medication."[60]

In addition to restricting the range of new drugs accepted for public coverage, Canada takes longer than other major industrialized countries to approve new drugs for use. In 1999 the approval process took an average of 591 days — more than nineteen months — almost seven months longer than in the United States.[61] These protracted approval times make Canadians wait longer for the benefits of new treatments and raise the cost and risk of developing new therapies.

According to Paul Lucas, president and chief executive officer of Glaxo Wellcome Inc., the inability of pharmaceutical companies to get timely access for their innovations, together with Canada's shaky performance in the protection of intellectual property, threatens both the quality of health care and the country's reputation as a place to invest. "Despite significant investment in Canada," he says, "our patent protection lags behind the United States, Japan, and other leading countries. At the provincial level, it is increasingly difficult to get our new products reimbursed through provincial drug plans, even after we demonstrate the value of these new innovations to patients and the health care system. My concern is the perception that Canada is not keeping up. It is talking innovation and talking productivity, but it does not yet have the policy frameworks in place to do the job. When you're behind, you can't just run as fast as everybody else. You've got to run faster."[62]

Although pharmaceutical research and development investments in Canada have grown dramatically over the past decade, this country continues to fall behind its G-7 competitors. According to Canada's Research-Based Pharmaceutical Companies, pharmaceutical research and development investment in the United States is now thirty-seven times greater than in Canada. "Price controls, lengthy delays in drug reviews and the refusal of provincial drug plans to reimburse seniors for new and more effective pharmaceuticals all contribute to placing Canada at a competitive disadvantage for research investment and impede the ability of Canadian patients to access the best new therapies . . . Since the introduction of prescription drug price controls in Canada a decade ago, prices of available prescription medicines in Canada have become among the lowest in the developed world. But Canadians are paying, with their health, for drug price controls and restrictions on the availability of new drugs."[63]

Claudio Bussandri, president and chief executive officer of Medis

Health and Pharmaceutical Services Inc., suggests that the American health care system may be more fragmented, but the profit motive provides a greater incentive to move quickly in adopting new technologies that can improve the quality of care while reducing costs. "The Americans understand that investment in technology will yield a payback. Here, each of the provinces has budget constraints. On paper they understand that investments in technology are necessary and will save them money, but they don't follow through in practice. We've launched a number of pilot projects in hospitals and sometimes covered the costs for two or three years. But after we prove that our services provide real savings and we want to start charging a modest fee, they say they can't afford it. The American system has its own inefficiencies, but they more readily understand that investment in systems or technologies will pay back their costs. The fact that everything here is government-mandated means there's more red tape. Persuading governments and health institutions to buy into new ideas takes a lot longer."[64]

This reluctance to embrace innovation is not limited to health care. Investments in infrastructure in particular tend to put short-term job creation ahead of long-term economic benefit to taxpayers. The Ontario government broke with tradition when it decided to finance a new highway bypassing Toronto as a toll road in partnership with private interests. Highway 407, subsequently sold in its entirety to an international consortium that includes Canada's SNC-Lavalin Group Inc., did more than act as a proving ground for new toll technology that uses transponders and cameras for automatic billing instead of toll booths. Because the private sector partners were responsible for costs over the entire life cycle of the highway, they opted for construction techniques and materials that were more expensive initially, but would result in a road that lasted longer and would need less maintenance. Roads that need frequent repair have attractions for elected officials by providing a recurring requirement for construction contracts and politically visible job creation. But when highways are built by owners who have to worry about the financial, as opposed to the political, returns on their investment, they opt for greater efficiency.

Jacques Lamarre, president and chief executive officer of SNC-Lavalin, says he sees governments shifting towards better economic decisions because their citizens are now demanding to know how much it really costs to get the services they want. "The Highway 407 contract was the rare occasion where I saw a government that did not keep for itself any political discretion on who would get the job. They made the decision only on the numbers. I have a lot of respect for that kind of government."[65]

External purchasing is one option that makes the costs and benefits of different alternatives more transparent. But contracting out need not be the only path to public sector innovation. In particular, as suggested by the Centre for Collaborative Government, the use of new technologies could have a huge impact on both the cost and the effectiveness of government services:

> *Information technology such as electronic service delivery, e-commerce, and 24-hour telephone and kiosk services is one important tool for improving service delivery. It can fundamentally change the way that services are provided to the public. It has the power to improve communications and access (broader audiences and easier dissemination of information and services), to improve efficiency and effectiveness (single-window one-stop service delivery), and to increase citizen participation and influence in government decision- and policy-making (interactive policy development and on-line discussion groups). These powerful attributes can make it a good candidate for improving service delivery at the citizen level, where more public involvement can be a way of strengthening the protection of rights.*[66]

In this context, it is instructive to consider what happened when the government of Ontario designed and tested a system of automated kiosks for delivering services — a network similar to the automated tellers used by banks. The efficiencies of ATMs are well known. In banking, one American study said that the cost of a transaction at an automated teller is just 3 percent of the cost of providing the same transaction through a branch. ServiceOntario started modestly, offering transportation services such as licence plate sticker renewals and fine payments. A range of services offered by other departments was added as the benefits became clear. The system was designed in partnership with IBM Canada Ltd., which built and owned the terminals and received a fee per transaction. The government shared the risk by guaranteeing a minimum volume, giving both sides a stake in encouraging increased use of the terminals. An initial pilot project was quickly expanded to a network of sixty-four terminals across the province. Then the problems began.

The first issue involved the $1 service fee for using the machines. Kim

CREATING AN INNOVATION SOCIETY

Devooght, the IBM government executive in charge of the project and now general manager, federal public sector, IBM Canada Ltd., has noted that even modest service fees for using automated kiosks have a big impact on usage. In Arizona, for instance, only 4 percent of the population used electronic service delivery while an initial $6.95 fee was in place. When the fee was dropped, usage jumped to 21 percent. "All things being equal, government should encourage the public to use the channels that are the least cost to the system," Devooght said. "It doesn't make sense to put user fees on the most efficient channel."[67]

That was not the only problem. The machines were initially installed in government service outlets — but, in one office, the staff hung an "out of order" sign on the machine because they feared it would lead to job losses. The kiosks were moved to shopping malls. Public servants were not the only ones to feel threatened by change. The ServiceOntario kiosks also compete with a network of franchised motor vehicle licence offices. These privately owned outlets were at one time patronage vehicles, and even though operators are no longer politically appointed, they remain a potent lobby group. Since every transaction going through a machine is a lost customer to these outlets, they succeeded not only in blocking the expansion of the kiosk network beyond sixty-four machines but in preventing the government from advertising even the existence of the machines, much less their potential convenience.

The lesson is clear. New technologies offer opportunities for governments to simplify service delivery, reduce duplication, integrate programs, improve the speed and quality of service, and do it all at a lower cost to taxpayers. But even the modest degree of innovation involved in automating services requires strong political leadership. The benefits to all citizens could be immense. As Paul Thomas of the University of Manitoba put it, "a glittering array of innovations holds the potential to improve relationships between governments and citizens in various roles: as customers (Web sites, electronic transactions, e-mail, etc.), clients (electronic benefits transfer, smart cards, one-stop shopping, data linking, etc.), and as active citizens (opinion polls, Web sites, networks, etc.). Ideally, information technology will contribute to the revitalization of government, making public bureaucracies more accessible, trustworthy and more proficient by supporting better policy learning, knowledge generation, information management, service delivery and democratic practice."[68]

Standing in the way of such innovations are the realities of our political system. Thomas notes that Canadians profess a desire for leadership, but tend overwhelmingly to blame politicians when government initiatives go wrong. "Today, many Canadians subscribe to a negative stereotype of politics and politicians. At its worst, politics is seen to involve grasping for power for its own sake, opportunistic, unprincipled and self-interested behaviour, an inflated sense of self-importance, corruption and patronage, the avoidance of responsibility and accountability, and the mindless denigration of one's political opponents and their ideas. Some measure of scepticism towards politics and politicians is healthy in a democracy, but a deep and persistent cynicism towards all things political deprives the governance process of the skills, wisdom and legitimacy that only political activities can provide."[69]

The result in Canada, as elsewhere, is a public service culture that tends to live in fear of making mistakes rather than trying to innovate. As authors David Osborne and Peter Plastrik put it in *Banishing Bureaucracy*, government organizations are creatures of the political process. "They become footballs in political contests, kicked from one end of the field to another. They undergo hostile scrutiny from legislators, lobbyists, interest groups, and the media . . . In response, organizations learn to defend themselves. Sometimes they ignore and ward off the outside world; at other times, they kowtow and please. Typically, they blame elected officials and interest groups for whatever is wrong with governments. And because they are afraid they will be blamed when things go badly, they take few chances."[70]

In 1999 a series of roundtable discussions hosted by the federal government in partnership with the Institute for Public Administration of Canada, the Business Council on National Issues, the Public Policy Forum, and the Conference Board of Canada came to a similar conclusion. The talks involved federal and provincial public servants and elected officials, along with academics and representatives of business and non-profit organizations. According to the final report by Kenneth Kernaghan, the evolution of politics as a "blood sport" and the reluctance of politicians to tolerate mistakes discourages initiatives that involve the taking of risk:

> *It is unlikely that elected officials, especially ministers, will be amused by public exposure of mistakes made by innovative, risk-taking public servants, no matter how honourable the public servants' intentions. Opposition politicians are poised to pounce on any government errors that will help to enhance*

> their political fortunes . . . However, successful government reform depends significantly on innovative behaviour by public servants — and innovation often involves risk-taking. If elected officials, on both sides of the legislature, do not tolerate mistakes arising from reasonable risk-taking, then public organizations will not perform at the highest possible level, and pride in the public service — and public servants' pride in themselves — will suffer.[71]

Brian Davies, a senior vice-president at the Royal Bank of Canada and co-chair of the roundtables, later commented that we need to encourage public servants to manage, rather than avoid, risk. "To avoid all risks stifles innovation and truly dampens the pride and job satisfaction that comes from being creative. But taking risks also leads to some failures. I fear that the political culture in Canada of late is far too intolerant of administrative failures of *any* magnitude, in *any area*. These attitudes must change, and the change must be led by the elected officials who oversee the public service." On the other hand, he suggested, public servants should not use the fear of political consequences as an excuse for avoiding good motivational management. "This defeatism about being able to be creative or innovative in personnel practices is symptomatic of poor management practices overall. 'Risk aversion' leads to no 'managed risk taking' whatsoever."[72]

Most Canadians think more highly of public servants than the public servants themselves realize. A 1998 survey of Canadians' attitudes to public sector service suggested that we understand the difficulty of the diverse tasks we hand to governments and that we are reasonably satisfied with many of the services we receive. Respondents rated fire departments and public libraries as offering better service than supermarkets, ranked police services ahead of telephone companies, and Canada Post ahead of banks. Yet key services such as public education, hospitals, and road maintenance ranked much lower in terms of citizen satisfaction. In giving their ratings, 54 percent of respondents agreed that "governments have a more difficult task than the private sector." Such recognition, however, did not reduce their expectations. Fully 42 percent still felt they should get a higher level of service from government than from the private sector, and another 53 percent said it should be at least as good.[73]

Charles Handy, one of the world's most respected management thinkers, suggests that, in a democracy, political leaders tend to be followers, and governments therefore are unlikely to be innovative. "I think in a democracy you can't step too far out in front of where everybody is or you won't get elected," he says. "So what politicians tend to do is to sense where the majority would be in about a year's time . . . The innovations in society do not come from governments or politicians . . . they come from private institutions, basically businesses that see an opportunity to make a difference and make money."[74]

In today's world, however, the biggest risk even for politicians is to do nothing. Just as in the private sector, the speed of change makes the probability of failure in any specific initiative higher than ever. But for leaders of companies and of countries, the rewards for smart choices have grown as well. Taking risks does not guarantee success, but refusing to take risks ensures failure.

If Canada as a whole is to triumph in the global economy, governments must look beyond the challenge of simply managing resources more efficiently. In building a culture of innovation, we need to look first at how different levels of government can build more effective relationships with each other and with citizens, and then at how all the sectors of our society can work together in new and better ways.

■ Innovation in Governance

Canadian federalism has proven itself to be an amazingly flexible vehicle for meeting the evolving needs of Canadians. Progress, however, tends to be slow and uneven. The Social Union Agreement promised a new era of cooperation, but did not prevent new rounds of conflict over health care funding. The health care accord of September 2000 dealt with the funding issue, but left only a weak commitment to reporting and accountability on a national basis. The Council of Ministers of Education, Canada, is still struggling to promote pan-Canadian cohesion in education, but has at least broken the logjam of unanimity by enabling new ideas to be developed by consortia of like-minded provinces. Cooperation and consultation among environment and energy ministers on global climate change negotiations did not prevent their consensus from being tossed out the window in the heat of the haggling in Kyoto.

Nothing illustrates the tortured progress of intergovernmental relations in Canada more vividly than the Agreement on Internal Trade. Robert Knox, the executive director of the federal Internal Trade Secretariat during the negotiations that produced the AIT in 1993 and 1994, recently concluded that the substance of the deal is relatively solid, but its structure is "built on quicksand" and has failed to ensure free trade within Canada. There are still clearer and more enforceable rules between Canada and the United States or Mexico than between British Columbia and Ontario.

In particular, he has suggested, the process for resolving disputes is "byzantine, expensive, time-consuming and, ultimately, pointless." Governments can flaunt it freely, because the only way to enforce decisions is for one provincial government to retaliate against another by erecting still more barriers to trade. To salvage the agreement, he recommends four steps. First, the overall agreement must be simplified and contradictions removed. Second, dysfunctional chapters such as those on investment, consumer standards, natural resource processing, energy, and transportation must be overhauled. Third, the dispute resolution process must be made shorter and simpler and be handed over to third party adjudicators. Finally, the consequences of violating the deal have to become more serious, perhaps by allowing aggrieved parties to sue offending provinces for damages.[75]

Donald Savoie has suggested that the endless rounds of jurisdictional conflict are leading to a centralization of power within the federal government. "In Canada national unity concerns and the nature of federal-provincial relations tend, in a perverse fashion, to favour the centre of government in Ottawa. They dominate our policy agenda and permeate government decision making to such an extent that the centre of government is only willing to trust itself to oversee their overall management." What is more, he suggests, "there is no indication that the one person who holds all the cards, the prime minister, and the central agencies which enable him to bring effective political authority to the centre, are about to change things."[76]

The process of governing is not immune from the forces of globalization and technological change. As Paul Thomas puts it, "power remains significantly concentrated in the hands of the prime minister and the cabinet, but government operates today within a web of multiple linkages to other governmental and non-governmental institutions, actors and processes. As a result, the core executive of the state has become the site of complex interactions in the policy process. Continuous flux, multiple interconnections, shared power and the necessity for collaboration are the new realities of governance."[77]

Harvey Lazar, director of the Institute of Intergovernmental Relations at Queen's University, has pointed out that the days when federal and provincial governments could work independently are long gone because the issues that matter to citizens do not respect jurisdictional boundaries. He suggests that governments should take four key steps in their efforts to work together more effectively. First, they must try to spring fewer surprises on one another. Second, the federal government must stop dealing with big structural issues within "the political hothouse of its annual budget cycle." Third, the concept of mutual respect has to become embedded in all dealings between the two orders of government. And, finally, there needs to be clear agreement on key goals of public policy, notably economic efficiency and equity among people and between regions. "Effective partnerships require trust among the partners. Such trust is very hard to build when there is no agreed sense of purpose or at least an agreed set of ground rules for managing both collaboration and conflict."[78]

In the meantime, as governments continue to lurch from one turf battle to the next, technology is putting powerful new tools into the hands of individual citizens. Just as e-commerce and the Internet are changing the balance of power between companies and consumers, they are having an impact on the relationship between governments and people as citizens and voters. The Alliance for Converging Technologies (now known as Digital 4Sight) suggested in 1999 that young, educated, and Internet-savvy citizens are emerging as key players in the future of government. "The advent of digital politics is already visible in the growth of online campaigning and Internet-based grassroots organizing. This will ultimately rewrite the rules of political competition and lobbying. The technologies that are adopted for political organizing must be harnessed in support of broader government and political objectives."[79]

People want more choices and more control over the details of their lives — and global integration and new technologies are helping them get it. But as Joseph Nye Jr., dean of the John F. Kennedy School of Government at Harvard University, has noted, the proliferation of choices for individuals can undermine traditional roles of government in ensuring equality of opportunity. "The more people can make micro-choices and control their own lives the better. But as we pursue that, it is worth remembering that the larger policy choices we make will have a lot to do with the quality of the communities we live in and whether there are public goods shared in those communities. In that sense, as we watch the way in which these new forces are changing our democracies — and they are changing — it's worth remembering that some of the policy choices we make will determine whether they're all for the good or some may be for the worse."[80]

In response to the growing influence of Internet-empowered citizens, governments are rushing to embrace a new model of governance, usually dubbed the "citizen-centred" approach. As we have already discussed, this attitude goes far beyond the question of how governments provide services. According to Frank Graves, president of Ekos Research Associates Inc., the citizen-centred approach concentrates on access to opportunity rather than equality of outcomes; on partnering with other sectors rather than acting as parent; on horizontal cooperation rather than vertical control; on coordination rather than delivery; and on results and outcomes rather than resources and inputs.[81]

Real progress towards citizen-centred governance depends on the direct engagement of individual citizens, not just of interest groups. Research by the Canadian Policy Research Networks Inc. has shown that citizens have a real impact when they get involved in setting goals and choosing benchmarks for measuring progress towards those goals. For instance, in a survey of various attempts to assemble a set of indicators that would measure quality of life, CPRN noted a marked difference between those that involved significant citizen participation and those that did not. Those that did not engage citizens produced sets of indicators heavily weighted towards health and economic security. Community and citizen-driven projects, by contrast, included a broader range of indicators that gave much greater importance to the environment and the community, physical security, education, and culture.[82]

There is more to building an innovative democracy, however, than simply enabling large numbers of people to participate in the process. As Clifford Cobb and Craig Rixford of the American organization Redefining Progress note: "Many indicators groups seem to start with the implicit and tenuous assumption that procedural justice will automatically bring about substantive justice. According to this view, social indicators will lead to better social outcomes if they are developed by a broad representation of community members. In practice, however, an insistence on achieving a consensus of stakeholders or citizens usually produces a set of indicators that do little to challenge prevailing practices."[83]

To sum up the resulting dilemma, the process of globalization has made many people fearful of losing control over their lives at the same time as it has given them new power as both consumers and citizens. Amid worries that multinational corporations are achieving dominance over nation states, individual citizens are demanding and achieving greater influence over both political and corporate governance. And, in the very process of building a better model of society through more effective citizen engagement, we risk eviscerating bold and innovative leadership through consensus-driven resistance to change.

This dilemma does not mean we should or could try to drive the development of a new Canada without the engagement and support of citizens. Rather, it means that leaders in government, business, and the non-profit sector have to be much more effective in working together to achieve the goals Canadians share. As technology transforms work and as jobs move with increasing ease around the world, we need to recruit leaders across the full spectrum of public life, leaders who are generalists and who bridge the gaps between sectors. As a paper from the John F. Kennedy School of Government at Harvard put it, the stakes are high:

> Perceptions differ on the large-scale social effects of this digitized economy. The pessimistic view sees displaced workers, frayed bonds of civic identity, and inequitable distributions of income and wealth. The optimistic scenario sees the greater productivity enabled by networking as the creator of tangible benefits throughout society — at least in the long term. To realize the optimistic vision, however, government leaders will need to forge sustaining partnerships with the private sector to create both educational and employment opportunities in accordance with the competitive dynamics of the global economy.[84]

■ Innovation in Society

In essence, the speed of global change means that simply rethinking the size, role, and efficiency of government is not enough. We have to re-examine our social contract, the implicit web of obligations and responsibilities that binds us together as a country and as a society. But as Harvey Lazar observed with respect to intergovernmental relationships, before we can build more effective partnerships across sectors, we first must recognize that people as diverse as social activists, business leaders, and public servants do, in fact, have shared goals. In particular, we need to develop a better understanding of the convergence of interests within our society, the vital links between economic and social success.

Canadians have already learned the hard way that governments are not the answer to all our problems, any more than unfettered markets can be expected to produce an equitable society. Governments and the private sector both have important roles to play — cooperative roles — in building a better society. But we cannot expect to come up with a successful Canadian model of economic and social success unless our concept of partnership crosses all sectors of society. Sherri Torjman of the Caledon Institute described it this way in 1998: "There is a growing sense that bureaucracies and the compartmentalized way in which governments typically address social needs often create more problems than they resolve. Governments are organized to deal with human problems as if these can be separated into distinct social, health, education and economic categories . . . Most public spending is directed towards a component of a particular issue or towards the alleviation of crisis in the form of remedial intervention after a problem has occurred. Partnerships that involve different sectors represent an important step in recognizing the complexities of most social, economic and environmental issues."[85]

The key to reinforcing Canada's ability to deal with these complexities is the engagement of the 175,000 non-profit organizations through which some 7.5 million Canadians contribute more than a billion hours of volunteer labour every year. Voluntary organizations enrich public policy debate by creating greater awareness of the issues affecting Canada's most marginalized citizens. They are able to deliver services to segments of society that neither business nor government can reach. They are a source of innovative ideas for improving service delivery. They reinforce the concept of citizenship by providing ways for people to express their commitment to making our society a better place: "Life's rapid pace and increasing changes can often lead people to retreat inwardly, when the real challenge is to reach out and participate in community-initiated action. The sector's bridge-building endeavors promote understanding, awareness, inclusion, and social justice — locally, regionally, nationally and around the world."[86]

At the same time, global economic integration and technological change are pushing the corporate sector to expand links with the voluntary sector. Corporate restructuring and the resulting wave of global mergers and acquisitions have weakened some of the traditional ties between corporations and the communities in which they operate. But even as the Internet gives consumers the power to squeeze profit margins by seeking out the best quality at the lowest price anywhere in the world, so it enables concerned citizens to expose unethical or illegal corporate behaviour no matter where it may occur.

Corporations realize that maintaining their credibility and managing their reputations on a worldwide front have become vital strategic issues that affect shareholder value. Demonstrating good corporate citizenship therefore becomes, at the very least, a condition for maintaining a licence to operate within any modern society. As we discussed in the previous chapter, a company's reputation and behaviour are increasingly relevant to its ability to recruit and retain the people it needs to compete in the global economy.

This heightened attention to the strategic importance of corporate community investment comes at a time when public expectations of the private sector are rising. The policy thrusts of the past two decades — freer trade and investment, tax reform, balanced budgets, and the battle against inflation — have brought benefits to all Canadians, but they are seen as having been driven by business interests. One of the consequences of budget squeezing by Canadian governments was decreased support for many organizations in the voluntary sector. Another was increased demand for social services from those same organizations. Since governments are the major funders for many charitable organizations, the voluntary sector was hit simultaneously by growing demand and shrinking financial resources.

This crisis led to sharply increased competition for support from the corporate sector. But direct corporate donations make up only a small fraction of the money received by the non-profit sector, so modest cuts in government funding meant shortfalls that even a dramatic rise in corporate donations could not overcome. And, even as charities had to compete more intensely for corporate support, they found that governments had become competitors for the same funds, trying to stretch their budgets by tapping companies for contributions to public-private partnerships. "Today the charitable sector faces many of the challenges that the public and private sectors have had to deal with over the past decade," according to a paper from the Imagine program of the Canadian Centre for Philanthropy.[87]

Major companies receive thousands of applications for funding every year. Just reviewing these applications is expensive, and many have little hope of approval because they do not fit the company's priorities. Charities are equally frustrated: the application process is growing more complex, yet many companies do not publish their criteria for donations. This breakdown in communications in the process of meeting day-to-day needs hurts the relationship between the corporate and the voluntary sectors — a relationship that is changing from one based on philanthropy to one founded on true partnerships. As Imagine put it:

> Partnerships are more complex than the traditional philanthropic gift framework that most charities are familiar with. Charities often have neither the experience nor the skill sets necessary to negotiate sophisticated partnership contracts or agreements. In the absence of clear guidelines and agreed standards such as measurement of outcomes and recognition of sponsors, frustrations and misunderstandings often arise. Charities also need to be willing [to make] and capable of forming partnerships with other non-profit organizations when necessary, and must be prepared to recognize more fully the contribution of business.[88]

The trend towards greater measurement and accountability marks a major change for the voluntary sector. Traditionally, it was enough that an organization identified a social problem and made a visible contribution to dealing with it. Now funders want to quantify the goals and measure progress. Yet the expertise of most voluntary organizations is in delivering results rather than measuring them. Especially in smaller organizations, there is neither the time nor the ability to meet demands for detailed data gathering and analysis.

Business investments in the community are driven by results rather than needs. Corporate funders want to know not only that the projects in which they invest will make a difference in people's lives but that these projects will do so more effectively than available alternatives. Voluntary organizations seeking funding are faced with demands for both cost efficiency and results. Evaluation does not have to be elaborate. The smaller the project, the simpler the goals and the measurement ought to be. Still, one way or another, the more that non-profit agencies look to corporations for funding, the more they are being expected to behave entrepreneurially.

Through this stressful and uneven process, both the private and the non-profit sectors are gradually coming to terms with the real meaning of partnership. Traditional philanthropy, based on arm's-length donations to good causes, leaves the recipient in charge of how the money is spent and how services are delivered. Corporate sponsorships, in contrast, give clear overall authority to the sponsor. The struggle today is to develop relationships in which both parties bring value to the table and work together in pursuit of shared goals.

While there remains a need to boost the overall contributions the private sector makes to community development, more effective partnerships could help companies and communities alike realize more value from the resources that are available. Through such a value-added approach, Imagine suggests, companies "are able to align their giving with their mission, skills, competencies, and employee and customer interests in a way that provides real returns for the company, charities and the community."[89]

The federal government–voluntary sector roundtables of the past two years have led to action on many of the resulting twenty-six recommendations. The government in mid-2000 committed $90 million in additional funding and other actions intended to strengthen the financial, human resource, knowledge, and structural capacity of the voluntary sector. It has also agreed to improve the regulatory framework governing the sector. These changes will, in turn, help the process of reshaping relationships between the private and the voluntary sectors that are being spearheaded by Imagine.

Critical to success in this realignment of relationships and responsibilities is recognition that the commitment of resources to the non-profit sector by business and government alike is not charity. It is an investment in structural change within our society. "The fact is, many recipients of business largesse often don't need charity; they need change. Not spare change, but real change — sustainable, replicable, institutionalized change that transforms their schools, their job prospects, and their neighborhoods. And that means getting business deeply involved in non-traditional ways," said Harvard University professor Rosabeth Moss Kanter in a 1999 article for the *Harvard Business Review*.[90] True innovation within society, she suggested, is able to flourish only if each sector is contributing what it does best. Traditional charity and volunteer work is still important, but rarely the best way to foster innovation in society. Businesses that want to make a real contribution to the social sector must look less to their budgets than to their core competencies. The results can be impressive:

CREATING AN INNOVATION SOCIETY

partnerships that not only produce measurable results but build capabilities and foster enduring improvements within the community. In this model, businesses can win, too, reaping public recognition as well as new products, new ideas, and new business opportunities.

Companies in Canada, as in the United States, have traditionally offered support for the social sector in two ways: through direct donations of cash and gifts in kind, and as catalysts for volunteer activities by employees. These methods are both useful, but, as Moss Kanter points out, they tend not to engage the unique skills and capabilities of a business. "It is important that businesses understand why the old models of corporate support don't create sustainable change. In partnership with government and non-profits, businesses need to go beyond the traditional models to tackle the much tougher task of innovation."[91]

Canadian communities are rich with examples of innovative and effective projects and partnerships driven by creative and entrepreneurial people. High-profile ceremonies such as the New Spirit of Community awards from Imagine and the Conference Board of Canada's recognition of outstanding business-education partnerships highlight success stories and help to inspire the spread of the best practices. But, despite the profusion of creative thinkers within our communities, we have yet to build a true society of innovation.

To build such a society requires continued structural change across the public, private, and non-profit sectors as well as a fundamental shift in attitude, one that embraces change for the opportunities it provides rather than fearing change for its threats. It requires a shared understanding at the gut level that none of us succeeds alone, that our social and economic progress are inextricably intertwined. We have to get over dated attitudes — that giving counts only if it hurts or that seeking to maximize profits benefits only shareholders.

Corporations can do more to build community success in ways that help their bottom line and sustain their growth. At the same time, governments can support both better social outcomes and more robust economic growth. And individual citizens and community-based voluntary organizations can be entrepreneurial without losing their souls. The challenge we face as Canadians is global. We're in it together. Every one of us has to contribute our creativity as we build the innovative society we will need to achieve our dreams together.

■ Accelerating Innovation

Accelerating the process of innovation in our society is critical to achieving Canada's social and economic goals. As the United States Council on Competitiveness put it in 1998, speed is everything in the New Economy. Technology cycle times are so rapid that no corporate executive can remain complacent and still hang on to industry leadership. Countries are playing leapfrog, with places like Bangalore, India, emerging as major high-technology hubs in the space of a decade. And the faster the pace of change, the more opportunities there are for new competitors to crash the party. "The line between global leader and also-ran has become very thin. . . . Leadership can shift within a few generations, and — especially in infotech — a generation can be as little as two or three years."[92]

An economy based on innovation must be rooted in a society dedicated to change. Any dedicated gardener knows that aggressive pruning is vital in promoting vigorous new growth. This strategy is equally important for countries wishing to promote vigorous growth in jobs and incomes in the knowledge economy of the twenty-first century. Despite the frenzied pace of global mergers and acquisitions, large companies have been shrinking as a share of total employment. This diminution does not mean that companies have stopped growing big. By 1999, for instance, the companies in the Fortune 500 employed roughly 5 million fewer people than in 1980, even though total employment in the United States had grown by 34 million. This figure does not mean that 5 million people lost their jobs — it is just that the membership of this top 500 group had changed dramatically. Its new members, including the likes of Microsoft, Cisco, and Intel, simply needed fewer employees to produce the kind of sales volume necessary to dominate the economy. Employment at these companies has grown dramatically, but they need fewer people for their size precisely because they are so much more productive.

Fostering more of these highly innovative, very productive, and fast-growing companies is the key to increasing both the overall number of jobs and average incomes. In "The State New Economy Index," for instance, the Progressive Policy Institute compared the strategies of American states with their success in achieving growth in recent years. The single most important factor in job creation was the number of companies known as gazelles — firms that increased their sales by at least 20 percent a year for four consecutive years. These companies accounted for almost three-quarters of all net new jobs. The more gazelles a state fostered, the more jobs it created. But the institute also found that herds of galloping gazelles were inevitably accompanied by fields of corporate corpses. The more often that companies failed as well as started up, the faster a state succeeded overall in generating more jobs. "Innovation and change mean uncertainty and disruption. But it is becoming increasingly clear that dynamism is critical to growth. (You can't have upward mobility if no one is on the move.)"

It is no coincidence that, in 1999, the United States, enjoying its longest stretch of economic expansion ever and, with unemployment at historic lows, reported a record number of layoffs. Capital has to shift out of old industries in order to fuel the growth of new, more productive, and better-paid jobs in other sectors. Companies have to take more risk — and therefore fail more often — if they want to achieve rapid growth. The institute concluded: "As markets fragment, technology accelerates and competition comes from unexpected places, learning, creativity and adaptation have become the principal sources of competitive advantage in many industries. Enabling constant innovation needs to become the goal of all organizations committed to prospering. Similarly, the goal for states must be to foster innovation and adaptation — in infrastructure, in institutions and on the part of individuals."[93]

This is a lesson that Canada's business leaders are taking to heart. In the words of BCE's Jean Monty: "If you don't get off your old horse to get onto the new one, you'll die with the old horse. As a society, we have to be able to shift our emphasis from old industries to new ones."[94] The Royal Bank's John Cleghorn agrees that tremendous opportunities will be opening up for Canadians in the early years of the new century. To seize those opportunities, however, we have to look at how Canada can turn its relatively small size into a plus in the competition for investment and jobs. "The advantage we have as a small country is that we should be able to move more quickly than others. But we have not geared ourselves up to be a rapid-deployment, mobile, flexible business environment. There's a perception that we're a good place to do business, but we don't have a market that is spawning the kind of innovation we're going to need if we want to be a leader ten years out."[95]

3M is a company renowned for its dedication to innovation, one that sets aside 15 percent of its employees' time and resources for undirected work and deliberately designs its buildings to force people to meet and talk. At an innovation conference in Toronto in November 2000, 3M Canada president and general manager Alex Cirillo suggested that a major difference between Canadians and Americans is the degree to which they believe they can be innovative. "Most of the barriers to innovation are self-imposed constraints. There is an important cultural issue that Canada has to face."[96]

Canada does have important strengths. We have plenty of smart, well-educated people, a solid social and economic infrastructure, and a firm base of expertise and capital across a wide range of industries. What we need now is a new attitude, one that embraces innovation and change as the keys to building better lives for all Canadians. As Finance Minister Paul Martin put it in his 2000 budget: "Together, we will build an economy based on innovation. For that, ultimately, is the only means by which a modern nation can control its future."[97]

Once we have made a real commitment to building an economy and a society that thrive on change, we can make Canada a magnet for new investment and the home base of choice for global enterprises.

6

BUILDING GLOBAL CHAMPIONS

> *There are arguably four stages to being a big global company. The first was corporate colonialism, under which companies either used foreign outposts as "dumb terminals" to distribute domestic goods or, through either laziness or a desire to be local, let those outposts develop lives of their own . . . The second stage, which most big companies had already passed through by the 1980s, might be described as the cheap-hands stage, in which big companies integrated their manufacturing along global lines but often did not bother to adapt them too much to local needs. The third stage might be described as the transnational one, when companies begin to use their foreign subsidiaries for ideas as well as production: they also tailor global products to local needs. The fourth stage has less to do with structure than state of mind: Businesses become genuinely multicultural multinationals in which the nationality of employees ceases to matter.[1]*
>
> — JOHN MICKLETHWAIT AND ADRIAN WOOLDRIDGE,
> A FUTURE PERFECT, *2000*

◄ ◄ ◄

The process of globalization is infectious. Companies that serve clients globally demand similar capability from their own suppliers. The traditional full-service country subsidiary is fading away as production is consolidated into plants that serve customers across continents and around the world. Management functions, too, are clustering as companies develop global centres of expertise that bring together people from many different countries. And, as companies collaborate and consolidate across borders, corporate cultures are evolving in ways that reduce the influence of their legal home base.

According to the United Nations Conference on Trade and Development (UNCTAD), the number of transnational companies continues to grow rapidly: 63,000 parent companies with 690,000 foreign affiliates by 1998.[2] These numbers keep growing, despite the well-publicized wave of cross-border mergers and acquisitions sweeping the world — 6,000 of them in 1999 alone — with a total value of $720 billion (U.S.). That value was up 35 percent from the previous year, and from $100 billion in 1987. Based on several mega-deals already announced, UNCTAD's mid-2000 World Investment Report estimated that the merger and acquisition total for 2000 could surpass $1 trillion. The pace of cross-border consolidation is unnerving to many national governments, and their regulatory bodies seem increasingly inclined to block or put conditions on major transactions. Nonetheless, UNCTAD suggests that "what is already happening may only be the beginning of a massive consolidation process at the regional and global levels."[3]

Mergers and acquisitions, however, are just one aspect of a global evolution in corporate strategy. Dezsö Horváth, dean of the Schulich School of Business at York University, has noted that, for a growing number of transnational corporations, the home country is no longer sacred territory. Instead, these companies are adopting "complex integration strategies" that allow any part of their activities to take place anywhere in the world. "These permit value-adding operations and sourcing to be carried out wherever they are most profitable. With complex integration, any affiliate or parent firm, regardless of its location, may itself or in combination with other affiliates perform functions for the firm as a whole."[4]

The challenge for Canada, therefore, goes beyond fostering home-grown global enterprises. This evolution of corporate strategy means that Canada must put greater focus on attracting international business investment in plants, laboratories, and head office functions serving the global market. In particular, it must aim to build up centres of expertise that provide an attractive base for carrying out high-value, rather than low-value, functions within the operations of increasingly multicultural

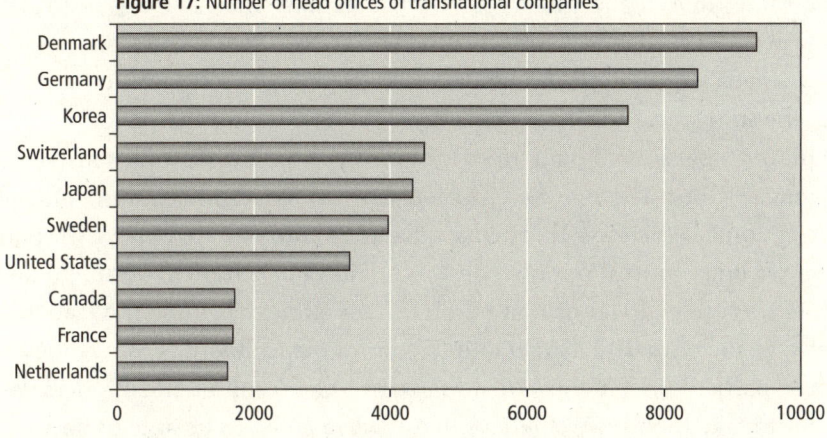

Figure 17: Number of head offices of transnational companies

transnational corporations. Our record to date is poor both in attracting such investment and in ensuring that Canadian companies engage in the global marketplace. Despite our integration with the larger North American market, UNCTAD figures suggest that Canada has fallen behind Belgium, Sweden, and the Netherlands as a host for foreign investment, and that it is home to fewer multinational corporations than Denmark, Sweden, Switzerland, or South Korea (see fig. 17).

What does it take for a country to attract investment in this increasingly borderless world of multinational and multicultural enterprises? What are our most important strengths and weaknesses — and how can we improve our odds of becoming home base to a growing number of high-paying jobs and successful enterprises within a global market? Given the triumphs and frustrations of our existing global champions, what it will take to make Canada a magnet for investment and jobs in the knowledge economy of the twenty-first century?

■ Global Champions in Action

Canada is already home to a solid core of companies that are not merely surviving but flourishing within the global economy. The problem is that Canada does not have enough of them.

Nortel Networks has shown what can be achieved from a Canadian base. Once the sleepy captive equipment-maker for a monopoly telephone company, it has transformed into a major global force in high technology. Others have followed its lead, quickly growing to global scale through acquisitions — JDS Uniphase in optical fibres, for instance. At the same time, many Canadian companies have instead been acquired, as when Newbridge Networks was taken over by French-based Alcatel.

Canada's leading players are all engaged actively in expansion abroad for the simple reason that Canada does not have enough room for them to achieve global scale. Bombardier Inc., for instance, has become another of Canada's global champions — in aerospace, mass transit equipment, and recreational vehicles — through acquisitions abroad. "We believe strongly that we must control our own destiny," said Robert Brown, president and chief executive officer of Bombardier. "Our strategy is to be the leader in selected niches in the market and to control the technology that relates to those particular segments. We don't want to be component suppliers. We want to take the risk. We believe that if we're going to be able to have the profit margins we need to prosper, we have to control the technology. And to do that, we have to be geographically diversified as well."[5]

The consolidation among manufacturers is leading to similar consolidation in transportation services. The railway business in North America, for instance, has seen a procession of mergers and acquisitions aimed at reducing costs while giving shippers seamless access to suppliers and customers across the continent. Canadian National has been a major participant, forging a pair of major merger deals in the United States. The first, with Illinois Central, extended its network of track south through the centre of the United States. The second, with Burlington Northern Santa Fe, would have made the combined operation one of the biggest in the continent. Even though this merger was blocked by American regulators, the growth imperative remains. "I believe that, in order to be a centre of excellence, we have to operate on a continental basis," said Paul Tellier, president and chief executive officer of Canadian National. "Either we will become a significant regional railroad or we become a continental player. If we don't become a continental player, it's going to have a major impact on Canadian shippers."[6]

Some companies have grown to positions of global leadership without ever establishing a major business base within Canada. Much of Canada's physical infrastructure is controlled by governments at the provincial and municipal level. Government procurement in turn frequently gives local companies an edge — despite the country's supposed commitment to a common internal market. As a result, major engineering firms such as SNC-Lavalin have built most of their business abroad. "When we compare ourselves with other engineering and construction firms in the world, people are always amazed to see the size of our international business, because our base in Canada is so small," said president and chief executive officer Jacques Lamarre. "Certainly a more unified Canadian construction market would help us become more competitive, but we like the way the world is heading, and we feel we have a major strategic advantage in satisfying the needs of the world in the future."[7] Even SNC-Lavalin's biggest investment at home, the purchase of Highway 407 from the government of Ontario, involves international links, in this case a partnership with an experienced toll-road operator based in Spain, Cintra Concesiones de Infraestructuras de Transporte. In an era in which governments are increasingly looking to the private sector to own and operate, as well as build, infrastructure, Canadian companies need to achieve both the scale to make major investments and the ability to form alliances and partnerships on a global basis.

Mergers and acquisitions are not always necessary for growth, as demonstrated by companies such as oil-sands specialist Suncor Energy Inc. But president and chief executive officer Rick George noted that the only alternative to being very big is to be very good within a narrow specialty. "If you want to survive as an independent player in the global economy, you have to pursue your specific advantage and do what others are not doing or can't do. We haven't made acquisitions of any size. No mergers, just focusing on what we do, so as to be the best at it in the world and drive it home. If you want to be successful, you really have got to find your niche and excel."[8]

As the global evolution of the financial services industry is making clear, however, size is becoming increasingly important even for niche players. "We have seen a tremendous pick-up in technology spending by our competitors around the world, and with the Internet and the advantage it gives to those who move first, settling for second is not good enough," said Charles Baillie, chairman and chief executive officer of TD Bank Financial Group. "The Internet has made scale much more important. We see it with our discount broker. We have had to move really quickly. In the space of a year, we had to double what we spend on our technology and double what we spend on our advertising. We have to get to be one of the top three or four names across North America. If we don't spend and get the brand known, others will pass us by. We have to do things on a much bigger scale than we really dreamed of before, and even if we're really good, it's incredibly uphill in this new world."[9]

John Cleghorn, chairman and chief executive officer, Royal Bank of Canada, suggested that whether or not Canadian companies want to go global, the depth, breadth, and quality of service needed to succeed abroad will be essential to survival and growth at home. "Canadians ultimately are going to want the best provider of financial services. They are not going to care about nationality. That has already been proven in mutual funds, which is a pretty broad-based product. There's no reason why it would not be so in credit cards. We've got to be good not just in Canada. We have to be good in a North American context."[10]

The recent spate of demutualization in the insurance industry is another sign of the drive for efficiencies through consolidation. Going public makes it possible for former mutual companies to raise the capital they will need for acquisitions, whether within Canada or beyond. "We want to create a world-class company that is based here in Canada," said Dominic D'Alessandro, president and chief executive officer of Manulife Financial. "To do that, we have to compete everywhere in the world. We can't build it on the Canadian population base. We can't ever have enough market in Canada to make us a player in the world league. Out of necessity, we have to expand abroad."[11]

Canadian ownership is not essential to the creation of global businesses from a Canadian base. Canadian subsidiaries have demonstrated an encouraging ability to nail down worldwide responsibilities within a global corporation. Pratt & Whitney Canada Corp., for instance, has for decades had a world product mandate for small aircraft engines, and through that mandate has won considerable autonomy. "We have never had a project we wanted to do that we have not been allowed to do," said former chairman and chief executive officer David Caplan. "As we grew and developed, we created a success. We were small, but we were more focused and we did the job. We kept going and we stayed profitable. We have earned our status, and through several generations of management the parent company has never tampered with the mandate. We have even been able to expand it."[12]

Other Canadian subsidiaries have been able to evolve into relatively autonomous centres of expertise within global corporations. In the previous chapter we mentioned two — Nestlé Canada Inc. in food products and HSBC Bank Canada in financial services — that have developed roles as global centres for product innovation and test marketing. Another is IBM Canada, which, having established a reputation for delivering solid results on a national basis, was successful in bidding for broader responsibilities when the parent company began organizing more operations along continental lines. "We have doubled the overall number of executives in Canada in the last two years and tripled the number of female executives," noted John Wetmore, president and chief executive officer of IBM Canada in late 1999. "Many of these people have responsibilities beyond Canada and focus on North America or worldwide mandates." In addition to becoming home to more executives with continental and global responsibilities, the Canadian subsidiary was able to win the job of providing telephone technical support to customers across North America. "In just two years, we built up a call centre in Toronto with 1,500 people in it. This is not low-level work. This requires university graduates. The technical talent that we have in Canada is phenomenal. And the diversity I would stack up against any city in the world. We speak twenty-three languages out of that call centre," Wetmore added. "The integration and the movement that is going on in the world has great potential to hurt Canada, but is also gives us the opportunity to play, if we are aggressive, innovative, and think things through. We have to be flexible, recognize worldwide economics, and pick our spots to develop roles for the Canadian subsidiary within the global corporation. It's a double-edged sword."[13]

Cross-border partnerships have also proved to be a sound foundation for the growth of Canadian-based global companies. Finning International Inc., for instance, started its life as a Caterpillar dealer in British Columbia, selling and servicing that brand of heavy equipment for the province's mining and forestry sectors. Over the years, Finning not only built a successful dealership in British Columbia but expanded its territory into Alberta and the North, and then persuaded the American manufacturer to let it take over dealerships in Chile and Britain. The result is a $2.5 billion company — and a fifty-year business relationship — built on the power of a simple dealership agreement that could be cancelled on ninety days' notice.[14]

Partnerships also play a role in the growth of Canadian jobs in the high technology sector. INTRIA-HP got its start with a decision by the Canadian Imperial Bank of Commerce (CIBC) to outsource some of its data processing. This work was highly specialized, requiring totally secure and extremely reliable processing of large volumes of data at very high speeds. These needs, however, are not unique to banking. From automotive manufacturing to e-commerce, a growing number of global companies need similar speed and reliability. The result was a joint venture between CIBC and Hewlett Packard, one that took advantage of the bank's existing data-processing facilities and expertise in combination with the American computer giant's sales network and globally respected brand. INTRIA-HP's potential customers are the largest corporations in the United States and around the world, but it is providing its services entirely from a Canadian base.

According to INTRIA-HP president Dan Branda, the cost of communications is quickly becoming insensitive to distance, so the company could operate globally — and could have located its computing centre anywhere. Toronto won out for two reasons. First, each of the two buildings housing its operations includes $100 million worth of equipment — facilities that already existed in Toronto and would have had to be built from scratch in another location. Second, even when the company assumed a Canadian dollar at par with its American counterpart, it found it could recruit plenty of engineers at lower cost than in the United States. "In our business model, when I deliver services to the United States, I can come in at about 70 percent of the cost." The challenge is to grow the company quickly to global scale. "What we aim to do with these centres is to go after the American as well as Canadian markets from a Canadian base. The objective is to get critical mass, and Canada by itself does not compare well to the United States. However, by adding U.S. business to our mix, we can attain the critical mass necessary to reach our goal of becoming a megacentre."[15]

Stories like these suggest that Canada is doing pretty well in moving full speed into the global economy. But the overall statistics tell a different tale, one of global engagement that is far too narrowly based. Industry Canada has noted that the top five exporters alone account for more than one-fifth of the country's export sales, and that the top fifty are responsible for almost half of Canada's exports. Only 10 percent of all small and medium-sized businesses are engaged in exports at all, and they account for just a tiny fraction of the country's sales abroad.[16]

Further signs of Canada's vulnerability can be seen in its equity markets. While Canadian stock markets did relatively well in 2000, they under-performed badly in comparison with American and global benchmarks through the previous decade. In June 2000 the Toronto Stock Exchange 300 composite index briefly achieved parity with the Dow

Jones Industrial Average after lagging consistently for almost five years. But, as the *Financial Post* pointed out, the long-term record remains poor. From 1977, when the TSE 300 was relaunched at 1,000, it appeared to have matched the Dow twenty-three years later with a cumulative gain of 920 percent, compared with 940 percent for the American benchmark. Still, the broader Standard and Poor's 500 index gained 1,401 percent over the same period. And, after factoring in the 31 percent decline in the relative value of the Canadian dollar, the American dollar return on the TSE fell to 603 percent.[17]

The resulting backwater status of Canadian equity markets continues to leave many Canadian companies highly vulnerable in an era of global consolidation. A dollar of earnings in the hands of a Canadian company has been persistently worth less than the same dollar of earnings in the hands of American competitors. In a buy-or-be-bought era of mergers and acquisitions, low stock prices, combined with a low Canadian dollar, make foreign takeovers and big-ticket global investments by Canadian companies prohibitively expensive. By the same token, profitable leading-edge Canadian companies look invitingly cheap to foreign buyers able to raise cheaper capital on more buoyant markets. "The combination of the low value of the dollar plus the low price-to-earnings multiples in the market makes it very difficult for Canadian companies to invest in growth," said John Mayberry, president and chief executive officer of Dofasco Inc. "Investments that would have been affordable become bet-the-farm investments. Because Canadians tend to be a conservative lot by nature, those investments are often not made. Everyone becomes a sitting duck."[18]

"In essence, a weak currency is your market cap," agreed the Royal Bank's John Cleghorn. "What the world is saying is that you have a depreciated asset value. That is very harmful in an era of global consolidation, because your company's shares are the currency you use to make acquisitions. If a Canadian company is undervalued because our currency is undervalued, it is very tough to compete with American companies that have share prices based on higher earnings multiples and a stronger, more stable currency."[19]

In 1999, amid the global frenzy of mergers, acquisitions, and consolidations, a heavily discounted Canadian dollar and a host of undervalued assets finally prompted a wave of foreign takeovers of Canadian companies. In that same year, however, Canadian investors were shovelling a net $23 billion into foreign securities. That outflow set a new record and

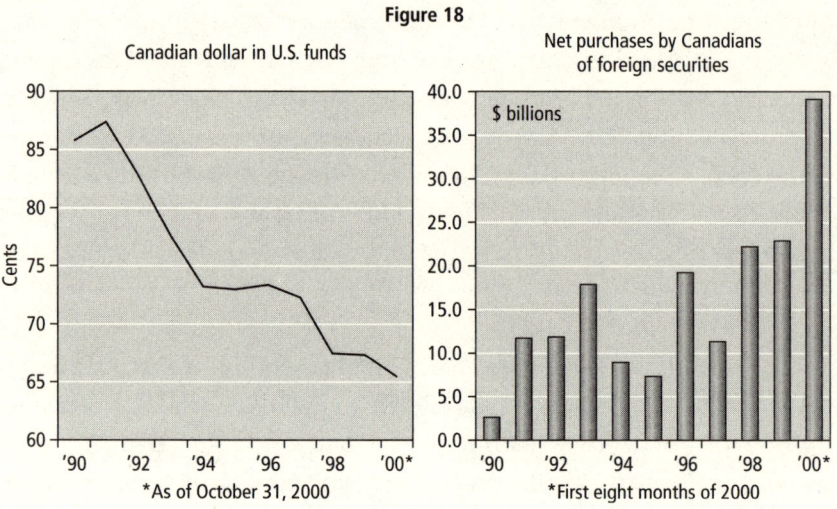

Figure 18

brought the cumulative total for the 1990s to $135 billion. The exodus of capital then accelerated further in 2000. In the first eight months of 2000, Canadians put a net $39.1 billion into foreign securities, with the vast majority going into foreign stocks (see fig. 18).[20] Some of the 2000 outflow can be attributed to the February 2000 budget provisions that increased the foreign content limit within Registered Retirement Savings Plans and pension plans. From an investor's point of view, global diversification is a sensible strategy. Outflows on this scale, however, suggest that too many Canadians have lost faith in the ability of Canadian companies to deliver competitive returns from a Canadian base.

This inability to attract Canadian investors has, in turn, led many Canadian companies to put more emphasis on marketing their virtues abroad and listing their stocks on American and other foreign exchanges. Only by getting noticed and tapping into the larger pools of capital in the United States and elsewhere can Canadian-based firms raise money cheaply enough to grow to a global scale. As a result, many widely held Canadian companies now have a substantial level of foreign shareholders. By 1999, according to the *National Post* Business 500, foreigners owned 39 percent of Alcan, 46 percent of Moore Corp., 54 percent of Inco, 87 percent of Potash Corp. of Saskatchewan, 35 percent of Alberta Energy Co. Ltd., 56 percent of Agrium, and 63 percent of Placer Dome Inc. — all within the 100 largest companies in Canada.[21]

While foreign investors are showing increased interest in successful Canadian companies, Canada is not fostering enough such enterprises.

Tsun-Yan Hsieh and Stephanie Coyles of McKinsey & Co. have noted that, as of early 2000, only two of the top 150 global corporations by market capitalization were based in Canada. What is more, the market value of one of the two, BCE Inc., was largely due to the value of its since-spun-off controlling stake in the other, Nortel Networks. Although almost half of the global 150 had head offices in the United States, six were based in the Netherlands and five in Switzerland. "Successful companies like Nortel and Bombardier demonstrate daily that Canada can and does produce global champions," they write. "Our challenge is in producing even greater numbers of Canadian global champions at a more rapid pace than ever before . . . The need for concerted action to address Canada's leadership challenge has never been greater. Canadian companies that don't specialize and establish a global presence risk being taken over by more focused players with superior performance or by larger companies with significant assets; both can lever their much stronger share price currencies to do so. Current restrictive ownership regulations will only delay the inevitable consolidation and change in leadership."[22]

■ Why Champions Matter

With Canada's economic growth as strong as it has been over the past few years, are such worries overblown? Hsieh and Coyles argue persuasively that, without a concerted effort to create more global champions, we could jeopardize the prosperity of an entire generation. They suggest that global champions are critical to a country's performance for three reasons: they create a disproportionate share of wealth; they invest disproportionately in their home countries; and they form hubs of activity that are critical in spawning smaller ventures and attracting and retaining people, ideas, and capital in the knowledge economy. Let us look at each of these assertions in turn.

There is no question that companies able to forge positions of global leadership have done extraordinarily well in recent years. The 1990s were hot for stock markets generally, but the biggest have done best. Between 1994 and 1999 world market capitalization more than doubled, from $15 trillion to $33 trillion. But the value of the 150 largest companies by market capitalization grew even faster, increasing their share of the total from 27 percent to 34 percent. These 150 companies created $7.2 trillion in market value over that five-year period — two and a half times greater than the growth in Canada's gross domestic product (GDP). These figures represent the degree of wealth created for investors — but this growth also flowed through to employees, suppliers, and communities through higher-quality jobs, higher salaries, and higher-value contracts.[23]

This view is consistent with the observations made by Industry Canada researchers of trends in innovation and productivity in Canadian companies. As we saw in the previous chapter, it is the larger and foreign-owned firms that have generally been on the forefront of adopting new technologies and investing in greater productivity. However, the critical observation of the department's most recent work was that the behaviour of foreign-owned multinationals was virtually identical to that of Canadian-based global companies: it is global engagement, not ownership, that leads to greater investment in enhancing productivity.

The conclusion is obvious. To deliver the high-value jobs and rising incomes that flow from productivity and innovation, Canadian companies must compete globally both in selling their products and in attracting investors. To ignore the world, to remain content with being a big fish in the Canadian pond, can at best provide an illusion of stability in the short term and a guarantee of declining fortunes for Canadian investors and employees alike over the longer term. "I don't think that Canadian companies can build fences around Canada and say we will fly within our own sphere," said James Stanford, chairman of the board of Petro-Canada. "The world just won't allow that to happen. People will demand and get access to Canadian opportunities, and Canadian corporations must be equally aggressive in demanding access to opportunities around the world. But once they get that access, they have to be able to compete."[24]

Moving to Hsieh and Coyles' second rationale for fostering global champions, there is persuasive evidence that the location of a global company's home base still matters. They note, for example, that Finland's cellular telephone–maker Nokia still maintains 48 percent of its employees in its home country, even though only 3.5 percent of its sales are made there. Similarly, Canada's Nortel still conducts almost half its research and development here, even though the Canadian share of its global sales has dropped below 10 percent. However, as Micklethwait and Wooldridge suggest, global corporations are moving into a new stage of development, one in which their traditional loyalties to a home country are weakening as they serve customers and integrate employees and managers around the world.

The experience of Canadian champions sends up some warning signs in this respect. At Nortel, for instance, while 90 percent of the top 400 executives are still Canadians, almost all have moved abroad — many for personal reasons that can be justified, but were not required, by the growth of the company's operations worldwide. At Bombardier, core head-office functions remain firmly rooted in Montreal, but the heavy subsidies offered by foreign governments for aerospace work have led to a steady decline in Canadian content in each generation of the airplanes it makes.

Even within a truly global corporation, the decisions of individuals in key roles remain influenced by where they live. The experience of Air Liquide, a French-based company specializing in industrial and medical gases, is instructive. With 29,000 employees spread through 125 subsidiaries in sixty countries, the company has been making conscious efforts to shift towards a truly global corporate culture. It actively recruits managers from beyond its home country and moves them around the world with increasing frequency. While its headquarters remains in Paris, the company is adopting English as its official language worldwide. Nonetheless, the company has found that the location in which managers live and work still has a powerful impact on their decisions.

In 1999 Air Liquide invested in two major expansion projects in Canada — an $85 million air separation unit in Hamilton and a $150 million plant in Edmonton. The engineering teams building these plants both reported to the same executive, a Canadian based in Houston. But the project managers themselves were based at two different locations, the one for the Hamilton project in France and the one for the Edmonton project in Houston. When the company did a detailed comparison of the two projects, it discovered that the European content that went into the Hamilton project was twice that of the Edmonton project. Furthermore, the Edmonton plant designed by the Houston team had much greater American content. "It's the same company with the same expertise. We like to think that we're global," said Marc Fortier, former head of subsidiary Air Liquide Canada and now the Paris-based vice-president of worldwide energy services. "And yet our two plants were being built with components sourced from different locations. In many cases, we found that our engineers, our experts, continue to order parts from the suppliers they know. So it's not the head office location that matters so much as where the critical decision are made."[25]

In other words, what matters most is the location where top executives choose to work. "You tend to support the communities where you hang your hat. That is the natural gravitation," said David O'Brien, chairman, president, and chief executive officer of Canadian Pacific Limited. "You have a view of the world that is fashioned to some degree by where you live. And that affects the decisions you make about where to locate your business functions."[26]

This observation leads to Hsieh and Coyles' third reason why global champions are so important to a country's ability to create wealth: their role as a hub that helps smaller businesses to grow and acts as a source of ideas, people, and capital. This impact is especially evident in the high technology sector. Hsieh and Coyles noted that in just three years, from 1997 through 1999, Intel invested $2.5 billion (U.S.) in some 250 other ventures.[27] One of its partnerships was with Canada's Research in Motion. The Canadian company went to Intel looking for a chip to power two-way pagers, ones with keyboards that would let users send as well as receive e-mail. Intel made a modest cash investment, but its major contribution was to develop a new low-power version of its old 386 chip. RIM got the chip it needed as well as a capital injection; Intel got a whole new market for an old product line; the partnership was chosen as the winner of the 1999 Canadian-American Business Achievement Award; and the runaway success of RIM's Blackberry pagers made it the hottest performing stock on the Toronto Stock Exchange that year.

In earlier work for the Business Council on National Issues, Hsieh and Coyles noted a similar pattern of three generations of new ventures involving either direct investment or people from Northern Telecom and Bell Northern Research, now Nortel Networks. The first generation created thirty-seven companies, including JDS Fitel (now JDS Uniphase) and Skystone Systems, since sold to Cisco. The second generation created twenty-one more companies, including Mitel. And the third generation added another twenty-four companies, including Newbridge and Corel. Many of these companies, in turn, have spawned further spinoffs. Together they have created a meaningful high technology hub in the Ottawa region.[28]

The head offices of global corporations can provide a significant boost even to growing companies in completely different industries. Montreal-based CGI Group Inc., for instance, has grown rapidly into a global player in computer services. But president and chief executive officer Serge Godin noted that the presence of global company head offices in CGI's home city of Montreal gave his company a crucial leg up into international markets. "One of the companies in Canada which dealt the most with CGI when we started was Alcan. Because they were here in Montreal, it was easy. We were meeting frequently, having lunch in the same restaurants. We were able to create a relationship over the years, and they have become one of the largest clients we have today. If Alcan had not been based in Montreal when we were still a small company, we would not have had the same access . . . We could say that the economy is going very well," Mr. Godin concluded, "but we are losing our head offices. It's damaging, highly damaging. When we have a head office somewhere, we have a relationship with the community, we have friends. A decision to move a head office is almost always a terminal act. It's not going to come back."[29]

A global champion's role as a hub goes beyond its impact on industrial growth either through investment or through supplier purchases. It is also a critical hub for its community. "If you're raising money, I don't care what it's for, it's a lot easier to raise money if the CEO is there," said James Arnett, former president and chief executive officer of Molson Inc. "Every time you lose a head office, you lose funding for the arts and other forms of community support. It's a brain drain and it's a brain drainer. The best people tend to end up in a head office or want to get into a head office."[30] "I think head offices are very important," agreed Paul Desmarais Jr., chairman and co-chief executive officer, Power Corporation of Canada. "I think we are learning this in the province of Quebec. Head offices have left the province and it has changed Montreal dramatically. It's a question of capital and decision-making. It's obvious you want them here."[31]

On this score, the signs for Canada are ominous. As we saw previously, 40 percent of the BCNI's member chief executives put the odds at 50/50 or higher that their own job functions would leave Canada within a decade. That degree of pessimism suggests that Canada may have a hard time hanging on to its existing champions, much less fostering the number of new ones needed to achieve the country's economic and social goals.

"We need champions. We need global headquarters in Canada. They attract research, they support universities, they support community organizations, and they drive economic progress," said Jean Monty, president and chief executive officer of BCE Inc. "We are still trying to work from a Montreal base, but we're doing it out of conviction as individuals. It would be a lot easier to start hedging our bets and focus our growth in friendlier environments. Some companies have done that. That was their choice.

Others like us are doing their best to build in a very difficult environment."[32] Robert Peterson, chairman, president, and chief executive officer of Imperial Oil Limited agrees. "What we're talking about is our ability as a nation to compete for the mobile resources that exist, whether they be people, ideas, or money. Where we are disadvantaged is that we are next door to the Energizer bunny and he moves faster than we do. I don't think it's inevitable that every head office moves, but if the economic penalty for being in Canada is perceived to be too high, why would you stay?"[33]

Global economic integration and the shift to knowledge-based work make the presence of global champions more important than ever to our country's economic and social progress. These same forces, however, make key corporate functions and high-value operations more mobile and therefore more challenging both to attract and to retain. "The old economy has its basis in the land. The major footprint of the railway is in Canada, and it won't move," said David O'Brien of Canadian Pacific. "Other sectors like our shipping business and hotel business are more portable. When you have hotels everywhere you can set up shop anywhere. Over time you'll go where it makes sense to run that business, in terms of where it's nice to live, where the business conditions are good and where you can attract good people to a head office function. Those will be the driving factors."[34]

Other executives support this view. "Canada urgently needs to rethink where it wants to be in the new economy," said Jacques Bougie of Alcan. "If as Canadians we continue to be complacent, before long we won't be a significant force. We will be talking about the ex-Canada, what Canada used to be. We will revert to being hewers of wood and drawers of water. We will no longer be a top-tier economy."[35] And Charles Sirois, chairman of the board and chief executive officer of Telesystem Ltd., has this to say: "If you want a country where you will be able to maintain your lifestyle and your quality of life, you have no choice but to be a major actor in the new economy. We can be a leader in lumber, in mining, in aluminum parts, and in car production. Fine. But I'm willing to bet you that all that together will represent less than 30 percent of the total value of the economy in less than ten years from now. The forest will not move. The mine will not move," he continued, "but the new economy can move. The new economy is driven by creativity, innovation, and entrepreneurship. What should a government do? Nothing other than create the right environment."[36]

Canadian and foreign-owned companies that operate in the global arena face identical pressures, and they are shaping their growth strategies and investment decisions accordingly. Put another way, the factors that will encourage Canadian enterprises to flourish from a Canadian base will be equally effective in persuading foreign companies to choose this country as the preferred location for global centres of expertise. Before we look at how Canada can make a more compelling case for itself as the home base of choice for global enterprises regardless of ownership, we need to take a closer look at the factors that are influencing investment decisions today — and where Canada is falling short.

■ The Troubles with Canada

The 1999 BCNI survey of member chief executives, which, as we have seen, returned a pessimistic view of the future of Canada's head office functions, also probed in detail the factors that affect business investment decisions. It found that, overall, a company considering where to locate a new investment looks, first, at the rate of taxation, followed by the cost and availability of critical inputs, and, finally, the quality of infrastructure and the country risk factors. Infrastructure is seen as Canada's greatest competitive advantage. We are a low-risk place to do business and are open to trade, with the decided geographic advantage of being next door to the American market. Our supply of skilled workers and the quality of our social infrastructure was also rated as a significant plus. But the size and role of government, and especially the resulting burden of taxation, stood out as a major problem area.

Any strategy for enhancing Canada's ability to attract more investment in high-value activities must build on our strengths. At the same time, it is critical to deal decisively with the greatest barriers to progress. There is a clear perception that Canada is relying too heavily on old-economy strengths such as cheap land and plentiful natural resources. Despite our solid education infrastructure, there are warning lights about the future supply of highly skilled people. The supply and cost of capital, as demonstrated by the long-term under-performance of Canadian equities, is clearly a serious problem. And several other issues, both international and domestic, threaten the future growth of Canadian companies across a wide range of industries.

In interviews with dozens of leading chief executives, one of the most common worries concerned the way Canadian policies discourage corporate growth in an era where global reach is becoming critical to survival in many industries. "In Canada, we have yet to thoroughly embrace the virtue of going global," said Jacques Lamarre of SNC-Lavalin. "The United States encourages transnational enterprise. As a result, the companies there have a strategic advantage. We need to improve our domestic laws and regulations if we want Canadian companies to have a fair chance in the world market."[37]

Nowhere is the reluctance to enable Canadian companies to achieve global scale more evident than in the financial services sector. "The impersonal market forces that are creating a global system of financial services cannot be stopped or 'walled off.' The only effective Canadian policy responses to deal with them are ones that create an internationally competitive system in Canada," said economist Edward Neufeld in a paper for the Institute of Intergovernmental Relations at Queen's University.[38] If current merger and tax policies continue even as foreign penetration of the Canadian market grows, he concluded, "the chances are that this would cause the banks to lose a substantial share of their own domestic market and become inconsequential players internationally, ending with eventual absorption by foreign banks. Even their chances of evolving into significant niche players in Canada would be minimal because niche players themselves have become international in scope. Such an outcome would be irreversible and it is difficult to see how it would serve Canada's national interests. It would be a very high price to pay for whatever short-term advantages are seen in perpetuating such policies."[39]

"We're number two in the world in discount brokerage, and we do have a shot if we're fast enough to overcome some of the disadvantages of having the bank mergers turned down," added Charles Baillie of TD Bank. "But I think that we all have to achieve greater scale, or in a few years we won't have head offices in Canada and we'll be part of global empires controlled by foreigners."[40] Youssef Nasr of HSBC agreed: "Brand names are going to become more important in the world of e-commerce. While the Canadian banks without any doubt will have the brand name in Canada, they will not have it on a global basis."[41] Former Nesbitt Burns chief executive Jack Lawrence offers a blunt assessment of federal government opposition to bank mergers: "We had a window of opportunity and it was slammed shut. The decision was bad public policy — it virtually killed the opportunity for Canadian banks to be global players."[42]

It is critical for governments to rethink the role they play in encouraging the development of global champions operating from a Canadian base. Part of this process must include a re-examination of competition policy. According to Lawson Hunter, a former head of the federal competition bureau who is now a partner at Stikeman Elliott, Canada's competition laws remain respectable, but need to be updated. In particular, he suggested in a paper for the BCNI, "high-tech or knowledge-based industries are occupying an increasingly large proportion of Canada's and the world's economy. Antitrust laws must adapt to this change to ensure that old paradigms do not prevent needed change and the efficient functioning of markets in these industries . . . If Canada is to develop its potential in the new millennium, its antitrust laws must properly account for innovation and change."

Hunter recommended three changes to Canada's competition legislation. First, it should require the commissioner of competition to consider efficiency savings as a factor in deciding whether to challenge a merger. Second, to ensure that Canadian firms can achieve global scale, the law should make it clear that efficiencies are to be counted wherever they occur, and not just in Canada. Third, the importance of efficiency gains on the ability of Canadian business to compete internationally should become a relevant consideration in any merger evaluation. "Our current law and policy is close to being at the forefront of policy developments globally, and has been so for the last 15 years. But we must ensure that we stay with the pack, if not one or two steps ahead of it. These changes are designed to help Canada grow, adapt and become more productive through the application of enlightened competition policies," Mr. Hunter concluded.[43]

"Time and time again, companies would really like to have expanded across Canada, but the regulatory impediments have overwhelmed the arguments for greater efficiencies of bringing Canadian firms together to enable them to compete globally," said Paul Tellier of Canadian National. "Because of the large number of obstacles, attitudes and deeply entrenched suspicions, a lot of businesses have been driven south."[44] Stephen Snyder, president and chief executive officer of TransAlta Corporation concurred: "The big challenge for us is growth," he said. "Provincial regulations make east-west growth extremely difficult. We're already large in our home province. We were forced to go international, but with at least one arm, if not our legs, tied behind our back."[45]

"Canada needs much more critical mass in various clusters of enterprises," noted Marc Fortier of Air Liquide. "Our domestic market is very small, and yet we decide to keep our champions fragmented. The way to alleviate consumers' concern is to create very big, strong Canadian companies that, from a home base, can compete worldwide. And then you allow other large companies to come and compete in Canada. We are afraid in Canada of creating champions because we're suspicious of success. We say small is beautiful. We are prepared to be second best, or third best. This is not acceptable."[46]

The unwillingness to recognize the importance of scale to global competitiveness is not the only impediment to attracting more investment and fostering corporate growth. Chief executives point to a wide range of other issues that have significant impact, as we shall see.

▼ Government Subsidies

Business subsidies, or "corporate welfare," became a significant issue in the autumn 2000 federal election campaign. Echoing the 1970s "corporate welfare bums" theme of the New Democratic Party, the 2000 campaign saw the Canadian Alliance at the other end of the political spectrum highlighting the need to turn off the spending taps. The 1999 BCNI member survey suggested that, in most cases, subsidies to business have relatively little impact on investment decisions. And, as we have argued already, governments that want to stimulate investment efficiently are usually better to use the tax system rather than cash handouts.

The exception to this general observation, however, comes in sectors with high political visibility that also have a history of heavy government involvement. The most obvious and relevant example for Canada is the aerospace sector. In most countries, the development of aerospace companies has been strongly linked both to the necessities of national defence and to the imperatives of national pride. Military procurement has subsidized the development of new technologies for commercial use, and a wide range of other programs support every phase of the industry, from research to export sales. The competition Canada faces in this sector provides compelling evidence of why Canada needs to support a strong framework of multilateral agreements. Only by working within the World Trade Organization can it hope to get and enforce tougher restrictions on such subsidies. In the meantime, our unwillingness to compete has significant consequences.

The record of Bombardier in becoming a leading player in aerospace as well as mass transit and recreational vehicles shows that government support does not always stand in the way of the evolution of a global champion. It can, however, strongly influence how many and what kinds of jobs remain in Canada as the company expands. "We would prefer not to have any support," says Robert Brown, president and chief executive officer of Bombardier. "The reality is that we're competing against people that have defence support plus other generous programs. At the same time, Canada's program attracts tremendous criticism even though it is the least competitive program available in any jurisdiction I deal with. I've got people willing to give me money in Europe and Asia, wherever I go. It's the same deal they are willing to give their domestic companies, but it is a quantum factor better than I can get here."[47]

Other aerospace companies are pursuing similar strategies. For American manufacturers, the opening up of China, Russia, and Eastern Europe represents a particular opportunity to marry low costs with established capability. "The capability is not obvious. It still has to be developed. But it is there," said David Caplan of Pratt & Whitney Canada. "We have had a supplier in Poland since the late 1970s. Now we have a plant and a wholly owned subsidiary with about 600 employees there. We are opening a joint venture in China geared to parts manufacturing. And we are looking into Russia very seriously, both because of their ability to manufacture at lower cost and because we want to be part of that environment as it rebuilds its infrastructure and moves into its next stage of aerospace development."

Given its small domestic market and its lack of military procurement and research, Canada's progress in aerospace has been impressive. "Canada has no right to hold the position it does in the world of aerospace," Caplan added. "It is number four in the world, and without a military budget, that is incredible."[48] However, the positive numbers on sales mask a steady decline in Canadian value-added — a trend that has serious implications for the number and quality of jobs in the Canadian industry in the years ahead.

With each succeeding generation of aircraft Bombardier has developed, the proportion of Canadian content has been falling. For its Global Express, every part of the manufacturing process went outside Canada, except the final assembly and the cockpit. The fuselage, for example, is made in Ireland; the wings, the most complex and critical component of any aircraft design, are manufactured in Japan. "If you look at the value-added in the Canadian aerospace industry, it is falling by three to four percentage points a year," Brown added. Furthermore, the aerospace sector, like the automotive industry, is delegating more and more responsibility to its suppliers. Instead of buying individual parts and doing all the assembly in-house, airplane manufacturers are buying major components and systems from outside suppliers and limiting their own manufacturing role to final assembly. As part of its efforts to stay cost competitive, Bombardier is also looking to its major suppliers to share the risk of developing new products.

That involvement is bad news for smaller Canadian companies that have traditionally sold individual parts or subsystems, because the suppliers who can handle both the technology and the risks of major system development are abroad and subsidized — in Japan, Spain, France, Germany, Italy, and other countries, in addition to the United States. "We have reduced the number of suppliers we deal with from about 2,000 to just 200. These suppliers provide entire systems and guarantee their work. We have tried to put our Canadian parts suppliers into contact with these system-level suppliers, but they face extremely tough competition in trying to sell to foreign companies," Brown said. "Rather than fight for a level playing field on subsidies, we are organizing ourselves in a way that places much of the work out and around the world. As a company, we are not doing badly, but the value-added here is going down, and that bothers me. Even though I head a global company, I strongly believe in the community in which I live. I want Canadian children to have a shot at a job like I have, and to be able to grow in their own environment. But because of the nationalistic approach that other countries take in our industry, I am worried that our children will not have the chance to achieve their potential."[49]

The experience of the aerospace sector suggests an important message for Canadian policy-makers. Where public subsidies are necessary to keep Canadian companies in the game, we should either do them right or not at all. Half-hearted half-measures are costly and futile, adding to the cost of government, but insufficient to stem the tide of declining Canadian content in the industry. This message reinforces a more general point about subsidies: they are an inefficient way to encourage the growth of Canadian enterprises. Where subsidies may be necessary in the short term because of the behaviour of international competitors, Canada should work within the context of global trade rules to eliminate them globally. And where no international reason for subsidies exists, as in many of our efforts at regional development, we should recognize that there are better ways to stimulate growth in jobs and incomes and get rid of them unilaterally. To the extent that governments feel compelled to offer corporate subsidies at all, they should at least focus their efforts and make them effective in areas in which Canadian companies are struggling to compete with the pocketbooks of bigger and richer governments abroad.

▼ Defence and Security

The end of the Cold War did nothing to ease American concerns about leakage of sensitive technology to other countries. And while the risks of superpower confrontations may have faded, the United States is increasingly concerned with the security of its own borders, whether against rogue states launching missiles or against terrorists, drug smugglers, and illegal immigration.

Canada received a serious jolt in 1999 when it was accused of being a conduit for leaking technological secrets. The immediate political issue was eventually resolved, but the impact of the dispute lingers on. Even in the short term, Canadian companies were effectively shut out of the American defence market, and those dependent on American suppliers or technology faced troubling restrictions and delays. More seriously, even the Canadian subsidiaries of American companies found their operations restricted. At Pratt & Whitney Canada, for instance, responsibilities for certain operations and projects became limited after the company was forced to restrict contacts between Canadians and some American employees and to reconfigure the corporate intranet to limit access by Canadian employees.[50] In addition to the immediate impact, such conflicts reinforce the broader perception that investing in Canadian-based global mandates is a riskier proposition than investing directly in the United States.

▼ Intellectual Property

Treatment of intellectual property is an issue that involves both dangers and opportunities for Canada. Nowhere is this more evident than in the pharmaceutical industry. Canada's move to extend patent protection in the 1980s led to a major expansion of research operations. Its affirmation of twenty-year patent coverage in 1998 added momentum to research investments and led to expansions in Canadian-based manufacturing, the vast majority of it for export.

Today, though, the world's research-based pharmaceutical companies see Canada's commitment to innovation being undermined on several fronts. The first is in a lack of willingness to enforce patent protection; instead, Canada quietly encourages generic manufacturers to exploit loopholes in the rules. Second, as discussed in the previous chapter, is the lengthy approval process for new drugs and for obtaining coverage under provincial drug plans. The third is pricing, which is now governed by the Patented Medicine Price Review Board. Establishment of the board was a trade-off for patent protection; it was justified by relatively high prices at the time, but as a result Canadian prices have fallen well below the global median. It is now American consumers who can be seen cross-border shopping for pharmaceutical bargains in Canada.

As with manufacturing in many other industries, global companies are consolidating their operations so that a handful of plants make their products for customers worldwide. How Canada moves forward in encouraging innovation within its borders could determine whether it flourishes as a global centre of research and manufacturing or withers into a minor market. "Our talent is well recognized. Our ability to deliver has been well recognized. Our ability to innovate as a company has been recognized. That leaves us well positioned to be a key player in Glaxo Wellcome's worldwide operation," said Paul Lucas of Glaxo Wellcome. "To capitalize on this opportunity, we need Ottawa to support aggressively knowledge-based industries like pharmaceuticals."[51]

As we see it, the key issue goes beyond the question of whether Canada has competitive provisions for protecting intellectual property. The real question is whether our country follows through on its promises. Canada's credibility is at risk.

▼ Internal Trade

Even though Canada is a small market in the global context, jealousies and disputes between the federal and provincial governments continue to fragment both the country's efficiency and its reputation. As we discussed earlier, significant internal barriers to the movement of people, goods, and services and capital persist, and despite signing an Agreement on Internal Trade, governments have given the removal of the remaining barriers a low priority. Restricting people's ability to live and work where they please discourages movement and reinforces regions of high unemployment and dependency. Policies supposedly intended to protect jobs and opportunity for residents of each province instead fragment the Canadian marketplace and leave Canadian enterprises smaller and less competitive. "We have the disunited provinces of Canada," said James Shepard, former chief executive officer of Finning International Inc. "The most unfree trade area in the Western hemisphere is within Canada, province to province. We have freer trade with Washington than we do with Alberta. That's another dimension that works against us."[52] And, added David O'Brien of Canadian Pacific, "it is bad enough that we have a small economy relative to the United States. But then we slice it about ten different ways and make ourselves smaller and smaller."[53]

Even policies that are designed to capture Canadians' mutual support and caring can have destructive consequences. Just as generous welfare provisions can discourage the search for earned income, so the structure of Canada's equalization transfers create their own version of a welfare trap. When the governments of have-not provinces do succeed in generating new sources of provincial revenue, much of the gain is deducted from the money they receive from the federal government through equalization. This system takes away much of their incentive to encourage development, unless it has an immediate and concrete impact in terms of job creation.

Seymour Schulich, chairman and chief executive officer of Franco-Nevada Mining Corporation Limited, cites the behaviour of Newfoundland and Labrador as one recent example. The provincial government first promised a ten-year tax holiday for businesses creating new ventures in the province — and then withdrew that support after the discovery of the Voisey's Bay nickel deposit. The province went on to refuse permission to develop Voisey's Bay without a guarantee that all ores would be smelted within the province rather than elsewhere in Canada. The result was a standoff — no mine, no smelter, and no jobs.

Schulich suggests that such efforts to keep jobs and economic activity within the boundaries of a single province end up hurting both the economy and the reputation of the entire country. "Capital today flows like water to places where it's wanted, welcome, and able to earn a fair return for its providers."[54]

▼ *Political Strife*

The disputes over internal trade issues are part of a broader pattern of political conflict. In particular, the prolonged uncertainty over the future of Quebec within Canada has been highly damaging to Canada's image and to the country's ability to attract investment. More than half of the respondents (52 percent) to the 1999 BCNI survey of member chief executives said that uncertainty over Quebec's future had had at least a moderate impact (4 or more on a scale of 1 to 7) on their companies' decisions to continue investing in Canada. Almost half, 44 percent, rated the impact at 5 or higher. While companies based in Quebec were more likely to indicate that their Canadian investments had been affected, responses indicating a significant impact came from Canadian and foreign-owned companies alike. When it comes to global branding, anything that affects a part of our country affects the reputation of the whole.[55]

The truth of this statement was confirmed in October 2000 by Moody's, the international credit-rating agency. A report by senior analyst Steven Hess said bluntly that Canada cannot qualify for Moody's top AAA rating until it deals with two problems. The first is its high level of public debt, which is now falling steadily as a percentage of GDP. But the second issue preventing Canada from achieving a top-level credit rating is the issue of Quebec separatism. "Canada is the only major advanced economy where national unity is an issue," Hess wrote. "Even if the risk to Canada's credit quality from Quebec secession may be viewed as small, separatism is present to a greater degree than elsewhere."[56]

The continuing conflicts between First Nations and the federal and provincial governments also hurt investment and economic activity. While the damage here is more localized, influencing investment primarily in the resource sector, such conflicts affect the reputation of the entire country and give investors in all industries one more excuse to look elsewhere first.

▼ Environmental Regulation

Canada's global reputation as a vast land of natural beauty offering a superb quality of life is one of its most positive attributes in attracting people and investment. The country is committed to maintaining these qualities and has, as a result, been a leader both in environmental regulation and in environmental technology.

Canada's reputation as a place to invest, however, is being hurt by its environmental regulation. The damage does not flow from the letter of its laws and regulations, but from the way they are applied. The chief executives we talked to had relatively few concerns about the strictness of Canadian rules. If anything, jurisdictions in the United States often have tougher standards and enforcement, but the rules there are seen as relatively transparent and consistent. What bothers corporate investors is the

Canadian process for environmental approvals, a process that is far too uncertain, time-consuming, and political. "In the United States, you fill in an application. The rules are known. They check to see whether your proposal meets the rules, and what you have to change to make it fit. They give you your permit. And then when you start up, they come back and check. If you have not complied with the rules, they shut you down," said Roger Phillips, president and chief executive officer of IPSCO Inc. "In Canada, if we want to make a 30 percent increase in our steel-works capacity, we will go through an environmental process that will last a minimum of 24 months, and more likely 36 months."[57]

▼ Labour Regulations

Entrenched work rules and a reputation for labour strife haunt Canada's reputation abroad and discourage new investment. "We have so many rigidities still in our system that it is scary," said David O'Brien of Canadian Pacific. "To take just one example, at our last set of negotiations with the union representing employees at one of our hotel properties, they came forward with a shopping list of demands. Their opening position was that they didn't want to work weekends or nights. This is in a hotel. It's preposterous. You can't run a hotel and not be open at night. But there is an attitude, not always in the rank and file, sometimes just in the leadership, that you face in many places in Canada."[58]

▼ Cost of Doing Business

All the factors mentioned here influence Canada's ability to attract investment in two ways: by affecting financial returns through behaviour that raises the cost of doing business here; and by hurting our reputation as a country that wants to be home to successful global businesses. We will turn shortly to Canada's reputation and what we can do to build the Canadian brand, but first we must understand the cost-based realities of global business.

The cost challenge is most obvious within the resource sector that has been the backbone of Canada's economy in the past. Neither the presence of energy and resources nor the availability of financing, skilled labour, or even leading-edge technology can ensure the survival of competitive advantage. "We have this historic advantage of resource base, of trees and food and fish and fuel. All of those things have been the centrepiece of the economy for most of the last fifty years. But those resources aren't unique any more. We cannot produce any good or service that's unique to Canada at a better price," said Robert Peterson of Imperial Oil.[59]

In the aluminum business, for instance, modern smelting technology is available off the shelf. Anyone can buy that technology and hire an engineering firm to build a state-of-the-art smelter anywhere in the world. Construction is cheaper in warmer climates. Labour is cheaper in the developing world. And governments eager to attract such investment offer incentives that can range from very low-cost energy and subsidized infrastructure to lower tax rates and lax environmental standards. Justifying an expansion in Canada becomes difficult. "I'm in a very simple business. It's cost, cost, cost until you are blue in the face," said Alcan's Jacques Bougie. "Our challenge is to earn our cost of capital at metal prices that have been falling in real terms and will continue to fall."[60]

As we have seen in our discussion of innovation and productivity, Canada does have a temporary cost advantage when it comes to the availability of highly skilled labour. But much of that advantage stems from the abysmal performance of the Canadian dollar and the resulting wage cut that all Canadians have suffered in comparison with their southern neighbours. At the same time, the level of skills available in many other parts of the world is rising impressively. From Eastern Europe to South Asia, talented people are eagerly seeking new opportunities, so that even Canada's current cost advantages will be fleeting.

As we strive to give Canada the edge it will need to attract more investment in the high-value activities that create well-paid jobs, we cannot ignore the importance of taxation. In the BCNI survey, taxation rated as the single most important factor affecting business location decisions, and as Canada's greatest disadvantage in the competition for investment. Improving the competitiveness of both our tax rates and our tax structure will not of itself turn Canada into an instant magnet for new investment — but unless we address our most serious shortcomings on this front, much of our effort in developing human advantage and fostering innovation will come to naught.

■ The Power of Positive Tax Policy

We have discussed previously the impact of tax rates on Canada's ability to attract and retain skilled people and to foster entrepreneurial activity. But in the struggle to make Canada an attractive home base for successful global enterprises and well-paid global citizens, no single policy can have more influence than corporate taxation.

The problems with Canada's tax rates and structure on the corporate side are similar to those we have outlined with respect to personal taxation. Corporate income tax rates are too high in comparison with those levied by key competitors. These income tax rates are, in turn, compounded by a complex and growing web of other taxes — on capital, on property, on inputs such as fuel, and so on — that make doing business in this country more expensive. And most dangerous of all, the structure of our corporate income tax system is biased against globally active companies in the service sector, the main engine of highly paid jobs in the knowledge economy. In the words of Israel Asper, executive chairman of the board of CanWest Global Communications Corp., "Forget about our rates, our tax structure is anti-development. At best, it reflects a lack of understanding among politicians and officials about how the real world of commerce works. At worst, it betrays a destructive anti-business bias."[61]

The combination of high rates and a perverse tax structure is deadly in a world in which business investment decisions are increasingly sensitive to differences in taxation. For instance, a 1998 paper for the National Bureau of Economic Research by Rosanne Altshuler, Harry Grubert, and T. Scott Newton examined investment decisions by American manufacturing affiliates in fifty-eight countries. They concluded that a 10 percent increase in corporate taxes in 1984 would have led to a 15 percent drop in foreign investment — and that figure doubled to a 30 percent loss by 1992.[62] The implication is that both the negative impact of uncompetitive corporate taxes and the potential gains from a tax cut doubled in just eight years. And, given the extent of global economic integration since 1992, the impact is likely to be even more significant today.

There are two reasons for this growing sensitivity. The first has to do with business costs. A high tax burden raises the cost of doing business and reduces expected returns on investment. Where a country offers other compelling advantages that are linked to geography — a superb resource base or access to a major market — a significant tax gap can be sustained. But the world today offers investors an unparalleled array of investment opportunities. Government subsidies and targeted incentives such as tax holidays can make a difference in the final stages of a major investment decision, but countries with high tax regimes these days do not even make the short list for consideration. "Canada's tax rates are impacting the country," said John Wetmore, president and chief executive officer, IBM Canada Ltd. "Many participants in our industry are locating and growing in low-tax jurisdictions, and Canada is not as attractive in terms of its tax rates."[63]

The second reason that high taxes have become so damaging to investment is more pragmatic. They simply do not pay. Companies operating in many jurisdictions will, as a matter of course, take whatever legal means are available to realize as much profit as possible in lower-tax jurisdictions. Countries with lower tax rates can actually end up receiving more money in corporate income tax revenue, simply because companies based there generate more profits. "Canada is undoubtedly one of the high tax regimes that we're in," said John Willson, former chief executive officer of Placer Dome Inc. "The United States is much more attractive. So is Chile. So is Australia, not to mention Papua New Guinea. We spend a great deal of time and energy trying to make sure that we produce money in a jurisdiction where we can find some shelter from heavy tax burdens."[64]

There is, of course, a sinister side to this multinational activity, one that flows from technological progress. As *The Economist* observed in the summer of 2000: "The Internet has the potential to increase tax competition, not least by making it easier for multinationals to shift their activities to low-tax regimes, such as Caribbean tax havens, that are physically a long way from their customers, but virtually are only a mouse-click away." The difference between tax havens and the governments of major industrialized countries is, however, merely one of degree. Ireland has opposed harmonized corporate tax rates because its low rates give it a competitive edge, *The Economist* noted. Britain has blocked a savings-tax directive out of fear that it might hurt activity in the financial centre of London. Luxembourg and Switzerland continue to be reluctant to share information with foreign tax authorities because they want to maintain their reputation for discretion. And the United States resists taxation of e-commerce because, as a net exporter, it has the most to gain from keeping the Internet tax-free.[65]

Even for governments willing and determined to capture their fair share of corporate income tax revenue, the task is becoming steadily more difficult. A high proportion of international trade involves intra-company transactions — purchases and sales of products between related corporations. One vehicle for reducing taxes owed in a high-tax jurisdiction is to set the prices on cross-border transactions in a way that produces more profit in the lower-tax jurisdiction. Tax authorities in all countries, of course, monitor such transactions and do their best to ensure that transfer pricing reflects fair market value.

This task was difficult enough when the major transborder flows involved relatively uniform products like steel ingots or even automobiles. Putting a fair market value on management services provided by a parent company to a subsidiary is much more difficult. And even that pales in comparison with the difficulty of establishing a value for intellectual property, such as computer software, that has not yet been developed to the point at which it can be sold to customers. What is more, both countries involved in any particular transaction want as much of the action as possible for their own coffers. Like tax havens at the extreme, some may be willing to trade off losses on the income tax revenue side in return for more economic activity that is taxable in other ways.

Peter Cook of the *Globe and Mail* has suggested that all high-tax countries will face a growing problem as transnational companies become seamless international organizations with teams of workers passing around projects through the Internet or internal company Intranets. "Where will this activity be taxed? It is not clear. But almost certainly it will not be taxed where taxes are highest. Technology is giving us the makings of a whole new method of evading high taxes; physically, we will not have to journey across a border if many of us start working for companies or doing work that is, by definition, borderless. Which means, sooner or later, the big taxers in Europe and Canada will have to rethink big taxes."[66]

In 1998 the report of the Technical Committee on Business Taxation commissioned by the federal government highlighted the structural problems of business taxation and issued detailed recommendations for resolving them. However, the committee was crippled by a mandate that insisted on revenue neutrality. In a country where some industries faced competitive burdens and others highly uncompetitive ones, this approach would have created as many losers as winners and made every sector equally uncompetitive. Jack Mintz, who chaired that committee, is now president and chief executive officer of the C.D. Howe Institute. In 1999 he took a look at how the world had changed even in the short time since the committee report was published and shelved by the government. He found that, in just three years, Canada had gone from being middle of the road in its corporate tax rates to the second highest in the G-7.

Germany, France, Sweden, Spain, Ireland, Australia, and Japan: the list of countries cutting corporate taxes keeps growing. Governments of the left and right alike have realized that a competitive corporate tax structure is the single most effective way to attract new investment in leading-edge industries. Mintz concluded that the speed and extent of corporate tax reductions in other countries, combined with the growing mobility of capital in the global economy, pose a serious threat to Canada's future growth. Canada's high business-tax burden reduces its competitiveness even after factoring in the benefits of its public services and infrastructure. "Although it is important — and politically popular — to reduce personal taxes, it is the business tax system that creates the greatest leverage in improving productivity and growth of incomes in Canada, as other countries such as Ireland have found out."[67]

In the 1980s Ireland had an unemployment rate that reached 18 percent, a national debt equal to 125 percent of GDP, and a loss of population of 1,000 a week. Since dramatically slashing corporate tax rates early this decade, it has enjoyed the fastest economic growth in the industrialized world. Technology-based employers now account for about 10 percent of its workforce and 20 percent of its GDP.[68] By 2000, one-third of all the personal computers sold in Europe were being made in Ireland. Nineteen of the top twenty-five computer companies in the world had set up shop there, including Microsoft Corp., IBM Corp., Hewlett Packard Corp., Dell Computer Corp., and Canada's Nortel Networks. By the spring of that year, the Organisation for Economic Co-operation and Development reported that Ireland had surpassed the United States as the world's leading exporter of computer software, selling products worth close to $5 billion a year.[69]

The Irish experience has generated a great deal of controversy. Those who like to dismiss taxation as irrelevant, for instance, point to the country's access to extensive subsidies from the European Union as a key element in its 1990s growth surge. We would note, however, that other lower-income members of the European Union had access to the same subsidy scheme, yet failed to match Ireland's record. According to the World Economic Forum, Ireland's average annual growth rate between 1993 and 1998 was 7.59 percent, second only to China. Portugal, in contrast, ranked twenty-fifth on the five-year growth rate, at just 2.36 percent, and Greece was forty-third, at just 1.45 percent a year. Canada, for that matter, was barely ahead of Greece, in thirty-seventh spot at real annual growth of 1.69 percent.[70]

We would agree that factors other than corporate tax cuts were an essential part of the Irish miracle. A policy of strategic investment in education and human capital development was certainly critical to ensuring a better supply of highly skilled workers. That investment in education, however, does not explain the reversal of Ireland's brain drain. The fact that Ireland is now desperately recruiting from abroad indicates, instead, that the pace of business investment has outstripped the supply of human capital. As we have suggested in earlier chapters, investing in education and training remains good public policy and an essential part of building competitive advantage for Canada, as for other countries. But Ireland's investments in education did not and could not alone drive the flow of investment that has doubled the standard of living of Irish citizens in just ten years.

What made a difference in Ireland was the decision not simply to reduce corporate taxes dramatically but to take this course as part of a concerted national strategy with broad public support. As Fred McMahon described it in his book *Road to Growth*, "the strategy is to reduce costs in the economy, to allow investors to reap increased profits. In Ireland and the Netherlands, this was accomplished through tax reductions and co-operation between unions, business and government in holding down wage growth. Even the union leadership argued in favour of wage moderation on the grounds that profits needed to be improved." Tax cutting and wage restraint to improve competitiveness are often attacked as "a race to the bottom" that leaves individual wage earners worse off. The experience of Ireland, and of another recent success story, the Netherlands, shows that the opposite tends to be true. McMahon notes that "real wages in Ireland and the Netherlands grew more rapidly after unions shifted from tough bargaining to a policy of wage moderation explicitly intended to increase business profits. This had two positive effects on longer-term wage growth. As investment, attracted by profits, increased, so too did the capital/labour ratio. This naturally made workers more productive and their labour more valuable. And, as employment grew, learning-by-doing and other forms of training also increased the value of labour. This created the room for real increases in wages that did not cut into profits, holding open the door to further investments and wage increases."[71]

John Bruton, Ireland's prime minister from 1994 to 1997, has noted that, if anything, EU subsidies impeded necessary adjustments in the country's economy, especially in propping up uneconomic agricultural businesses. He also confirms the importance of labour market flexibility, suggesting that if Ireland had had to stick to a standard European policy on unemployment benefits and minimum wages, it "would probably have killed off the Celtic Tiger at birth." And he emphasizes the importance to business investment of predictable and consistent policies that can flow only from social consensus. But he agrees that the major driver of Ireland's growth comes down to its strategy on taxation: "Achieving economic success is not simply a question of cutting taxes. It is a question of cutting the right taxes. The lesson of Irish economic history is that one should have a low and predictable rate of tax on the factors that generate growth. Companies and people at work generate growth. That is why the priority should be on reducing taxes on working people and on profits, rather than on reducing taxes on other activities. Ireland still has a pretty high rate of taxation on goods purchased in shops, but this has not inhibited economic growth."[72]

All taxes distort activity and reduce output to some extent. But, as discussed earlier, the federal Department of Finance has estimated that a dollar of corporate income tax may have as much as nine times the impact on economic growth as a dollar of sales tax. Others have come up with different estimates of the marginal impact of various forms of taxation, but the pattern is consistent. If the objective is to stimulate economic growth, cutting corporate taxes is the most effective strategy.

Despite the fact that its average corporate tax rate is less than one-third of Canada's, Ireland collects more money from this source as a percentage of GDP than Canada does. Corporate tax cuts would have a clear impact on investment, productivity, and economic growth and can be delivered at very low cost to governments, even in the short term. Mintz recommended a three-pronged approach in this country. First, he said, Canada should cut its corporate income tax rates below those in the United States. Second, he repeated a key thrust of the Technical Committee's report and called for improving the neutrality and simplicity of the business tax system. This reform would mean that the service sector, where most new jobs are being created, would get proportionately greater tax relief. Third, he said that the federal and, in particular, the provincial and municipal levels of government should reduce their reliance on inefficient profit-insensitive taxes that have little relation to the costs of public services provided to business.[73]

Richard Harris of Simon Fraser University has pointed out an additional incentive for cutting corporate tax rates within the context of a knowledge-based economy. In this environment, skilled labour and physical capital (such as new machinery and equipment) are complementary inputs. A country with more people who have higher skill levels will see greater productivity growth and attract more capital investment. And a country that attracts more investment in productivity-enhancing technologies is one that provides more work opportunities for highly skilled people. This scenario has important implications for the tax system. Lower corporate taxes will improve the odds for investment in the leading-edge technology that creates more high-skill opportunities. Personal income tax rates affect individual decisions about whether to invest time and money in more education, decisions that affect another important factor in investment choices — the supply of highly skilled people. "Consequently, a cut in income taxes which raises the return to human capital acquisition may raise the growth rate both by encouraging more human capital formation and by attracting an inflow of new investment. Both of these are growth enhancing," Harris concluded.[74] In other words, the benefits of boosting investment in education and cutting taxes would be reinforced if we did both at the same time.

The 2000 federal budget took an important step in principle by recognizing that corporate tax rates matter. But even the commitment in the October budget update to speed up corporate tax cuts remains slow and tentative in comparison with the tax cuts already under way and in place in other countries. In effect, Canada has promised to cut our general corporate tax rate over a four-year period to a level our competitors already have achieved. Also, while this plan will cut rates for the highest-taxed industries in Canada, it provides no relief to the resource sector and others whose treatment under the old regime was relatively favourable but whose rates are still out of line with those of their global competitors.

Some provincial governments, however, are accelerating the pace of tax reduction. Ontario leaped ahead of the pack in its spring 2000 budget with corporate tax reductions that included a small-business rate of just 4 percent. But Alberta leapfrogged over Ontario in September, announcing that it would cut its general corporate tax rate from 15.5 percent to 8 percent by 2004, a level that would be less than half paid by companies in neighbouring British Columbia. Alberta also will be cutting its small-business rate to 3 percent and helping to encourage growth by doubling the income ceiling for the small business rate to $400,000. Alberta treasurer Steve West said his goal was to make the province one of the most competitive tax regions in North America. "These cuts will send a message that Alberta is the place to set up shop."[75]

Canada is clearly moving in the right direction. On the whole, however, our competitors have been moving much faster. If Canada wants to gain a real competitive advantage in attracting business investment, it must both extend and accelerate its tax cut plans. We recognize the political difficulties involved in proposing such corporate tax breaks. Any opinion poll would find that, given a choice between cutting their own tax bills or those of a faceless corporation, most people would prefer to put money directly into their own pockets. Ultimately, however, smart tax policy is what will leave all Canadians better off.

We also accept that tax cuts have to be made as part of a broader strategy for attracting investment. As we have discussed here, other factors matter too, including the cost and supply of skilled labour, market size, market access, and transportation infrastructure. However, as the Conference Board of Canada has pointed out, many of these factors are subject to a host of variables that cannot be controlled by governments. "Taxation, on the other hand, falls completely within the domain of various levels of government. Taxation policy can influence the economic environment, which in turn can affect the competitive position of a country in the global market. As such, a competitive and stable taxation policy has the potential to be an effective tool for the Canadian government to promote investment and economic activity in the country."

Furthermore, the Conference Board concluded, tax policy affects not just the economic environment but also the country's reputation with investors. Despite its recent moves to cut tax rates, Canada retains the image of being a high-tax country. "In an era of 'globalization' characterized by emerging market economies, fierce competition for scarce foreign investment, and the relative ease with which capital can move from one jurisdiction to another, perceptions play a vital role in investment decisions. The taxation policy of a country has the potential to influence these perceptions."[76]

■ The Need for a Winning Attitude

Canada cannot change its weather, but most of the other barriers to business investment identified by the BCNI survey and our interviews are within our country's power to address. The changes that are needed will not come easily, though, and that challenge leads to the critical final ingredient: a winning attitude.

Howard Mann took on the job of president and chief executive officer of McCain Foods Limited in Canada after building an impressive record in Britain. After assuming his post in Toronto, he noticed an interesting difference in behaviour between Canadians and Britons. In his native land, people march up escalators with the same energy they would bring to a regular staircase. In Canada, most people seem to step on and then stand in place while the escalator moves them up. The difference in behaviour struck him as an apt metaphor for the Canadian tendency to rely on governments without worrying about the cost. "Canada has an Escalator Economy. Stand on it and be carried to the top. Don't run up it. If Canada wants to compete with the United States and the rest of the world, the government has to help people to run, by making them accountable for their own demand for public spending."[77]

If Canada wants more investment, more jobs, and higher incomes, standing around and waiting for prosperity to arrive will not work. "People think everything is fine, that Canada is in great shape, that we are number one in the world and everybody loves us. Yet we are standing on quicksand," said Ronald Mannix, chairman of Coril Holdings Ltd. "Complacency is our greatest enemy."[78] No matter how determined we are to move quickly and decisively, we do have to be realistic in our expectations. We won't fix everything overnight, but neither can we gold-plate our social programs until we've grown our tax base enough to cover the bills. At the same time, we have to take more pride in what we already have achieved.

Robert Brown of Bombardier is always struck by the attitude Canadians have towards the mode of transportation chosen by our political leaders when travelling abroad. "The president of France, he takes a Falcon. He is proud to step off that airplane. He's trying to sell one to anyone who greets him. The prime minister of Britain would take the Concorde to demonstrate British technology and strength. In the United States, they have no qualms about showing up in a Gulfstream or a Boeing, because they are proud that this is a product that is made in their country and they see themselves as helping to sell more of that product. Yet our politicians are so heavily criticized for flying in Canadian-made jets that basically they won't use them. How can that be? Why is it that any time a politician uses one of our business jets, it becomes a front-page story about government extravagance?"[79]

"The global competition for investment is like a baseball game. We've already got two strikes against us. Another strike and we're out," said Pierre Brunet, former co-chairman and co-chief executive officer, National Bank Financial Inc. "We are not doing enough to create an atmosphere that is helpful for investment, but as part of improving that atmosphere, we have to build up the country's strength and pride."[80]

Along with pride goes confidence. Canada will always be a small player economically next door to the United States. But that is the whole point of setting an independent course and building a compelling brand for ourselves. Just because we always will be small does not mean we can't be good. Indeed, if we do not believe in our ability to play in the big leagues and win, we are essentially resigning ourselves to farm team status — and a farm team standard of living. "Do we really need a plethora of protections to be Canadians?" asked BCE's Jean Monty. "I don't think we have enough faith in ourselves. The Americans are going to walk all over us if we don't deal with them from a position of economic strength."[81]

"One of the things we've got to come to grips with as a country is that we actually can compete with Americans," said Sanford Riley, president and chief executive officer of Investors Group Inc. "For too long, we have been saddled with an inferiority complex. In some ways, we are our own worst enemies. If Canadians had more confidence in their ability to compete, they would be able to compete more effectively. Part of the problem with the border is that it is a psychological issue. Some people feel that you have to be on the other side of the border to be successful."[82]

Finally, if we want people to be successful on the Canadian side of the border, we have to welcome the money and the people who make success happen, no matter where they may be from. We have already seen how important Canadian-based multinationals and foreign-owned companies have been for the growth of productivity, the pace of innovation, and the diffusion of new technologies throughout our economy. We cannot hope to achieve our dream of a distinctly successful Canadian society by putting up barriers, by going back to the "guilty until proven beneficial" days of the Foreign Investment Review Agency.

That open door does not mean we should ignore the way companies behave within our society. The issue that should concern us, however, has nothing to do with the passports held by shareholders and everything to do with how the companies doing business here are helping Canadians to achieve their full potential in the global market. "In Canada, we should worry less about the nationality of capital and worry more about the behaviour of capital," said David Culver, chairman of CAI Capital Corporation and a former chief executive of Alcan Aluminium Limited. "I say that our country is better off with a good foreign investment that is well run than we are with a Canadian investment that is poorly run."[83]

In the knowledge-based economy, throwing out the welcome mat for investment dollars is not enough. Investment returns are driven by people, and those people have to feel welcome, too. This is a need that goes beyond competitive salaries, taxation, and social programs. This final piece of the puzzle speaks directly to social attitudes towards success — and it is especially important if Canada wants to attract and retain the kind of leading-edge entrepreneurial talent that is driving growth in the knowledge economy.

Cognetics Inc., a Massachusetts-based company founded by business and economic researchers from the Massachusetts Institute of Technology, studies the process by which individual companies grow and facilitate job creation. In its 1999 report "Entrepreneurial Hot Spots: The Best Places in America to Start and Grow a Company," Cognetics looked at which cities and regions in the United States were most successful in attracting fast-growing companies, and at the factors driving the location of these gazelles in every sector of the economy. It identified four "hard" determinants that are key to attracting and supporting such enterprises. Traditional factor costs — the local price for everything from labour to transportation and energy — appear all but irrelevant. What does matter is the presence of universities, skilled labour, and good airports. In addition, the region must be "a nice place to live."

We have already discussed the importance of universities as crucibles for both ideas and talent, as well as the importance of expanding our human advantage. The impact of airports with good domestic and international connections is striking, but echoes comments we heard in our interviews with the chief executives of larger companies. Top managers now spend a great deal of their time on the road. Consequently, the ease of travel and the length of time taken in trips to visit company operations, customers, suppliers, and investors are clearly factors in decisions about where to locate and whether to move head offices and strategic corporate functions.

Even more intriguing was the Cognetics finding about the importance of quality of life. This result is both good news and bad news for Canada. On the one hand, while we cannot do much about our climate, the report underscores the advantages our existing social infrastructure gives us — relatively low-density living, short commutes, high-quality schools, colleges, and universities, safe streets, well-supported cultural institutions, and so on. On the other hand, the report says that quality of life is crucial because skilled labour is essentially mobile — a fact that reinforces the importance of showing value for money, providing more of the good things in life without excessive taxation.

What may be most challenging for Canadians is the kicker in the Cognetics study, the significance of what it calls the "soft determinants" of entrepreneurial investment. If trying to define quality of life is hard, evaluating the impact of attitudes and culture may seem almost impossible. But the report's description has a resonance that speaks to the gulf in attitudes between American and Canadian society. As Cognetics put it, entrepreneurs tend to have big egos; moreover, they are unconventional and challenge the existing order. They are doing their best to steal market share, and to do that they steal people from existing businesses and get rich doing it. "Not all communities welcome somewhat crazy upstarts who steal their customers and their labor force, and, in the process, become wealthier than anyone else in town — particularly if they let you know it. Said another way, tolerance and recognition of new and different people doing new and different things is the hallmark of a place in which entrepreneurs will start and grow companies. Such wild and crazy people want to be wanted. They want to be recognized and respected for what they have done. They will gravitate to places that revere them and will avoid places that treat them badly."[84]

Canada can point to the success stories of many entrepreneurs who have built globally competitive ventures within our borders. The question is not whether such success is possible, but how to foster more of it. To persuade more of our talented people to pursue their dreams here, and to attract people with money and ideas to see Canada as their preferred base for growth, we have to look at our own attitude to successful people. If we do not, all our efforts to foster better schools and universities, better transportation and communications infrastructure, and even a better quality of life, will not suffice.

Not everybody welcomes constant challenges to the existing order. Given the disruptions involved, such resistance to change and to agents of change is not surprising. But in the end, as Cognetics suggests, the soft cultural dimension of a community is at least as important as all those hard determinants of investment decisions. Communities that choose to emphasize preservation of the existing order and to spurn those who would challenge it should not expect to attract the kind of investment that drives dynamic economic growth.

■ We Are Canadian

Having a good product is vital to sustainable success in any business. But whether the goal is to market beer or to market a country, image and branding matter too. "The fact of the matter is that people will identify with a brand because they want the lifestyle that the brand symbolizes," noted James Arnett, former chief executive officer of Molson Inc. in an interview on November 9, 1999. "It's a badge. If you're drinking with your friends, you position yourself by the beer you're drinking. A Heineken is a very different signal than a Budweiser or a Kokanee."

What image do we want to plant in the minds of foreign investors when they think of Canada? Should we be positioning Canada as attractive because it is so much like the United States and has such good access to its market, but a little bit different in ways that are nice? Or should we be basing our pitch on distinct advantages that emphasize our differences? For the moment, the Canadian way seems to be to muddle through, and the result is a brand that's bland.

Bland is not all bad. In a 2000 follow-up to their 1989 study of Canada's image abroad, Nicolas Papadopoulos and Louise Heslop of Carleton University noted that the image foreign buyers have of Canadians as a people produces a "halo effect" that rubs off on Canadian-made products. Only a few of the more than 6,000 respondents to their fifteen-country survey could name more than two products Canada makes, and most could not name a single Canadian brand or company. Yet, as Papadopoulos and Heslop put it, the resulting attitude could be expressed as follows: "I don't know what you make, but I think so highly of you that I guess whatever it is must be reasonably OK." Even when foreign buyers have never before seen a Canadian-made product and are aware of our strengths only in natural resources, Papadopoulos and Heslop conclude that stressing a product's Canadian origin would help. "In a global market where firms need to run twice as fast as before to stay in the same place,

Canadian products seem to be losing some ground in terms of buyer mind share. However, they are also associated with an extremely strong country image that, if used inventively in marketing strategies, may be able to contribute significantly to their international competitiveness."[85]

The BCNI has for years been a champion of the Canadian brand abroad. In recent years its presentation on Canada at the World Economic Forum in Davos has been entitled "Northern Renaissance." Such private sector messages can be very effective, often more so than ones seen as government propaganda. But the credibility of our messages abroad has always flowed from hard facts — good news and bad news alike. We have talked with enthusiasm about positive developments in our country, but we always temper our sales pitch with frank acknowledgement of the areas in which our country still needs to pull up its socks.

The fact is, we do have a strong base on which to build a global brand. We start, of course, with the obvious signs of today's economic strength. Our economy is creating jobs, incomes are rising, and governments have, for the most part, left deficits behind them. Inflation and interest rates remain low. Our superb trade performance in recent years demonstrates the benefits to Canadians and foreign investors alike of our excellent access to the rest of the North American market. Our well-educated workforce offers a plentiful supply of skilled labour. And, for better or for worse, our low dollar means that the skills we offer are cheap, at least in comparison with those in the United States.

Second, we can point to our extensive public infrastructure. The network of ports and airports, railways and highways that keep our country together is well integrated into the North American system. Our communications infrastructure and costs are among the best in the world. To that list we can add our good schools, public health care, social safety net, clean air and water, safe streets, and all the other elements of social infrastructure so important to quality of life.

Third, we are leaders in governance. We share a federal form of government with many other countries, but have managed to make it work not only across vast territories but also across a broad range of cultures. Through our history, we have enabled English and French to create a country, together with the people of our First Nations and more recent immigrants from around the world. In a world reeling from tribalism, we are a multicultural success story. We are not a melting pot of homogeneous patriotism, but a society in which people of all cultures and backgrounds can fulfill their potential and achieve their dreams without leaving their heritage behind.

In Canadian hands, federalism has demonstrated its ability to adapt to changing needs and to meld the interests of diverse groups and regions. This record has, in turn, been made possible by the independence and professionalism of our public service at all levels of government. And the integrity of our governments has been reinforced by a superb and independent legal infrastructure, including a judiciary whose expertise is respected and sought out by other countries worldwide.

Finally, Canadians reflect exemplary values. Our citizens, our enterprises, and our governments are respected for their honesty and integrity. We have been a force for peace in a world of conflict. We have been leaders in promoting human rights, labour standards, and sustainable development both at home and abroad. Our engagement as global citizens has given our country an influence in world affairs out of all proportion to our military or our economic clout.

These are all qualities that contribute to Canada's repeated ranking as the best place in the world to live. Despite that record, Canada's brand in the minds of global investors is much like that of its beers: good and dependable, but not well known and fuzzily positioned. We are too expensive to compete with the bargain brands, even if we wanted to. And we're not exciting enough to attract a loyal following at a premium price. Those who try us like us, but most don't even notice our label as they scan shelves packed with offerings from around the world. To ensure that we sustain both our economic and our social success, we need to build a brand that makes people excited. It's not enough to be good; we have to stand out. That does not mean we should try to be the best at everything, but it does mean that we must be more than a pale imitation. We have to create an image — backed up by reality — that is genuinely distinct.

Other small countries that have succeeded in establishing a global brand and attracting investment from around the world have much in common, including a strong social infrastructure and a high quality of life. But despite their similarities, each offers at least one compelling characteristic that is unique. Ireland, as we have discussed, chose dramatically lower corporate income tax rates. The Netherlands combined a legal environment that was very friendly to head offices with special personal tax treatment of expatriates working for those head offices. Switzerland shares a border and a language with its larger neighbours Germany, France, and

Italy but continues to build on its centuries-old reputation for absolute neutrality, absolute political and monetary stability, and a firm commitment to law and order.

Canada's reputation as a global conciliator and peacekeeper has given us disproportionate influence in circles such as the United Nations, but we need a more compelling characteristic if we want to stand out as a destination for talented people and global investment. It seems to us that the multicultural reality of Canada's society could give us that edge and enable us to become the meeting place for international cooperation in business, the preferred base for what Micklethwait and Wooldridge called the fourth stage of the global corporation. We have built a nation of diversity and tolerance. Where else in the world could the employees of a truly multicultural head office feel more at home than within the Canadian community? We think this should be Canada's objective — not just to attract factories, as in Ireland, or legal entities, as in the Netherlands, or bank accounts, as in Switzerland — but to become the home of choice for centres of expertise within global companies, a place where ideas and people and capital from all parts of the world come together and grow in harmony.

The fact that no city in Canada can challenge the scale and influence of a New York, London, or Tokyo does not mean that we are out of the running in attracting head offices and other key jobs within global enterprises. Consider, for instance, Minneapolis–St. Paul. It has many of Canada's disadvantages — a relatively distant northern location with a climate to match — yet it has become home to twelve Fortune 500 companies, including well-known names such as manufacturing powerhouse 3M, retail giants Dayton Hudson and SUPERVALU Inc., Northwest Airlines, Honeywell, and General Mills. Among other indicators of the resulting economic health are a 2 percent unemployment rate and an average per capita income that is almost $5,000 a year higher than the national average, yet one of the lowest costs of living among major American cities.

What drives this success? The local chamber of commerce points to indicators such as graduation rates — 15 percentage points higher than the national average for high school, and 7 points higher for four-year college programs. It includes a major hub airport, the eleventh busiest in the country, but also just twenty minutes from downtown. It boasts the second-lowest rate of traffic congestion in the country and the shortest average commuting times of all major American centres. And it emphasizes its extensive network of parks and recreation facilities along with a wide range of cultural attractions.[86]

There is nothing in this recipe that a Canadian city could not duplicate. Many of the factors that make a city like Minneapolis–St. Paul attractive as a location for large and small companies alike already exist across a range of Canadian locations. Most of the remaining shortcomings could be addressed through action at the local level as well as at the provincial and national levels. "You could create the environment that now exists in Boston in Toronto or Montreal," noted John Roth of Nortel. "You would not be disadvantaged by the border. Nortel has proven that. We are a Canadian company, but we do business as easily in the United States as within Canada. That is what free trade allowed. The problems we have are of Canada's own making. If the governments want to have more Nortels, they have to create the right environment for them. If they do not, they are basically going to end up selling harvesting rights for Crown land."[87]

In its 2000 list of the world's most desirable cities in which to live, William M. Mercer Companies LLC ranked Vancouver as tied for first place with Zurich, Vienna, and Berne. Based on thirty-nine indicators of quality of life, ranging from political, economic, and environmental factors to health, safety, education, transportation, and other public services, Toronto also made the top twenty in the world (tied for fifteenth). However, as Mercer warned in releasing the results, "at the very top of the scale, there is little to differentiate the highest-scoring cities."[88]

Maintaining a superb quality of life in Canadian communities is vital, but we cannot create a compelling global brand based on quality of life alone. In the competition for investment and talent today, being nice is not enough. Clean air, safe streets, and good schools all help, but many others offer those attributes too. We have to get the economic substance right as well. "There are two sides to globalization. On one side, there are strongly positive factors . . . improvements to people's standard of living, the benefits of new technologies and of trade liberalization," said Edward Newall, former chief executive officer of both NOVA Corporation and DuPont Canada. "The other side of that coin, however, is reduced control over the direction of your economy — unless you're smart enough to realize that the only way to win is to put an environment in place that is demonstrably better than the other places people and companies could go."[89]

Canadians in both the private and the public sectors must not be shy about our many strengths. Just as business and government leaders have used the Team Canada concept to enhance trade performance, so we need to work together to build Canada's profile and win greater recognition of our country's potential as the preferred location for investment in global enterprises. We have to be proud of what we have achieved together and tell the world about our confidence in Canada's future.

At the same time, however, we must address our weaknesses. We have to bring down our sky-high mountain of public debt. We have to reinforce confidence in the stability and ultimate strength of the Canadian dollar. We have to boost our lagging pace of investment in research and development. We have to become far more effective at turning new ideas into innovative businesses. And we have to rethink a tax structure that is undermining our competitiveness, endangering our base of human capital, and discouraging Canadians and foreigners alike from seeing this country as a viable location for successful global enterprises.

Most multinational corporations are still at what Micklethwait and Wooldridge would call the third stage of their evolution. They are global in scope. They use their operations abroad to generate ideas as well as to produce. They tailor global products to meet local preferences. But they still have firm roots within a national economy, roots that give the home country an edge in retaining a disproportionate share of that company's top jobs and high-value-added operations. For that reason, Canada must seek to grow more of its own champions. We must enable and encourage companies founded and based here to flourish on the world stage.

But the deeper challenge and, for Canada, the greater opportunity flow from the continuing evolution of corporate structure and strategy. As more multinational corporations become truly multicultural institutions, Canada should position itself as the logical place for such companies to establish and grow global centres of expertise. Gaining an edge in the competition for such centres has two dimensions, one financial and one human. The prerequisite for attracting investments of financial capital remains a powerfully attractive economic environment. The second element, however, is to establish just as attractive an environment for human capital. Canada must be a profitable place to do business; it must also be an attractive place to live. Neither condition alone will suffice. To be a magnet for investment and to build global champions, our social and economic recipes must blend seamlessly.

7

WALKING TALL AMONG NATIONS

> *Canadians hold deeply that we must pursue our values internationally. They want to promote them for their own sake, but they also understand that our values and rights will not be safeguarded if they are not enshrined throughout the international environment . . . They understand that our economic and security interests are served by the widest possible respect for the environment, human rights, participatory government, free markets and the rule of law.*[1]
>
> — DEPARTMENT OF FOREIGN AFFAIRS AND INTERNATIONAL TRADE, 1999

◀ ◀ ◀

If Canadians can be winners in the global economy by concentrating on Canada's domestic concerns, challenges, and opportunities in a global context, how can they be a powerful and constructive force *among* nations?

To project influence beyond our borders, we must first ensure that our own house is in order. This lesson is as old as history itself. There are countless examples of societies, nations, and empires that have extended their reach well beyond their frontiers, only to see their power wane owing to financial and moral rot at home. This theme has been a constant in the thinking of the Business Council on National Issues. It was reflected in the council's message in December 1983 to the Royal Commission on the Economic Union and Development Prospects for Canada. "In the face of a rapidly changing international environment, Canada must stake out its place as a competitor with global aspirations. We will be frustrated in this objective unless we move decisively to fix our domestic policies. We must wage war against deficits, curb inflation, achieve higher levels of productivity, improve the value-added of our exports, and reach out boldly to new markets. If we fail, we will be condemned to be bit players as other countries pass us by."[2]

As we have seen in previous chapters, Canadians have taken giant strides to deal with the weaknesses that, over the past three decades, have hobbled our domestic economic performance. The back of inflation has been broken, deficits have given way to surpluses, free trade has given greater vigour to our export sector, the overall tax burden has begun to fall, and deregulation and privatization have ushered in a more market-sensitive environment and, in its wake, a growing number of entrepreneurial successes. A stronger and more competitive domestic economy, together with a world-class social and governmental infrastructure, has positioned Canadians as potentially significant players in global society — all not a moment too soon.

■ The Responsibility to Engage

We believe that Canadians should build on these strengths, engage vigorously as global citizens, and work hard to extend Canada's influence and recognition in the global arena. Some are bound to dismiss this suggestion as pretentious, as un-Canadian, as somehow inconsistent with our self-proclaimed middle-power status. We disagree for several reasons.

First, it is in our interests to aspire to walk tall among nations. As we pointed out in the preceding chapter, we now live in an environment where country "brands" matter more than ever. In such an environment, selling our products and ideas is easier if we are known, appreciated, and respected — just as attracting investment and people to Canada is in large part a function of how desirable it is to live and work here.

Second, as Canadians we have a responsibility to engage in the global commons. Canadian media theorist Marshall McLuhan spoke of this responsibility well in advance of the Internet age. Writing in 1964, he said: "As electrically contracted, the globe is no more than a village. Electric speed in bringing all social and political functions together in a sudden implosion has heightened human awareness of responsibility to an intense degree." More recently, World Bank president James Wolfensohn offered a challenging interpretation of country and individual responsibility in the face of a globalized world. Speaking to members of the Business Council on National Issues in Washington, DC, on April 8, 1997, he said: "Neither countries nor individuals can any longer afford to think or act in isolation. A globalized world and a bewildering array of global issues demand our attention and our active involvement."

A third reason why Canada and Canadians should not shy away from active engagement globally is that we have much to contribute. At the individual level, Canadian writers, scientists, doctors, jurists, educators, business people, diplomats, soldiers, peace officers, musicians, and athletes possess qualities that are in demand the world over. At the country level, the maple leaf is a respected symbol that connotes honesty, competence, and efficiency in many fields of endeavour — in diplomacy, peacekeeping, development assistance, and international business.

A fourth reason for reaching out more emphatically into the world is that the Canadian "model" is worth exporting. Canadian governance, encompassing a parliamentary system, a professional and non-partisan public service, and a balanced federation, is a global asset of distinction. Canadian values are no less worthy, a point emphasized by the Canadian government in the statement cited at the opening of this chapter.

The attractions of the Canadian model are enhanced by another reality — our distinctive culture — which has been influenced by our history and geography, forged through compromise, marked by tolerance, and manifested in a vibrant multiculturalism. Canada's multiculturalism is a sign of the growing power of "hybridity" — an asset G. Pascal Zachary of the *Wall Street Journal* described as a source of vitality and creativity and the key to success in a globalized world.[3] In short, Canadians have learned to live together and are moving ever closer to one another at a time when many countries are flying apart. There is a lesson for the rest of the world in the success of the Canadian multicultural experiment.

In addition to these reasons for striving to be seen and heard on the global stage, Canadians can count on yet another advantage. Canada is not a superpower: it does not carry the stigma of a colonialist past, nor does it harbour any hegemonic aspirations. Canadians are not feared or mistrusted. To put it in the vernacular, Canadians are generally seen throughout the world as "good guys."

The flip side to this rosy view of Canada can be found in the plethora of misconceptions about the country, and here we offer a sample collected in the United States and in various other parts of the world. "Canada is somewhere north of here"; "Nortel Networks is an American company";

"Canada's health care system is socialist"; "All I know about Canada is that they have great hockey players"; "Canada is an exporter mainly of raw resources"; "I didn't know Canada had an army"; "Canadians are boring." These simple and erroneous views of Canada and Canadians suggest that, despite all our advantages, virtues, and achievements, we suffer from a weak country brand and that we are paying a price for it.

What issues are most relevant to our role and responsibilities in the world, and how can we build on our strengths and project them more convincingly?

■ Multilateral Trade and Canadian Prosperity

We begin with the multilateral trading system, a critical component of the global economy and one central to Canada's interests. Canada played a leading role in establishing the General Agreement on Tariffs and Trade (GATT). An enthusiastic Canadian government, together with twenty-two other countries, agreed to launch GATT on October 30, 1947. Although the much more ambitious International Trade Organization that was to administer GATT provisions was scuttled, largely due to United States congressional opposition, GATT lived on, initially not as an organization, but as a set of detailed "rules and obligations designed generally to prevent nations from pursuing 'beggar-thy-neighbor' trade policies which would be self-defeating if emulated by other nations."[4] Fifty years later, World Trade Organization director general Renato Ruggiero reflected on GATT's solid, albeit conservative, achievements:

> In many ways the formula of addressing the challenge of international trade cooperation on a professional, rather than a political, basis proceeded admirably. In the anonymity provided by Geneva, government officials worked quietly to promote their governments' trade interests. All had similar objectives: make trade freer, more stable, and more predictable, but not too quickly and without creating too many political problems.
>
> Much was accomplished. Barriers came down, but gradually. Rules were formulated, but implemented judiciously. Exports and imports grew, but at a pace that allowed for orderly adjustment. Problems were solved, but pragmatically. The reach and depth of the rules gradually expanded as governments gained increasing confidence in the multilateral system.[5]

Canada saw in early GATT rules the hope that they would expand its share of the world economy. Initially, the agreement did open Canada's markets significantly, but, over time, the benefits diminished. "By the end of the Kennedy Round," wrote Michael Hart, "they [Canadian tariffs] were among the highest in the industrialized world. The Canadian economy remained more sheltered than those of the United States and Europe. This strategy may have been good short-term politics, but proved to be poor long-term economics" (see fig. 19).[6] Hart went on to identify perceptively the consequences of a skewed Canadian trade policy:

> While the Canadian economy boomed, it did not become more outwardly oriented. For the three postwar decades, the Canadian economy remained at roughly the same level of international integration. Foreign direct investment in Canada, largely by American firms, helped to ensure that most of the goods Canadians consumed were produced at home. Canadian exports continued to be heavily concentrated in the resource sector, although some progress was made in upgrading some of these resources in Canada before exporting them to world markets. Canadian trade policy contributed to this pattern. Through the first six rounds of GATT negotiations, Canada zealously maintained high levels of protection for its manufacturing sector. The result was an inwardly focussed, foreign-committed manufacturing sector and an outwardly focussed, also foreign-dominated resource sector.[7]

As Canada entered the 1980s it became increasingly clear to business and government leaders that a protectionist stance was no longer prudent

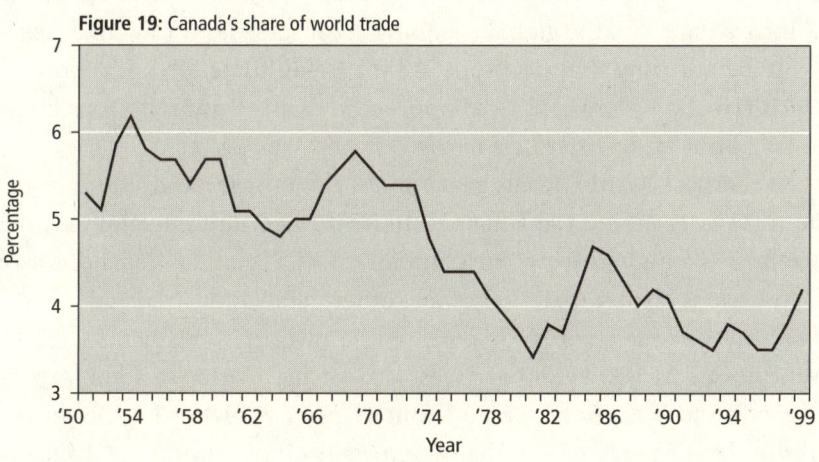

Figure 19: Canada's share of world trade

or feasible. This realization led to a profound transformation in attitude towards trade policy that manifested itself most dramatically in the historic reversal of Canadian business towards free trade with the United States, a subject we address later in this chapter. Throughout the 1980s and 1990s, trade became a powerful engine of growth. Total trade, inclusive of exports, imports, and goods and services, rocketed from less than 50 percent of GDP to over 80 percent. Although there is no doubt that a favourable exchange rate stimulated exports considerably during this period, the most striking aspect of this story is the degree to which Canada's economic structure has changed. The economy is more open, less dependent on the export of natural resources, and more knowledge-oriented and diversified. Canadian direct investment abroad now exceeds inbound foreign direct investment, and Canadian firms are more globally oriented and competitive.

The United States has been both the source and the destination of much of Canada's international trade activity, leading some to suggest that the multilateral trade system and its coordinating body, the World Trade Organization (WTO), are not deserving of the priority they command in Canadian trade policy circles. We disagree with this suggestion. GATT and its successor, the WTO, combine to have a strongly unifying effect on global commerce, extolling the virtues of openness and the rule of law. We would go further and argue that a strong multilateral trade system and an effective WTO should be one of Canada's highest strategic priorities. In the words of Robert Wolfe of the School of Policy Studies at Queen's University: "The WTO matters for Canada. It is our principal trade agreement with the world, and it plays a central role in stabilizing an increasingly volatile global economy . . . It safeguards Canadian sovereignty by ensuring that decisions are made multilaterally in a forum in which Canada has a voice — as opposed to being imposed on us by the power of our trading partners in the U.S. and Europe."[8]

As the post-Seattle debate rages about the policies and future role of the WTO, why should Canadians embrace further multilateral trade liberalization as a high priority? First and foremost, Canadian dependence on open trade is greater than that of any other major industrialized country. Every day, Canada records some $2.2 billion worth of business — exports and imports of goods and services — with the world. In total, exports of goods and services increased about 11 percent in 1999 to reach $410 billion, or 43 percent of Canada's gross domestic product. Given that approximately one job in three depends on exports, the 427,000 net new jobs created in 1999 reflects the beneficial impact of Canada's vibrant external commerce. Clearly, Canadians have a major stake in keeping the global economy open.

Second, multilateral trade liberalization has been a powerful catalyst for non-inflationary growth. The effects on the United States are instructive. Fred Bergsten of the Institute of International Economics points out that "lower import prices explain virtually all the decline in inflation between 1996 and 2000 . . . This decline in inflation alleviated the need for higher interest rates and tighter monetary policy . . . It thus permitted at least one and a half to two additional percentage points of economic growth that would otherwise not have been attainable."[9]

A third reason for vigorously advancing the cause of multilateral trade liberalization is that Canada stands to benefit in a number of specific ways. Further tariff reductions, and in some cases their complete elimination on a sector-by-sector basis, will improve market access for Canadian exports. Improved transparency in areas of government procurement will open up opportunities for Canadian suppliers. So will easier access in areas such as professional, business, financial, telecommunications, computer, environmental, energy, and transportation services.

A cornerstone of the WTO process is the dispute settlement mechanism, and here, too, Canada has a strong interest in ensuring that it operates more effectively, and that it is more transparent and inclusive. Institutional reforms that will allow the WTO to work more closely with other international organizations to improve coherence, complementarity, and coordination also will serve Canada's interests. In addition, Canada has a stake in making new rules that establish rights and obligations in areas inadequately covered by, or not yet subject to, WTO provisions. High on this list of priorities are intellectual property rights and rules governing competition policy.

Agriculture remains a thorny issue. WTO members in the Uruguay Round committed themselves to restart negotiations by the year 2000 to promote "progressive reductions" in agricultural supports and protection. Interpretations of the meaning of this term are as numerous as the member countries themselves. Export subsidies remain a serious problem, and the Cairns Group, of which Canada is a member, and the United States have proposed their elimination. Domestic subsidies were reduced in the last round, but many countries argue that these disciplines are being circumvented. Clearly there is much to be done on the agricultural front, and here Canada's stake is significant.

Finally, there is the issue of investment. Many investment issues are outside the area of WTO discipline, and investment incentives and export performance requirements continue to distort trade and investment flows among WTO member countries. The appetite for engaging in broad WTO negotiations on investment is weak in many countries, given the failure of the negotiations led by the Organisation of Economic Co-operation and Development on a multilateral agreement on investment. Here Canada's goals are directly tied to the agendas of developing countries. Given the importance of foreign direct investment to economic growth in these countries, it is they who should champion a WTO-wide investment pact while Canada presses for its establishment.

■ Global Social Priorities and Environmental Imperatives

Aspiring to walk tall in the global community also means according a high priority to fighting global poverty and disease. Healthy, well-nourished, and educated people are the basis of prosperous economies and stable states. Every year Canadians invest some $2 billion abroad in support of child protection, health and nutrition, and the war against HIV/AIDS. This is not enough: we should do more. Indeed, the whole of the industrialized world must do more. Relatively modest investments in primary health care, proper nutrition, water, and sanitation can make a huge difference in reducing poverty and improving quality of life. Canada is a contributor to initiatives launched by the United Nations and the World Bank, including the Roll Back Malaria campaign, the Global Stop Tuberculosis Initiative, and the Global Alliance for Vaccines and Immunization.

The global HIV/AIDS pandemic is killing more people than any other infectious disease and is spreading rapidly. Over 35 million people are infected worldwide, and more than 14 million people already have died from the disease. Canada's priorities here are the right ones: more vigorous education initiatives, improved reproductive health care, and enhanced support for vaccine development. But here again, Canada and the industrialized countries must do more.

Most Canadians are ignorant about the importance of development assistance. They see it as a form of charity, as an act of *noblesse oblige*. But global issues can no longer be easily compartmentalized and segregated. As Wolfensohn has argued repeatedly and eloquently, all mankind is part of an integrated whole. Canada must once again aspire to be a leader in championing the cause of development assistance. One major focus should be on building the "capacity" of developing countries to engage in the global economy. This participation requires much more than money for disaster relief, disease prevention, and physical infrastructure. Many of the poorest countries in the world need expertise, above all, in making democratic institutions work. They need help in building the political, legal, and financial infrastructure that is necessary to make any country a realistic candidate for greater flows of private sector investment. Here Canada can make a real difference. We are respected and trusted, and we have the know-how. In addition to being more generous, we must integrate our development priorities and strategies more successfully into our international trade and foreign policies.

Canada's effectiveness in developing countries will be greatly enhanced if Canadians play a leadership role in advancing trade liberalization there. As Jeffrey Schott rightly pointed out, "first and most fundamental, developing countries gain from the strengthening of the rules-based system. As the western partners in the trading system, they benefit the most when the major trading partners play by a common set of rules."[10] He went on to argue that WTO negotiations help developing countries undertake and "lock in" domestic reforms needed to advance their development objectives. In addition, they gain from reductions in agricultural subsidies and in peak tariffs in OECD countries.[11]

A clean and healthy environment should be among Canada's highest global priorities. Daniel C. Estey of Yale University ranked Canada seventh in overall sustainability in a preliminary assessment of global environmental indicators tabled at the 2000 Annual Meeting of the World Economic Forum in Davos. Since then, Canada has moved up to third place next to first-place Norway and second-place Finland. This improvement is encouraging, but we can and should do even better. Sustainability is intimately connected with quality of life. Quality of life is obviously about economic prosperity, about opportunities to learn, work, and grow. But it is also about the quality of air and water, natural spaces, and safe livable communities. The oft-repeated phrase "we do not inherit this earth from our ancestors, we borrow it from our children" is a sobering message to which we subscribe.

We also support the view that Canada should be a world leader in linking economic growth with sustainability. Canadians should set the standard in enhancing our natural capital — not just natural resources such as oil, minerals, forests, and fish but also precious ecological systems such as waterways and wetlands. Our stock of natural capital is, in reality, the basis for all economic activity. If we devalue that stock — through over-harvesting, pollution, or waste — both the environment and the economy will be at risk.[12] We need to live off the interest, not run down the principal. As environmentalist Paul Hawken reminds us, the economy is a wholly owned subsidiary of the ecology, not the other way around.[13]

The world's current population of 6 billion is already testing the carrying capacity of the global ecosystem. It is estimated to grow to 9 or 10 billion before the mid-point of this century. To respond to the material demands of this expanded population, we will have to increase significantly the value and usefulness that we extract from every barrel of oil, tonne of steel, and litre of water. This is man's *ultimate* productivity challenge. The encouraging news is that, with foresight, ingenuity, and the innovative harnessing of market-based solutions, it can be done. It may take some radical experiments and original thinking, but this kind of transformation is essential to protecting the global environment and providing a better quality of life for citizens of the world.

Some people have called this "the next industrial revolution" — the adaptation of technology, information systems, and new approaches to substantially transform the current systems of production and use of energy, materials, and goods.[14] A few companies are already experimenting with closed-loop systems — ones where materials are used and reused to add value, with no waste stream at the end. In effect, they are redefining their businesses to provide the services that consumers value, rather than merely making products to be consumed. A number of transnational companies are investing heavily in solar, wind, and other renewable resources because they now consider themselves in the energy *service* business — and not necessarily in the oil and gas business.

The attainment of global sustainability is a challenge of staggering proportions, but Canada and Canadian business should aspire to lead in its realization. Both government and business leaders demonstrated creativity and commitment in the lead-up to the 1992 Earth Summit in Rio de Janeiro. They should do the same now as preparations begin for the World Summit on Sustainable Development in Johannesburg, South

Africa, in 2002. As an energy-intensive economy and a major exporter of resource-based products, leadership will carry certain costs. But the very intensity of our energy and resource use presents a clear incentive for Canadian companies to pursue strategies geared to environmental innovation. The increasing competitiveness in these markets means that we must find ways to improve material and energy efficiency and to lower our costs.

Canadian companies are taking the sustainability challenge seriously because it makes good sense to do so — both as global citizens and as managers charged with generating competitive returns for shareholders. It is already clear that irresponsible corporate behaviour has repercussions that can affect financial results as well as global reputation. More to the point, a positive reputation for environmental responsibility is becoming a vital element in attracting customers, employees, and investors. Doing the right thing for the global ecosystem is a necessary element in any successful strategy for sustainable growth in shareholder value.

One of the greatest environmental challenges facing the international community is the threat of global climate change. While there is much that is not yet fully understood about the earth's climate system — and the contribution of human activity to changes in climate — it is a risk that must be seriously addressed. As we write, the global plan to implement the Kyoto Protocol is still being hotly debated. At the sixth Conference of the Parties to the United Nations Framework Convention on Climate Change (COP-6) in November 2000 at The Hague, the international community failed to produce a clear path forward on how, and to what extent, the protocol should be implemented. Canada took considerable criticism from the media, environmentalists, and other governments for its supposed part in the breakdown of the talks. We believe much of that criticism is misplaced. At COP-6, Canada, the United States, and other members of the so-called Umbrella Group argued for the use of international emissions trading to assist countries in meeting emissions reduction goals. They also suggested that credits should be earned for efforts to sequester carbon through enhanced management of forests and agricultural soils. These ideas were not recent inventions; indeed, they are integral parts of the agreement reached in Kyoto three years ago. Having taken on extremely ambitious targets, it is critical that developed countries have the flexibility to pursue the most cost-effective strategies.

The use of market instruments (the "Kyoto Mechanisms") has three distinct advantages: they can facilitate the engagement of the private sector in efforts to reduce global emissions of greenhouse gases; they will spur innovative approaches and new technologies that will be invaluable over the longer term; and they can deliver much needed technology and skills to developing countries, which will soon generate more than half of global greenhouse gas emissions. Similarly, the use of "sinks" not only removes carbon effectively from the atmosphere but also provides an added stimulus to the proper management of forest and agricultural lands in Canada and in other parts of the world, resulting in additional benefits beyond climate change. "Although often couched in terms of protecting the environmental integrity of the Kyoto Protocol, the arguments of many other countries at The Hague also reflected a desire to secure economic advantage."

Most Canadian business leaders engaged in the climate change debate do not regard the failure at The Hague as a reason for delay or inaction. They are moving ahead with prudent investments in energy efficiency, alternative energy sources, and new technologies that can improve industrial productivity and contribute to environmental goals. Notwithstanding this recent setback in the international negotiations, it is critical that Canada continue to play a leadership role in forging an economically defensible, long-term, and truly global approach to this issue.

As we have said, business can be a positive force for change in the global drive for more sustainable forms of development. Business can lead by example, in showing what can be done responsibly and cost effectively. It can work with governments, community leaders, and other stakeholders to design market-oriented policies that support enhanced environmental and economic performance. It can lend expertise and experience to educate employees, customers, and suppliers, bringing them to early and meaningful action. And in conjunction with the efforts of all citizens, it can reinforce Canada's brand as a force for responsible environmental leadership at the global level.

■ Canada and the United States

Any attempt to define Canada's global role and aspirations must factor in the hugely important relationship with the United States. In part, Canada's identity is shaped by how we see ourselves in contrast with the United States, and by how others perceive that difference. Still, the bonds between Canadians and Americans are deep in a historical, social, cultural, and economic context.

The economic dimension of the bilateral relationship is of impressive proportions. During the past decade, two-way trade has grown at an annual pace of 10.2 percent, raising the level of flows in goods and services from $235.2 billion a year in 1989 to over $622.7 billion in 1999. This figure represents over $1.7 billion of business per day. The United States accounts for over four-fifths of Canadian exports and three-quarters of imports entering Canada. From an American perspective, Canada does not loom quite so large, reflecting the different size of the two economies. Nonetheless, Canada carries an economic weight in the United States market well above its weight in global markets. For example, Canada's share of total imports into the United States rivals that of all the countries of the European Union combined and is well ahead of Japan's.

The stunning growth in two-way trade between Canada and the United States would not have been possible without the Free Trade Agreement (FTA) and its successor, the North American Free Trade Agreement (NAFTA). The FTA in turn would not have been possible in its time without the vision and initiative of Canada's business leaders who, in the early 1980s, abandoned their long-entrenched opposition to free trade in favour of a comprehensive agreement. When members of the Business Council on National Issues met to discuss the concept in Toronto on January 21, 1982, not a single Canadian government or political party supported the idea of a comprehensive free trade agreement. The chief executives decided, nevertheless, "to study the issue and to test the waters."[15] No one present at the meeting voiced disagreement with the proposition that "a comprehensive agreement that liberalizes trade across the board is worth pursuing. It offers the promise of substantial increased commerce between our two countries, improved access for our exports, more competitive companies and workers, and an improved rules-based regime to deal with disputes."[16]

Following the January 21, 1982, meeting, the first priority was to win support for a full-scale agreement among the member chief executives of the BCNI itself. The council's Task Force on Industrial Development and International Trade spearheaded the work, which garnered the early and prominent support of Noranda chief executive Alfred Powis. By September 1982 a consensus was established within BCNI circles to continue to push for free trade within the context of a "Trade Enhancement Agreement." The next priority was to attempt to win over federal decision-makers at both the political and the official level. Efforts on this front were largely unsuccessful. BCNI proposals were dismissed as unrealistic and politically unsaleable, although a member of the Trudeau cabinet, Edward Lumley, communicated quiet but unofficial support, as did Derek Burney, then a senior official in the Department of Foreign Affairs. The third priority was to gain support from senior American business leaders who were members of the Business Roundtable. Here, too, the BCNI's efforts were rebuffed. It was not until September 1984 that the proposal received a responsive hearing.

In the two-year period from 1982 to 1984, allies and converts to the free-trade cause grew in number. Independently of the BCNI, the Royal Commission on the Economic Union and Development Prospects for Canada, under the able chairmanship of former Liberal cabinet minister Donald MacDonald, was preparing to deliver a decisive vote of confidence in favour of free trade. Throughout much of this period, however, political sensitivities were such that the words "free trade" were usually avoided. Instead, the lexicon demanded substitutes such as "enhanced trade" or "freer trade." The chief executive of the Royal Bank of Canada, Rowland Frazee, who was chairman of the BCNI at the time and a tireless advocate of trade liberalization, summed up his frustration with the doublespeak. "Whatever we call it, the course we must follow is clear — tariffs must come down, investment must flow more freely and disputes must be settled in accordance with the rule of law. This is how we must define the future of the Canada–United States relationship."

A myth persists, mainly in nationalist circles in Canada, that the Americans foisted the free-trade initiative on unwilling Canadians. While it is true that United States ambassador Paul Robinson was an enthusiastic advocate and U.S. trade representative William Brock expressed genuine interest in BCNI proposals, the United States administration as a whole remained largely unengaged until the autumn of 1984. Vice President George Bush manifested this indifference at a private meeting in Ottawa with members of the Business Council on National Issues on March 23, 1983. When the BCNI suggested that a comprehensive free-trade agreement would be in the interests of both Americans and Canadians, he expressed interest, but acknowledged that he had never previously considered the idea."[17]

The reason for offering specifics on the role of the business community in embracing the rationale of free trade with the United States is to explain the profound change in attitudes that has helped to shape a new economic order in Canada over the last two decades. The war on inflation, the battle against deficits and debt, the drive to achieve consumption-based tax reform, the quest for privatization and deregulation, and the struggle for tax competitiveness have all been advanced by the decision of Canadians to endorse the FTA in the historic election of 1988. In the words of Donald MacDonald, "What the Canada–U.S. Free Trade Agreement did was offer Canada a process to adjust to a much more competitive world."[18]

The change in attitude that fuelled the powerful shift in Canadian business towards free trade was mirrored in a new political consensus as well. When the BCNI created the Canadian Alliance for Trade and Job Opportunities, which became the principal private-sector advocacy coalition in favour of free trade in the lead-up to the 1988 federal election, it invited two distinguished political leaders to co-chair the initiative — Donald MacDonald and Peter Lougheed, a former Conservative premier of Alberta. Earlier in the decade, Lougheed had been one of the first premiers to grasp the potential for a free-trade agreement with the Americans.[19] They proved to be powerful and effective advocates: "In the titanic struggle to win the hearts and minds of Canadians in favour of this all important free trade agreement," commented one observer at the time, "Canada's business leadership is fortunate to count as allies two respected political leaders of profoundly different traditions, perspectives and geographical roots. They represent the vanguard of what will be a certain re-alignment of mainstream party views towards the issue of free trade in this country."[20]

After more than a decade, what can be said of the impact of the FTA? Professor Richard Lipsey offers the following assessment:

> *None of the dire predictions of the opponents came to pass. . . . Canadian exports have expanded greatly . . . proving that Canadian industry was ready to compete on equal terms both with the Americans and the rest of the world. Canada had an export-led recovery from the deep worldwide recession of the early 1990s . . . Significant adjustment occurred as inefficient areas of production contracted and efficient areas expanded . . . Canada got a dispute mechanism that by and large has worked well . . . Canada has been protected against the upsurge of U.S. protectionist sentiment . . . And increasing amounts of foreign direct investment entered Canada over the first years of the FTA, indicating a willingness of foreign firms to locate in Canada to serve the North American market if costs and other economic calculations justified that decision.[21]*

Canadian business leaders have been unequivocal in their endorsement of the overall effects of the FTA. The perspectives of three seasoned veterans who experienced the impact of the FTA on their enterprises are instructive. Noranda's Alfred Powis said, "the free-trade agreement and the lengthy debate that preceded it brought the hard reality of global competitiveness to our front door." NOVA Chemicals chairman Ted Newall pointed out that "the FTA in effect created a single market for products, services, talent, and ideas. It made us much more outward-oriented and competitive by compelling us to benchmark ourselves against the best that the United States could muster." Former Alcan chief executive David Culver offered the following assessment: "The Canada–United States Free Trade Agreement has had an indisputably positive influence on our exports, on the efficiency of our production and on the effectiveness of the rules-based relationship with our most important trading partner. But its greatest impact has been on the Canadian psyche. In embracing the FTA as a country, we proved that we had the confidence to graduate to world status."

Interviews with Canadian chief executives participating in the BCNI's Canada Global Leadership Initiative in 1999 bolstered an already strong consensus on the results of the FTA. The evidence most often cited is the explosion in bilateral trade and investment; the exponential rise in strategic alliances, mergers, and acquisitions; the deepening integration of capital markets; and the increasing two-way flow of people, products, and innovation.

So far, so good — but what about the future of the Canada–United States relationship? This is one of the most complex and perplexing questions facing Canadians. We are not helped by the sense of complacency that permeates thinking on the issue. Ten years of extraordinary economic performance in the United States, mirrored by good economic times in Canada, have led many to believe that the status quo in the bilateral relationship is just fine. Derek Burney, CAE Inc. president and chief executive officer and former Canadian ambassador to the United States, warns against complacency: "Benign neglect of the USA by Canada can be very damaging to our well being. Managing this complex relationship has to be a top priority for our government, whether they like it or not."[22]

Michael Hart identifies a number of issues that should be addressed if Canada and the United States are to reap the full benefits of deepening bilateral integration:

- for *customs and border administration*, more progress needs to be made on various initiatives to facilitate, streamline, and even eliminate the need for customs clearance of both people and goods;
- for *tariffs and related programs*, such as rules of origin, industry on both sides of the border would benefit from the reduction and harmonization of Most Favoured Nation (MFN) tariff levels, obviating the need for many of these programs;
- for *product and process standards*, much more progress can be made in developing either common standards or greater acceptance of equivalence, mutual recognition, common testing protocols, and similar provisions;
- for *services*, there is room to move beyond commitments on market access to greater reliance on common standards and mutual recognition; sectoral discussions related to financial, transportation, telecommunications, and professional services would also provide further scope for reducing discrimination and for enhancing trade and investment opportunities, and for increasing healthy competition on a broader basis;
- for *government procurement*, the rules could advance from the limited entities method pursued in the GATT/WTO Procurement Agreement, and expanded in the FTA/NAFTA, to a full national treatment approach, mandating that governments throughout the region purchase goods and services for their own use on a non-discriminatory, fully competitive basis, at least insofar as North American suppliers are concerned;
- for *trade remedies* — anti-dumping and countervailing duties — rules could evolve beyond WTO-like procedural safeguards to common rules about competition and subsidies, thereby reducing the scope for anti-competitive harassment and procedures;
- for *competition policy*, more effort could be devoted to setting out common goals and providing a basis for cooperative enforcement procedures;
- for *investment*, provisions should move further down the track of enforcement of jointly agreed rules of behaviour by the domestic courts; and
- *institutionally*, the two governments may need to move beyond the ad hoc intergovernmental arrangements of the FTA and NAFTA towards more permanent supranational institutions.[23]

Increasingly, the economic dimension of the Canada–United States relationship is pressured by the forces of convergence. More and more, foreign policy, security, and immigration issues are affecting, and being affected by, economic and business issues. George Haynal, the assistant deputy minister in Canada's Department of Foreign Affairs and International Trade responsible for relations with the United States, explained this merging-of-issues phenomenon: "A process of policy convergence is already well in train. It is becoming more intense. Its end product is still hard to identify, but clearly it is building a level of integration that extends beyond the economy . . . The question is less whether we need to negotiate new instruments to further the process, but whether the public realm is capable of keeping up with emerging forces pushing us into deeper integration."[24]

The need to better understand and manage the convergence challenge has been a focal point of the BCNI's Canada Global Leadership Initiative. The initiative was driven in part by concerns of Canada's chief executives about growing problems and divergences in the context of the Canada–United States relationship: the gap in standard of living and productivity performance; Canada's declining share of foreign direct investment; the relative weakness of the Canadian dollar; the increasing number of firms and individuals going south in search of better opportunities and a more market-friendly environment; declining respect for the effectiveness of Canada's securities administration; and fears in the United States that Canada is too lax in protecting sensitive military products and services, and too fainthearted in dealing with narcotics smuggling, money laundering, and other international criminal activity.

The greater part of this book has been dedicated to countering these problems with the right blend of domestic policies, combined with strong leadership and the marshalling of political will. In the search for remedies, it is also important to deal with what economist John Helliwell has called the "border effect." Despite multilateral and bilateral efforts to diminish the impact of the border, he calculates that the propensity for Canadian firms to buy and sell domestically is twelve times higher than their propensity to do business internationally.[25] In contrast, Hart points out that the Autopact has virtually eliminated the border effect for trade in automotive products for the states and provinces in which the auto industry is concentrated.[26]

Economic statistics aside, the border effect is clearly diminishing owing to increased bilateral interchange of every kind. *Time* magazine journalist Stephen Handelman discussed the "new intimacy" in the Canada–United States relationship. Referring to a meeting of Canadian premiers and American governors in Brandon, Manitoba, in May 1999, he wrote: "They had a lot to be comradely about. During each minute that they laughed and sang in Brandon, Canada and the U.S. conducted more than $1 million in two-way trade. During the two days of meetings, roughly 1.1 million Canadians and Americans — of the 200 million who do so every year — crossed the 5,060 km border to live, work or play. As a result, a new relationship is being forged between Canada and the U.S. that will increasingly shape the future of both countries."[27]

A key element of a winning strategy for North America is to further reduce the border effect. The Canada Global Leadership Initiative crystallized concerns about the "Canada discount," magnified by Canada–United States imbalances. The increasingly worrisome evidence can be seen in the relatively weak Canadian currency, the brain drain, the depreciated value of Canadian assets (making them easy targets for American acquirers), and the productivity and innovation gap between the two countries. Increased integration with the United States would help Canadians close the gap. Economist Richard Harris drove this point home in a fall 2000 analysis:

> The phenomenal U.S. growth during the 1990s, with low inflation and low unemployment, has had a two-fold effect. First, it has quashed a lot of doubts by anti-market proponents as to the performance and merits of U.S.-style market capitalism. Historically, [Canadian] antipathy towards this model of economic development has precluded getting too close to the U.S. Second, the fact that the U.S. has done so well relative to Canada has raised the export dependency of Canada on the U.S. and increased the potential benefits to catch up with the U.S. Together with a lack of progress on the multilateral front this implies that deeper Canada–United States integration is the only realistic option for progress in developing significant market access.[28]

How to confront this reality in a way that best serves Canadian interests is one of the most important and complex challenges facing the country. According to Derek Burney, a reliance on rules should guide the future course of the relationship: "History demonstrates that we can harness our proximity to the U.S. to our advantage without compromising our identity or our right to disagree. We are best served by rules, agreements, and treaties which reflect genuine compromise and help temper the enormous power imbalance and by a sense of priority and political will which reinforce the importance of the relationship."[29]

Within BCNI circles, the debate is ongoing over the best strategy for responding to "the next chapter" in Canadian–American relations. Should it be one of incrementalism, based on negotiating specific issues as they arise, or, alternatively, one that is broad, sweeping, and comprehensive? The case for incrementalism is that it is process-oriented, rules-based, and carries with it a low profile and a manageable level of political risk. The problem with this approach is that it does not work well: in the early 1980s, for example, when the Trudeau government pursued the idea of sectoral initiatives with the Americans, the United States political system found it difficult to accommodate the specific concerns of a foreign government. Solutions tended to reflect a strong American bias. In the past, advocates of the issue-by-issue approach counted on a perceived special relationship between Canada and the United States to help facilitate such negotiations. This presumption can no longer be counted on.

Today, Americans see themselves as besieged by special pleaders, demanding concessions in return for which the benefits are minuscule or non-existent. The outcome of the November 6, 2000, national election, denying both Democrats and Republicans a decisive victory and revealing sharp divisions within the country, will not make it easier to engage the administration or the Congress.

We are of the view that a broad, sweeping, and comprehensive initiative is the only viable strategy and the one that will best serve Canada's national interest. Nothing less has any hope of attracting the attention of political leaders in the United States. To mount such an initiative will require that a wide range of issues be put on the table for discussion and negotiation. Hart has provided an example of Canadian and American trade interests that would be logical candidates for discussion (see fig. 20).[30]

We recognize that a Canadian initiative for a broader and deeper two-way economic agreement between Canada and the United States would attract opposition at home. To allay these fears and to gain mainstream political support in Canada, political leaders would need to explain the benefits thoroughly and objectively. They would have to differentiate between an initiative aimed at knocking down trade, investment, and regulatory barriers and a more far-reaching option, such as a customs union or a common market leading to an economic union. A customs union

Figure 20: Canadian and U.S. medium-term bilateral trade interests

Canada	United States
• trade remedy law • government procurement preferences • security-based restrictions • border restrictions (e.g., temporary entry, customs procedures) • state and federal agricultural programs and practices • standards-related issues • competition policy • investment restrictions • dispute settlement provisions	• agricultural supply management • Canadian content and similar cultural policies • border restrictions (e.g., refugee policies, customs procedures) • provincial and federal agricultural programs and practices • intellectual property–rights issues • telecommunications • investment restrictions

would involve the creation of a common external trade policy and the free movement of goods and services within the treaty area. A common market would involve the free movement of goods, services, capital, and technology as a precursor to an economic union. In turn, an economic union would introduce a unified monetary policy and currency and allow for the free movement of people within the union's borders.

Although the common market and economic union options would deliver important economic advantages, they would carry with them the requirement for shared political and economic institutions. They also would demand a very considerable ceding of sovereignty. Inevitably, they would lead to demands for exchange rate fixity, as economists Thomas Courchene, Richard Harris, and others have advocated. The floating exchange rate for the Canadian dollar is disappointing, they argue. It has been prone to major misalignments, as its current weakness demonstrates, which puts Canada at a disadvantage in the North American competition for physical and human capital investment. A formal North American Monetary Union, they suggest, would offer important benefits for macroeconomic stability and financial integration.[31] Economist and Nobel laureate Robert Mundell makes his preference clear: "Other things being equal — including inflation rates — large currency areas are more stable and resistant to shocks than small currency areas. In a monetary union or fixed exchange rate arrangement between a large and a small country, most of the gain goes to the small country."[32]

As authors, we share a long-standing commitment to the virtues of a floating exchange rate, and we are not alone. Former Bank of Canada governor Gordon Thiessen, like his immediate predecessors, has been a stout defender. In addition, a vast number of economic thinkers are ready to defend the float, among them another Nobel laureate, Milton Friedman. Friedman's rebuttal of Mundell is based on a "different strokes for different folks" thesis that recognizes the significant differences in the makeup of the two economies as well as the implications for sovereignty.[33]

Political support for a common market or an economic union is minuscule in Canada and virtually non-existent in the United States. The idea of monetary union, in contrast, commands a small degree of interest and support in Canada, but none to speak of in the United States. Whether the impact of globalization and continuing north-south integration will kindle interest in both countries in moving towards much deeper levels of integration remains to be seen. The absence of political support for these options should not preclude their thorough study and evaluation, however, along with a vigorous public debate. In the meantime, the Canadian government should engage in an urgent re-examination of its attitudes, policies, and strategies for dealing with the United States. To continue in passive management of the relationship would be irresponsible. At the level of the prime minister, the cabinet, and most senior echelons of the public service, the United States deserves a higher degree of focus and a better-defined, more proactive strategy. The suggestion has been made in BCNI circles that the prime minister or the minister of foreign affairs should chair a special committee of ministers to manage strategies and issues dedicated solely to the United States.[34] A greater number of top-notch people and considerably expanded financial resources are needed to implement the strategy, and improved coordination of efforts within federal and provincial levels of government is critical.

In the United States itself, a much stronger and more visible Canadian presence is urgently needed. The resources available to Canada's embassy in Washington and to Canadian consulates throughout the United States should be increased significantly. Coordination of efforts with Canadian companies and business organizations in marketing the Canada brand should be stepped up. Canadians are not without friends and allies in the new Bush administration and in the Congress. These links must be nourished and reinforced. In this regard, we are encouraged by affirmations made following the November 2000 federal election by Canada's new minister of foreign affairs, John Manley, and by international trade minister Pierre Pettigrew that bolstering Canada's presence in the United States will be their highest priority.

At the top of a new and invigorated agenda should be the negotiation of a comprehensive initiative aimed at erasing remaining trade, investment, and regulatory barriers between the two countries. The agenda must also take into account the reality of convergence. Foreign policy, security, and immigration issues must be incorporated into the overarching strategy for dealing with the United States.

The strategy must also be sensitive to a relatively new but exceedingly important factor — Mexico. A little more than a decade ago, Canadian political and business leaders would not have predicted that a reformed Mexico, in short order, would become a partner in the Canada–United States Free Trade Agreement. When senior Mexican business leaders met with BCNI representatives in Toronto in 1989 to seek advice on how best to advance their country's aspirations to become a free-trade partner, the response on the part of Canadian chief executives was one of incredulity.[35] Mexico was perceived as an inward-looking developing country with a relatively closed economy and a troubled history with its northern neighbour.

With the signing of the North American Free Trade Agreement on December 17, 1992, Mexico accelerated its agenda of economic reforms. Its presence within NAFTA helped it survive the peso crisis of 1994 and, since then, it has made remarkable progress. Mexico is now the second largest national trading partner of the United States after Canada, and Mexican political leaders and officials are openly predicting that, in trade terms, Mexico will eclipse Canada within the decade. The likelihood of this happening was reinforced recently by the United States ambassador to Canada, Gordon Giffin: "Mexico might be our largest trading partner in the next five years . . . certainly in the next ten, they might be."[36] On the political radar of the United States, Mexico is a much more pressing preoccupation than Canada. Some 20 million Americans have family ties to Mexico, and the flow of drugs and illegal migrants into the United States is a source of major concern to American policy-makers.

The Mexico factor may well inhibit efforts at expanding and deepening cross-border trade and investment ties between Canada and the United States. While political and business leaders in the United States might see real merit in accelerating economic integration with their Canadian counterparts, sensitivities towards Mexico may cause them to drag their feet or to insist that the process be trilateralized. Trilateralization would virtually guarantee that progress would be slow and, in the near term, limited in scope. But this concern should not deter Canada from vigorously pursuing the United States strategy we are advocating. The building of a new "special relationship" will be difficult, but not impossible, if we in Canada are prepared to advance our vision for deeper integration with a clear plan, sustained effort, and the necessary resources. Ambassador Giffin echoes the need for action, urging Canadians to adopt "a coherent, planned, strategic approach."[37]

As for Mexico, significant opportunities beckon. On December 1, 2000, Vicente Fox was sworn in as president. A leader with vision and impressive political skills, he has promised far-reaching reforms aimed at achieving higher and more equitable economic growth and a more open society. At both the political and the private sector levels, there are important and growing synergies between Mexico and Canada that will benefit both countries.

■ Pursuing Smart Regional Strategies

So far, we have discussed Canada's priorities in the multilateral and North American contexts. Some would say this outreach is enough; we cannot do much more. We reject this notion. Globalization has opened up the entire world to Canadian ideas and products, and we must respond to opportunities wherever they are. But some countries, regions, and markets deserve more attention than others. We begin with the European Union.

▼ Canada and the European Union

By any measure, the European Union is a political and economic heavyweight combining fifteen countries, a population of 375 million, GDP in excess of $12 trillion, and 19 percent of world exports. Deeply rooted historical ties, Canada's sense of attachment to Europe, and the desire of a succession of Canadian political leaders to reverse the relative decline of Canada-Europe trade and investment vis-à-vis the United States prompted a number of government-led initiatives in the 1990s. In the autumn of 1994 International Trade Minister Roy MacLaren proposed a free-trade arrangement between Canada and the European Union that would prepare the ground for a more ambitious pact between NAFTA and the European Union. Several months later, Prime Minister Jean Chrétien went even further to propose a NAFTA–EU free-trade agreement. Canada's heady ambitions were soon to suffer a setback, however. A fishing dispute, the "turbot war" involving Canada and Spain, plunged relations between Canada and the European Union into a chill. When representatives from Washington and Brussels launched bilateral discussions in the autumn of 1995, Canada's attempts at trilateralizing the talks were rebuffed. The Europeans and the Americans reached an accord and, after some delays, an accord with Canada followed in December 1996.

In October 1997, Prime Minister Chrétien again called for a transatlantic free-trade zone, which failed to ignite interest on the part of the European Union, although Canada was actively engaged in attempting to forge a trade pact with the countries of the European Free Trade Association (EFTA) — Norway, Switzerland, Iceland, and Liechtenstein. In 1998 the Americans and Europeans managed to cobble together the Transatlantic Economic Partnership initiative, in which they pledged to join forces to improve market access for goods, services, and agricultural products and to promote bilateral and multilateral trade reform. Not to be left behind, Canada and the European Union in December 1998 concluded an EU–Canada Trade Initiative similar to the Transatlantic Economic Partnership.

Behind this tangle of negotiations and agreements lies growing concern and frustration in Canadian political and business circles. It is clear that the interests of the two economic superpowers dominate the transatlantic agenda and that Canada is considered a sideshow. The level of discontent with the status quo was expressed in strong terms by Donald MacDonald: "The EU has rejected Canadian proposals for free trade negotiations. We are simply not important enough to them. Canada has found it a more positive investment of time and effort to negotiate with partners elsewhere than Europe."[38] So far, attempts at trilateralizing the agenda have failed, owing to resistance from both the Americans and the Europeans. In the meantime, Canada and the United States are pursuing parallel but separate tracks in their economic relations with the European Union. Both countries have agreed with their European counterparts to take joint action on multilateral matters and to enhance bilateral co-operation in such areas as mutual recognition, services, government procurement, intellectual property, competition policy, cultural co-operation, and business dialogue. But real advances have been minuscule, as tensions and differences on major issues such as agriculture prevent any significant leap forward.

In the meantime, Mexico and the European Union reached an agreement in November 1999 that will free bilateral trade in industrial goods by 2007, and in agricultural products by 2010. The agreement does not stop there: it covers dispute settlement, government procurement, services, investment, competition policy, and intellectual property. Startled Canadians and Americans were told that the European Union was prepared to deal with Mexico because agriculture and culture were not significant impediments. The message here is clear for Canada: either we accept that closer trade and investment ties with Europe must follow in lock-step with the United States or, as a country, we must pursue our bilateral ambitions with the Europeans with greater vigour, insistence, and creativity. We favour the latter course. An ever-larger and more prosperous European Union is an essential partner for Canada politically, and a critical player in terms of trade, investment, and economic cooperation. Two-way trade between Canada and the European Union at somewhat less than $50 billion in 1999 is no match in the face of the Canada–United States equivalent. But the real message here is that the potential for much expanded links is so significant that half-measures will not do any longer. This conviction prompted a strong appeal to EU Trade Commissioner Pascal Lamy at a meeting with Canadian business leaders in Ottawa following the December 2000 Canada–European Union Summit. Lamy was encouraged "to recognize the strategic value of a Canada–European Union free-trade pact as a precursor to a comprehensive transatlantic agreement involving the United States."[39]

Canada's strategy vis-à-vis the European Union must be comprehensive, with important economic and political dimensions. Canadian political scientist Donald Barry has made the case for such a strategy:

> Canada needs to develop a broader agenda if it is to engage and hold the EU's attention. That agenda should go beyond economic cooperation to take account of the Union's growing importance as a political actor. It should embrace such issues as circumpolar relations (grounded in Canada's interest in the north and the emerging Northern Dimension of EU policy), human security (arising out of Canada's human security agenda and the Union's Justice and Home Affairs, and democratic development concerns), and conflict prevention, peace enforcement, and peace-building (based on Canada's long-standing involvement in peacekeeping and the EU's incipient Common Foreign and Security Policy).[40]

In December 2000 Jacques Chirac, president of France and president of the European Union, spoke of the vast potential for dialogue and cooperation that is opening to Canada and the European Union:

> We must capitalize on the potential and meet the challenges of new technology, expand exchanges between our students and scientists, pay special attention to the expectations of our civil societies and consumers, fight together against crime infiltrating our borders, promote a consistent approach to development assistance, and foster joint participation by our armed forces and police in operations to keep the peace. These are the issues that unite Europeans and Canadians now and in the future.[41]

We identify squarely with the growing number of influential Canadians who yearn for a deeper transatlantic bond and claim that simple dialogue and cooperation on these issues are not good enough. But this bond is only the stuff of dreams unless Canadian political and business leaders are prepared to do what it takes to consummate a marriage — for which, at present, there is a singular lack of appetite on both sides of the Atlantic.

▼ Canada and the Asia Connection

In the 1990s it was common to envisage the twenty-first century as "the Pacific century." The Asian financial crisis in 1997/98, however, and Japan's inability to emerge from its decade-long economic malaise cooled some of the ardour of the most enthusiastic of the Asia boosters.

We are convinced that Asia's long-term prospects are very attractive and that Canada must continue to identify the Pacific rim countries as a strategic priority for trade, investment, and economic cooperation. This is one of the key reasons for Canada's involvement, with active business support, in the Asia Pacific Economic Cooperation (APEC) initiative. Outstanding economic performers such as Hong Kong, Singapore, Taiwan, and, despite its recent difficulties, Korea should remind us of the region's potential for growth and innovation. To these we would add the growing importance of the linked economies of Australia and New Zealand.

A centrepiece of Canada's Asia strategy must be Japan. The second-largest economy in the world, Japan has a gross domestic product about half that of the United States and equal to the combined markets of Britain, France, and Italy. Per capita income, even after a decade of slow growth and economic turmoil, remains one of the highest in the world. Japanese investment abroad has grown steadily over the past decade and a half, as export-oriented firms have moved some operations out of Japan to lower-cost locations or to be closer to markets or desired technologies.

Japan continues to face serious economic difficulties, and there is a possibility that the situation may worsen. However, when the Japanese economy recovers and the significant reforms already in place take a deeper hold, we expect Japan to renew its steady growth and show once again its remarkable capacity to adjust and adapt. As it does, Canadian firms will want to be in a position to be part of that process, as suppliers of technology and inputs, as investment partners, and through joint ventures in third markets.

In single-country terms, Japan is now Canada's second-largest trading partner and its fourth largest source of foreign direct investment. At the political level, the relationship is largely free of friction, and the two countries enjoy a positive image of one another. The disquieting aspect of the relationship is that it is stagnating in economic terms. Put another way, the relationship has lost its economic momentum. The value of bilateral trade flows over the past decade has been essentially flat, bilateral investment flows remain at extraordinarily low levels, and, despite the growth of the knowledge-based economy, the mix of products being traded has changed only marginally over the past decade.

Concern about this stagnation drove the BCNI and Japan's leading business association, the Keidanren, to launch a joint exercise in 1999 to examine ways to expand trade, investment, and business cooperation between the two countries. At the Tokyo meeting of the Canada Japan Business Committee on May 15, 2000, the two organizations presented their findings and recommendations. They called for stepped-up sectoral co-operation and indicated an openness to examine the potential for free trade between the two countries. The disappointing performance of the Japanese economy over the past decade and the persistent inability of Japan to break out of its economic malaise has prompted some Japanese to call for a fundamental reassessment of the country's staunch commitment to an exclusively multilateral approach to trade agreements. The setback in Seattle in 1999 and the fact that Japan is one of the few developed countries that does not partake in a regional free-trade arrangement have served as a catalyst for the reassessment of current policies. One signal of Japanese intentions has been the opening of negotiations between Japan and Singapore aimed at concluding what in effect would be the first of Japan's bilateral free-trade agreements.

At the Tokyo meeting of the Canada Japan Business Committee, the BCNI underscored the growing economic convergence between the two countries — a theme the council had first raised in May 1991 on the occasion of a BCNI-led CEO mission to Japan. In its May 2000 recommendations the BCNI called for the adoption of free trade between Canada and Japan within five to seven years, based on tariff-free trade on virtually all industrial and agricultural products, the elimination of discretionary licensing, full application of non-discriminatory investment principles, and deeper commitments on trade in services than under the current WTO agreement. The council called for a fresh and modern interpretation of the relationship: "The old model of a resource-rich, labour-poor economy finding complementarities with a resource-poor, labour-rich partner no longer responds to reality."[42]

While the reaction of the Keidanren to the proposals of Canadian business leaders has stirred some real interest in Japanese business circles, the attitude of the Japanese government has been cautious and non-committal. Officials in some ministries, such as Trade and Industry (MITI), have quietly expressed interest. Others, such as Foreign Affairs (MFA), have been quite negative. It would be a mistake to put Japan and the European Union in the same category as far as Canada's aspirations for transoceanic free-trade arrangements are concerned, but in one respect there is a similarity: both Japan and the European Union will not easily be convinced of the merits of free trade with Canada. Seeking a deeper and more balanced relationship with the Japanese is well worth the effort. CN chief executive Paul Tellier, speaking in his capacity as co-chairman of the Canada Japan Business Committee, explained it this way: "Japan is the world's second-largest economy and Canada's second-largest trading partner. If we are smart, we will build on our relationship with the Japanese. Results will take time, but they are worth the investment."

▼ Key Emerging Markets

We have stressed throughout this book the need for choices and, while every real opportunity wherever it may exist in any part of the world should not be ignored, some key economies and markets will justify a special effort. We have made the case for North America, the European Union, and Japan. We would add three emerging economies to the priority list by virtue of their size, long-term economic potential, and growing political influence: the People's Republic of China, India, and Brazil. These countries are not easy to deal with, but they merit sustained effort and a long-term view. Each of the three offers up a rich diversity of markets within its borders. All three have been the target of Team Canada missions led by the prime minister and involving provincial government leaders and business representatives. To date, the return on the time and effort invested has been relatively small. But the case for courting opportunities among these potential economic heavyweights of the decades to come reinforces the adage that "smart capital has foresight and patience."

The People's Republic of China continues to be a global leader in attracting foreign direct investment. Chinese accession to the WTO will further spur trade and investment opportunities for those countries and businesses willing to sustain their China commitment. Canada and China currently enjoy a positive political and economic relationship. Strong links between the Hong Kong Chinese and their Canadian counterparts further enhance these ties. The importance of the China connection to Canada is underscored by the fact that yet another Team Canada mission is planning to visit Beijing, Shanghai, and Hong Kong in February 2001.

India attracts ten times less foreign investment than China does, and its exports are also considerably smaller. A major problem is the slow pace of reform in India, accentuated by several impediments to improved competitiveness — high costs for power and borrowing, red tape and corruption, high taxes, slow transport, and inflexible labour markets. Still, India's business class is determined to push for deeper and more rapid reforms. Clearly, the country's considerable potential cannot be ignored.

Canada's current relations with Brazil are chilly because of the acrimonious dispute involving Bombardier and the Brazilian aircraft manufacturer Embraer. Once the dispute is resolved, it will take some time to heal the relationship. With the long term in mind, Canada should make the effort. Brazil has important links to other South American economies in which Canada has an interest — particularly Argentina and Canada's free-trade partner, Chile. Brazil is also a key player in the Free Trade Area Agreement of the Americas initiative (FTAA), which will gather heads of governments at a Summit of the Americas in Quebec City in April 2001, chaired by Prime Minister Chrétien.

Canada's commitment to the FTAA process and goals (free trade by 2005 or sooner) is especially worthwhile given the long-term potential of the Latin American economies. Latecomers, Canadians are now political and economic players in the hemisphere, and if we play our cards right, our influence there will grow significantly over the next decade.

■ The Need for Focus

One of the greatest temptations in international economic affairs is for countries to try to do too much. Canada's attractive geostrategic position and its multiplicity of links, whether defined by the Atlantic, the Pacific, the Arctic, the hemisphere, the Commonwealth, or the francophonie, can easily lead to over-stretch. The same applies to companies that fail to take account of their limitations, or that do not recognize where their most important interests lie.

Walking tall means picking your avenues carefully and ensuring that your chosen destinations can be reached, with plenty of resources to secure your presence when you get there. Too many avenues or too many destinations will lead to confusion and exhaustion. In this chapter, we have challenged Canada and Canadians to engage vigorously as global players because we have something to offer the world and because it is in our interest to do so. But we have also suggested an approach based on priorities that make sense. They can be summarized as follows:

- pursuing an open multilateral trading system with effective and credible institutions as the country's highest strategic priority within a global context;
- demonstrating leadership in the development and support of global social priorities and environmental standards, with an emphasis on helping developing countries build the capacity to meet the challenge of governance and economic growth;
- taking the next steps in shaping Canada's relationship with its most important bilateral partner by far, the United States, within the context of a North America strategy, which includes Mexico;
- going well beyond the status quo in reshaping and strengthening key regional relationships, with the European Union and Japan having the highest priority;
- focusing on the most important emerging economies — specifically, China, India, and Brazil; and
- building on vigorous leadership in North America to extend Canadian influence in the western hemisphere through the Free Trade Area Agreement of the Americas initiative.

Achieving significant results in all these areas will require more than just focus. It will require leadership on the part of Canada's politicians, corporate community, educators, and many others. It will require much improvement in the coordination of effort and resources. It will also require a supportive foreign policy and a credible defence capability — both subjects that are beyond the purview of this book. Suffice it to say that Canada's aspirations to walk tall among nations will require a foreign policy that clearly embraces the doctrine of internationalism and recognizes isolationism for what it is — a silly and virtually impossible concept in a globalized world.

Canada must participate fully in global affairs, and that means having the strategy, the people, and the financial resources to do the job properly. The panorama of global affairs today is vast: in addition to exercising traditional diplomacy, it includes dealing with development, the environment, human rights, crime, terrorism, illicit immigration, conflict prevention and peacekeeping, and, in some cases, the need to wage war as our forces did at the time of the Kosovo crisis. A leadership role in global affairs, even from a middle-power position, does not come cheap — a fact that a succession of governments in Ottawa seems to have forgotten. It must also rest on a broad degree of understanding, engagement, and support from the Canadian public at large — a situation that does not exist in the country today and needs to be remedied.

Some argue that Canada's historical attachment to internationalism has been eroded because trade and investment have assumed positions of pre-eminence in our conduct of foreign affairs. But these two emphases should be complementary, not contradictory. We are strongly of the view that the vigorous pursuit of trade and investment liberalization globally is a powerful instrument of democratization, development, and conflict prevention.

If strategies, people, financial resources, and commitment are essential to an effective foreign policy, the same can be said for Canada's defence capability. Sadly, our armed forces continue to face a decline in effectiveness, and the morale of our troops is low. Canada contributes only 1.1 percent of GDP to defence. This rate is one of the lowest in the world, and the second-lowest in the North Atlantic Treaty Organization, where the average is 2.1 percent. In the words of the Conference of Defence Associations Institute: "There is a growing perception among allies that Canada has neither the will nor the resources to engage in anything more challenging than low-level peacekeeping . . . Canada has become in recent years less influential in international affairs, which can be linked in part to its military shortfalls. This has impacted negatively on both Canadian diplomacy and trade."[43]

Walking tall among nations requires that you have the wherewithal to defend your national interests. It also requires that, at the very least, you carry your weight in international circles — in the exercise of collective security or in the conduct of peacekeeping. Canada is capable of doing neither in an effective or a sustained way. This state of affairs is an embarrassment, one that will stand in the way of achieving our national goals and global responsibilities.

In our brief discussion of Canada's foreign policy and defence requirements, we have stressed the need for urgent and clear thinking, better public understanding and engagement, improved resources, and the resolve to integrate these critically important, credibility dependant assets into the country's mainstream. Professor Douglas Bland of the School of Policy Studies at Queen's University has appealed for a new and integrated approach that we strongly endorse:

> *Several converging, critical factors ought to compel Parliament to open comprehensive deliberations on Canada's foreign and defence policies. Canada faces continuous internal threats from globalized crime, terrorists, the drug trade, and illicit migration. External policies are pressured by fundamental transformations in international organizations and shifting political arrangements in Europe, Asia, and Latin America. Changing ideas about foreign policy and defence goals in the United States demand a Canadian response beyond indignation . . . If Canada is to protect itself from and help redress those problems and to be taken seriously in Washington, it must offer credible hard as well as soft national security options to Canadians and the international community."*[44]

8

HOW CANADIANS CAN TRIUMPH

If we want Canada to be a leader in the economy of tomorrow, we cannot succeed only by following others to where they have been. We have to learn from others — in North America, Europe, or Asia — but then we have to do better. As a small country within a competitive world, we are the ones who must try harder, who must anticipate rather than react, who must create change rather than adapt to it.[1]

— DAVID O'BRIEN, CHAIRMAN, BUSINESS COUNCIL ON NATIONAL ISSUES,
APRIL 5, 2000

◄ ◄ ◄

Canada is a country twice blessed, first by its vast lands and resources, and second by the talent and spirit of the millions of people who have chosen to make it their home. Canadians may be small in number, but that need not be a disadvantage in a world where nimbleness and flexibility are key virtues. We have a solid base on which to build, but we can aspire to do much more.

The first step in honing the northern edge that will power our progress is to agree on our shared goals, on what it is that we hope to accomplish together. Many of our ancestors, like many of the current generation of immigrants, came to this land with a common dream — to build better lives for themselves and their children. This remains our fundamental goal today. The question is what we mean by better lives — and how much better we should strive to make them.

In setting goals for ourselves, it is important to be ambitious. It is true that people who want more, when they already have so much, can be portrayed as greedy. For the most part, Canadians tend to regard "greed is good" as a creed that may work for some on Wall Street, but has no attraction for them. We, like most Canadians, believe strongly in the importance of caring and sharing, across regions and among people. But we see shared progress as an essential element in forging Canada's unique identity and as a foundation for global success. We make no apologies for being ambitious — ambitious not for ourselves but for our country.

Canada has achieved much in its relatively brief history, and we are rightly proud of our accomplishments together. But the welfare of mankind has never been improved by people who were satisfied with the status quo. As long as our efforts are part of building a better world, one that leads to a higher quality of life for all people in all countries, we should not be ashamed of being ambitious. For all the progress people have made within our borders and around the world, too many have been left behind. We can serve the less fortunate best by taking our place in the vanguard of global progress, showing by example how much people everywhere can aspire to achieve.

■ Setting Ambitious Goals

The goals we advocate here are targets to be achieved over the next ten years. Some of the structural changes and reforms that we propose will require at least that length of time before they achieve their full impact. Yet a decade is a short enough period that, if we want to achieve these ambitious expectations, we will need to begin vigorous action right away. The new millennium began on a strong economic note, yet, as 2001 dawned, there were signs of rapid deceleration in growth. The year was barely a week old when New York investment dealer Morgan Stanley Dean Witter & Co. declared that a recession already had begun in the United States. Chief economist Stephen Roach added that there was a 45 percent chance that the American slowdown would lead to a global recession before the year was out. A day later, CIBC chief economist Jeff Rubin slashed his growth projection for the Canadian economy in 2001 from 3 percent to just 1.6 percent, adding that he expected the Canadian manufacturing sector to follow its American counterpart into recession. Even if the good economic news of the past few years comes to a crashing halt in Canada in 2001, we remain confident that Canadians can make significant and sustained gains over the course of the next decade. Making the right choices will pay dividends through good times and bad.

In defining our goals, we start with broad measures of economic growth. This is not to say that economic goals take precedence over social ones; rather, social progress is much more difficult, if not impossible, to sustain without steady increases in our country's capacity to generate wealth. The obvious goal would be to match the real per capita gross domestic product of the United States. Surely, on average, Canadians should be able to aspire at least to an equal standard of living with people living on the other side of an all-but-invisible border. This objective does not mean that we must match American policies or their relatively unequal distribution of income. But there is no reason why, as a basic national goal, Canadians should not aim to match the United States in the size of its economy per person.

Achieving this goal within ten years will be extremely difficult. Industry Canada has calculated that, by 1999, the gap in real per capita GDP had grown to $6,700 (U.S.). Assuming that American and Canadian per capita GDP continues to grow at their respective annual trend rates of 2.1 percent and 1.3 percent, the gap would widen to $11,200 (U.S.) by 2010. Even if Canada manages to match the American rate of growth, the gap in the per capita standard of living would widen in that decade to $8,500 (U.S.). To close the gap entirely by 2010, Canadian per capita GDP would have to grow at more than double the American rate, at 4.3 percent annually.[2] Given the current rate of population growth, such an objective implies a sustained rate of overall economic growth exceeding 5 percent per year in real terms.

Such growth rates are not impossible. Canada's performance in 2000 was running close to that pace, and Ireland's astounding record during the 1990s showed that it is possible to sustain an even higher rate of growth over a decade-long period. Nonetheless, this rate of expansion would represent an extraordinary achievement.

If closing the per capita income gap in a decade seems too ambitious, let us settle on a slightly more modest but still challenging benchmark: sustained real growth in gross domestic product of 4 percent per year for the next decade. Our progress in 2000 shows that we are capable of exceeding such a growth rate during good years, and the challenge lies in maintaining a high average level of growth despite the inevitable periodic downturns. Assuming that Canada's population continues to grow at its current pace, such a rate of economic growth would still imply real growth in the standard of living of each Canadian of better than 3 percent annually. And, over the course of a decade, this growth would boost the size of our economy by almost half and the economic standard of living of each Canadian by more than a third.

Assuming that the American trend rate in per capita growth remains stable, such a goal also implies that Canada would outperform the United States by about one percentage point a year. This difference is roughly equivalent to the margin by which the United States outperformed Canada over the past decade. Outperforming the United States by any margin will be challenging enough, and the close integration of the Canadian and American economies means that exceeding the American rate of growth by a wide margin over a prolonged period will be even more difficult than trying to exceed the performance of other industrialized countries. But outperform the Americans we can and we must.

The next challenge is to make sure that such substantial gains are well shared. In the past, Canada has done remarkably well in maintaining a relatively modest spread between the best and the worst off in our society. After taxes and government transfers, the families in the top 20 percent have been left with about five times the income of those in the bottom 20 percent. There is nothing magic about this proportion, but it reflects the reality of Canadian society for the past two decades. We can presume that it is consistent with Canadian values of caring and sharing.

Canadians, like many others around the world, are struggling with methods by which to define poverty, and, in particular, whether to define it in terms of relative equality of income or an absolute standard of living. Rather than framing our goal as one of moving a set percentage of low-income families out of poverty, we suggest a simpler benchmark. In essence, we believe that Canada must demonstrate that faster growth can be shared by all. Specifically, the real disposable incomes of the worst-off 20 percent of Canadian families — their incomes after taxes, government transfers, and inflation — should grow over the next ten years at least as quickly as that of the average Canadian. Given our economic growth target, the real standard of living of Canada's lower-income families would then rise by more than a third within the next decade.

Such progress would not necessarily eliminate all instances of poverty even by today's various definitions, but it would have a significant impact. For instance, Statistics Canada's Low-Income Cut-Off varies by family size and place of residence. In 1998 a family of four was considered low income if its after-tax income fell below $27,890 in a city of 500,000 people or more, or below $18,285 in a rural area. The average low-income family fell short of its LICO by $6,638.[3] Boosting the incomes of low-income families by a third would move a large proportion above their respective cut-offs — and would clearly represent real progress by any definition.

There is no question that well-distributed and sustained economic growth of this magnitude would allow real progress in improving the quality of life of all Canadians. But how do we make such growth more than wishful thinking? The key, as we have said repeatedly, is to invest in people, in new ideas, and in new tools. We must also establish some key benchmarks that will help us to see whether we are on track towards the scale of growth we hope to achieve.

As we discussed earlier, the primary driver of higher incomes for Canadians must be higher productivity — the ability to get more value out of any input, from an hour of labour to a dollar's worth of new equipment. If we aspire to outperform the United States or any other country in terms of economic growth and family income, we must also aspire to outperform in boosting productivity. Our target for the next decade should be to boost productivity by one percentage point a year faster than in the United States, again effectively reversing the pattern of the past decade. To surpass this benchmark, Canadians must become much more aggressive in developing and adopting new technologies and in fostering innovation in every sector of our society.

The federal government has already adopted some useful targets that will encourage more innovation. For instance, the government has set a goal of doubling public sector investment in research and development by the end of the decade. We concur, and add that our goal should be to foster equivalent growth in private sector investment in R&D. We also have to make sure that our research leads to functional innovation and market success. In practical terms, we must boost our rate of patent applications to one of the top five in the world on a per capita basis. Given the importance of critical mass to the development of clusters of innovation, this ranking is the minimum to which we, as a smaller country, must aspire.

The next step is to ensure that more of our good ideas evolve into fast-growing enterprises — the global champions of tomorrow. Our rate of participation in entrepreneurial ventures is already high. Where we need to improve is in the availability of capital for growth. Our goal here should be to match or exceed the per capita rate of venture capital disbursements in that most entrepreneurial of cultures, the United States.

We will not succeed in creating a culture of innovation and in driving productivity to new heights without continuing improvements in the education and skills of all Canadians. Where people are concerned, what matters is our progress in helping more Canadians attain higher standards of education and functional competence. Canada already does well in basic education, but must do better. We suggest, as a minimum target, that, by 2010, more than 90 percent of Canadian children should complete the full high school curriculum on time or within one year of their normal graduation date. In the longer term, we should aim to reduce the proportion of 25- to 29-year-olds with less than a high school education to below 5 percent from 13 percent in 1998.

We should also improve the quality of what our children learn. As a national goal, we should try to move Canadians into the top spot in assessments of literacy and numeracy by the Organisation of Economic Co-operation and Development. Furthermore, given that the latest results from international math and science tests suggest that we have already become one of the better-performing countries, we should aim to be number one in these subjects as well. Only by shooting for the stars can we inspire the kind of innovation in our schools that will be needed to become the best in the world.

We need to ensure that all Canadians have access to and participate in meaningful lifelong learning. In part, we should maintain a strong rate of growth in the proportion of Canadians between the ages of 25 and 29 who have completed university. This figure rose from 17 percent to 26 percent between 1990 and 1998. Even if the growth rate levels off, we should be able to raise the proportion of university graduates to more than a third of young Canadians by 2010. The majority of Canadians still will not complete university studies, but participation in some form of post-secondary learning, whether through community colleges, apprenticeship programs, or private institutions, should become almost automatic for high-school graduates. Does this goal risk over-investment in post-secondary education, the possibility of producing more college and university graduates than our economy can absorb? In the short term, yes. But investing in human capital never produces a negative return. At worst, an oversupply of talented and skilled graduates may depress their earnings temporarily while creating another powerful attraction for global investors.

Once Canadians enter the labour force, every person should have access to continuous learning opportunities, whether provided directly by employers or indirectly through financial support for independent learning. Setting benchmarks for training is difficult because a great deal of learning occurs informally on the job, especially in smaller firms. However, as we develop better means of assessing and recognizing different forms of learning, we will be able to shape more effective strategies for boosting the rate of participation in training and lifelong learning.

The final set of targets relates to the third critical element in boosting innovation, productivity, and incomes: our ability to attract capital and to make Canada the home base of choice for global enterprises. Canada today invests far more abroad than it attracts in foreign investment. We need a healthier balance. Assuming that our share of global outflows remains stable, this means aiming to double our share of global inflows, from about 2.5 percent to 5 percent. Attracting this amount of foreign investment over the course of the next decade will only be possible if we succeed in winning a great many more continental and global mandates from multinational corporations, Canadian and foreign-owned alike. These mandates must extend across a wide range of industries and encompass both the production of goods and the provision of high-value services based in world-leading centres of expertise.

At the same time, we need to redouble our efforts to broaden the global engagement of Canadian enterprises of all sizes. To build more global champions, we must begin by expanding dramatically the number of Canadian companies that choose to grow beyond our borders. Our goal on this front should be highly ambitious — to triple the number of Canadian-based multinationals by 2010.

Except with respect to education and income distribution, indicators of social progress are noticeably absent from this list. It is obvious that Canadians share a wide range of social goals, from timely access to comprehensive and high-quality public health care to low crime rates, clean air and water, and extensive opportunities for cultural and recreational activities. As the federal government constantly reminds us, the United Nations keeps ranking Canada as number one in the world in quality of life, although the index cited is essentially based on just three groups of indicators: economic, education, and health. A broader set of benchmarks to measure our progress in delivering a higher quality of life for all Canadians is both possible and desirable.

But we must keep in mind that such benchmarks are primarily static indicators of outcomes rather than dynamic indicators of our ability to improve outcomes over time. The benchmarks we have outlined, targets for progress in innovation, education, and investment, are the enablers of social progress. If Canada can make economic gains on the scale we believe possible, we will have immensely greater ability to meet a broad range of social priorities. We focus on economic gains not because we think social goals are less important, but because developing the base is a precondition for having more resources to share in meeting our social goals.

Some of the benchmarks we have suggested may seem farfetched. But we recall the scepticism that greeted members of the Business Council on National Issues in the early 1990s when they outlined a series of policy priorities that, they suggested, could make Canada the top-performing economy in the G-7 by the end of the decade. Many of those policy suggestions were in fact adopted, and by 2000 that seemingly impossible goal had been achieved.

The growth goal we have set out here is at least as ambitious, and the benchmarks we have suggested will have to be part of achieving our desired pace of growth. We have deliberately set goals that will stretch us to our limits and perhaps beyond, goals that may prove impossible to achieve no matter what we do. To have any hope of achieving them, Canadians must show that the determination of the early 1990s was no fluke, and that we are capable of working hard together to build on our successes and deliver even better results for all Canadians.

While surpassing any of the benchmarks we have suggested will be tough, our goals are mutually reinforcing. Success on any one front will strengthen our ability to attain our goals on others. What will become most important is consistency — the will to stay with our goals through thick times and thin. As one of Canada's best-known entrepreneurs, Ron Southern, put it: "I figured out that Hemingway's novel *The Old Man and the Sea* evocatively echoed the message that to be great you have to last. It's a simplistic thing, but in every walk of life, we see something come up and then disappear, like a shooting star. To create something of permanence means having one's own objective, a reasoned judgement of what you can accomplish — not a fad, and not an unreasonable hurdle for your people."[4] We believe that the goals laid out here will not only generate enduring improvements in the quality of life of all Canadians but are within our grasp. There is no excuse for aspiring to less.

■ Twelve Ways to Sharpen Canada's Edge

Having set our sights high, we must consider what actions will be most effective in putting us on the right track. We suggest twelve strategic thrusts aimed at improving fiscal management, enhancing Canada's human advantage, building a stronger Canadian community, and establishing global leadership. Each of these thrusts could improve Canada's prospects significantly within the next decade. Each one also offers the potential for actions that could be taken quickly and that could set the stage for more ambitious undertakings down the road.

In limiting our focus to these twelve ways of sharpening the Canadian edge in the struggle for global triumph, we are making some basic assumptions about existing policies and trends. We assume, for instance, that the Bank of Canada will continue to manage monetary policy in a way that keeps inflation low and promotes the stability of the Canadian dollar — an approach we believe will be reinforced by the appointment of David Dodge as governor of the Bank of Canada. We also assume that the federal and provincial governments will continue to make budgets that are at least balanced, and will not revert to a policy of spiralling deficits. And we are confident that the broad trend in government towards greater reliance on market forces and less red tape will not be reversed. In short, we are making the basic assumption that the progress Canada has already made towards global success will not come undone.

▼ 1 Aggressive Debt Reduction

The one fiscal priority that has seen considerable progress in the past year is prudent management of public debt. We discussed earlier the persuasive arguments for a more active debt-reduction strategy during strong economic times. The environment of growing economic uncertainty during the latter months of 2000 also reinforced the dangers to the fiscal outlook of continuing to carry an excessive load.

The surpluses of recent years at the federal and provincial level, combined with robust economic growth, have made a noticeable dent in the size of our collective debt relative to our economy. Finance Minister Paul Martin's October 2000 budget update projected that Canada's debt would fall to less than 40 percent of gross domestic product within five years, a laudable improvement. Furthermore, the surge in revenues has led to substantial repayments during the 1999/2000 and 2000/1 fiscal years. Debt repayment, however, has been limited to the residual — whatever happens to be left over in the kitty at the end of the year after all possibilities for splurging have been exhausted.

We feel it is pointless to legislate debt repayment because sensible fiscal policy must leave plenty of room for the flexibility needed to deal with an unexpected nasty downturn. However, we would set a debt repayment target, one sufficient to knock the federal debt-to-GDP ratio down to about 25 percent by 2010. The ability to meet this target will depend primarily on maintaining robust economic growth. We would argue, however, that the government should also reduce the principal owing by an average of about $10 billion a year. When growth is strong, as in the 1999/2000 fiscal year, the payments should continue to be higher; when growth slows, repayments might be smaller. This flexible approach has the additional virtue of acting counter to the economic cycle, of preventing the government from excessively stimulating the economy during periods of high growth and leaving room for pump-priming during tough times. But to be effective, it must be applied consistently.

▼ 2 Structural Tax Reform

In terms of fiscal strategy, the fundamental area for action lies in taxation. Until 2000 the most urgent concerns of the business community revolved around Canada's uncompetitive rates of personal and corporate income tax and the need to bring these rates down significantly. The combined actions included in the February 2000 budget and the October budget update had a significant impact in easing these concerns.

Don Drummond, former associate deputy minister of finance and now chief economist of the Toronto-Dominion Bank, recently noted that, by 2004, the overall Canadian tax burden as a share of GDP will be back to where it was in 1979 and close to where the G-7 average is today. Canada's tax burden remains considerably higher than that of the United States, and corporate tax policies are still a serious problem.

While corporate income tax rates are scheduled to fall towards the G-7 average, Canadian enterprises are also subject to a range of other levies that, together, put them at a disadvantage with respect to international competitors and discourage business investment in our country. Drummond singled out the federal and provincial taxes on capital, which are especially high on financial institutions. Alberta is scheduled to eliminate its capital tax on financial institutions by April 2001, but in other provinces this levy ranges from 0.9 percent in Ontario to 4 percent in Newfoundland. Overall, he said, capital taxes in Canada are equivalent to an additional 3.6 percent charge on corporate incomes, compared with just 1 percent in the United States. We concur with his simple recommendation that capital taxes be eliminated.[5]

Similarly, more work needs to be done on the personal tax side. After all the announced cuts in personal taxes are in place, Canada will still have the highest personal income-tax burden in the G-7. That said, the cuts that have been announced will narrow the Canada-United States gap considerably and give Canada an advantage in certain aspects of taxation relevant to entrepreneurship and fast-growing companies.

At this stage, we think the emphasis in public debate on taxation needs to shift from tax reduction to tax reform. Our most serious competitive problem as a country no longer flows predominantly from the overall size of our tax burden, but from what we tax most heavily. As we have discussed at length, corporate income taxes have a much more dramatic impact on reducing or boosting investment and economic activity than taxes on payroll. Similarly, personal income taxes, and especially taxation of investment and savings, impose a greater cost on economic growth than taxation of consumption. What Canada must consider now is a fundamental shift of its tax structure from an income to a consumption base.

The most direct way to achieve such a shift at the federal level would be to dramatically reduce personal income taxes while raising the GST. However, there are practical objections to such a shift. Consumption taxes, for instance, are less progressive in structure than current income tax rates. These flaws can be offset. We already use GST tax credits to offset the burden of consumption taxes on lower-income Canadians. These credits could be raised proportionately. Even though much higher value-added taxes are the norm in socially progressive countries in Europe, the biggest obstacle to such a structural shift in taxation in Canada is political. The history and visibility of the GST is such that, regardless of economic logic, any attempt to raise the GST dramatically would be doomed.

There are other options for shifting the structure of personal taxation towards a consumption base. Many of the tax cuts already announced and in place reflect such a shift. The biggest cuts have been in personal income tax. Even though no other taxes have been raised, the share of tax revenue flowing from the GST will rise. Similarly, the cuts in the capital gains inclusion rate have meant even greater cuts in taxation of investment income as opposed to consumption. Simply continuing to cut taxes on personal and corporate incomes will achieve some of the structural shift that is necessary.

Other proposals that would boost incentives for saving, whether by raising limits for RRSPs and RESPs or by creating tax-sheltered individual learning accounts, all have the practical impact of reducing the taxation of savings and investment. This reduction in turn shifts the income tax burden more heavily towards income that people choose to spend rather than save. Taking this theme to the extreme, we could allow Canadians to make unlimited deductible contributions into RRSP-style savings vehicles. At that point, we would effectively be taxing people not on how much money they earned but on how much money they did not save — in short, on their consumption. A hard-driving entrepreneur would be taxed not when he earned a million dollars, but only when he chose to live like a millionaire instead of ploughing his money back into greater investment and job creation. And we would be taxing people on their consumption through a system of progressive tax rates in a way that would also capture money spent outside the country — a tax base that the GST misses.

In one way or another, such a structural shift in taxation will play a critical role in any successful plan to accelerate Canada's economic growth in the decade ahead. As Jonathan Kesselman put it in a November 2000 study for the Institute for Research on Public Policy, all the comparative international studies show consistently that taxing smarter is more important than taxing less when trying to promote economic growth. Greater relative reliance on GST-style taxes and payroll taxes, or a shift in personal taxation to place a heavier burden on income consumed than on income saved, would pay real economic dividends.

While allowing well-off people to defer taxes and pile up assets may provide an appearance of unfairness relative to low-income earners who cannot afford to save, Kesselman noted that boosting the rate of savings in our economy would set in train a series of long-term effects. In the end, tax reform along these lines would actually improve income distribution within our society. "Tax or other policies that spur savings and capital accumulation will raise skilled wages, but raise unskilled wages even more, thus compressing the skill premium and reducing inequality."[6] Bigger tax breaks for savings, in other words, actually lead to greater equality in the distribution of wages and salaries.

▼ 3 Smart Public Spending

Governments have an important role in responding to a wide range of needs in our society. At the same time, governments, through their revenue base, are no less vulnerable to global competition than are private enterprises. It is vital for governments to ensure that the taxes they charge are put to good use.

There are areas in which governments will have to increase spending in the years ahead. We have already mentioned the likely trend in health care spending, which was reinforced in December 2000 by the Canadian Institute for Health Information. It noted that, after the lean years of the mid-1990s, public spending on health care rose 6.7 percent in 1999 and was forecast to jump a further 7.7 percent in 2000, for a total that year of $67.7 billion. The September 2000 deal to boost federal transfer payments to the provinces is likely to mean continuing large increases in health care budgets in the next few years.

Such growing demands for core services put even greater pressure on governments to look for more effective ways to spend. Reducing the incidence and duration of poverty remains a high priority for federal and provincial governments alike. In the dying days of 2000 there was speculation that the re-elected Liberal government in Ottawa would initiate some form of guaranteed annual income. A single program would replace the patchwork of income supports that two layers of government now provide. Although this idea has many attractions in principle, four decades of study by governments around the world have suggested that it involves even more problems in practice. Given the multiple jurisdictions involved and the diverse circumstances affecting those in poverty, a one-size-fits-all income support program is unlikely to be the most effective approach. However, the need for improvement in existing programs remains urgent, and the fight against poverty should be seen as fertile territory for policy innovation.

Another sphere of government intervention crying out for innovation is Aboriginal affairs. The conflicts over ownership of and access to land and resources are both troubling and economically damaging. The costs of existing programs are huge, and the outcome in terms of the education levels and incomes of Aboriginal people is dismaying. What is more, the demographics of Aboriginal communities have frightening implications for the country as a whole if we fail to prevent another generation of dependency.

As we seek to free up resources for emerging or growing priorities and to inject a spirit of innovation into public sector activities, it will be critical to foster a commitment to continuous improvement. Governments must evaluate constantly, look at what works well and what does not, and be willing to pull the plug on what does not. This evaluation goes beyond the question of effective administration to the more important one of value for money.

We have already discussed the shortcomings of many of the attempts to subsidize businesses, particularly through regional development programs. We have also suggested that, except where necessary to maintain a level playing field against international competitors, such subsidies could be abolished. The money saved should be used instead to provide across-the-board reductions in the corporate income tax burden — a much more cost-effective way to stimulate business investment in competitive enterprises. This approach is consistent with the goal of restructuring the tax base to give Canada a compelling advantage in fostering more entrepreneurial ventures that expand onto the world stage and in attracting foreign investment and profitable multinational operations within the global economy.

In more general terms, we must remain constantly aware of the difference between spending that involves current consumption and spending that represents an investment in future growth, one that will provide a measurable return to taxpayers over time. The Finance Committee of the House of Commons has called for a "productivity covenant," an approach that would examine all proposals for new spending in terms of their impact on productivity growth and, therefore, on the economic well-being of all Canadians.

Even where a government proposal could have a positive impact and is judged more important than other program priorities, it must be weighed against alternative forms of delivery. Could the same benefits be obtained at lower cost by contracting out? Have possible partnerships been considered? More important, could the same or better results be obtained more efficiently through the tax system? The same questions must be asked regularly about existing government initiatives to ensure that innovative possibilities are not overlooked and that available resources are refocused to meet changing priorities in the most effective manner.

▼ 4 Public School Reform

Our existing systems of public education work well for most students, but we must do better if we are to equip all Canadians for global success. Our recommendations for school reform are focused on the need to motivate students to stay in school at least through high school graduation and to ensure that they leave school with the core skills needed to function effectively as global citizens.

To achieve the goals we set earlier in terms of graduation rates and student achievement, we need to start with a more comprehensive assessment of what our children are learning and how well they are learning it. To improve their achievement, we need to link that assessment to accountability, so we can reward the teachers and administrators who make a real difference and direct additional resources towards troubled children and institutions. We have to reinforce accountability with greater investment in the professional development of teachers, to keep them on the cutting edge of knowledge as they prepare our children for a world in which much of that knowledge will already be obsolete. Finally, we need to devolve much more authority to individual schools, to make sure that, while every school is accountable for the achievements of its students, teachers and principals have as much flexibility as possible to meet the particular needs of their students and to work with members of their communities.

At the next meeting of first ministers, the federal and provincial governments should make a joint commitment to improve the quality of basic education in Canada and the achievement level of all students. This commitment should include the development of minimum standards for high school graduation. In addition, provinces should agree to harmonize and share publicly their assessments of student achievement levels at all ages; and federal government, in concert with First Nations, should take the lead in developing innovative programs aimed at improving education outcomes for Aboriginal youth.

The business community has important roles to play as well. Businesses have no interest in meddling in curriculum or teaching methods, but can offer expertise in managing change. They can provide additional resources and knowledge; they can offer guidance and experience to young people through vehicles such as mentoring, internships, and work experience programs; and they can get involved in a wide range of partnerships with governments and educators. Above all, business leaders can speak powerfully and frequently in support of public education, helping to build a genuine consensus for constructive change.

The approach we have suggested to school reform is not designed to save money. Overall spending may increase, and spending in key areas must increase. But this combination of measures, if put in place within an environment of respect among parents, educators, administrators, and political leaders, is likely to produce significant increases in student achievement. The payoff, for our children and for our country, would be huge.

▼ 5 Access to Lifelong Learning

Beyond high school, the critical area for action is in overcoming barriers to access to opportunities for learning. Here the need for government action has less to do with how public institutions are run and more to do with how education and training are financed. We have suggested a number of possible ways to decrease the financial risk to the individual. We would like to emphasize two measures, one to encourage people to save for education, and the second to enable people to reduce their burden of debt over time.

Enhancing the Registered Education Savings Plan concept to allow all individuals to save for their own future education and training is a good start; and converting the tax-prepaid model of the RESP to an RRSP-style plan with deductible contributions could make it even more effective. An alternative approach would be to provide matching contributions, as the federal government already does with RESPs for children and as the Liberal Party election platform suggested in the autumn of 2000 for Registered Individual Learning Accounts. Still, even with matching contributions to assist lower-income Canadians to save, the costs of extended periods of study will require many Canadians to borrow money. Though existing rules provide tax relief on interest payments, we suggest that tax policy should go much further in sharing the risks and benefits of education. A tax credit equal to a significant portion of the principal of a student loan each year would enable all students to finance their education without taking on a lifelong burden of debt. At the same time, providing gradual forgiveness of the principal over many years would ensure that only those students who put their skills to work and pay taxes in Canada will receive relief. Those who take their taxpayer-subsidized education and earn greater rewards elsewhere would have to repay the full amount. As the portion of education costs covered by tuition fees increases, as seems likely, and as the size of the average student loan follows suit, this incentive will become ever more effective.

Tax policy could also come into play in the provision of learning opportunities by employers. Until now, training has been treated largely as another business expense. If anything, employer-paid education has been tagged as a taxable benefit to employees, a policy that was finally stopped in the late 1990s. Governments that want to encourage corporate investment in employee training, or more broadly in support of education and early child development in their communities, could tilt the tax rules to provide an additional incentive. One possibility we suggested earlier was to allow a super-deduction of relevant expenses. Another idea, perhaps preferable in the context of government plans to match contributions to individual learning accounts, would be to allow employers to make matching contributions to employee learning accounts as a non-taxable benefit.

▼ 6 Accelerated Immigration

Canada has always been a magnet for immigrants. People from many countries and cultures have flocked to our shores in search of opportunity, and the resulting diversity of our society is a vital element in both the Canadian soul and Canada's economic potential. Our generous treatment of refugee claimants is complex and costly, but it is linked to our determination to offer hope to the oppressed. Our model of social and economic development also draws would-be migrants from all corners of the globe, but especially from less-developed countries.

The demand for access to the opportunities our country offers is so great that the primary function of Canada's immigration officials has become one of screening out applicants. But in the increasingly intense global war for talent, we must also see our immigration rules and officials as key partners in the campaign to attract people with the skills most highly sought by globally oriented companies. Such individuals have many options, and they refuse to consider relocation to countries that impose barriers to their entry.

Canadian companies are increasingly active in recruiting scarce talent abroad. They need immigration officials to help them market Canada's many virtues and assist employers to bring in the talent they require. Furthermore, as the Expert Panel on Skills recommended, all foreign students who are completing a university degree program in Canada should be offered Canadian landed immigrant status within six months of graduation. Finally, the evaluation of prospective immigrants' skills should be carried out before their entry into Canada to facilitate their rapid integration into the economy once they arrive.

▼ 7 Intergovernmental Collaboration

Almost every major challenge we have discussed in this book cuts across jurisdictional boundaries. Whether negotiating international agreements, coordinating tax reform, or improving the effectiveness of health care and education, our federal and provincial governments will have to work closely together.

The degree of interdependence requires cooperation based on respect, not coercion or gamesmanship. It requires coordination, but not uniformity. The federal government must respect the diversity of the federation and the authority of provincial and territorial governments to act in the best interests of their residents. At the same time, the provinces and territories have a moral duty to all Canadians to work together in the interests of the country as a whole.

We would suggest that the experience of the past two decades shows conclusively that our energies are better spent in working on practical solutions within our eminently flexible federal framework than in grappling with the fractious abstractions of the written constitution. This having been said, at some point as Canadians we must confront our constitutional responsibilities. As Gordon Robertson, the former clerk of the Privy Council, has long advocated, constructive steps must be taken to win Quebec's support for the constitution and to bring about meaningful Senate reform. Until this happens and these issues are resolved, Canada's future will not be assured.[7]

Commitment to the goal of Quebec independence, embraced by the province's Parti Québécois government, remains a potentially lethal threat to the integrity of Canada. The decision in January 2001 of popular premier Lucien Bouchard to resign and to quit politics in the face of fading support for independence has reduced the credibility of the threat somewhat. But the threat remains nevertheless, and will until the majority in the Quebec National Assembly is in the hands of Quebecers strongly committed to Canada. Quebec Liberal leader Jean Charest and his party offer such an alternative, but whatever the outcome of the next provincial election, Quebec's concerns will not be resolved easily or quickly. In the meantime, we must move ahead with the kinds of strategies that will produce early and substantial benefits for all Canadians.

We have seen remarkable progress in the ability of different levels of government to work together constructively. We have seen the evolution of various federal-provincial and interprovincial bodies, of regular meetings that bring together officials and ministers on critical files such as labour market policies, environmental issues, and education. Without belittling the strides that have been made, we have much further to go. To prove that federal and provincial governments really can deal with the vital interests of Canadians, we throw out a challenge in three areas: health care, education, and internal trade. In each of these areas, the goals are clear. Canadians want to be confident they can get prompt access to quality public health care whenever and wherever they need it. Parents from coast to coast want access to pre-school care that prepares their children for a lifetime of learning and to schools that equip them for success as global citizens. And businesses with ambitions need to be shown that this country really does provide a clear and effective single market as a base for global expansion.

The intergovernmental issues that remain are not disputes over these goals, but over the best means of delivering what Canadians want and expect. Some needs vary by province and by region, flowing from the diversity of our geography and people. There are also legitimate national goals and roles. They involve the harmonization of rules and regulations affecting commerce and labour mobility, for instance, or the need for better information about the quality of health care being delivered and the effectiveness of the various approaches being tried in different jurisdictions. In education, we believe we should be able to agree on the minimum set of knowledge and skills that all Canadian children should possess by the time they graduate from high school. What is more, effective measurement of their achievements against a common standard would be a vital tool in helping all provinces assess their efforts to improve the way schools are run in every jurisdiction.

How well the federal and provincial governments work together on these three challenges will have a fundamental bearing on the broader survival of Canada as a viable country with a distinct culture. Their progress, or lack of it, will either restore confidence in public institutions and reinvigorate citizen engagement with the enterprise of nation-building or lead to continuing deterioration in people's faith in government. The record-low voter turnout in the autumn 2000 election was just another symptom of a troubling level of disengagement. As individuals, Canadians and citizens of other industrialized countries have a growing number of options for meeting their needs. If governments in Canada fail to prove their relevance and effectiveness, a growing number of Canadians will ignore or bypass them, to the detriment of the country as a whole.

▼ 8 Trust and Transparency

This need for an engaged citizenry leads to a broader challenge for all Canadian governments, from federal down to municipal. Delivering better services and providing better value for money is the least that today's empowered citizens demand. To restore faith in our democratic institutions, there must be a broader thrust towards openness and trust.

In part, this realignment will require more public discussion and deliberation. Public consultation is entrenched in the political process, but meaningful engagement is relatively rare. At the same time, broad consultation is not a substitute for leadership. The consensus tends not to opt for change without powerful persuasion. Governments must engage, listen, and take into account what everyone has to say, but also take bold decisions where necessary. To maintain legitimacy in such instances, it is vital that people retain trust in the institution even when they disagree with its actions.

As Peter Dobell noted in a recent study for the Institute for Research on Public Policy, the House of Commons in particular is declining in stature and in influence as power shifts to the executive. This shift is happening in Canada to an extent greater than in any other British-type legislature. "The House of Commons used to be the cockpit in which national policy was probed and defended. Fifty years ago, the Prime Minister and ministers sat in the chamber during most debates. They did so because, before the development of polling, MPs were respected as the voice and ears of Canadians."[8] Members of Parliament are increasingly seen as irrelevant in the public eye, while, within the public service, "Parliament is seen, and at times referred to, as a *minor process obstacle*, rather than being regarded as an institution capable of validating and improving legislation."[9]

Dobell made a variety of recommendations, especially with respect to strengthening the role of parliamentary committees. Among others, he suggested that the chairs of committees be elected by a double majority

— a majority of both opposition and government members. He also recommended that more committees be chaired by opposition MPs and that committee chairs receive extra pay. In addition, he noted a particularly important innovation already adopted by the British House of Commons and the Quebec National Assembly. In these bodies, when a bill is referred to committee, the responsible minister does not merely make a token appearance to present the bill, but actually joins the committee for all its deliberations. As a result, ministers can assess personally when amendments are desirable, and amendments are both more frequent and more effective.

We suggest a further measure at the federal level as a means of enhancing public trust in our institutions of government. The time has come for greater public scrutiny and review of key appointments, especially to arm's-length institutions such as the Supreme Court of Canada and the Federal Court of Canada, the Bank of Canada, and quasi-judicial or regulatory bodies such as the Canadian Radio-Television and Telecommunications Commission. We also recommend public review of the appointment of directors of crown corporations — and delegation to those boards of the authority to choose their chief executives.

There are many other ways to improve the workings of the federal parliament and provincial legislatures. Useful recommendations have come from all parties over the years. The most recent set of proposals came from the Canadian Alliance in January 2001, highlighting in particular the advantages of more free votes in parliament. By making confidence votes the exception rather than the rule, individual MPs would be able to reflect the interests of their constituents more effectively without leading to the fall of the government. Any of the suggestions we have mentioned here would be useful in rebuilding the effectiveness of our democratic institutions. The missing ingredient has been the courage to act.

Public trust depends on openness. Every time an Access to Information request is returned three months late with pages of information blacked out, it sends one more signal that politicians and public servants are so afraid of embarrassment that they are unwilling to trust Canadians with the facts. If they want Canadians to be proud of their work, respect their achievements, and trust their judgment, they must behave accordingly. In the political context, openness can be embarrassing when mistakes are made. At the same time, more open disclosure of the process leading to decision-making enables everybody to gain a better understanding of the way a decision was reached. It also allows broader participation in analyzing what went wrong and how to do a better job next time. We should not expect governments to be perfect, and we must, like our elected representatives, become more tolerant of honest attempts at innovation that fail. But greater disclosure of the process is a precondition for tolerance.

Such openness would have one further benefit. Ideas that are shared earlier in the legislative process would broaden the opportunity for constructive engagement by both citizens and their elected representatives from all parties. The focus of discussion could shift much more readily from partisan bickering to collaboration, and legislation could be vetted for weaknesses before the fact instead of being buried in finger-pointing and recriminations at a later stage. Parliamentary committees are among the few forums at the federal level in which genuine discussion takes place. Their role would be greatly enhanced if they became places for discussion of possibilities rather than of amendments to decisions already taken. This suggestion reflects another of Dobell's recommendations: that parliamentary committees be invited to consider more bills at the draft stage, along with more green papers that lay out policy options rather than decisions. Using such an approach — already in place in Britain and Australia — the government would not lose its power and responsibility for making final decisions, but, rather, would encourage greater collaboration across party lines. In one way or another, broader engagement of both citizens and elected representatives is key to making Parliament and provincial legislatures more effective institutions.

▼ 9 Cohesive Communities

In the knowledge economy, profitability depends on the commitment and support of people with drive, ideas, and skills. To attract such people, companies must pursue goals that inspire, offer a working environment infused with compatible values, and base their operations in communities that offer a high quality of life. The challenge of building vibrant Canadian communities must involve more than government action. All sectors of society must be part of the process.

Canada's major corporations are leaders in community investment throughout the country. They have always been among the most generous donors to non-profit organizations. Increasingly, though, their community investment strategies are evolving beyond arm's-length donations. They are driving many of the most innovative and effective partnerships emerging within our communities. The challenge at this point is to broaden the base of participation in social innovation, to convince a greater number of businesses and voluntary sector organizations that a more comprehensive approach to corporate citizenship could bring significant benefit to social outcomes and to bottom lines.

Canadian communities are already rich with creative thinkers and terrific partnerships. As expressed in a 1998 paper for the Caledon Institute of Social Policy, "our challenge is to keep learning from one another, testing new ideas, improving on the better partnerships and working to build new and stronger relationships within a true community of enterprise."[10]

While strengthening this spirit of innovation will help us to address the full range of social issues we face, we would highlight the challenge of improving early child development as a particularly appropriate test-bed for new approaches to building stronger communities. There is no better crucible for an innovation society based on collective action than the way we prepare our children for a lifetime of learning. Parents want the best for their children and for those of neighbours, friends, and fellow citizens. We know that intelligent investment in parenting and in child development can pay huge dividends. We also know that the needs of communities and families vary widely.

Canada today is a laboratory for early child development. Because of provincial jurisdiction over education, the services and programs available differ widely across the country, from $5-a-day childcare in Quebec to user-pay kindergartens in British Columbia. We endorse the conclusion reached by Fraser Mustard and Margaret McCain in their study for the Ontario government — that new one-size-fits-all programs are not the answer. But we are also aware that a comprehensive and flexible network of community-based childcare will not emerge spontaneously. Provincial government initiatives are high profile and are generating intense debate. All of us have a responsibility to look at what seems to be working best and at how we can reinforce that approach to success in our own workplaces and communities. Early child development, of course, is but one of many areas in which there is potential for greater collaboration across all sectors of society, but a focus on success for all children would lay the foundation for even stronger and more vibrant communities to be shared by the next generation of Canadians.

▼ **10** *Global Trade and Investment*

The multilateral framework for liberalizing trade and investment is under siege. The protests at the World Trade Organization in Seattle have been followed by disruptions at every major gathering of government leaders. The real breakdowns in negotiations flow not from the protests, but from disagreements among governments with conflicting interests. The reality remains that progress towards freer global trade and investment has stalled.

This situation is perilous for Canada. As an economy highly dependent on trade and investment flows, Canada has a huge stake both in enhanced access to markets worldwide and in the effective rule of law. The existing progress in liberalizing cross-border flows has had a wide range of benefits for Canadians. Among others, it has opened up new markets, stimulated non-inflationary growth, and protected Canadian exporters from abuse by larger players.

Canada must act on two fronts. First, it must be vigorous within international bodies such as the World Trade Organization as an advocate for continued progress in liberalization. Canadian businesses have an important role to play in offering their wholehearted support for the efforts of political leaders and officials who are trying to restore momentum to a vital global process. In addition, governments and business must work together in Canada and around the world to promote a better understanding of globalization and to demonstrate the benefits of trade and investment liberalization. In particular, they must ensure that these benefits are not restricted to the few, but enhance the welfare of people in all nations.

In this respect, we talked earlier about the importance of reinforcing commercial ties with a commitment to building social capacity in less-developed nations. Our efforts to export our know-how in constructing democratic institutions and social infrastructure are at least as important in the long run as our marketing of goods and services abroad. We say this not simply because we believe all Canadians have responsibilities as global citizens, but because, in a world of interdependence, stronger social and economic development in all countries can only rebound to the advantage of Canadians as well. To have greater influence in world affairs, we must retain and enhance the respect with which Canadians are seen in every sphere of human achievement — and that respect will also underpin our success in building the Canadian brand and in providing an attractive base for global enterprise. Essential to achieving greater influence for Canada is a dynamic foreign policy dedicated to full global engagement, and a credible defence capability able to protect national interests at home and abroad.

▼ 11 North American and Regional Strategies

The process of economic convergence within North America is well under way. That process will continue and intensify no matter what course Canadians choose to pursue. The Canada–United States Free Trade Agreement and the North American Free Trade Agreement accelerated that convergence and produced huge benefits for Canada. But many challenges remain and new issues continue to crop up. The question for us as a country is how to manage the process of convergence in future so that it will continue to produce the best possible results for Canadians.

Many of the current border issues could be resolved incrementally and, where such progress is possible, it should proceed quickly. We fear, however, that the changing political and security landscape globally, together with demographic shifts within the United States, have put Canada's unique relationship with the United States at risk. That relationship has been of great value to Canadians and Americans alike. It would be foolish to let it wither. But to maintain and strengthen that relationship, we must move beyond incrementalism. It may be that we will ultimately fail, that we will decide we are unwilling to compromise our strategies and priorities sufficiently to justify the tangible and intangible benefits we gain from greater integration. Nevertheless, we believe a broad and sweeping initiative aimed, in the first instance, at eliminating existing trade, investment, and regulatory barriers is the only way to re-invigorate the spirit of that relationship and to capture the imagination of citizens and political leaders on both sides of the border.

Broader and deeper integration, while retaining the essential elements of sovereignty, is our overall goal. Many uncertainties must be resolved, from the range of issues to be tackled to the question of how to integrate Mexico's aspirations. But the time has come to begin work on the next great continental project — to explore options and to lay down a foundation in defining Canada's interests and roles within North America.

A North American strategy must be complemented by smart regional strategies aimed at closer integration with the European Union and Japan, a vigorous role on Canada's part in the hemisphere, and the special targeting of major emerging markets such as China, India, and Brazil.

▼ 12 Environmental Leadership

As an energy-intensive economy and major resource exporter, Canada has no choice but to be a world leader in environmental stewardship. Our first priority is to lead by example in managing and enhancing our natural capital. At the same time, we must be leaders in environmental innovation — in developing new and better ways to extract more value from every kilogram of resources we use.

According to global measurements, Canada's environmental performance ranks among the highest of any country. Still, our reputation for environmental leadership has been tarnished in recent years. Some of the criticism has been driven more by competitors seeking commercial advantage in the international marketplace than by genuine concern for sustainable development. Valid or not, this criticism of Canada's motives and degree of commitment to environmental responsibility is beginning to have a real impact on the value of the Canadian brand. If not answered, such criticism could affect both the influence of our country in world affairs and the economic prospects of our enterprises in every industry.

Canadian companies have taken their environmental responsibilities seriously. They have engaged actively in the development of new technologies and in the process of putting those technologies to work at home and abroad. Still, businesses in Canada must do more, not just from altruism but as an essential element in building shareholder value. They can continue to lead by example, showing others what can be done both responsibly and cost effectively. They can become more active in helping employees, customers, and suppliers to understand the need for early action and to see its benefits. More broadly, the corporate community can play a valuable role in building consensus within Canadian society on how Canada can enhance its reputation for global leadership on environmental issues.

The discussions ahead will require ingenuity from Canadians in all walks of life. The behaviour of all Canadians must change if we are to meet our responsibilities as global citizens. The challenge is to make a real difference in reducing the damage Canadians do to our environment in ways that reinforce Canada's global brand and enhance our prospects for economic growth.

■ The Innovation Imperative

Each of the twelve strategic thrusts we have suggested would have a meaningful impact on our ability to accelerate economic growth and to ensure that the benefits of that growth are shared within our society.

- An aggressive but flexible debt reduction strategy will steadily reduce risk and free up public resources over time, while avoiding excessive economic stimulus during boom times.
- Structural tax reform will maintain the revenue stream that Canadian governments require to meet the needs of Canadians, but will also enhance the country's ability to attract capital, encourage business investment and innovation, and persuade more individuals to invest in their own education and in entrepreneurial ventures.
- Smarter public spending will tilt government activity away from current consumption and lead to investment in building the country's capacity for growth, again enhancing growth and the ability to pay for the range and quality of public services that matter most to Canadians.
- Public school reform that improves student achievement will build the supply of well-educated Canadians and improve Canada's attractiveness to foreign and domestic investors. At the same time, ensuring that more Canadian children finish high school equipped with the skills they need to prosper in the information economy will reduce the number of Canadians condemned to a lifetime of dependency — boosting their incomes and reducing the need for public spending on income support.
- Access to lifelong learning for all Canadians will reinforce the supply of cutting-edge skills available in Canada. The tax policies that are most likely to be effective in expanding participation in lifelong learning will also help to tilt the overall tax structure in the right direction, encouraging investment rather than consumption.
- Accelerated immigration, a conscious and coordinated effort to market Canada's virtues to highly skilled people worldwide and to facilitate their entry into our economy, will reinforce Canada's ability to attract investment, especially in multicultural enterprises serving the global market.
- Active collaboration among governments will ensure smart spending and a competitive tax structure. Creation of a true common market will accelerate business investment, while collaboration in improving edu-

cation and ensuring access to lifelong learning are essential to more rapid development of Canada's human potential.
- Reform of our public institutions to increase transparency and rebuild trust will make Canada a more attractive place in which to live, work, and invest. It will also improve the process of developing good legislation, making public policy more likely to reflect the long-term interests of Canadians rather than short-term partisan benefits.
- More cohesive communities that encourage collaboration across the public, private, and voluntary sectors will make the most of our collective resources in meeting today's complex social challenges. Re-invigorating our communities also will play an important role in enhancing Canada's brand as a home of choice for skilled and mobile people within the global economy.
- Strengthening the multilateral framework for trade and investment will ensure that Canada remains able to protect its interests against unilateral action by larger and more powerful competitors. It must also retain the access to major markets that is critical to attracting investment in global mandates.
- A sweeping re-evaluation of Canada's strategy within North America will be essential in building a distinctive advantage within a converging continental economy, one that will enable our country to boost its share of North American and global investment, the fuel for business creation and growth. Strengthening Canada's political and commercial relationships with key economic players in Europe, Asia, and the western hemisphere, and with important emerging markets, will yield significant political and economic dividends.
- Global leadership in responsible and innovative approaches to environmental policy will enhance Canada's brand in the eyes of investors, customers, and skilled employees alike, while stimulating the creativity and innovation that will boost private sector productivity.

We do not claim that this list is comprehensive. Many other actions within both the public and private sectors could contribute to building human advantage, fostering new ideas, and attracting financial capital. We have touched on others in the course of our detailed discussion in earlier chapters. But we think that the strategic thrusts we have suggested here are especially important in giving Canadians the kind of edge that is needed to achieve the scale of growth in jobs and incomes we think is possible.

We also have to be clear that even sweeping progress on all of these fronts cannot guarantee that we surpass the ambitious goals set out earlier. Canada's progress, as always, will be affected by the overall growth of the global economy, and in particular by the ups and downs of our major trading partner to the south. What adopting these strategic thrusts will do is to improve our relative performance, to maximize the gains that Canadians are able to achieve within the global context.

Effective action on any of these fronts, however, cannot be achieved through cautious, piecemeal efforts; it can only flow from a fundamental commitment to innovation in everything we do and in every sector of our society. Canadians have many reasons to be satisfied with the status quo, but today we have only two choices. We can be passive players in a world of change, trickle-down recipients of the benefits of innovation by others, or we can become active participants and leaders in the effervescent advance of human achievement.

The lesson of the past decade on this point is clear: leadership pays. Those who take the risks, turn breakthrough ideas into products and processes, and create entire new markets are the ones who reap a disproportionate share of the rewards. Late adopters avoid many of the mistakes made by those on the leading edge, but pay a stiff price for their hesitation. First, they must pay to access the intellectual property of others. More dangerously, delay at one stage leads to delay in future stages of exploiting the potential of new technologies. What is more, leaders attract leaders. On the cutting edge of human progress, like attracts like with frightening speed. To abandon the struggle for leadership in any area of achievement is to abandon the hope of attracting or retaining a critical mass of world-leading talent in that field.

In terms of innovation, Canada's national strategy to date, such as it is, has been driven primarily by government action. To drive more research, the federal government has boosted grants through its agencies and funded new research chairs and infrastructure. To drive more private sector R&D, it has established the most generous tax credits in the industrialized world. To encourage more entrepreneurial investment, it has discovered the power of reduced capital gains taxation. All these measures are important tools, but they miss the point of a national strategy geared to innovation.

Innovation is first and foremost driven by attitude. It is an attitude that rejects the idea that the way we do things today is the best possible way. It is an attitude that insists that we can and we must do better. It is an attitude that requires the confidence to dispense with heavy-handed regulation, to embrace wide-open competition, to welcome investment from abroad, and to cast away restrictions on who can own how much of what. It is an attitude that finds joy in disruption, not because of the pain disruption causes, but because of the benefits it brings. It is an attitude that will not stand still, that bounces irrepressibly towards a better future. It is an attitude that must infuse every part of our society if we are to succeed in meeting ambitious goals for our economic and social progress as a country.

Some critics will suggest that our recommendations focus too heavily on what governments should or should not do. To them, we would suggest that, when talking about strategies for a country, it is inevitable that public policy will play a central role. We believe that the nation state still matters, that people can still enhance their collective well-being by banding together along territorial lines. Global integration and technological change are creating more alternatives for collective action that crosses geographic boundaries — as the Internet-savvy non-governmental organization (NGO) community demonstrates repeatedly in putting together protests against globalization. But in providing a sound foundation for advancing quality of life within physical communities, countries matter — and their governments matter too.

The role of governments is critical in defining the boundaries and characteristics of a state, but they remain creatures of their citizens. A nation state is more than the sum of its governments. It is an expression of collective will, a vehicle that enables people to work together in realizing their potential and achieving their dreams. In seeking to create a greater collective advantage for Canadians, all of us — as voters, citizens, consumers, residents, community members, neighbours and friends to others, parents and children, employers or employees, paid or unpaid, investors or borrowers — must be part of the solution.

This theme was emphasized by new federal Industry Minister Brian Tobin during his first meeting with members of the BCNI in January 2001. Whether in strengthening our relationship with the United States, continuously re-evaluating the competitiveness of our tax structure, or creating conditions that attract and retain highly skilled people, it is essential for business and government to work together. Though the two sectors will not always agree, he made it clear that both share the goal of a stronger and more prosperous Canada and must focus on reinforcing each other's contribution to that overarching goal.

We agree wholeheartedly. Members of the business community have many important roles to play in contributing to Canadian growth and prosperity. Indeed, rather than putting too much responsibility on governments, other critics may suggest that we have lost sight of the fundamental responsibility of business managers to deliver the maximum possible return to shareholders. We have talked about the contributions that business leaders can make in addressing everything from fiscal management and community investment to education and environmental stewardship. We see these roles not in conflict with the duty to shareholders, but as essential elements in sustaining and raising profitability over the long term.

In setting business strategy, the hard financial calculation cannot be ignored, but successful corporate strategy in the information age is increasingly based on intangibles — and that reality makes a company's reputation more important than ever. Operating within the boundaries of the law is not enough to convince customers, partners, shareholders, employees, governments, and communities that a company is worthy of their trust and participation. All these publics have growing expectations, and if their demands are not always consistent they are no less powerful for their inconsistency.

To continue to grow profitably from a Canadian base, business owners and managers in this country must become more aggressive and sophisticated in their business strategies. Those that have yet to do so must reach out beyond our borders, both in expanding their markets and in seeking out new possibilities for collaboration. As Alcan did with CGI, Canada's global champions must continue to help younger enterprises move onto the global stage. As larger enterprises did in ensuring economy-wide readiness for Y2K, they have a responsibility to persuade their customers and suppliers to invest in new technologies and exploit their potential in arenas such as e-commerce. Employers of all sizes must enhance their management of human resources to encourage employees to contribute ideas, to reward them for taking risks, and to develop their skills and knowledge.

At the same time, Canadian businesses must be innovative in meeting the broader issues flowing from the process of globalization. They must address concerns about the liberalization of trade and investment. They must help to show how freer flows of people, money, goods, and services make a real difference in attacking the age-old scourges of sickness and famine, in ensuring the growth of social capacity in less-developed nations, and in improving the standard of living of rich and poor alike. They must continue to be innovators in sustainable development, providing voluntary leadership in finding the best way to mesh profitability and economic growth with responsible management of the global ecosphere. Equally, at home, business leaders must encourage innovation across the public and non-profit sectors as well as within their own enterprises. If Canada is to provide a compelling home base for the global champions of tomorrow, business leaders must become more visible in their efforts to support better delivery of public services and more effective democratic institutions.

The pace of innovation within Canada's enterprises will be driven, in turn, by the way Canadians choose to invest. Many Canadians claim to believe that our country has what it takes to be the best in the world. Yet our actions as investors suggest we have no such faith in the ability of Canada or Canadian enterprises to prosper in a competitive world. With a few exceptions, our pension funds have been much slower to grasp the potential returns from venture capital investment than their counterparts in the United States. As beneficiaries of institutional investments and as individuals, we have to be prepared to put our money — the future of our families — where our mouths are, to take greater risks in backing Canadian ventures aimed at world-leading innovation and global reach.

Employees in all sectors have a vital role to play as well. Skilled people know they have a growing range of options at home and abroad. The explosive growth of the high technology sector has persuaded many talented people to take big risks in the hope of greater returns. As a country, we need to harness that entrepreneurial attitude, to persuade more young graduates and more of our globally experienced managers to choose the higher risk, but potentially greater returns, of helping to turn our small country into a global force. Just as we must persuade more Canadians to invest their money in home-grown enterprises, so we must convince more people to invest their time and effort, their intellectual capital, in Canadian enterprises and Canadian society.

In this respect, there is a special need for courageous leadership within the more traditional sectors of our economy and in the public sector in which organized labour still plays a significant role. Too many labour leaders are caught up in the ideological debates of yesterday. We understand that the defensive stance of many unions is driven by the desire to protect their members from some of the negative consequences of continental and global integration. But the experience of progressive and successful countries such as Ireland and the Netherlands shows that co-operation among business, organized labour, and government can pay significant dividends. Reactionary union leaders who try to avoid risk and resist innovative approaches damage the prospects of their members and their organizations. Employees have many common interests and should work together, within a single employer and across our society. But unions, too, need to evolve, to become active participants in addressing the challenges of innovation.

The need for significant evolution applies just as strongly to the managers of public sector institutions. We cannot expect our schools to become engines of innovation if elected officials, public servants, and school board administrators are unwilling to abandon industrial-era policies and bargaining positions. Our colleges and universities cannot prepare Canadians for roles as innovative employees, managers, and investors in global enterprises unless they become more adept at responding to the changing needs of students and employers alike. And managers in the health care sector, elected and appointed, must work with all players in the system to break down the barriers to innovation that limit Canadians' access to the best and most cost-effective treatments available.

We have talked at length about the necessity for innovation in all government activities. We need public servants who will take the smart risks that will drive progress. We need managers who will support the professional development required to let employees make good choices and foster a working environment that attracts creative people. We need political leadership that is willing to acknowledge mistakes and fix them, without discouraging honest effort and worthwhile risk, and to reward public servants for innovative behaviour.

This argument in turn leads to the responsibilities all of us have as citizens. We should have high expectations of our governments as service providers, just as we demand high quality, low prices, and attentive service from the companies with which we do business. But citizens are more than voters who may or may not cast a ballot once every few years. As Canadians, we enjoy many privileges and, equally, we have responsibilities not just to pay taxes but to make our democracy work. We have a duty to think about the future of our country and the challenges we face, to offer ideas for solving our problems, to discuss our own ideas and those of others, and to cooperate in turning talk into effective action. We need to be active at every level, from debating major issues that affect the country as a whole to serving as volunteers within our communities and our schools. The quality of life we build as a country will directly reflect the extent to which individual citizens from coast to coast choose to make a difference.

■ Northern Edge: The Will to Win

Novelist and essayist John Ralston Saul has been vitriolic in his attacks on the business community for championing the cause of freer trade and global economic integration. In particular, he and others of his ilk portray those who dare to see opportunity for Canadians within the reality of a converging continental economy as colonialist lackeys intent on "turning our backs on our own northernness" to ape mindlessly the behaviour of the dominant empire of our day. In his view, "those obsessed by free market flows" are simply incapable of creativity and innovation. "For most of our élite, the north-south argument is a passive expression of their desire for a life of reaction not action."[11]

In our view, this is defeatist drivel. Continental economic integration should spur us to build distinctive advantages, not act as an excuse for craven imitation of our southern neighbour. It is possible to believe in the benefits of free markets and still be a Canadian nationalist. Caring is not in conflict with great ambition. Innovation is a means of reinforcing traditional values, not rejecting them. We can be proud of what we have achieved together as a country and still see the need for change.

Global integration does pose a threat to both the standard of living we have come to enjoy and the values and cultural traditions we cherish. But, as always, the best defence for Canada's model of society is a strong economic offence. The time has come to stop huddling in fear of losing our culture and, instead, to make Canada's model the envy of the world.

We have taken two essential steps in the past two decades. The first was the leap of faith into freer trade with the United States, a decisive strategy to accelerate continental economic integration and to expose Canadian companies to the opportunities and competitive realities of the vast market to our south. The second was the battle to end the futility of spiralling deficits and to put our fiscal house in order. Both struggles were divisive and disruptive, but the results, as positive as they have been, must not be the end of Canada's drive for a better future. Indeed, we see these two steps as the prelude to greatness.

Global leadership, however, is not a mineral deposit safely stored within our borders waiting to be exploited. Rather, leadership flows from a state of mind that sees no limits to what Canadians can achieve, that is prepared to take on the best in the world and emerge triumphant. Around the world, we see individual Canadians who have achieved superstar status in every field of human endeavour. Canadian enterprises have shown they are capable of penetrating every market in the world and beating out larger and more powerful competitors. What we have not yet demonstrated is the will to excel as a country.

The essential ingredients are all in place. We have the people, the ideas, the skills, the resources, the capital, the technology, and the infrastructure. What we must do now is bring all these elements together to forge a country and a society shaped for success in the twenty-first century.

Other advanced countries share many of our best attributes: strong democratic institutions, a robust social safety net, a clean environment, a superb transportation and communications infrastructure, a highly educated population, access to major markets, and communities with a high quality of life. What Canada can offer in addition is the world's most successful multicultural society. As multinational companies serving the global market evolve into increasingly multicultural institutions, the diversity and tolerance of Canadian society could become our unique selling proposition, the key characteristic that will make us stand out as the preferred alternative amid many attractive possibilities.

A society that works, an economy that works, the home of choice for global champions: we have the makings of a compelling brand. Success in our quest is far from guaranteed, but our parents strove to build better lives for us and we owe no less to our children. Canada's potential is immense. The avenues for realizing that potential are clear. The only missing ingredients are the will to win and the determination not to waste a minute more. The blade is ready and our northern edge waits to be honed. Using it to maximum advantage is the key to the triumph of Canadians in the global economy of tomorrow.

NOTES

■ Introduction: On the Edge

1 Business Council on National Issues, "Global Champion or Falling Star? The Choice Canada Must Make," statement at the CEO Summit 2000, Toronto, April 5, 2000, 2.
2 Ibid., 4.
3 Jack Mintz, "Government Policy and the Canadian Advantage," *Canadian Business Economics* 8, 2 (August 2000): 8.
4 David Hale, "Will American Economic and Financial Performance Perpetuate American Economic Dominance in the 21st Century?" paper presented to the Atlantic Conference, Chicago Conference on Foreign Relations, Puerto Rico, November 11, 2000, 18.
5 Pierre Fortin, *The Canadian Standard of Living: Is There a Way Up?* C.D. Howe Institute Benefactors Lecture, Montreal, October 19, 1999, 8.
6 Conference Board of Canada, "Performance and Potential, 2000–2001: Seeking 'Made in Canada' Solutions," October 2000, 2.
7 Eric Beauchesne, "Canadians taxed into global poorhouse," *Ottawa Citizen*, July 20, 2000.
8 Mintz, "Government Policy and the Canadian Advantage," 8.
9 Bob Howlett, ed., *Hong Kong — A New Era* (Hong Kong, China: Hong Kong Government, 1997), 43.
10 Hong Kong Economic and Trade Office, "CE urges Canadian companies to do more in Asia," *Hong Kong Update* (August 2000): 1–2.
11 Conference Board of "Canada, Performance and Potential," 2.
12 David Olive, *No Guts, No Glory: How Canada's Greatest CEOs Built Their Empires* (Toronto: McGraw-Hill Ryerson Limited, 2000), 215.
13 Gregory N. Mankiw, *Principles of Economics* (New York and Toronto: The Dryden Press, Harcourt Brace, 1997), 11.
14 Charles Fishman, "The War for Talent," *Fast Company*, issue 16 (August 1998): 104. "www.fastcompany.com/online/16/mckinsey.html".
15 The Honourable Paul Martin, "Speech to the Toronto Board of Trade," Toronto, September 14, 2000.
16 Lester C. Thurow, *Building Wealth: The New Rules for Individuals, Companies and Nations in a Knowledge-Based Economy* (New York: HarperCollins, 1999), 148.
17 John Yochelson, "A Perspective on U.S. Innovation," presentation to the Business Council on National Issues, Toronto, April 14, 1999.
18 Michael Porter and Scott Stern, "The New Challenge to America's Prosperity: Findings from the Innovation Index," Council on Competitiveness, 1999, 3–4.

19 The Honourable Paul Martin, "The Budget Speech 2000," February 28, 2000, 9.
20 Paul D. Reynolds, Michael Hay, William D. Bygrave, and Erkko Autio, "Global Entrepreneurship Monitor, 2000 Executive Report," Kauffman Centre for Entrepreneurial Leadership at the Ewing Marion Kauffman Foundation, 1999, 32–33.
21 Canadian E-Business Opportunities Roundtable, "Fast Forward: Accelerating Canada's Leadership in the Internet Economy," Boston Consulting Group (Canada), January 2000.
22 Vito Tanzi and Ludger Shuknecht, *Public Spending in the Twentieth Century: A Global Perspective* (Cambridge: Cambridge University Press, 2000).
23 Mintz, "Government Policy and the Canadian Advantage," 7.
24 Business Council on National Issues, "Global Champion or Falling Star? The Choice Canada Must Make," statement at the CEO Summit 2000, Toronto, April 5, 2000.
25 Ibid.
26 David S. Landes, *The Wealth and Poverty of Nations* (New York: W.W. Norton, 1998).

■ Chapter 1: Riding the Globalization Wave

1 Kofi Annan, Address to participants at the Millennium Forum, United Nations, New York, May 22, 2000, 2.
2 Alan Greenspan, "Globalization," remarks at the Banco de Mexico 75th Anniversary Conference, Stabilization and Monetary Policy: The International Experience, Mexico City, Mexico, November 14, 2000, 4.
3 Thomas L. Friedman, *The Lexus and the Olive Tree* (New York: First Anchor Books, 2000), 20.
4 Ibid., 47.
5 *The Economist*, "A Survey of The New Economy" (September 23, 2000): 5.
6 David Hale, "Will American Economic and Financial Performance Perpetuate American Economic Dominance in the 21st Century?" paper presented to the Atlantic Conference, Chicago Conference on Foreign Relations, Puerto Rico, November 11, 2000, 2.
7 Ibid., 1.
8 Mike Moore, "The Backlash against Globalization?" address to Liberal International, Ottawa, October 26, 2000, 1.
9 John Micklethwait and Adrian Wooldridge, *A Future Perfect: The Challenges and Hidden Promise of Globalization* (New York: Crown Publishers, 2000), 23.
10 Ibid.
11 Anthony Giddens, *Runaway World: How Globalization Is Reshaping Our Lives* (New York: Routledge, 2000), 19.
12 Friedman, *The Lexus and the Olive Tree*, 81.
13 Charles P. Kindleberger, *World Economic Primacy, 1500–1990* (New York and Oxford: Oxford University Press, 1966).
14 David S. Landes, *The Wealth and Poverty of Nations* (New York and London: W. W. Norton, 1998), 215.
15 Lester C. Thurow, *Building Wealth* (New York: HarperCollins, 1999), 50.
16 Bill Gates, *The Speed of Thought* (New York: Warner Books, 1999), xiii.
17 Jay Mazur, "Labour's New Internationalism," *Foreign Affairs* 79 (January/February 2000): 80.
18 CLC International, *Global Solidarity: A Trade Union International Agenda* (July 11, 2000): 1.
19 Nicholas Negroponte, *Being Digital* (New York: Vintage Books, 1996), 47.
20 Friedman, *The Lexus and the Olive Tree*, 227.
21 "Economic Freedom of the World: 2000 Annual Report," The Fraser Institute, The Hong Kong Centre for Economic Research, and The Cato Institute.

Notes

22 Thomas d'Aquino, address to Global Business Forum, Banff, Canada, September 21, 2000.
23 Thurow, *Building Wealth*, 83.
24 Thomas J. Courchene, "A Mission Statement for Canada," *Policy Options* (July/August 2000): 10.
25 William Thorsell column, *Globe and Mail*, February 2000.
26 David Dollar and Aart Kraay, "Growth Is Good for the Poor," Economic Growth Research, World Bank Group, 2000.
27 George Soros, "Open Society: Reforming Global Capitalism," address to the State of the World Forum, New York, September 5, 2000.
28 Alan Greenspan, "Global Economic Integration: Opportunities and Challenges," remarks to symposium sponsored by the Federal Reserve Bank of Kansas City, Jackson Hole, Wyoming, August 25, 2000.
29 Friedman, *The Lexus and the Olive Tree*, 42.
30 Jeffrey J. Schott, ed., *The WTO after Seattle* (Washington, DC: Institute for International Economics, 2000), 5.
31 John Micklethwait and Adrian Wooldridge, *A Future Perfect: The Challenges and Hidden Promise of Globalization* (New York: Crown Publishers, 2000), 275.
32 The Honourable Pierre Pettigrew, "Seattle — Globalization vs. Internationalization: A Collision between Two Worlds," address to the Global Forum 2000, Washington, DC, May 15, 2000.
33 David Cameron and Janice Gross Stein, "Globalization, Culture and Society: The State as Place Amidst Shifting Spaces," *Canadian Public Policy*, vol. xxvi, special supplement, (August 2000): S31–32.
34 "The case for globalization," *The Economist* (September 23, 2000): 19.
35 Mike Moore, "The Backlash against Globalization?" address to Liberal International, Ottawa, October 26, 2000, 3.
36 Aaron Bernstein, "Too Much Corporate Power," *BusinessWeek* (September 11, 2000): 147.
37 Paul Raeburn, Sheridan Prasso, Auzanne Timmons, Michael Shari, "Whose Globe?" *BusinessWeek* (November 6, 2000): 90.
38 *OECD Principles of Corporate Governance*, Paris, May 10, 1999, 1.
39 Thomas d'Aquino, "Marching towards Prosperity: The National and Global Challenge," address to the Autumn General Meeting, Business Council on National Issues, Toronto, November 1, 2000, 9–10.
40 Micklethwait and Wooldridge, *A Future Perfect*, 335.

■ Chapter 2: Making Smart Choices

1 Organisation for Economic Co-operation and Development, *OECD Economic Outlook* 67 (June 2000): 275.
2 John McCallum, "Five reasons to reduce federal government debt," Royal Bank of Canada, Economics Department, *Current Analysis* (September 2000).
3 Department of Finance Canada, "Economic Statement and Budget Update," October 18, 2000, 12.
4 David Stewart-Patterson, "Tax cut delay will not pay," Business Council on National Issues (BNCI), *Opinions*, February 1999.
5 International Institute for Management Development (IMD), *World Competitiveness Yearbook 2000*, 404.
6 Caroline Hughes Tuohy, Colleen M. Flood, and Mark Stabile, "How Does Private Financing Affect Public Health Care Systems? Marshalling the Evidence from OECD Nations," paper presented to Ontario Medical Association Roundtable, October 17, 2000. Authors' calculations based on table 1.

7 BNCI, "Creating Opportunity, Building Prosperity: A Tax Reduction Strategy for Canadians," October 1998.
8 Organisation for Economic Co-operation and Development, *OECD Economic Surveys, Canada 1997*, November 1997, table 23, 85.
9 Thomas Courchene, *A State of Minds: Towards a Human Capital Future for Canadians* (draft, forthcoming).
10 Jonathan Kesselman, "Flat Taxes, Dual Taxes, Smart Taxes: Making the Best Choices," Institute for Research on Public Policy, *Policy Matters*, vol. 1, no. 7 (November 2000): 52.
11 Department of Finance Canada, "Economic Statement and Budget Update," October 2000, 29, 33, 86.
12 Vito Tanzi and Ludger Schuknecht, *Public Spending in the Twentieth Century: A Global Perspective* (Cambridge: Cambridge University Press, 2000), 253.
13 Conference Board of Canada, "Canadians' Values and Attitudes on Canada's Health Care System: A Synthesis of Survey Results," October 2000, 4-5.
14 Kevin Lynch, "Improving Canada's Productivity Performance: The Key to Higher Living Standards," Presentation, January 18, 2000, 4.
15 Ibid., 3.
16 John McCallum, "Will Canada Matter in 2020?" Royal Bank of Canada, Economics Department, *Current Analysis*, May 2000, 2.
17 BNCI, "Global Champion or Falling Star? The Choice Canada Must Make," statement at the CEO Summit 2000, Toronto, April 5, 2000, 16.
18 Robert D. Brown, "The Impact of the U.S. on Canada's Tax Strategy," *Isuma: Canadian Journal of Policy Research* 1 (spring 2000): 73.
19 Muriel Harrison, Letter to the Editor, *Ottawa Citizen*, December 29, 1979. In *To the Editor: A Century of Letters* (Ottawa: The Ottawa Citizen, 2000), 284.
20 Verena Menec, Noralou Roos, Deborah Nowicki, Leonard MacWilliam, Greg Finlayson, and Charlyn Black, "Seasonal Patterns of Winnipeg Hospital Use," Manitoba Centre for Health Policy and Evaluation, October 1999, 3, "www.umanitoba.ca/centres/mchpe/reports".
21 André Picard, "Manitoba develops six-month ER cure," *Globe and Mail*, June 29, 2000, A5.
22 Marni Brownell, Noralou P. Roos, and Charles Burchill, "Monitoring the Winnipeg Hospital System: 1990-91 Through 1996-97," Manitoba Centre for Health Policy and Evaluation, February 1999, 1-3.
23 Marni Brownell and Cheryl Hamilton, "Winnipeg Hospital Bed Closures: Problem or Progress," summary of ibid., "www.umanitoba.ca/centres/mchpe/reports.htm".
24 Samuel B. Sheps et al., "Hospital Downsizing and Trends in Health Care Use among Elderly People in British Columbia," *Canadian Medical Association Journal* 163, 4 (August 22, 2000): 397-401.
25 Noralou P. Roos, "The Disconnect between the Data and the Headlines," ibid., 411-12.
26 Michael Decter, "A Plan to End the Hospital Crisis," *Maclean's* (January 17, 2000): 28.
27 Provincial and Territorial Ministers of Health, "Understanding Canada's Health Care Costs: Interim Report," June 2000, 21-27.
28 Brian Lee Crowley, David Zitner, and Nancy Faraday-Smith, "Operating in the Dark: The Gathering Crisis in Canada Public Health Care System," Atlantic Institute for Market Studies, November 1999, 1.
29 A. Charles Baillie, "Health Care in Canada: Preserving a Competitive Advantage," speech to the Vancouver Board of Trade, April 15, 1999.
30 Government of Ontario, "Report Shows Health Care Costs Could Double," news release, Office of the Premier, June 9, 2000.
31 Provincial and Territorial Ministers of Health, "Understanding Canada's Health Care Costs," v.
32 John Zhao, Doug Drew, and T. Scott Murray, "Brain Drain and Brain Gain: The

NOTES

Migration of Knowledge Workers from and to Canada," *Statistics Canada Education Quarterly Review* 6, 3 (2000): 17-19.
33 David Dodge, "Reflections on the Role of Fiscal Policy: The Doug Purvis Memorial Lecture," *Canadian Public Policy* 24, 3 (1998): 287.
34 Auditor General of Canada, 1998 Report, chap. 6: "Population Aging and Information for Parliament: Understanding the Choices," exhibit 6.12.
35 Canadian Medical Association, "In Search of Sustainability: Prospects for Canada's Health Care System," Reports to General Council 2000, A37-40.
36 Conference Board of Canada, "The Future Cost of Health Care in Ontario," October 2000, 2.2.
37 World Health Organization, *World Health Report 2000*, "Health Systems: Improving Performance," 4.
38 Provincial and Territorial Ministers of Health, "Understanding Canada's Health Care Costs," 56.
39 Brad Evenson, "Health care spending in Canada rises to $95B," *National Post*, December 12, 2000.
40 Hugh Scully, "Health-care system cannot survive," *National Post*, May 5, 2000, A18.
41 Mark Kennedy, "Limit medicare coverage or system will die," *Ottawa Citizen*, June 19, 2000, A1.
42 Mark Kennedy, "Canadian health care 30th in world," *Ottawa Citizen*, June 21, 2000, A1; see also World Health Organization, *World Health Report 2000*, annex table 1.
43 Tuohy, Flood, and Stabile, "How Does Private Financing Affect Health Care Systems?" 2-5.
44 Tom Kent, "What Should Be Done about Medicare," The Caledon Institute of Social Policy, August 2000, 10.
45 David Gratzer, *Code Blue: Reviving Canada's Health Care System* (Toronto: ECW Press, 1999).
46 Conference Board of Canada, "Canadians' Values and Attitudes," table 2, 12.
47 Brown, "The Impact of the U.S. on Canada's Tax Strategy," 76.
48 Constitution Act, 1982 [en. by the Canada Act 1982 (U.K.), c. 3, s. 36], 2.
49 Robert Gibbens, "Developers revolt against Quebec's tech city subsidy," *Financial Post*, October 25, 2000, C5.
50 Fred McMahon, *Retreat from Growth: Atlantic Canada and the Negative Sum Economy* (Halifax: Atlantic Institute for Market Studies, 2000), xii-xiii.
51 Operation ONLINE Inc., "www.online.nf.ca".
52 McMahon, *Retreat from Growth*, ix.
53 Dale Orr, "If Americans Can Operate an Economy at 4% Unemployment, Why Can't We?" WEFA Inc., July 2000.
54 Robert Mundell, in McMahon, *Retreat from Growth*, v.
55 Auditor General of Canada, *2000 Report*, chap. 11: "Human Resources Development Canada, Grants and Contributions, October 2000," 11-17.
56 Rick Szostak, "Lessons from the HRDC Scandal," Institute for Research on Public Policy, *Policy Options*, June 2000, 66.
57 Auditor General of Canada, *2000 Report*, chap. 11, 11-49.
58 Ibid., 11, 51-2.
59 Ben Cherniavsky, "The Economics of Job-Creation Programs: What We Know," C.D. Howe Institute Backgrounder, July 25, 2000, 7.
60 Christopher Sarlo, *Poverty in Canada* (Vancouver: The Fraser Institute, 1994), 193-94.
61 Statistics Canada, "Family Income 1998," *The Daily*, June 12, 2000.
62 Ibid.
63 Ross Finnie, "The Dynamics of Poverty in Canada: What We Know, What We Can Do," C.D. Howe Institute Commentary No. 145, September 2000, 32.

64 BCNI, "Creating Opportunity, Building Prosperity: A Tax Reduction Strategy for Canadians," 18.
65 Alexa McDonough, "Straight answers on questions of values," *Ottawa Citizen*, July 10, 2000, A13.
66 House of Commons, Standing Committee on Finance, "Productivity with a Purpose: Improving the Standard of Living of Canadians," 1999.

■ Chapter 3: Developing Human Advantage

1 Jean C. Monty, speech to the Collegium of Work and Learning, Toronto, May 2, 2000.
2 Statistics Canada and Council of Ministers of Education, Canada, *Education Indicators in Canada: Report of the Pan-Canadian Education Indicators Program 1999* (Ottawa, 2000), 3–5.
3 Organisation for Economic Co-operation and Development (OECD), *Literacy in the Information Age: The Final Report from the International Adult Literacy Survey* (Paris, June 2000).
4 Michael Bloom, Marie Burrows, Brenda Lafleur, and Robert Squires, "The Economic Benefits of Improving Literacy Skills in the Workplace," Conference Board of Canada, May 1997, 7.
5 Sean Fine, "Are the schools failing boys?" *Globe and Mail*, September 5, 2000, A1.
6 Government of Ontario, *Early Years Study: Final Report*, April 1999, 9.
7 John T. Bruer, *The Myth of the First Three Years* (New York: The Free Press, 1999), 207.
8 Government of Canada, *The Budget Plan 2000* (Ottawa, 2000), 135.
9 Business Council on National Issues (BCNI), "Creating Opportunity, Building Prosperity: A Tax Reduction Strategy for Canadians," October 1998, 18.
10 Kenneth J. Boessenkool and James B. Davies, "Giving Mom and Dad a Break: Returning Fairness to Families in Canada's Tax and Transfer System," C.D. Howe Institute, Commentary No. 117, November 1998, 27–28.
11 Canadian Alliance, "A Time for Change: An Agenda of Respect for All Canadians," autumn 2000, 10.
12 Mary Gordon, "Home Is Where the Start Is," *Education Canada* 39, 4 (winter 2000): 44–47.
13 Government of Ontario, *Early Years Study*, 150.
14 Dr. Fraser Mustard, interview with authors, January 20, 2000.
15 Jennifer Lewington, "So Many Reforms, So Little to Show," *Education Canada* 38, 3 (fall 1998): 18.
16 Jean-Pascal Souque, "Focus on Competencies: Training and Development Practices, Expenditures and Trends," Conference Board of Canada, Members' Briefing, December 1996.
17 Helen Raham, "Education K–12 Policy for Canadian Global Leadership," Society for the Advancement of Excellence in Education, September 1999, 14.
18 Penny Milton, "Commitment to Success for All," *Education Canada* 38, 3 (fall 1998): 32.
19 Council on Competitiveness, *Going Global: The New Shape of American Innovation* (Washington, DC, September 1998), 8.
20 OECD, *Overcoming Failure at School 1998* (Paris, 1998).
21 For a detailed look at the range of information available about schools in Britain, see the BBC Web site at "news.bbc.co.uk/hi/english/education/league_tables".
22 Raham, "Education," 21–22.
23 Brian Caldwell and Don Haywood, *The Future of Schools: Lessons from the Reform of Public Education* (London: Falmer Press, 1998).

NOTES

24. C. Wylie, "Self-Managing Schools in New Zealand: Seven Years On — What Have We Learnt?" New Zealand Council for Educational Research, September 1997.
25. Province of Ontario, Report of the Royal Commission on Learning, *For the Love of Learning* (Toronto, 1994) (short version).
26. Albert Shanker, cited in Katherine Wagner, "National Standards," Society for the Advancement of Excellence in Education, "www.saee.bc.ca/policywa.html".
27. Edward B. Rust Jr., "The Business Roundtable Responds to Today's High-Stakes Testing Poll Released by the American Association of School Administrators," The Business Roundtable news release, June 22, 2000, "www.brt.org/document.cfm/441".
28. Raham, "Education," 6–7.
29. Siobhan Gorman, "How Should Teachers Be Evaluated?" *National Journal* 12, 4 (1999): 3,479.
30. J.E. Stone, "Value-Added Assessment: An Accountability Revolution," in *Better Teachers, Better Schools* (Washington, DC: The Thomas B. Fordham Foundation, 1999), 245.
31. American Federation of Teachers, "The Use of Student Test Scores in the Evaluation of Teachers," Educational Issues Policy Brief No. 11, October 1999, 3.
32. British Columbia Teachers Federation, "AGM Opposes Foundation Skills Assessment," *Issue Alert* 12, 2 (April 6, 2000).
33. Canadian Teachers Federation Web site, "www.ctf-fce.ca/e/what/other/assessment/high-stakes.htm".
34. BBC News Online, "Merit pay deadline passes," June 6, 2000; "Teachers' bonus in best schools," May 23, 2000, "www.news.bbc.co.uk.hi.english.indepth/education/2000/teachers_pay".
35. "Pay for Performance: An Issue Brief for Business Leaders," The Business Roundtable, "www.brt.org.document.cfm/403".
36. Raham, "Education," 23.
37. Society for the Advancement of Excellence in Education, "Mixed Progress on Performance Pay," News Bulletin on Education Change, August 2000, "www.saee.bc.ca/edudigest.html".
38. Helen Raham, "Cooperative Performance Incentive Plans," Society for the Advancement of Excellence in Education, *Education Analyst* 3, 1 (winter 2000): 5.
39. Raham, "Education," 24.
40. D.S. Smith, "Parent-Generated Home Study in Canada," *The Canadian School Executive* 15, 8 (February 1996).
41. Raham, "Education," 10.
42. Daniel J. Brown, "The Impact of Parental Choice on Three Canadian Public Schools," University of British Columbia, 1999.
43. Teachers for Excellence in Education, TEE, Report 7, 3 (October 2000): 2.
44. Joe Williams and Alan Borsuk, "City's school scene redefining public education," *Milwaukee Journal Sentinel*, January 17, 1999.
45. Helen Raham, "Linking Assessment and School Success: A Look at Practices and Results across North America," Society for the Advancement of Excellence in Education, April 1999.
46. David Grissmer, "Exploring Rapid Achievement Gains in North Carolina and Texas," The National Education Goals Panel, November 1998, "www.negp.gov/reports/grissmer.pdf".
47. Kevin Lynch, "Improving Canada's Productivity Performance: The Key to Higher Living Standards," *Industry Canada* (January 18, 2000): 14.
48. BNCI, "Jobs, Growth and Community: Large Enterprises at Work," June 1997, 24–25.
49. Human Resources Development Canada, *Job Futures 2000: World of Work, Overview of Labour Market Trends*, "www11.hrdc-drhc.gc.ca/doc/jf/trends/trends.shtml#8".

50 Micheline Bouchard, "The Knowledge Chain: Succeeding in the Information Age," speech to the Canadian Club, Toronto, January 1999.
51 Association of Universities and Colleges of Canada Web site: "www.aucc.ca/en/research/revenue.htm".
52 "Degree Deluge," *Maclean's* (May 31, 1999): 55.
53 Carman Miller, quoted in Patrick McDonagh, "To B.A. or Not to B.A.?" *McGill News* (fall 1999): 16.
54 Ibid., 35.
55 Corporate-Higher Education Forum, "It Pays to Stay," October 1997, 34.
56 Danielle Svetcov, "The Virtual Classroom vs. the Real One," *Forbes*, Best of the Web, (September 11, 2000): 50.
57 Christine Massey and Joanne Curry, "Online Post-Secondary Education: A Competitive Analysis," *Industry Canada* (March 1999).
58 Ibid.
59 Doug Hull, Industry Canada, interview with authors, December 3, 1999. See also "www.schoolnet.ca/campus".
60 W. Randall Kangas, "Return on Investment of a Land Grant University," University of Illinois at Urbana-Champaign, November 1996, "www.admin.uiuc.edu/NB/96.11/9611collegetip.html".
61 Abraham McLaughlin, "States compete to keep grads home as idea-driven economy drains brains," *National Post*, December 27, 1999, A14.
62 Progressive Conservative Party, PC Platform, Education and Learning, "www.pcparty.ca/policy/Full_policyindex_printable.asp".
63 Liberal Party of Canada, "Opportunity for All: The Liberal Plan for the Future of Canada," autumn 2000, 10.
64 BCNI, "Jobs, Growth and Community," 26.
65 The Honourable Paul Martin, Budget Speech, February 2000.
66 Society for the Advancement of Excellence in Education, "New School Rating System," *Education Analyst* 3, 3 (fall 2000): 3.
67 Council of Ministers of Education, Canada, *Education Indicators in Canada 1999*, 96.
68 Michael Mendelson and Ken Battle, "Aboriginal People in Canada's Labour Market," Caledon Institute of Social Policy, June 1999, 16.
69 Auditor General of Canada, *2000 Report*, chap. 4, "Indian and Northern Affairs Canada, Elementary and Secondary Education," 4–10.
70 Bob Rae, "Education: Refocusing the Debate," *Education Canada* 40, 1 (spring 2000): 48.
71 Stephen Lawton, "The Future of Teachers' Unions: A Call for Change," *Education Canada* 1, 1 (spring 2000): 22.
72 Helen Raham, "Reinventing Teacher Contracts," Society for the Advancement of Excellence in Education, *Education Analyst* 3, 3 (fall 2000): 4–5.
73 Quebec School Improvement Network Web site: "www.qesn.meq.gouv.qc.ca/schimprove/qscommit".
74 Canadian Education Association, "Shape the Future: Creating a Culture of Achievement in Canadian High Schools," 1999.
75 Margaret Wente, "Mommies drop dead! Canada's largest union is kicking parents out of the school," *Globe and Mail*, March 18, 2000, A26.
76 Maude Barlow and Heather-jane Robertson, *Class Struggle: The Assault on Canada's Schools* (Toronto: Key Porter, 1994), vi–viii.
77 Benjamin Levin, "Democracy and Schools: Educating for Citizenship," *Education Canada*, 40, 3 (fall 2000): 4–7.
78 John Mayberry, interview with authors, August 31, 1999.
79 Jean Monty, speech to Collegium of Work and Learning.

80 Conference Board of Canada, "What to Do before the Well Runs Dry: Managing Scarce Skills," March 2000, 7.
81 BCNI, "Jobs, Growth and Community," 28–33.
82 David Stewart-Patterson, "A Community of Enterprise," in *Perspectives on Partnership*, Caledon Institute of Social Policy (June 1998): 37–38.
83 Raham, "Education," 32–33.

■ Chapter 4: Competing for Talent

1 Don Tapscott, David Ticoll, and Alex Lowy, *Digital Capital: Harnessing the Power of Business Webs* (Cambridge: Harvard Business School Press, 2000), 180–81.
2 Ed Pierce, "Networking the World," *Ivey Business Journal* (November/December 1999): 22.
3 John Roth, interview with authors, November 12, 1999.
4 Pierce, "Networking the World," 24.
5 John Zhao, Doug Drew, and T. Scott Murray, "Brain Drain and Brain Gain: The Migration of Knowledge Workers from and to Canada," *Statistics Canada Education Quarterly Review* 6, 3 (2000): 10–13.
6 Don DeVoretz and Samuel Laryea, "Canadian Human Capital Transfers: The United States and Beyond," C.D. Howe Institute, October 1998, 8.
7 Zhao, Drew, and Murray, "Brain Drain and Brain Gain," 10–13.
8 Human Resources Development Canada and Statistics Canada, "South of the Border: Graduates from the Class of '95 Who Moved to the United States," 1999.
9 DeVoretz and Laryea, "Canadian Human Capital Transfers," 10.
10 Ibid., 23.
11 Shelly Branch, "You Hired 'Em. But Can You Keep 'Em?" *Fortune* (November 9, 1998): 247.
12 Human Resources Development Canada and Statistics Canada, "South of the Border."
13 Personnel Systems, "Today's Technology Graduate: Mobile, in Demand and Demanding!" 2000, "www.perssyst.com/survey/grad-results".
14 Canadian Advanced Technology Association, "Education for Export," 1996.
15 Human Resources Development Canada and Statistics Canada, "South of the Border."
16 David R. Graham, correspondence with authors, February 24, 2000.
17 Zhao, Drew, and Murray, "Brain Drain and Brain Gain," 13.
18 Ibid., table 4, 30.
19 Mike Blanchfield, "Brain drain swells to 5-year high," *National Post*, September 27, 2000, A1.
20 Business Council on National Issues, "Winning the Human Race: Developing and Retaining World-Class Talent," May 2000, 26–27.
21 Zhao, Drew, and Murray, "Brain Drain and Brain Gain," 23.
22 Ibid., 19.
23 Mark MacKinnon, "Give us your highly educated," *Globe and Mail*, May 24, 1999, B1.
24 Michelle Goldberg, "Barriers to Employment — Part I," presentation to Fourth International Metropolis Conference, Washington, DC, Ministry of Training, Colleges and Universities, Government of Ontario, December 1999.
25 Jean Monty, interview with authors, July 19, 1999.
26 Tony Fell, interview with authors, August 18, 1999.
27 Jeff Lipton, interview with authors, July 6, 1999.
28 Roger Phillips, interview with authors, August 20, 1999; IPSCO Inc. news release, January 15, 1999.
29 Daniel Schwanen, "Putting the Brain Drain in Context: Canada and the Global Competition for Scientists and Engineers," C.D. Howe Institute, April 2000, 12.

Notes

30 Paul Hill, "Brain drain not about taxes; it's about the seat of power," *Globe and Mail Report on Business*, January 18, 2000.
31 Edward Newall, interview with authors, November 4, 1999.
32 Youssef Nasr, interview with authors, July 5, 1999.
33 Jeff Lipton, interview with authors, July 6, 1999.
34 David Kerr, interview with authors, August 17, 1999.
35 Gwyn Morgan, interview with authors, September 8, 1999.
36 Michael Phelps, interview with authors, September 20, 1999.
37 Raymond McFeetors, interview with authors, August 19, 1999.
38 John Willson, interview with authors, September 20, 1999.
39 Steven Globerman, "Trade Liberalization and the Migration of Skilled Workers," *Perspectives on North American Free Trade*, Paper Number 3, Industry Canada (April 1999): 23.
40 John Van Brunt, interview with authors, September 7, 1999.
41 Robert Brown, interview with authors, August 10, 1999.
42 John Cleghorn, interview with authors, July 15, 1999.
43 Business Council on National Issues, "Global Champion or Falling Star? The Choice Canada Must Make," statement at the CEO Summit 2000, Toronto, April 5, 2000, 7.
44 David O'Brien, interview with authors, September 8, 1999.
45 The Honourable Mitchell Sharp, "Setting the Compass: Defining Public Service Values in Times of Change," speech, Winnipeg, February 5, 1998.
46 Joel Novek, "Employer of First Resort," Institute for Research on Public Policy, excerpt of March 1983 article republished in *Policy Options* (September 2000): 39.
47 Nancy Averill, "The New Public Service," presentation to Rediscovering Public Service Roundtable, Toronto, June 18, 1999.
48 Morley Gunderson, Douglas Hyatt, and Craig Riddell, "Pay Differences between the Government and Private Sectors: Labour Force Survey and Census Estimates," Canadian Policy Research Networks Inc., February 2000, iv.
49 Averill, "The New Public Service."
50 Advisory Committee on Senior Level Retention and Compensation, Second Report, Treasury Board of Canada Secretariat, March 2000.
51 Eva Ryten, "Canadian Health Care and the Brain Drain: Doctors and Nurses," paper presented at Fraser Institute conference, Vancouver, November 13, 1998, 9.
52 Ibid., 4.
53 Zhao, Drew, and Murray, "Brain Drain and Brain Gain," 17.
54 Victor Dirnfeld, "Canadian Physicians and the Brain Drain," presentation to the House of Commons Standing Committee on Finance, June 9, 1998.
55 Canadian Nurses Association, "CNA President Says National HHR Strategy Key to Sustainability of the System," July 20, 2000.
56 Ibid., "Rebuilding the Health System Starts with the Renewal of the Nursing Workforce," September 12, 2000.
57 Ibid., "Major Registered Nursing Shortage Looms," November 4, 1997.
58 Christine Tausig Ford, "Keeping Top Profs Gets Tougher," Association of Universities and Colleges of Canada, *University Affairs*, December 1997, "www.aucc.ca".
59 Leanne Elliott, "Revitalizing Universities through Faculty Renewal," Association of Universities and Colleges of Canada, *Research File* 4, 1 (2000): 2–3.
60 Ibid., 3–4.
61 Paul Beamish, "Knowledge Creators or Knowledge Retailers? Business School Research in Canada," Ivey Business School, 2000, 5.
62 Advisory Council on Science and Technology, "Stepping Up: Skills and Opportunities in the Knowledge Economy," report of the Expert Panel on Skills, 2000, 45–46.
63 James Shepard, interview with authors, July 5, 1999.

NOTES

64 Advisory Council on Science and Technology, *Stepping Up*, 46.
65 Ibid., 47.
66 Canadian Labour Force Development Board, "Prior Learning Assessment and Recognition: Learning has no Boundaries," undated, 1.
67 Tapscott, Ticoll, and Lowy, *Digital Capital*, 174.
68 Graham Lowe, "It pays to treat the workers well," *Toronto Star*, May 19, 2000, A25.
69 Business Council on National Issues, "Jobs, Growth and Community: Large Enterprises at Work," 1997, 28–33.
70 Beamish, "Knowledge Creators or Knowledge Retailers," 3–5.
71 Business Council on National Issues, "Creating Opportunity, Building Prosperity: A Tax Reduction Strategy for Canadians," 1998.
72 Lori Whewell, "Cross-Border Flows of Skilled Workers," presentation to Skills Development in the Knowledge-Based Economy Conference, Moncton, New Brunswick, June 23, 1999, 12.
73 Kerry Hawkins, interview with authors, December 8, 1999.
74 Jacques Lamarre, interview with authors, July 19, 1999.
75 Jeff Lipton, interview with authors, July 6, 1999.
76 Gwyn Morgan, interview with authors, September 8, 1999.
77 Hartley Richardson, interview with authors, August 19, 1999.
78 The Honourable Paul Martin, speech to the Toronto Board of Trade, September 14, 2000.

■ Chapter 5: Creating an Innovation Society

1 Council on Competitiveness, "Going Global: The New Shape of American Innovation," September 1998, 14–15.
2 Kevin Lynch, "Improving Canada's Productivity Performance: The Key to Higher Living Standards," presentation on behalf of Industry Canada, January 18, 2000, 9.
3 Gerry Schwartz, interviewed in *Ivey Business Journal* (July/August 2000): 28.
4 Lynch, "Improving Canada's Productivity Performance," 6.
5 Andrew Sharpe, "The Stylized Facts of the Canada–U.S. Manufacturing Productivity Gap," Centre for the Study of Living Standards, January 2000.
6 Lynch, "Improving Canada's Productivity Performance," 8.
7 Peter Bentley, interview with authors, September 20, 1999.
8 Donald Daly, "Small Business in Canada–U.S. Manufacturing Productivity and Cost Comparisons," Schulich School of Business, York University, January 2000, 36.
9 Surendra Gera, Wulong Gu, and Frank Lee, "Foreign Direct Investment and Productivity Growth: The Canadian Host-Country Experience," Working Paper No. 30, Industry Canada, 1999.
10 Daly, "Small Business in Canada–U.S. Manufacturing Productivity and Cost Comparisons," 16.
11 John Baldwin and Petr Hanel, "Multinationals and the Canadian Innovation Process," Statistics Canada, June 2000, 45.
12 Frank Cella, interview with authors, July 26, 1999.
13 Youssef Nasr, interview with authors, July 5, 1999.
14 Baldwin and Hanel, "Multinationals and the Canadian Innovation Process," 46.
15 John Mayberry, interview with authors, August 31, 1999.
16 Andrei Sulzenko, comments at Centre for the Study of Living Standards conference on the Canada–U.S. Manufacturing Gap, session 8, January 22, 2000.
17 Michael Porter and Scott Stern, "The New Challenge to America's Prosperity: Findings from the Innovation Index," Council on Competitiveness, 1999, 43–48.
18 Organisation for Economic Co-operation and Development, *Basic Science and Technology Statistics, 1999 Edition* (Paris: OECD, 2000).

NOTES

19 Paul Davenport, "Universities, Innovation and the Knowledge-Based Economy," Industry Canada Distinguished Lecture, CERF/IRPP Conference on Creating Canada's Advantage in the Information Age, May 5, 2000.
20 Manuel Trajtenberg, "Is Canada Missing the Technology Boat? Evidence from Patent Data," Centre for the Study of Living Standards — Industry Canada Conference on Canada in the 21st Century, Ottawa, Ontario, September 18, 1999, 16–17.
21 Davenport, "Universities, Innovation and the Knowledge-Based Economy."
22 David Strangway, "Releasing the Creative Energy of Canadian Researchers: Doing Things Differently," The Canada Foundation for Innovation, September 28, 1999, 8.
23 Hon. Henry Jackman, interview with authors, August 31, 1999.
24 Robert Berdahl, "Energizing the National Commitment to Education," in Porter and Stern, *The New Challenge to America's Prosperity*, 57.
25 Business Council on National Issues, "Risk and Reward: Creating a Canadian Culture of Innovation," working paper, May 2000, 11–12.
26 Liberal Party of Canada, *Opportunity for All: The Liberal Plan for the Future of Canada*, October 2000, 7.
27 Organisation for Economic Co-operation and Development, *Implementing the OECD Jobs Strategy: Assessing Performance and Policy* (Paris: OECD, 1999), 152.
28 Conference Board of Canada, "Collaborating for Innovation: 2nd Annual Innovation Report," Report 303-00 Detailed Findings, 2000, iii.
29 United States Senate Joint Economic Committee Staff Report, "Entrepreneurial Dynamism and the Success of U.S. High-Tech," October 1999, 31.
30 OECD, *Implementing the OECD Jobs Strategy*, 152.
31 Samuel Kortum and Josh Lerner, "Does Venture Capital Spur Innovation?" Boston University, Harvard University, and the National Bureau of Economic Research, November 1998, 3.
32 Paul Reynolds et al., "Global Entrepreneurship Monitor 2000 Executive Report," Babson College, London Business School, and Kauffman Center for Entrepreneurial Leadership, 2000, 16.
33 Gordon Sharwood, notes for presentation to Greater Toronto Area Liberal Caucus meeting, June 18, 1999.
34 Jeff Lipton, interview with authors, July 6, 1999.
35 Mary Macdonald, "Promising new times for venture capital," *Globe and Mail*, January 22, 2000.
36 Canadian Labour and Business Centre, "Pension funds as investors: Could they improve Canada's 'ability to fund bright new ideas developing here'?" *Working Together* (newsletter), February 2000, 3.
37 Organisation for Economic Co-operation and Development, *OECD Science, Technology and Industry Scoreboard 1999: Benchmarking Knowledge-Based Economies* (Paris: OECD, 2000), 54–55.
38 Karen Corkery and Angie Brennand, "Seed Stage Investment Activity in Canada," Expert Panel on the Commercialization of University Research, January 12, 1999.
39 Canadian E-Business Opportunities Roundtable, "Fast Forward: Accelerating Canada's Leadership in the Internet Economy," Boston Consulting Group (Canada), January 2000, 24–25.
40 Theresa Shutt and Hugh Williams, "Going to Market: The Cost of IPOs in Canada and the United States," Conference Board of Canada Members' Briefing 296-00, June 2000.
41 Canadian E-Business Opportunities Roundtable, "Fast Forward," 29.
42 Roger Martin, "Forget this TSE obsession and fix the capital markets," *Financial Post* (September 14, 2000): C19.
43 Business Council on National Issues, "Risk and Reward," 17–18.

NOTES

44 United States Senate Joint Economic Committee, "Entrepreneurial Dynamism," 29.
45 Ibid., 21.
46 John Roth, interview with authors, November 12, 1999.
47 William Sahlman, "The New Economy Is Stronger Than You Think," *Harvard Business Review* (November-December 1999).
48 Paul Reynolds et al., "Global Entrepreneurship Monitor 2000 Executive Report," 47.
49 John Cleghorn, interview with authors, July 15, 1999.
50 Paul Tellier, interview with authors, November 8, 1999.
51 "In praise of wealth," *National Post*, editorial, August 22, 2000, A17.
52 Prime Minister's Advisory Council on Science and Technology, "Stepping Up: Skills and Opportunity in the Knowledge Economy, Report of the Expert Panel on Skills, 2000," 68–69.
53 Robert Carroll et al., "Entrepreneurs, Income Taxes and Investment," Working Paper 6374, National Bureau of Economic Research, January 1998, 21–22.
54 Robert Carroll et al., "Income Taxes and Entrepreneurs' Use of Labor," Working Paper 6578, National Bureau of Economic Research, May 1998, 2.
55 Pierre Fortin, "The Canadian Standard of Living: Is There a Way Up?" C.D. Howe Institute Benefactors Lecture, 1999, Montreal, October 19, 1999, 97. Emphasis in original.
56 Paul J. Hill, interview with authors, December 7, 1999.
57 Standing Senate Committee on Banking, Trade and Commerce, "The Taxation of Capital Gains," Fifth Report, May 2000.
58 Howard Mann, correspondence with authors, November 14, 2000.
59 Canada's Research-Based Pharmaceutical Companies, "The Value of New Medicines," Backgrounder, September 2000, "www.canadapharm.org".
60 Wayne Millar, "Disparities in Prescription Drug Insurance Coverage," *Statistics Canada Health Reports* 10 (spring 1999): 11.
61 Canada's Research-Based Pharmaceutical Companies, "Drug Approval Times in Canada, 1999," June 2000, "www.canadapharm.org".
62 Paul Lucas, interview with authors, August 17, 1999.
63 Canada's Research-Based Pharmaceutical Companies, "Impacts of Drug Cost Containment and Price Controls in Canada," April 10, 2000, "www.canadapharm.org".
64 Claudio Bussandri, interview with authors, December 20, 1999.
65 Jacques Lamarre, interview with authors, July 19, 1999.
66 Centre for Collaborative Government, "Collaborative Government in the Post-Industrial Age: Five Discussion Pieces," May 2000, 18.
67 Kim Devooght, presentation to Crossing Boundaries 2, Roundtable 3, Ottawa, May 8, 2000.
68 Paul Thomas, introduction to *Change, Governance and Public Management: Alternative Service Delivery and Information Technology* (Ottawa: Public Policy Forum, 2000), 51–52.
69 Ibid., 28.
70 David Osborne and Peter Plastrik, *Banishing Bureaucracy: Five Strategies for Reinventing Government* (New York: Penguin Putnam, 1998), 257–58.
71 Kenneth Kernaghan, "Rediscovering Public Service: Recognizing the Value of an Essential Institution," Institute of Public Administration of Canada, 2000, 19–20.
72 Brian Davies, comments during panel discussion on "Rediscovering Public Service" at Institute for Public Administration of Canada conference, Ottawa, August 29, 2000.
73 Brian Marson, "How Canadians View Public Sector Service: Findings from the 1998 Citizens First Survey," Treasury Board of Canada, 1999.
74 Charles Handy, interviewed in *Ivey Business Journal* (July/August 2000): 35.

75 Robert Knox, "The Unpleasant Reality of Interprovincial Trade Disputes," The Fraser Institute, *Fraser Forum* (October 2000).
76 Donald Savoie, *Governing from the Centre: The Concentration of Power in Canadian Politics* (Toronto: University of Toronto Press, 1999), 362.
77 Thomas, introduction to *Change, Governance and Public Management*, 74-75.
78 Harvey Lazar, "Get your fiscal acts together," *Globe and Mail*, October 13, 2000.
79 Alliance for Converging Technologies, "Governance in the Digital Economy," 1999, 3.
80 Joseph Nye Jr., remarks to Members Meeting, Governance in the Digital Economy Program, Alliance for Converging Technologies, Cambridge, Mass., October 28, 1999.
81 Frank Graves, "Rethinking Government: Canadian Views of Emerging Issues," presentation to Institute for Public Administration of Canada conference, August 30, 2000.
82 Barbara Legowski, "A Sampling of Community- and Citizen-Driven Quality of Life/Societal Indicator Projects," Canadian Policy Research Networks Inc., March 7, 2000.
83 Clifford Cobb and Craig Rixford, "Lessons Learned from the History of Social Indicators," Redefining Progress, November 1998, 22.
84 Harvard Group on Network-Enabled Services and Government, "Eight Imperatives for Leaders in a Networked World," John F. Kennedy School of Government, Harvard University, 2000.
85 Sherri Torjman, "Partnerships: The Good, the Bad and the Uncertain," Caledon Institute of Social Policy, June 1998, 10-11.
86 Government of Canada / Voluntary Sector Joint Initiative, "Working Together: Report of the Joint Tables," August 1999, 17-18.
87 Canadian Centre for Philanthropy, "More than Charity: A New Agenda for Corporate Citizenship," June 1998, 6.
88 Ibid., 9.
89 Ibid., 8.
90 Rosabeth Moss Kanter, "From Spare Change to Real Change: The Social Sector as Beta Site for Business Innovation," *Harvard Business Review* (May/June 1999): 124.
91 Ibid., 125.
92 Council on Competitiveness, "Going Global," 10.
93 Progressive Policy Institute, "The State New Economy Index: Benchmarking Economic Transformation in the States," July 1999, "www.ld1cppi.org".
94 Jean Monty, interview with authors, July 19, 1999.
95 John Cleghorn, interview with authors, July 15, 1999.
96 Alex Cirillo Jr., remarks at Innovation 2000 conference, Conference Board of Canada, Toronto, November 2, 2000.
97 Hon. Paul Martin, Budget Speech, February 2000.

■ Chapter 6: Building Global Champions

1 John Micklethwait and Adrian Wooldridge, *A Future Perfect: The Challenge and Hidden Promise of Globalization* (New York: Crown Publishers, 2000), 135-36.
2 United Nations Conference on Trade and Development, "World Investment Report 2000: Cross-Border Mergers and Acquisitions and Development," July 2000, 1.
3 Ibid., 21.
4 Dezsö Horváth, "Canada and the Global Marketplace: Challenges and Opportunities," presentation to the Executive Program 2000, Schulich School of Business, York University, June 2000, 1-2.
5 Robert Brown, interview with authors, August 10, 1999.
6 Paul Tellier, interview with authors, November 8, 1999.
7 Jacques Lamarre, interview with authors, July 19, 1999.

NOTES

8 Rick George, interview with authors, September 7, 1999.
9 A. Charles Baillie, interview with authors, July 15, 1999.
10 John Cleghorn, interview with authors, July 15, 1999.
11 Dominic D'Alessandro, interview with authors, July 21, 1999.
12 David Caplan, interview with authors, September 2, 1999.
13 John Wetmore, interview with authors, July 21, 1999.
14 James Shepard, interview with authors, July 5, 1999.
15 Dan Branda, interview with authors, August 31, 1999.
16 Kevin Lynch, "Moving Canada Forward: Progress and Challenges," presentation on behalf of Industry Canada, February 13, 1997, 24.
17 William Hanley, "The also-ran index," *Financial Post*, July 26, 2000, D1.
18 John Mayberry, interview with authors, August 31, 1999.
19 John Cleghorn, interview with authors, July 15, 1999.
20 Statistics Canada, "Canada's international trade in securities, August 2000," *The Daily*, October 24, 2000.
21 *National Post Business Magazine*, June 2000, 96–97.
22 Tsun-Yan Hsieh and Stephanie Coyles, "Breaking Out of the Pack: Creating More Canadian Global Champions," *Ivey Business Journal* (May/June 2000): s34–36.
23 Ibid., s35.
24 James Stanford, interview with authors, July 21, 1999.
25 Marc Fortier, interview with authors, November 9, 1999.
26 David O'Brien, interview with authors, September 8, 1999.
27 Hsieh and Coyles, "Breaking Out of the Pack," s35.
28 "Going for Gold: Winning Corporate Strategies and Their Impact on Canada," working paper, April 2000, 20.
29 Serge Godin, interview with authors. September 2, 1999.
30 James Arnett, interview with authors, November 9, 1999.
31 Paul Desmarais Jr., interview with authors, July 28, 1999.
32 Jean Monty, interview with authors, July 19, 1999.
33 Robert Peterson, interview with authors, August 31, 1999.
34 David O'Brien, interview with authors, September 8, 1999.
35 Jacques Bougie, interview with authors, December 20, 1999.
36 Charles Sirois, interview with authors, November 10, 1999.
37 Jacques Lamarre, interview with authors, July 19, 1999.
38 Edward Neufeld, "What Kind of a Financial System Do Canadians Want? Implications of Globalization and Current Canadian Policies for the Future of the Canadian Financial System," School of Policy Studies, Queen's University, April 2000, 33.
39 Ibid., 38.
40 A. Charles Baillie, interview with authors, July 15, 1999.
41 Youssef Nasr, interview with authors, July 5, 1999.
42 R. John Lawrence, interview with authors, January 13, 2000.
43 Lawson Hunter, "Canada's Competition Policy — Its Role in Achieving Global Competitiveness," Business Council on National Issues, September 1999.
44 Paul Tellier, interview with authors, November 8, 1999.
45 Stephen Snyder, interview with authors, July 7, 1999.
46 Marc Fortier, interview with authors, November 9, 1999.
47 Robert Brown, interview with authors, August 10, 1999.
48 David Caplan, interview with authors, September 2, 1999.
49 Robert Brown, interview with authors, August 10, 1999.
50 David Caplan, interview with authors, September 2, 1999.
51 Paul Lucas, interview with authors, August 17, 1999.
52 James Shepard, interview with authors, July 5, 1999.

53 David O'Brien, interview with authors, September 8, 1999.
54 Seymour Schulich, interview with authors, August 17, 1999.
55 Business Council on National Issues, "Magnetic North: Powering Canada's Growth," 14.
56 Bloomberg News, "Separatism, debt blocking 'AAA' rating, Moody's says," *National Post*, October 20, 2000, A5.
57 Roger Phillips, interview with authors, August 20, 1999.
58 David O'Brien, interview with authors, September 8, 1999.
59 Robert Peterson, interview with authors, August 31, 1999.
60 Jacques Bougie, interview with authors, December 20, 1999.
61 Israel Asper, interview with authors, August 19, 1999.
62 Rosanne Altshuler, Harry Grubert, and T. Scott Newton, "Has U.S. Investment Abroad Become More Sensitive to Tax Rates?" Working Paper 6383, National Bureau of Economic Research, January 1998.
63 John Wetmore, interview with authors, July 21, 1999.
64 John Willson, interview with authors, September 20, 1999.
65 "The mystery of the vanishing taxpayer," *The Economist* (January 28, 2000).
66 Peter Cook, "The drive to make the world's tax havens unsafe," *Globe and Mail*, June 28, 2000, B10.
67 Jack Mintz, "Why Canada Must Undertake Business Tax Reform Soon," C.D. Howe Institute, October 1999, 2.
68 Richard Rapaport, "When Irish IT Is Smiling," *Forbes ASAP* (May 31, 1999): 114.
69 Barry Came, "The Celtic Tiger," *Maclean's* (August 21, 2000): 47.
70 World Economic Forum, "The Global Competitiveness Report 1999," 229.
71 Fred McMahon, *The Road to Growth* Atlantic Institute for Market Studies (2000): 12–13.
72 Ibid., 7–9.
73 Mintz, "Why Canada Must Undertake Business Tax Reform Soon," 3.
74 Richard Harris, "Making a Case for Tax Cuts," Business Council on National Issues, October 1999, 25.
75 Carol Howes and Claudia Cattaneo, "Business gets $1B tax break in Alberta," *Financial Post*, September 14, 2000, C1.
76 Mahmood Iqbal, "Implications of Taxes on Investment Decisions in Canada: Some Comparisons with OECD Countries," Report 213-97, Conference Board of Canada, October 1997, 16.
77 Howard Mann, interview with authors, August 3, 1999.
78 Ronald Mannix, interview with authors, September 9, 2000.
79 Robert Brown, interview with authors, August 10, 1999.
80 Pierre Brunet, interview with authors, September 2, 1999.
81 Jean Monty, interview with authors, July 19, 1999.
82 Sanford Riley, interview with authors, August 19, 1999.
83 David Culver, interview with authors, November 9, 1999.
84 David Birch, Anne Haggerty, and William Parsons, "Entrepreneurial Hot Spots: The Best Places in America to Start and Grow a Company," Cognetics Inc., 1999.
85 Nicolas Papadopoulos and Louise Heslop, "Countries as Brands: Canadian Products Abroad," *Ivey Business Journal* (November/December 2000): 36.
86 Greater Minneapolis Chamber of Commerce Web site, "www.minneapolischamber.org".
87 John Roth, interview with authors, November 12, 1999.
88 William M. Mercer Companies LLC, "Four Cities Share Top Ranking in Worldwide Quality of Living Survey," news release, January 13, 2000.
89 Edward Newall, interview with authors, November 4, 1999.

Notes

■ Chapter 7: Walking Tall among Nations

1. Department of Foreign Affairs and International Trade, "Canada in the World: Projecting Canadian Values and Culture," 1999, 1.
2. Thomas d'Aquino, remarks on behalf of the Business Council on National Issues to the Royal Commission on the Economic Union and Development Prospects for Canada, December 12, 1983, Ottawa.
3. G. Pascal Zachary, "The Global Me, New Cosmopolitans and the Competitive Edge: Picking Globalism's Winners and Losers," *Public Affairs Books* (July 2000).
4. John H. Jackson and William J. Davey, *Legal Problems of International Economic Relations*, American Casebook Series, 2nd ed. (Saint Paul, Minn.: West Publishing Co., 1986), 296.
5. Renato Ruggiero, foreword to Michael Hart, *Fifty Years of Canadian Statecraft: Canada at the GATT, 1947–1997* (Ottawa: Centre for Trade Policy and Law, 1998), vi–ix.
6. Hart, *Fifty Years of Canadian Statecraft*, 221.
7. Ibid., 222.
8. Robert Wolfe, "Confronting the Aftermath of Seattle: Canada Must Set Key Trade Priorities Now," working paper of the *Institute for Research on Public Policy* 1, 1 (2000): 1.
9. C. Fred Bergsten, "The United States Interest in New Global Trade Negotiations," in Jeffrey J. Schott, ed., *The WTO after Seattle* (Washington, DC: Institute for International Economics, 2000), 45.
10. Schott, *The WTO after Seattle*, 15.
11. Ibid., 15 and 16.
12. See Thomas d'Aquino, "Environment and Economy — Until Death Do Them Part," address to the Conference on Sustainable Development, Winnipeg, May 17, 1989.
13. Paul Hawken, address to Canada's Energy Efficiency Conference 2000, Ottawa, October 11, 2000.
14. See Paul Hawken, Amory Lovins, and Hunter Lovins, *Natural Capitalism: The Next Industrial Revolution* (London: Earthscan Publications, 1999).
15. The BCNI was encouraged to pursue the free trade idea by Liberal Senator George van Roggen, chairman of the Standing Senate Committee on Foreign Affairs.
16. Thomas d'Aquino, introduction of United States ambassador Paul Robinson at a meeting of the Business Council on National Issues, York Club, Toronto, January 21, 1982.
17. Meeting of select members of the BCNI with Vice President George Bush at the Château Laurier, Ottawa, March 23, 1983.
18. Donald S. MacDonald, "Leap of Faith," in L. Ian MacDonald, ed., *Free Trade: Risks and Rewards* (Montreal and Kingston: McGill-Queen's University Press, 2000), 53.
19. G. Bruce Doern and Brian W. Tomlin, *Faith and Fear: The Free Trade Story* (Toronto: Stoddart, 1991), 50.
20. Thomas d'Aquino, remarks to the Executive Committee, Canadian Alliance for Trade and Job Opportunities, Toronto, October 7, 1987.
21. Richard Lipsey, "The Canada–U.S. FTA: Real Results Versus Unreal Expectations," in MacDonald, ed., *Free Trade*, 104 and 105.
22. Derek Burney, "Accessing the U.S. Market," remarks to Aerospace Industry Association of Canada 39th Annual General Meeting, Ottawa, September 18, 2000, 5.
23. Michael Hart, "Disarming the 'Undefended' Border in Order to Preserve It: Canada, the United States and Deepening Economic Integration," paper prepared for the Business Council on National Issues Global Leadership Initiative, Ottawa, February 2000, 12.

24 Michael Hart et al., "Canada–US Free Trade: Is It Time for Round Two? A Virtual Roundtable," *Canadian Foreign Policy* 7, 3 (2000): 6.
25 John Helliwell, *How Much Do National Borders Matter?* (Washington, DC: Brookings Institution, 1998).
26 Hart, "Disarming the 'Undefended' Border in Order to Preserve It," 15.
27 Stephen Handelman, "Two Nations Indivisible," *Time*, Canadian edition (July 10, 2000): 22.
28 Richard G. Harris, "North American Economic Integration: Issues and a Research Agenda," background paper prepared for an Industry Canada Roundtable on North American Linkages, Ottawa, September 7, 2000.
29 Burney, "Accessing the U.S. Market."
30 Hart, "Disarming the 'Undefended' Border in Order to Preserve It," 21.
31 Thomas J. Courchene and Richard G. Harris, "From Fixing to Monetary Union: Options for North American Currency Integration," C.D. Howe Institute, June 22, 1999.
32 "Canada's dollar: to fix or not," an e-mail debate arranged by the *Financial Post* between Robert Mundell and Milton Friedman, *Financial Post*, December 12, 2000, C19.
33 Ibid.
34 Thomas d'Aquino, address to annual general meeting, Business Council on National Issues, Toronto, April 17, 1996.
35 Thomas d'Aquino, summary of a meeting with Mexican business leaders at the Four Seasons Hotel, Toronto, January 24, 1989.
36 Gordon Giffin, "Canada needs a 'coherent' trade plan," *Ottawa Citizen* (January 6, 2001): A3.
37 Ibid.
38 Donald S. MacDonald, "Foreigners like Canadians don't count within the European Union," Canada-European Union Joint Supplement, *The Hill Times*, December 11, 2000, 19.
39 Thomas d'Aquino, remarks at a meeting with EU Trade Commissioner Pascal Lamy and Minister for International Trade Pierre Pettigrew, Rideau Club, December 20, 2000.
40 Donald Barry, "Pursuing Free Trade: Canada, the Western Hemisphere, and the European Union," *International Journal* 55, 2 (2000): 300.
41 Jacques Chirac, "European Union and Canada are increasing their exchanges," Canada–European Union Joint Supplement, *The Hill Times*, December 11, 2000, 17.
42 Thomas d'Aquino, "Forging a dynamic Canada-Japan trade and investment strategy for the third millennium," a presentation to the 23rd annual meeting of the Canada Japan Business Committee, Tokyo, May 15, 2000, 7.
43 Conference of Defence Associations Institute, *Sustainability and Prosperity: The Benefits of Investment in Defence* (Ottawa, 2000), viii–ix.
44 Douglas Bland, "National security at home and abroad," *National Post* (January 4, 2001): A1.

■ Chapter 8: How Canadians Can Triumph

1 David O'Brien, "Building on Strength, Seizing Opportunity," speech to CEO Summit 2000, Toronto, April 5, 2000, 8.
2 Renée St-Jacques, "North American Linkages," presentation to the 2000 Policy Research Conference, Ottawa, November 30, 2000, 12.
3 Statistics Canada, "Family Income 1998," *The Daily*, June 12, 2000.
4 Ron Southern, quoted in Peter C. Newman, *Titans: How the New Canadian Establishment Seized Power* (Toronto: Penguin Books, 1998), 451.

NOTES

5 Don Drummond, "Canadian Economic Policy: What Will It Take to Make Canada a Growth Leader?" presentation to the Industry Canada Distinguished Speakers Series, Toronto, December 8, 2000.

6 Jonathan Kesselman, "Flat Taxes, Dual Taxes, Smart Taxes: Making the Best Choices," Institute for Research on Public Policy, *Policy Matters* 1, 7 (2000): 57.

7 Gordon Robertson, *Memoirs of a Very Civil Servant: Mackenzie King to Pierre Trudeau* (Toronto: University of Toronto Press, 2000). See also Ronald L. Watts and Douglas M. Brown, eds., *Options for a New Canada*, Institute of Intergovernmental Relations, Queen's University, and Business Council on National Issues (Toronto: University of Toronto Press, 1991).

8 Peter Dobell, "Reforming Parliamentary Practice: The Views of MPs," Institute for Research on Public Policy, *Policy Matters* 1, 9 (2000): 10. See also Thomas d'Aquino, G. Bruce Doern, and Cassandra Blair, *Parliamentary Democracy in Canada*, Issues for Reform (Toronto: Methuen, 1983).

9 Dobell, "Reforming Parliamentary Practice," 11.

10 David Stewart-Patterson, "A Community of Enterprise," in *Perspectives on Partnership*, Caledon Institute of Social Policy, June 1998, 39.

11 John Ralston Saul, *Reflections of a Siamese Twin: Canada at the End of the Twentieth Century* (Toronto: Viking, 1997), 157.

INDEX

Aboriginal peoples, 122, 126–27, 242, 309, 311
aerospace sector, 236–38
Agreement on Internal Trade (AIT), 161, 204–5, 240
agriculture, 269–70
Agrium Inc., 152, 226
Air Liquide, 229, 235–36
Alberta, 6
  education in, 105, 108, 111
  taxation in, 54, 251–52, 306
Alberta Energy Company Ltd., 151, 226. *See also* Morgan, Gwyn
Alcan, 226, 231, 232, 244. *See also* Bougie, Jacques; Culver, David
Altshuler, Rosanne, 245
American Federation of Teachers, 105, 107, 129
Arnett, James, 231, 257
Asia, 30, 289–91, 321
Asper, Israel, 38, 245
Association of Universities and Colleges of Canada, 115, 142, 159
Atlantic Canada, 78–81
attitudes, 22–23, 190–92, 252–57, 325–26
auditor general, 70, 82–83, 127
Australia, 74, 104, 194

Baillie, A. Charles, 67, 221, 234
Baldwin, John, 175, 177
Bank of Canada, 3, 52, 283–84, 305
banks, 234
Barlow, Maude, 132
Barry, Donald, 288
Baxter, David, 71

BCE Inc., 227, 231–32. *See also* Monty, Jean
Beamish, Paul, 159–60, 165
Beaudoin, Laurent, 8
Bentley, Peter, 174
Berdahl, Robert, 181
Bland, Douglas, 295
Boessenkool, Kenneth, 97–98
Bombardier Inc., 8, 152, 220, 229, 236–38, 253, 292. *See also* Beaudoin, Laurent; Brown, Robert
border effect, 280–81. *See also* cross-border transactions
Boston Consulting Group (BCG), 188
Bouchard, Lucien, 314
Bouchard, Micheline, 115
Bougie, Jacques, 28, 232, 244. *See also* Alcan
brain drain, 15–16, 138, 140–46, 149–51
  in education, 157, 159–60
  in health care, 69, 157–59
  and salaries, 138–39, 163–66
  and taxes, 143–44, 166–68
  ways to counter, 161–62
Branda, Dan, 224
Brazil, 291–92, 321
British Columbia, 95, 105, 107, 108
Brock, William, 276
Brody, William R., 102–3
Brown, Daniel, 111
Brown, Robert, 38, 152, 220, 237–38, 253. *See also* Bombardier Inc.
Brown, Robert D., 62–63, 77
Bruer, John, 96
Brunet, Pierre, 254
Bruton, John, 249–50
Burney, Derek, 276, 278, 281–82

353

Bush, George, 276
business, 23, 46. *See also* private sector; small business
  and change, 35, 46–47, 274
  and the community, 100, 165–66, 209–13, 231, 318–19
  and education, 122, 132–36
  location of, 227–32, 244, 255–57
Business Corporations Act, 178
Business Council on National Issues, 10, 23, 241–42. *See also* Canada Global Leadership Initiative
  and Canada's future, 258, 263, 304
  and the community, 89, 165
  and education, 102, 114, 122–23, 134, 135
  and employee issues, 152–53
  and employment issues, 231, 233
  and foreign investment, 233
  and free trade, 32, 37–38, 275–77, 282
  and government, 202, 236
  and new companies, 189, 230
  and research, 181
  summits organized by, 2, 22, 23, 30, 62
  surveys by, 14–15
  on taxation, 53–54, 97, 244
  and trading partners, 284, 285, 290–91
Business Roundtable Education Task Force, 105
business schools, 143, 159–60, 166
Bussandri, Claudio, 198–99

CAE Inc., 278. *See also* Burney, Derek
Cairns Group, 269
Caledon Institute of Social Policy, 74–75, 127, 209, 319
California, 108, 184
Cameron, David, 44–45
Canada. *See also individual provinces*
  advantages of, 48, 233, 258–61
  and Asia, 289–91, 321, 324
  and the European Union, 286–89, 321, 324
  goals for, 293, 297–304, 323–24
  image of, 257–62, 265–66
  leadership potential of, 20–21, 324
  and Mexico, 285–86, 324
  openness of, 37–38, 317, 324
  shortcomings of, 48, 224–25, 233–44, 262
  and United States, 20, 61–62, 274–86, 300, 321, 324

Canada Customs and Revenue Agency, 143–44
Canada–European Union Summit (2000), 288
Canada Global Leadership Initiative, 23, 27, 33, 278, 280, 281
Canada Japan Business Committee, 290–91
Canada–United States Free Trade Agreement, 32
Canadian Advanced Technology Association, 142
Canadian Alliance Party, 54, 56, 98, 236, 317
Canadian Centre for Philanthropy, 210. *See also* Imagine program
Canadian E-Business Opportunities Roundtable, 17–18, 188
Canadian Education Association, 102
Canadian Imperial Bank of Commerce (CIBC), 223–24. *See also* Rubin, Jeff
Canadian Institute for Health Information, 72, 309
Canadian Labour and Business Centre, 187
Canadian Labour Congress, 36
Canadian Labour Force Development Board (CLFDB), 163
Canadian Medical Association, 70–71, 73, 158
Canadian Millennium Scholarships Foundation, 126
Canadian National, 220. *See also* Tellier, Paul
Canadian Nurses Association, 158–59
Canadian Pacific, 232, 243. *See also* O'Brien, David
Canadian Policy Research Networks Inc., 155, 207
Canadians, 36, 191, 265
  attitude to success of, 190–92, 255–56
  and globalization, 39–41, 294
  and government, 253, 315–16
Canadian Teachers Federation, 107–8, 132
Canadian Union of Public Employees (CUPE), 131–32
Canadian Venture Capital Association, 186
Canfor Corporation, 174
CanWest Global Communications Corp., 38, 245
capital gains tax, 54, 193–96, 307–8, 325
capitalism, 30–32, 42, 47
capital tax, 306

INDEX

Caplan, David, 222, 237. *See also* Pratt & Whitney Canada Corp.
Career Edge, 134
Cargill Limited, 167
Carroll, Robert, 192–93
C.D. Howe Institute, 2, 83, 97, 140, 148
Cella, Frank, 175–76
CGI Group Inc., 230–31
Charest, Jean, 314
Cherniavsky, Ben, 83–84
child care, 98–100, 319
children, 40–41, 96–100. *See also* early childhood development; education
Child Tax Benefit, 96–97
China, 41, 237, 248, 291–92, 321
Chirac, Jacques, 288–89
Chrétien, Jean, 29, 286–87, 292
Cirillo, Alex, 216
Cleghorn, John, 152, 190–91, 215, 222, 225
Clinton, Bill, 44
Cobb, Clifford, 207
Cognetics Inc., 255–56
commercialization, 178, 181–82, 187–88
common market, 282–84
communities, 98–100, 125, 207
  business and, 89, 100, 165–66, 209–13, 231, 318–19
  and economic development, 23–24, 46, 324
competition, 36–37, 58–59
  policies dealing with, 235, 279
  for skilled workers, 149–60, 163–68
  and taxation, 56, 194
Conference Board of Canada, 6, 8
  opinions of, 183, 202, 213, 252
  studies by, 58, 71, 94, 102, 123, 134, 188
Conference of Defence Associations Institute, 294–95
Constitution Act (1982), 77–78
convergence of interests, 209, 280, 285, 321
Cook, Peter, 247
Corporate–Higher Education Forum (C-HEF), 117
Council of Canadians, 132
Council of Ministers of Education, Canada (CMEC), 93, 105, 125, 127, 204
Council of Ontario Universities, 116
Council on Competitiveness, 16, 171, 178–79, 214

Courchene, Thomas, 39, 56, 283
Coyles, Stephanie, 227–28, 230
creative destruction, 35, 178
cross-border transactions, 223–24, 246–47, 279, 282–83, 321
Crowley, Brian Lee, 67
Culver, David, 255, 278

D'Alessandro, Dominic, 222
Daly, Don, 174, 175
Davenport, Paul, 179
Davies, Brian, 203
Davies, James, 97–98
debt. *See* public debt
Decter, Michael, 65–66
defence, 122, 239, 294–95, 320–21
deficits, 50–51, 59
  reduction of, 3–4, 50, 330–31
demographics, 66, 68, 69, 129–30, 157–58
Department of Foreign Affairs and International Trade, 263, 280
Department of Indian Affairs and Northern Development, 126–27
Desautels, Denis, 82–83
Desmarais, Paul, Jr., 231
development assistance. *See* foreign aid; regional development
Devooght, Kim, 200–201
DeVoretz, Don, 140–41
Digital 4Sight, 137, 206
disease, 68, 270–71
distance learning. *See* Internet
Dobell, Peter, 316–18
Dodge, David, 69, 305
Dofasco Inc., 177. *See also* Mayberry, John
dollar, Canadian, 52
  and floating exchange rate, 283–84
  weakness of, 59, 166, 167, 172, 225, 244
Dollar, David, 41
Dow Jones Industrial Average, 224–25
downsizing, 214, 215
drugs. *See* pharmacare; pharmaceutical industry
Drummond, Don, 306

early childhood development, 95–100, 319
economic growth, 248, 268–69, 272
  in Canada, 6, 37, 59, 248, 299–300, 308
economic measures, 5–6, 299–300
The Economist, 3, 27–28, 45, 246
education, 13–14, 41, 88, 101–13, 311. *See also* lifelong learning; training

355

assessment of students in, 94–95, 104–6, 125–26, 302
assessment of teachers in, 103–4, 106–8
competition for talent in, 157, 159–60, 162, 166
government role in, 109, 115, 120–21, 124–27, 134–35, 204, 315
importance of, 38–39, 58, 162
and knowledge economy, 101–2, 249–51
post-secondary, 13, 14, 93–94, 114–23, 302, 329
reform of, 7–9, 103–4, 106–7, 302, 311–12, 323, 329
role of business in, 122, 132–36, 311–12
role of parents in, 109, 121, 130–32
role of teachers in, 106–7, 109, 117, 128, 311
E-L Financial Corporation Limited, 180
emigration. *See* brain drain
employment insurance, 22, 78–82
entrepreneurship, 190–92, 255–57. *See also* Global Entrepreneurship Monitor
in Canada, 185–86, 190, 301–2
and innovation, 184–92
support for, 17–18, 38, 325, 328
and taxation, 192–93
in United States, 186, 190
environment, 8, 41, 46. *See also* global warming; sustainability
as global priority, 271–72, 322, 324
and government, 204, 242–43
equalization, 77–79, 241
Estey, Daniel C., 271
European Union, 32, 248, 286–89, 321
Expert Panel on Skills, 161–63, 191–92, 313–14
exports, 19, 172, 224, 269

families, 99, 100, 109, 121, 130–32. *See also* children
federalism, 258–59
federal-provincial relations, 205–6, 240, 314–16, 323–24
Fell, Tony, 146
Financial Post, 225
Finnie, Ross, 86–87
Finning International Inc., 162, 223, 241. *See also* Shepard, James
First Nations. *See* Aboriginal peoples
Flood, Colleen, 53, 73–74

foreign aid, 20–21, 270–71
foreign investment
attracting, 19–20, 218–19, 254–55, 259, 262
in Canada, 19, 52, 175–77, 219, 225, 303
by Canadians, 19, 225–26
Fortier, Marc, 229, 235–36
Fortin, Pierre, 193
Fortune, 141
Forum of Labour Market Ministers, 161
Fox, Vicente, 35, 286
France, 6, 97
Franco-Nevada Mining Corporation Limited, 241
Fraser Institute, 37, 85
Frazee, Rowland, 276
free trade, 31–32, 268–70, 275–77. *See also specific free trade agreements*
Canadian role in, 271, 324
with Europe, 286–89
with Mexico, 285–86
in North America, 3, 20, 59, 321
and United States, 268–69, 275, 276, 330–31
Free Trade Agreement (FTA), 275, 277–79, 321
Free Trade Area Agreement of the Americas (FTAA), 292
Friedman, Milton, 284
Friedman, Thomas L., 27, 30, 36–37, 42

Gates, Bill, 35, 125
General Agreement on Tariffs and Trade (GATT), 266–67, 279
George, Rick, 221
Gera, Surendra, 175
Germany, 97, 194
Giffin, Gordon, 285–86
Glaxo Wellcome Inc., 198, 240. *See also* Lucas, Paul
global economy, 4, 33–40, 177, 325. *See also* globalization
Global Entrepreneurship Monitor (GEM), 17, 185, 190
globalization, 11–12, 25–30, 320. *See also* brain drain; jobs; mobility
backlash against, 41–46, 326
and Canada, 3–4, 48, 264–66, 303, 327–28
fears about, 40–41, 208
and government, 22, 54, 57–58

INDEX

and investment, 29–30, 225–26, 279, 320–21, 324
and responsibility, 46–48
global warming, 273–74
Globe and Mail, 101, 131–32, 247
Godin, Serge, 230–31
Gordon, Mary, 99
governance
    as Canadian advantage, 258–59, 265
    corporate, 46–47
    innovation in, 204–8
government, 21–22, 154, 209. *See also* federal-provincial relations
    and citizens, 22, 206–7, 212, 315–16
    contracting out by, 199–200, 310
    and the economy, 31, 37, 89, 253, 325–26
    and education, 109, 115, 120–21, 124–27, 134–35, 204, 315
    and globalization, 57–58, 279, 294
    and innovation, 34–35, 46, 180, 185, 196–204
    international role of, 44–45, 320–21
    need for talent in, 153–60
    and productivity, 9, 178
    restructuring of, 24, 63, 90, 154–55
    spending by, 50–60, 309–10, 323
Graham, David, 143
Gratzer, David, 75
Graves, Frank, 207
Great Britain, 34, 246. *See also* United Kingdom
Great-West Life Assurance Company, 151
Greenspan, Alan, 26, 42
Group of Twenty (G-20), 30
growth. *See* economic growth
Grubert, Harry, 245
GST, 55–57, 306–7
Gu, Wulong, 175

Hale, David, 4–5
Handelman, Stephen, 281
Handy, Charles, 203–4
Hanel, Petr, 175, 177
Harris, Mike, 67
Harris, Richard, 250–51, 281, 283
Hart, Michael, 267, 278–79, 280
Harvard Business Review, 190, 212–13
Harvard Developments Inc. – A Hill Company, 194
Harvard University, 143, 208
Hawken, Paul, 272

Hawkins, Kerry, 167
Hayek, Friedrich von, 31
Haynal, George, 280
Health Act, 74–75
health care, 12, 58, 315
    competition for talent in, 157–59, 166
    and innovation, 196–99, 329
    public spending on, 7, 53, 57, 60, 62–76, 309
    reform of, 63–66
    two-tier, 73–76
    in United States, 53, 60, 62–63
Helliwell, John, 280
Heslop, Louise, 257–58
Hess, Steven, 242
Hewlett Packard, 224
high technology. *See* technology sector
Highway 407, 199–200
Hill, Paul (Adaytum Software), 149–50
Hill, Paul J. (Harvard Developments Inc.), 194
Holtz-Eakin, Douglas, 192–93
Hong Kong, 7–8, 34–35, 37, 292
Horváth, Dezsö, 218
House of Commons, 91, 310, 316–17
HSBC Bank Canada, 150, 176–77, 222. *See also* Nasr, Youssef
Hsieh, Tsun-Yan, 227–28, 230
human capital, 9, 38–39, 46, 244, 251, 262. *See also* brain drain; education; jobs; mobility
Human Resources Development Canada (HRDC), 82–83, 114–15, 141–42
Hunter, Lawson, 235

IBM Canada Ltd., 200–201, 222–23. *See also* Wetmore, John
Imagine program, 210–12, 213
immigrants, 69, 99, 144–45
    recognizing skills of, 16, 145, 161–63
immigration, 15–16, 140, 313–14, 323
Imperial Oil Limited, 232, 244
Inco, 226
income, 9, 77, 87
    real, 6, 8, 61, 299–300
    redistribution of, 8, 77, 300
    supplements for, 96–97
Income Tax Act, 98
income taxes, 52–55, 167, 307
    corporate, 55, 193, 245, 250–51, 306–7, 310
    and entrepreneurs, 192–93

India, 41, 291-92, 321
Industry Canada, 119, 172, 178, 224, 299
    on job mobility, 114, 151-52, 167
    on productivity, 174-75, 228
inflation, 4, 59
information revolution, 29, 32
infrastructure
    as Canadian advantage, 258, 259
    innovative approaches to, 199-200
initial public offerings (IPOs), 18, 188
innovation, 5-6, 8-9, 228
    accelerating, 214-16, 301
    and entrepreneurs, 18, 184-92
    and the environment, 272-73, 322
    in governance, 204-8
    government and, 34-35, 46, 180, 185, 196-204
    and health care, 196-99, 329
    and productivity, 172-78, 214, 301, 325
    and research, 178-84
    in society, 208-13
    and taxation, 192-96
Institute for Public Administration of Canada, 202
Institute for Research on Public Policy, 308, 316
Intel, 230
intellectual property, 239-40, 247. *See also* patents; software industry
International Labour Organization, 44
International Monetary Fund, 44
Internet, 18
    and education, 13, 110, 112, 117-19, 126, 134
    and globalization, 28-29, 45, 246
    government services and, 200-201
    and politics, 206-7
INTRIA-HP, 223-24
investment, 9, 244. *See also* foreign investment; venture capital
    factors affecting, 233-45, 255-57, 260-61
    and globalization, 29-30, 225-26, 279, 320-21, 324
    and taxation, 56, 244-52
Investors Group Inc., 254
IPSCO Inc., 147-48, 243
Ireland, 6, 246, 248-50, 259, 299
Ivey Business Journal, 172

Jackman, Henry, 180-81
James Richardson & Sons, Limited, 169

Japan, 289-91
JDS Uniphase, 219, 230
jobs, 3, 148-49. *See also* brain drain; organized labour; mobility
    grants for creating, 82-83
    movement to U.S. of, 138-46, 149-51
    and taxation, 83-84, 151
John Paul II, 42
Jones International University, 118

Kangas, Randall, 120
Kanter, Rosabeth Moss, 212-13
Kent, Tom, 74-75
Kernaghan, Kenneth, 202-3
Kerr, David, 150-51
Kesselman, Jonathan, 56, 308
Keynes, John Maynard, 2, 31
Kindleberger, Charles P., 33, 38
knowledge economy, 6, 8, 69, 185. *See also* brain drain
    education needs in, 14, 15, 38-39, 101-2, 132-33
    taxation in, 250-51
Knox, Robert, 204-5
Kolber, Leo, 194
Kortum, Samuel, 185
Kraay, Aart, 41
Kyoto Protocol, 273-74

Labour-Sponsored Venture Capital Corporations, 186
Lamarre, Jacques, 167-68, 199-200, 220-21, 234. *See also* SNC-Lavalin Group
Landes, David S., 24, 34
Laryea, Samuel, 140-41
Latin America, 32, 291-92, 321
Lawrence, Jack, 234
Lawton, Stephen, 128
Lazar, Harvey, 206, 208-9
leadership
    global, 320-22, 324, 327-28, 331
    need for, 22, 168-70, 325
    political, 201-2, 294-95, 316
    strategies for, 305-24
Lee, Frank, 175
Lerner, Josh, 185
Levin, Ben, 132-33
Lewington, Jennifer, 101
Liberal Party of Canada, 4, 54, 121-22, 282, 309, 312
lifelong learning, 14-15, 39, 88, 115

INDEX

access to, 121–23, 126, 138, 302–3, 312–13, 323
business role in, 134, 164
government role in, 126
Lipsey, Richard, 277
Lipton, Jeff, 147, 150, 169, 186
literacy, 40–41, 94, 302. *See also* education
London Life Insurance Company, 151
Lougheed, Peter, 277
Lowe, Graham, 163–64
Low Income Cut-Off (LICO), 85–86, 97, 300–301
Lowy, Alex, 137
Lucas, Paul, 198, 240
Lumley, Edward, 276
Lynch, Kevin, 59–60

MacDonald, Donald, 276, 277, 287
Macdonald, Mary, 186–87
MacLaren, Roy, 286
Mahathir bin Muhammad, 29–30
Manitoba, 63–65, 131
Manley, John, 284
Mann, Howard, 195, 253
Mannix, Ronald, 253
manufacturing, 172–75, 177–78
Manulife Financial, 222
marginal tax rates, 88–89, 97
market capitalization, 227–28. *See also* venture capital
Martin, Paul, 17, 30, 170
 budget of (2000), 123, 216, 305, 306
 and deficit reduction, 3, 49
Martin, Roger, 188
Mayberry, John, 133, 177, 225
Mazur, Jay, 35–36
McCain, Margaret, 95–96, 99–100, 124, 319
McCain Foods Limited, 195, 253
McCallum, John, 51–52, 60–62
McDonough, Alexa, 90
McFeetors, Raymond, 151
McGill University, 142
McKinsey & Co., 13, 181, 227
McLuhan, Marshall, 264
McMahon, Fred, 79, 80–81, 249
Medis Health and Pharmaceutical Services Inc., 198–99
Mercosur, 32
mergers and acquisitions, 209–10, 220, 234
Mexico, 3, 20, 32, 35, 59, 285–86, 287–88, 321

Micklethwait, John, 43, 46–48, 217, 228
Miller, Carman, 116
Milton, Penny, 102
Mintz, Jack, 2–3, 22, 247–48, 250
mobility
 of capital, 29
 of jobs, 143, 146–53, 232
 of workforce, 54, 81, 120, 160–62, 165–66, 256
Monahan, Patrick, 142
MoneyHunt, 184
Monty, Jean, 36, 93, 133–34, 146, 215, 231–32, 254. *See also* BCE Inc.
Moody's, 242
Moore, Mike, 31, 45
Moore Corp., 226
Morgan, Gwyn, 151, 169
Morgan Stanley Dean Witter & Co., 298
multiculturalism, 258–60, 265, 331
multinational corporations, 31, 175, 217–19, 262. *See also* foreign investment
Mundell, Robert, 81, 283–84
Murphy, Rex, 45–46
Mustard, Fraser, 95–96, 99–100, 124, 319

NAFTA. *See* North American Free Trade Agreement
NASDAQ, 188
Nasr, Youssef, 150, 176–77, 234
National Bank Financial Inc., 254
National Board for Professional Teaching Standards, 108
National Bureau of Economic Research, 245
National Child Benefit, 96–97
National Education Goals Panel, 113
national identity, 61–62, 330
National Post, 191, 226
National Public Relations, 142
Negroponte, Nicholas, 36
Nestlé Canada Inc., 175–76, 222
Netherlands, 6, 74, 249, 259
Neufeld, Edward, 234
Newall, Edward (Ted), 150, 261, 278
Newbridge Networks, 220, 230
New Democratic Party (NDP), 54, 90
Newfoundland and Labrador, 80
Newton, T. Scott, 245
New York Stock Exchange, 188
New Zealand Council for Educational Research, 104

359

Nokia, 228
non-profit organizations. *See* voluntary sector
Noranda Inc., 150–51. *See also* Kerr, David; Powis, Alfred
Nortel Networks, 138–39, 149, 219, 227–30, 248, 261. *See also* Roth, John
North American Free Trade Agreement (NAFTA), 32, 185, 275, 279, 321
  and brain drain, 140–41
  and Europe, 286–87
North Atlantic Treaty Organization (NATO), 294
North Carolina, 113, 135
Norway, 6
NOVA Chemicals Corporation, 146–47. *See also* Lipton, Jeff; Newall, Edward
Nye, Joseph, Jr., 206–7

O'Brien, David, 33, 153, 230, 232, 241, 243, 297
Ohio, 112
Ontario, 54, 71, 99, 199–200, 251
Oregon, 108–9
Organisation for Economic Co-operation and Development (OECD), 47, 71, 103, 248, 270
  on literacy, 94, 302
  on research, 179, 183
  on venture capital, 185–88
organized labour, 156. *See also* jobs; mobility
  costs of, 172, 244, 249
  and education, 128–29, 131–32
  response to change of, 35–36, 243, 249–50, 328–29
Orr, Dale, 81
Osborne, David, 202
Osgoode Law School, 142

Papadopoulos, Nicolas, 257–58
parents. *See* families
Parliament. *See* House of Commons; Senate
Parti Québécois, 314
partnerships
  corporate-community, 210–13, 318–19
  cross-border, 223–24
  global, 221
  public sector–private sector, 310
Patented Medicine Price Review Board, 240
patents, 179–80, 185, 198, 239–40

peacekeeping. *See* defence
pension funds, 187, 328
performance, economic. *See* economic measures
Personnel Systems, 142
Peterson, Robert, 232, 244
Petro-Canada, 228
Pettigrew, Pierre, 43, 284
pharmacare, 66, 76, 240
pharmaceutical industry, 197–99, 239–40
Phelps, Michael, 151
philanthropy, 212. *See also* Imagine program
Phillips, Roger, 148, 243
Placer Dome Inc., 151, 226, 246
Plastrik, Peter, 202
Poland, 237
politics
  as barrier to investment, 241–42
  Canadian views of, 202, 316
Porter, Michael, 3
Postl, Brian, 64
Potash Corp. of Saskatchewan, 226
poverty, 12, 41
  in Canada, 84–90, 300–301, 309
  global, 40–41, 84, 270–71
Power Corporation of Canada, 231
Powis, Alfred, 275, 278
Pratt & Whitney Canada Corp., 222, 237, 239
Prime Minister's Advisory Council on Science and Technology, 161–62, 191–92
Prior Learning Assessment and Recognition (PLAR), 163
private sector
  collaboration within, 183–85, 324, 327
  and education, 116, 122–23, 125–26, 164
  investment by, 9, 211
  and job mobility, 146–53
  role of in society, 89–90, 209–13, 327–28
  support for research by, 180–81, 301
productivity, 8–9, 21, 59–60, 228, 249, 301, 310
  and innovation, 172–78, 214, 301, 325
  lack of in Canada, 59–61, 172–73
  and standard of living, 9, 61, 172
  in United States, 4, 173
Progressive Conservative Party, 4, 54, 121, 195–96
Progressive Policy Institute, 214–15

INDEX

prosperity, 6–7, 266–70, 327. *See also* wealth
public debt, 2–3, 51–59, 242
 reducing, 305–6, 323
public policy, 44–45, 202. *See also*
 government; regional development;
 social programs
public sector. *See* education; government;
 health care
public service, 201–3, 259, 329

quality of life, 7–8, 165, 326
 in Canada, 260–61, 303–4
 and citizen involvement, 207, 209–13
 and environment, 20–21, 271
 importance of, 255–56, 330
Quebec, 78, 105–6, 130–31, 317
 separatism in, 241–42, 314–15
Quebec School Improvement Network,
 130–31
Queen's University, 142

Rae, Bob, 128
Raham, Helen, 102, 111, 112, 128–29, 135
Ramlo, Andrew, 71
RAND Corporation, 113
R&D Challenge Fund (Ontario), 180
Redefining Progress, 207
regional development, 12, 77–84, 310
Registered Education Savings Plans
 (RESPs), 121, 308, 312
Registered Individual Learning Accounts,
 121–22, 312
Registered Retirement Savings Plans
 (RRSPs), 121, 226, 308
regulation, 16, 235, 242–43
research, 16, 116, 178–79. *See also* patents
 in Canada, 17, 175, 179, 239–40
 government role in, 9, 17, 58, 178, 180,
 182–84, 301, 325
 and innovation, 178–84
 revenue from, 181–82
Research-Based Pharmaceutical
 Companies (Rx&D), 197–98
Research in Motion (RIM), 230
resource sector, 174, 243–44, 251
Richardson, Hartley, 169
Rider, Mark, 192–93
Riley, Sanford, 254
Rixford, Craig, 207
Roach, Stephen, 298
Robertson, Gordon, 314
Robertson, Heather-jane, 132

Robinson, Paul, 276
Rock, Allan, 75
Roos, Noralou, 65
Rosen, Harvey, 192–93
Roth, John, 29, 38, 138–39, 190, 261. *See
 also* Nortel Networks
Royal Bank of Canada, 222, 225. *See also*
 Cleghorn, John; Davies, Brian; Fell,
 Tony; McCallum, John
Royal Commission on Learning
 (Ontario), 104–5
Royal Commission on the Economic
 Union and Development Prospects for
 Canada, 263–64, 276
Rubin, Jeff, 298
Ruggiero, Renato, 266
Russia, 237
Rust, Edward B., Jr., 105

Sahlman, William, 190
Sanders, William, 106
Sarlo, Christopher, 85
Saul, John Ralston, 330
savings, 121, 226, 308, 312
Savoie, Donald, 205
School Achievement Indicators program,
 105
schools, 101–13, 311–12. *See also* education
 choices in, 109–12
 as community resource, 99–100
Schott, Jeffrey J., 43, 271
Schulich, Seymour, 241
Schumpeter, Joseph, 5
Schwab, Klaus, 41–42
Schwanen, Daniel, 148–49
Schwartz, Gerry, 172
Scully, Hugh, 72–73
security. *See* defence
Senate, 194, 314
ServiceOntario, 200–201
service sector, 245, 250, 279
Shanker, Albert, 105
Sharp, Mitchell, 154
Sharpe, Andrew, 173
Sharwood, Gordon, 185–86
Shepard, James, 162, 241
Shuknecht, Ludger, 21, 57–58
Silicon Valley, 188–89
Sirois, Charles, 232
skills. *See* human capital
small business
 productivity in, 174–75, 193

training in, 123, 134–35
Smith, Nancy Faraday, 67
SNC-Lavalin Group Inc., 168, 199–200, 220–21. *See also* Lamarre, Jacques
Snyder, Stephen, 235
social capability, 33–34, 38
social programs, 7–8, 52, 53. *See also* education; health care; poverty
Social Union Agreement, 204
Society for the Advancement of Excellence in Education, 102. *See also* Raham, Helen
software industry, 176–77, 247, 248
Soros, George, 42
Southern, Ron, 304
sovereignty, 283, 321
sponsorships, corporate, 210–13
Stabile, Mark, 53, 73–74
Standard and Poor's, 225
standard of living, 41, 56, 61, 327–28. *See also* poverty; quality of life
  improving, 86–88, 299–300
  productivity and, 9, 61, 172
Stanford, James, 228
Stanford University, 182, 184
Statistics Canada, 140, 158, 175. *See also* Low Income Cut-Off (LICO)
Stein, Janice Gross, 44–45
stock markets, 5, 29, 224–25, 227–28. *See also individual stock exchanges*
stock options, 168, 195
Strangway, David, 180
Strong, Lawrence, 156–57
student loans. *See* universities
subsidiaries, 222–23
subsidies, 79, 196, 279. *See also* regional development
  and business, 4, 23, 78, 196, 236–39, 310
  in European Union, 248, 249
Sulzenko, Andrei, 178
Summit of the Americas (2001), 292
Suncor Energy Inc., 221
surpluses, 51–52
surveys, 14–15
  Current Population (U.S.), 140, 143
  health care, 65
  Highly Qualified Manpower, 154
  by Human Resources Development Canada, 141–42
sustainability, 20–21, 23, 271–73, 328
Switzerland, 246, 259–60
Szostak, Rick, 82

talent. *See* human capital
Tanzi, Vito, 21, 57–58
Tapscott, Don, 137, 164
tariffs, 4, 267, 269, 279. *See also* free trade
taxation, 55–56. *See also specific types of taxes*
  and business costs, 245–47
  and education, 121, 124
  and entrepreneurs, 185, 187–88, 192–93
  and families, 96–97, 100
  and human capital, 54, 83–84, 166–68
  and innovation, 192–96
  and investment, 56, 244–52, 308
  and productivity, 22, 244–52
  and public debt, 52–57
  reduction of, 24, 51, 53–54, 61, 97, 247–52, 306–7
  reform of, 97–98, 194–96, 250–52, 306–8, 323
  and regional development, 79
  and research, 17, 180–82
  and standard of living, 88–89
tax credits, 307, 312, 325. *See also specific tax credits*
Tax Reform Act (1986), 192–93
TD Bank, 221, 234. *See also* Baillie, A. Charles
teachers. *See* education
Technical Committee on Business Taxation, 247
technology. *See also* Internet; software industry
  in Canada, 4, 9, 174, 328
  economic impact of, 28, 178, 301
  and education, 110, 117–18, 184
  and globalization, 26, 27–28
  and health care, 68–72
  and politics, 206–7
technology sector, 4, 139, 188–89, 214, 248
Telesystem Ltd., 232
Tellier, Paul, 191, 220–21, 235, 291. *See also* Canadian National
Texas, 106, 113, 135
Thiessen, Gordon, 283–84
Thomas, Paul, 201, 205
Thomas B. Fordham Foundation, 106–7
Thorsell, William, 40
3M, 215–16
Thurow, Lester, 14, 34, 38
Ticoll, David, 137
Tobin, Brian, 326–27
tolerance, 256, 260

INDEX

Torjman, Sherri, 209
Toronto District School Board, 99
Toronto Stock Exchange, 188, 224–25
trade, 20, 315, 320–21. *See also* free trade; World Trade Organization
  internal, 37, 240–41
  and prosperity, 266–70
training, 58, 88. *See also* education; lifelong learning
  accessibility of, 15, 122–23, 126
  as benefit to business, 15, 134–35
  in education sector, 102, 311
  strategies for, 303, 313
Trajtenberg, Manuel, 179–80
TransAlta Corporation, 235
Transatlantic Economic Partnership, 287
transfer payments, 57, 309
transportation, 220, 221, 255, 258
Treasury Board, 155
trust, 316–18, 324
tuition fees. *See* universities
Tung Chee Hwa, 8, 34–35
Tuohy, Caroline, 53, 73–74

unemployment, 78–82, 250. *See also* employment insurance
union, 282–84
unions. *See* organized labour
United Kingdom, 31. *See also* Great Britain
  education in, 103–4, 108
  health care in, 73–74
  taxation in, 194
United Nations, 44, 84, 270, 273, 303
United Nations Conference on Trade and Development (UNCTAD), 218–19
United States, 3, 4, 29, 31, 60. *See also individual states*
  and Canada, 274–86, 321
  education in, 60, 105, 108–9, 118, 129, 135
  health care in, 53, 60, 62–63, 74
  productivity in, 4, 173–74
  salaries in, 138–39
  taxation in, 97, 194, 246
  as trading partner, 44, 285–88
United States Senate, 184, 189
universities, 255
  foreign students in, 313–14
  research in, 180–82, 187–88
  student loans for, 121, 312, 313
  tuition fees for, 115–16, 119–20, 312–13
University for Industry, 118

University of California at Berkeley, 181
University of Phoenix, 118
University of Texas at Austin, 166
Urban Futures Institute, 71

values, 46, 190
  of Canadians, 22–23, 259, 298
Van Brunt, John, 152
venture capital, 17, 187
  in Canada, 185–88, 328
  importance of, 185, 301–2
voluntary sector, 89–90, 134–35, 209–13, 318–19

Wall Street Journal, 265
Walter and Duncan Gordon Foundation, 131
Washington School Research Center, 125–26
wealth, 189–90, 299
Wente, Margaret, 131–32
West, Steve, 251–52
Westcoast Energy Inc., 151
Wetmore, John, 223, 245–46. *See also* IBM Canada Ltd.
William M. Mercer Companies LLC, 261
Willson, John, 151, 246
Wilson, Michael, 190
Wisconsin, 112
Wolfe, Robert, 268
Wolfensohn, James, 264–65, 271
Wooldridge, Adrian, 43, 46–48, 217, 228
workers. *See* human capital
World Bank, 41, 44, 72, 270
World Economic Forum (WEF), 5–6, 41–42, 248, 258, 271
World Health Organization (WHO), 73
World Summit on Sustainable Development (2002), 272–73
World Trade Organization (WTO), 44, 292
  and Canada, 20, 236, 268, 320
  and GATT, 266, 279
  negotiations of, 43, 269, 271
  protests against, 43–45, 320

Yankelovitch, Daniel, 46
YMCA Canada, 134–35
Yochelson, John, 16

Zachary, G. Pascal, 265
Zitner, David, 67